Bells and Bellfounding

'If God loves us, why did he turn us into bellfounders?'
Alan Hughes, former owner of the Whitechapel Bellfoundry

'I flatter myself that I have at length come to the full knowledge of bell casting. Master, I say, of my Art'.
Letter from John William Taylor, 1858

Front cover photo: *David Potter MBE, President of the York Minster Society of Change Ringers, standing under 'Great Peter', the bourdon bell at York Minster, cast by Taylor's in 1927. It is 8 ft 8 ins / 264 cm in diameter and weighs 10 tons 16 cwts 2 qrs 22 lbs / 12.13 US tons /11,009 kg*
Photo: David Potter collection

Bells & Bellfounding

A History
Church Bells
Carillons
John Taylor & Co. Bellfounders

Michael J. Milsom

Former Bellmaster at
John Taylor & Company,
Loughborough,
England

First published in 2017
Copyright © 2017 Michael J. Milsom

The right of Michael J. Milsom to be identified as the Author of this Work
has been asserted by him in accordance with the
Copyright, Designs and Patents Act 1988.

All rights reserved.
This book or any portion thereof may not be reproduced
or used in any manner whatsoever without the express written permission
of the author except for the use of brief quotations in a book review.

A CIP catalogue record for this book is available from the British Library

ISBN – 13: 978-1547239153
ISBN – 10: 1547239158

Printed by CreateSpace, an Amazon.com Company

Available from Amazon.com, CreateSpace.com, and other retail outlets

*This book is dedicated to my wife Jane,
without whose help, patience and technical expertise
it would never have seen the light of day.*

Contents

		Page
List of Illustrations		xi
Acknowledgments		xv
Preface		xvii
Introduction		1
Chapter 1	The Origins of Bells	9
Chapter 2	Making Moulds	19
Chapter 3	Finishing the Moulds, Pouring the Metal	29
Chapter 4	My Early Years	45
Chapter 5	Setting Down Roots	57
Chapter 6	The Cherry Orchard	67
Chapter 7	The Ringing Isle	81
Chapter 8	'Great Paul'	95
Chapter 9	Mine is Bigger than Yours!	107
Chapter 10	Carillons and Singing Towers	125
Chapter 11	Paradise Lost	139
Chapter 12	After 'Great Paul'	151
Chapter 13	Post 1919	161
Chapter 14	'A Thirsty Market'	173
Chapter 15	'A Thirsty Market', Act Two	189

			Page
Chapter 16	A Really Interesting Job		209
Chapter 17	Back in the Fold		217
Chapter 18	Some Special Jobs		227
Chapter 19	A Sweet and Pleasant Sound		241
Chapter 20	The Nitty Gritty		255
Chapter 21	Paul Taylor: Last of the Line		273
Postscript			289
Taylor Family History			293
General Bibliography			295
Sources of illustrations			301
Conversion Charts			307
About the Author			309

List of Illustrations

Front cover   'Great Peter' at York Minster

Preface
Page xvi   A plaque depicting John William Taylor I
Page xix   A sketch of the Taylor bellfoundry, 1881-1891

Introduction
Page 7   The Cathedral of the Transfiguration, Toronto

Chapter 1
Page 11   'The Great Temple Bell' in Beijing
Page 15   A Chinese crotal and a Russian monk ringing bells 'Zvon' style

Chapter 2
Page 23   A core mould in a pit in the French Cornille-Havard bellfoundry
Page 27   The 'Johannesglocke' (John bell) cast by F. Schilling & Son

Chapter 3
Page 31   Closing moulds on big bell at Taylor's
Page 35   Casting bells at Taylor's
Page 43   Indenting an inscription
                A case for a 36 tonne bell, Royal Eijsbouts.

Chapter 4
Page 49   Southwell Minster Cathedral
Page 55   Southwell Minster choirboys
                Southwell Minster choir area

Chapter 5
Page 61   Lettering a cope mould at Taylor's
Page 63   Making the cope mould for 'Great Peter' at York
Page 65   An eighty-eight note piano keyboard

Chapter 6
Page 69   Print / sketch of Taylor bellfoundry, 1869-1875
Page 75   'Big Ben I' cast by John Warner & Son
Page 79   St. Paul's Cathedral, London

Chapter 7
Page 83   A ringing bell assembled for testing
Page 87   The bellmetal plaque in Taylor's ringing chamber
               Bellringers at Bury St. Edmunds
Page 91   Taylor 1936 bells for Buckfast Abbey
               Bell at St. Mary's, North Creake in Norfolk

Chapter 8
Page 99   'Great Paul' assembled in the works for testing
Page 101   'Great Paul' securely fixed to the truck
               The 14 ton case
Page 105   French engineer and Paul Taylor

Chapter 9
Page 109   Russian 'Kolokov' bell
Page 115   Bells for Toronto at Fonderie Paccard
               Joan of Arc bell Rouen Cathedral
Page 119   'Great George' in Taylor bellfoundry yard
Page 121   Cyril Johnston and the 18 ton Riverside bell
Page 123   The John Murphy bellfoundry in Dublin

Chapter 10
Page 127   St. Rombold's Cathedral, Mechlin
Page 133   Set of clock jacks Gloucester, England.
               Mechanical drum dated 1855
Page 137   Jef Denyn commemorative bell

Chapter 11
Page 145   Llandaff Cathedral organ

Chapter 12
Page 155   Ronnie Edwards machining a bell, 1972
Page 157   John William Taylor I inspecting 'Great Bede'

Chapter 13
Page 165   'Great Peter' York Minster in bellfoundry
Page 167   Buckfast Abbey ring and bourdon bell
Page 171   'Great George', cast in 1940

Chapter 14
- Page 177   Largest 6ft 9ins bell for Yale University
                  Bell on lorry
- Page 181   Loughborough War Memorial carillon bells
                  Loughborough War Memorial
- Page 185   Bok Tower, Lake Wales, Florida
- Page 187   The Riverside church tower

Chapter 15
- Page 193   Frank Godfrey in works
                  Canberra carillon on lorry
- Page 199   Zutphen carillon tower
- Page 203   Washington Cathedral carillon in works

Chapter 16
- Page 211   1868 tuning machine at Taylor's
                  Tuning shop, about 1900
- Page 215   Canberra practice clavier.

Chapter 17
- Page 219   A collection of tuning forks
                  A professional reel to reel tape recorder
                  B & K acoustical measuring equipment
- Page 221   Bell on ringing up stand at Taylor's

Chapter 18
- Page 229   AC/DC 'Hell's bell' recording
- Page 231   Mobile recording studio and microphone placement in tuning shop
- Page 237   Di Shelley at Winscombe church
- Page 239   A general view of the works
                  A large case and core plate

Chapter 19
- Page 245   Hemony carillon, Amsterdam
- Page 249   'Great Paul' in works at Taylor's
- Page 253   Harold Marcon in tuning shop

Chapter 20
Page 259　　A modern view of the tuning shop
Page 263　　The AC/DC bell awaiting dispatch
Page 265　　Washington Cathedral carillon in works
Page 269　　John Gouwens, carillonneur
Page 271　　Paccard carillon bells at Rouen Cathedral
　　　　　　A Dutch carillon bell
　　　　　　A small Taylor carillon bell

Chapter 21
Page 275　　Denison Taylor and 'Lttle John' bell
Page 279　　Paul Taylor in tuning shop
Page 285　　Paul Taylor at the Washington clavier

Back Cover　Part of the John Taylor & Co. Museum

Acknowledgements

My sincere thanks are due to all the people who have contributed advice and information in the course of writing this book. George Dawson and Chris Pickford, who run the archive department of John Taylor & Company, have been extremely helpful and found time for me on numerous occasions in their very busy lives. George has patiently answered many queries, given me free access to archive material, and supplied a large number of photographs. Chris has suggested many new avenues of exploration, and both of them have corrected any glaring errors in numerous emails on various subjects.

Andrew Higson has commented on many questions I have asked him and kept me up to date with his experiences after he took over my job as bellmaster for twenty years.

Jed Flatters has read selected chapters to correct technical information and has also told me many things I did not know. His knowledge of Taylor's is truly amazing even taking into account he worked there for a very long time. As an accomplished bellringer, he has shared some keen observations regarding Taylor rings of bells.

Alan Buswell, who has put together an incredible data bank over many years regarding Gillett & Johnston tuning books, has given me valuable information relating to their Croydon foundry, as has Alan Hughes, formerly owner of the Whitechapel Bellfoundry.

John Gouwens is one of the rare breed of musicians who is not only renowned for his organ skills but is also a very gifted and extremely respected carillonneur apart from finding time to do some composing and teaching students at the Culver Academies in the USA. He has shared with me his experiences of playing various carillons in North America and Europe, and his skilful perception of what works, what doesn't, and why. He is heavily involved in the prestigious North American Guild of Carillonneurs.

I have been greatly aided by being given permission to quote from various publications and for the use of photographs.

Any errors are mine and mine alone, for which (unfortunately) I have to take full responsibility where they occur.

JOHN WILLIAM TAYLOR 1827-1906

Preface

The Bell never rings of itself; unless someone handles or moves it, it is dumb. (Latin: Nunquam aedepol temere tinniat tintinnabulum; Nisi quis illud tractat aut movet, mutum est, tacet.)

Titus Maccius Plautus (255 BC-185 BC) - Trinummus (IV, 2, 162)

In this book there is a brief history of how bells came into being for religious or other uses. It includes carillons that are nothing less than a very large musical instrument, and the start and development of change ringing in churches. I have endeavoured to present this in a somewhat humorous fashion that will hopefully generate a smile and make it interesting to people who know nothing about bells, rather than a dry recital of facts.

Apart from this, my book is intended to be a celebration of the amazing achievements of the Taylor bellfoundry at Loughborough, England. Robert Taylor, the first member of the Taylor family, embarked on his own personal journey to become a bellfounder in 1780. The unbroken involvement of members of the Taylor family continued until 1981 when Paul Taylor died. This didn't mean that at this point everything became humdrum without further development. Further endeavours at the bellfoundry to produce state of the art bells continued. Today, John Taylor & Co., in their present form, has by no means abandoned these aims and ambitions.

Obviously, this book can be considered to be highly biased towards the Taylor bellfoundry, but no apologies are necessary as every member of the family 'pushed the envelope' to greater heights, with the consequent recognition that they were very successful pioneers and always at the pinnacle of what could be achieved. In 1894-1896 they re-discovered the art of tuning bells that had been lost in 1680 on the death of Pieter Hemony, the renowned bellfounder in Holland who, with his brother Frans, had taken the tuning of bells to a new level. It wasn't a question of Taylor's going cap in hand to another bellfoundry in Europe, or anywhere else, and asking politely, 'Will you tell us how you do it please?' There was no-one to interrogate. All other bellfounders consequently had to play 'catch-up' to try to compete with Taylor's.

Left: *John William Taylor I (Senior), 1827-1906. He designed the custom built bellfoundry in Loughborough in 1859 and cast 'Great Paul' for St. Paul's Cathedral, London, in 1881. It weighs just less than seventeen tons and is still the largest bell in England. In 1896, after re-discovering the lost art of casting and tuning perfect bells, he designed the large fifteen ton tuning machine, the first one in the world.*
Photo: Taylor archives

As was the case with the Hemony brothers in Holland in the 17th century, bells coming out of Taylor's from 1896 were accepted by musicians as being absolutely first rate. This was the aim of John William Taylor I who was very musical and was trying to dramatically improve the sound of church bells. From travelling throughout Belgium and Holland with family members, and meeting musicians and persons knowledgeable in the properties that perfect bells should exhibit in theory, it soon became clear to him that their newfound expertise could also be used to produce tip-top carillons, unrivalled anywhere.

In 1896, John William Taylor I designed the first tuning machine in the world that was capable of machining a bell internally from top to bottom. It weighs fifteen tons and can take a bell almost six feet in diameter and was put in an entirely new extension to the foundry. The confirmation that this was exactly what they needed meant that two smaller machines were quickly ordered, and then an immense one in 1900 that could take bells up to ten feet in diameter. All four machines are still capable of being used today.

They needed the very large tuning machine as the custom designed foundry that was built in 1859 on a 'green-field' site known as *The Cherry Orchard* had soon expanded to be the largest in the world. Pressure of work and space meant that in 1875 an entirely new building was needed where all iron and bell casting was carried out with the initial capability of producing very large bells using their five and seven ton furnaces in tandem if necessary. When the magnificent nine foot six inch diameter bell 'Great Paul' was cast in 1881 weighing just less than seventeen tons, another twelve ton furnace was built. This bell for St. Paul's Cathedral had to be the correct musical note to match in with the glorious ring of twelve bells installed in 1878 for change-ringing. No bell this big had ever been cast in England (it is still the largest bell) and no other bell approaching this weight had been installed as a swinging bell. John William Taylor I and his son John William Taylor II refused to guarantee this bell would be a perfect match as no tuning was possible, but their professional pride and expertise, together with the casting of a test bell half the diameter, resulted in this bell being absolutely perfect. A fourth two ton furnace was built in 1892 taking the combined capacity of metal that they could melt down to over twenty-three tons. This ability put them in the forefront of European bellfounders once again.

Edmund Denison Taylor, who was a driving force and a very astute businessman until he retired in 1945, always bemoaned that Loughborough was a long way from London, well 'North of Watford'. The Croydon Gillett and Johnston bellfoundry started entering the carillon market in 1921. Cyril Johnston was very flamboyant and tried to play 'catch up' very quickly. As I narrate in a chapter of this book, Cyril and the John Warner foundry in London

Right: *An artist's sketch of the bellfoundry from between 1881, when the third ten ton furnace was built for 'Great Paul' (the chimney is the right hand one of the three), and 1891 when a fire destroyed part of the works including the clock and bell tower over the main entrance. Bellfoundry house can be seen far right.*
Photo: Taylor archive

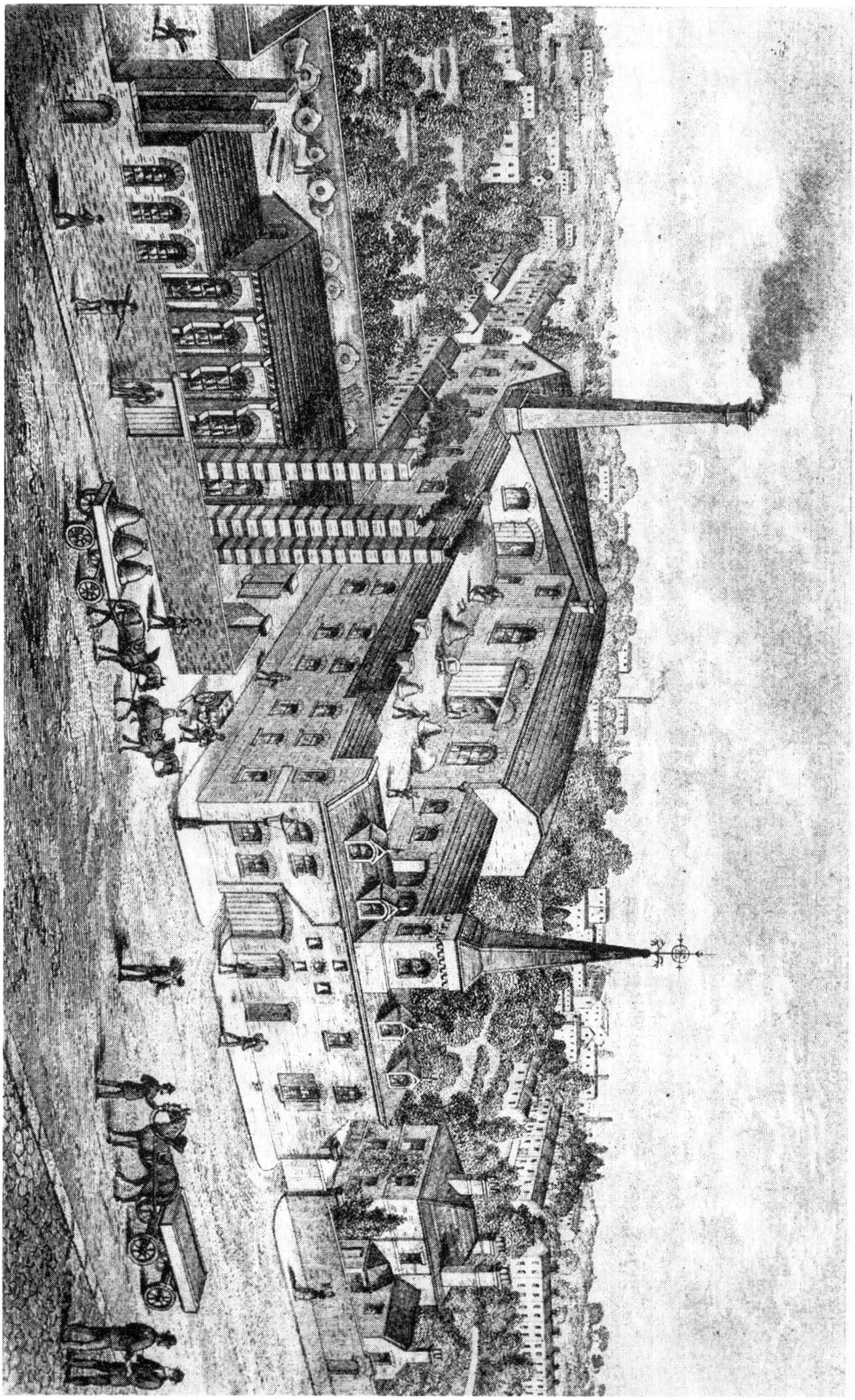

reputedly each obtained a Taylor bell and cut them in half to see if it gave them any short cuts. Cyril's nickname at Taylor's was consequently 'the great pirate'. Being an astute entrepreneur, he regularly swarmed over carillons installed by Taylor's and copied any new designs. He often proclaimed loudly that they were his own inventions, even when people knew he was lying.

Despite being so far from London, the Taylor family obtained a lot of work there. As early as 1851, Taylor's exhibited two bells at the Great Exhibition under Royal Patronage in Hyde Park. A skilled committee evaluated over one hundred bells from bellfounders in several countries, but John William was told his bells were 'superb' with a 'Certificate of Special Approbation' and a 'Prize Medal'. In 1854, when the new custom built foundry was not even on the cards, and they were working from a hotchpotch collection of buildings in another part of Loughborough, they clinched the order to recast fifteen bells at the Royal Exchange in London. They had been cast only a few years before, in 1845, by Charles & George Mears, the then owners of the London Whitechapel bellfoundry, but had always been considered poor castings and defective in tone. Apart from recasting all the bells, a new frame and a complete set of fittings were put in.

Taylor's then cast the set of twelve bells for St. Paul's cathedral, right in the centre of London, in 1878. When Queen Victoria celebrated her golden jubilee in 1887, Taylor's were again awarded a plum contract in London when they supplied a ring of ten bells, with the largest just over two tons, for the Imperial Institute.

Apart from in London, one of their flagship rings of twelve bells was cast in 1926 for York Minster. Once again, the existing ten bells were considered badly toned when supplied by Mears in 1843. In fact, they were considered worse than the previous twelve that had been recast! Although rehung in 1913 by John Warner & Co. from London, Taylor's recast them and supplied a new frame and a complete set of fittings. They still rank as one of the finest rings of bells in England to this day and are the fourth heaviest in the world. Another shining example of their expertise was when fourteen bells with an enormous swinging bell were installed at Buckfast Abbey in 1936. These replaced a previous set cast by John Warner in 1910 but not installed until 1922. In the space of thirteen years they were all scrapped.

As early as 1881, Taylor's were pushing for the adoption of cast iron frames for bells hung for change-ringing. When this type of framework was installed at the Cornish town of Camborne in 1882, the *Western News* reported, 'This is the first cast iron framework for a complete ring of bells that has been installed in England. ......the frame will be much more durable and not require such constant attention as a wooden one'. John William I soon boasted that his cast iron frames 'are more massive than those made by any London firm......but consequently the price may be a little higher'. This was another major step forward.

On the subject of single bells, I have a chapter that deals with large bells world-wide. As regards bells in Britain, of the heaviest ten bells in existence, eight of them come from

Taylor's. (I am excluding one bell that was formerly at the top of the list but is now no longer in use.) The extraordinary bell 'Great Paul' at St. Paul's cathedral in London currently needs new motors to drive it and an overhaul. The money for this has now been raised and the work is part of a major restoration project in 2018. The next largest bell, cast in 1940 and weighing fourteen and three quarter tons, is 'Great George' at Liverpool Cathedral.

Decades after Paul Taylor had tuned this bell and been to the opening ceremony he told me that 'it sounded magnificent'. This holds the record of the largest tuned bell in England, and the bell with the deepest musical note. It is also the same diameter as 'Great Paul'. The third heaviest bell is 'Big Ben II', cast by Mears from Whitechapel in 1858, that cracked after only two months of use. It does qualify to be the largest cracked bell in England. Next on the list of Taylor bells is the magnificent 1927 'Great Peter' at York Minster which, like 'Great Paul', has a musical note related to the ring of twelve bells cast the year before. It weighs just less than eleven tons and was supplied to replace a bell with lots of problems cast in 1845 by Mears. 'Heaviest' does not necessarily mean 'best', but going down the list there are many superb Taylor bells.

From 1875, when Taylor's built their new 'casting hall' to mould and cast iron and bronze, they had cast 2,553 tons of bells by 1906. From 1920-1929 the total was an amazing 1,099 tons. As so many carillons were being produced apart from church bells, Taylor's advertised for a works manager for 'about 100 men' in 1927.

Carillons are nothing less than enormous musical instruments that normally have between twenty-five and forty-nine bells, the closest comparison being large pipe organs. Skilled musicians called 'carillonneurs' attempt to achieve the most expression they can with loud and soft notes, as long as the linkages from the keyboard to the bells allow this. Taylor's were always striving to perfect these linkages and clapper design, and every new carillon incorporated the latest improvements to help the carillonneurs.

In 1920, the year before Cyril Johnston decided he was going to enter the carillon market, the thirty-nine bell Taylor carillon at Armagh in Ireland had just been installed. A letter was received at the bellfoundry from Anton Nauwelaerts, the carillonneur from Bruges in Belgium, who had been invited to play three recitals a day for four days. He wrote, 'It is really a pleasure to play on such a carillon as all the bells are so well tuned, with such a perfect mechanism and easy moving keyboard. Every clapper answers as he is commanded. I really am jealous of the man who always has to play here'. Cyril Johnston always tried hard to keep up as more and more Taylor carillons became state of the art over the years.

A very famous American carillonneur, Milford Myre, gave the first recital on a flagship Taylor carillon installed at Washington Cathedral in 1963, with the largest bell of the total of forty-nine weighing ten tons. The size of bells and range was almost identical to the superb 1927 Taylor carillon in Florida where he was then carillonneur, but he also was very jealous when he told Taylor's that the Washington carillon was the most responsive carillon he had ever encountered. It is the third heaviest in the world.

Having a 'range' of four octaves of bells (so forty-nine in total) was considered the ideal maximum as the spacing of the batons (keys) on the clavier keyboard meant the carillonneur could just reach either end. Cyril Johnston, when he had to move a 1925 carillon of his from one church to another in New York in 1929, expanded it to seventy-two bells, so six octaves. The largest bell at just over eighteen tons is the heaviest exported bell cast in England. Unfortunately, he had to have three goes at this bell because of a rogue musical note. He was also asked by the consultant to recast twenty-eight of the smallest bells from 1925 that were adjudged inaudible. The client was John D. Rockefeller Jr. and cost was not the prime consideration.

This carillon, and another almost identical one for the same client at Chicago, did nothing to make carillons more attractive or increase their 'playability'. The enormous bells had to be operated by air pistons as no carillonneur could manually pull the clappers into the bells, and the additional bells at the top end were rarely used as the batons were completely out of reach! Apart from this, the small ones at the New York carillon, even after being recast, were still almost inaudible at street level. Cyril wasn't overly concerned about all these problems as he was charging Rockefeller very large sums of money!

In 1968 the British Government decided to present Canberra with a carillon in a superb location to mark the fiftieth anniversary of Canberra being the Australian capital. Taylor's reputation was still extremely high, so it was not a difficult decision that a carillon from Taylor's would make a wonderful gift, and it was duly opened by Queen Elizabeth. In 1992, it was decided that a ten ton bell was the ideal commemorative gift from the UK to the people of Malta, in recognition of the 7,000 Maltese who lost their lives in World War II. The order for this bell, to be known as the 'Memorial Siege Bell', had to be given to Taylor's as they already had a considerably larger furnace capacity than the Whitechapel Bellfoundry.

A much less happy state of affairs took place in 2012 when the opening ceremony of the London Olympic Games was being planned. It was designed to celebrate the historical and industrial legacy of Britain. An enormous bell was suggested, and Taylor's gave a quote that had to take into account that another large furnace would need to be converted to burn oil, but their total furnace capacity was over twenty-five tons. They were astounded to learn that Whitechapel had clinched the order for a twenty-two and a half ton bell that was impossible for them to even remotely consider attempting to cast themselves, and their quote was more money. They sub-contracted this bell to the Royal Eijsbouts foundry in Holland. Danny Boyle, the artistic director of the opening ceremony, had a lot on his plate so probably didn't think through the implications. There was a precedent from 1995 when Whitechapel had four large carillon bells cast by the same company in Holland for the Wellington New Zealand carillon, as each of them were far too big for their furnaces.

This Dutch foundry had entered the market in a big way after World War II when they started casting bells in 1947. Under the leadership of André Lehr, who had joined them as a young man in 1949 to be their tuner, they became a real force to be reckoned with. Like Paul Taylor, André was a musician, a gifted engineer, and very knowledgeable regarding the acoustics of bells. He became an extremely respected bellfounder, so there were no complaints regarding their expertise. They had already cast a thirty-six tonne bell for a monastery in Japan in 2006. This is the largest swinging bell in the world until the fifty tonne bell cast in Poland in 2017, for a basilica in Brazil, is operational.

Although Whitechapel drew out the external and internal profile of the bell, it was made in Holland using their normal Dutch moulding techniques, very different from the way bells are made in England, and it was cast and tuned there. This bell does have 'Whitechapel' in large letters, but to my mind it is as relevant as having 'M&S' or 'Sainsbury' on it. Kathryn and Alan Hughes were the current owners of the Whitechapel bellfoundry, and Kathryn even referred to 'M&S' in an interview with the *Daily Mail* when she said, 'If an M&S outfit is made in China, it is still M&S clothing'. She then deviated from the truth in another somewhat critical interview with Anita Singh from *The Telegraph*. She is quoted as saying, 'Yes, the bell is being cast elsewhere... but it's our design, our profile, our lettering, and the same logo we have used since 1570. The only bit being done abroad is the pouring of the metal', but this wasn't true. Another newspaper headline read *Olympic clanger sees bell go Dutch for manufacture*. A pretty good headline that said it all! Nicky Morgan, the then MP for Loughborough, also criticised the decision and pointed to Loughborough's strong Olympic links as Loughborough University is the pre-Games base for Team GB. 'I am disappointed. Taylor's is a fantastic company.' What did Whitechapel gain from this? It didn't enhance their reputation as bellfounders, and they did nothing to the bell once it was taken out of the crate it came in. They made money out of this project of course, which I still see as being very badly conceived and surely not at all 'cricket'. In May 2016, the bell and framework was moved to just outside the Olympic stadium in the Queen Elizabeth Park, but there are no plans for it to be rung at any future date. Initially the largest imported bell, it is now relegated to being the largest Dutch sculpture.

Apart from my homage to the Taylor bellfoundry, I have broken this up with some autobiographical details. I am lucky that in my early childhood I became a very skilled cathedral chorister and then went on to be involved in high quality audio equipment. This helped me to make the transition into bellfounding, whereas every member of the Taylor family had lived and breathed it for over 200 years. Paul Taylor (1914-1981) was sometimes impatient with me when explaining some complicated procedure or calculation. Very gifted people verging on being geniuses often find it difficult when lesser mortals are struggling to understand their aims and technical achievements. He always explained it again, with copious puffs on his pipe! Paul Taylor was a truly remarkable man, but sadly he was the last of the Taylor line of exceptional bellfounders, always well in front of any other competitors. His only son and intended heir tragically died in 1961, aged seven, from childhood leukaemia which at that time was incurable.

Mike Milsom

Bellmaster, John Taylor & Company, 1977-1988

Introduction: Making Bells is Easy Peasy!

'As astonished as a bell founder'
Old French saying

Bellfounding would seem to be fairly straightforward. To make a bell you need an internal and external mould that fit snugly together with a space in between for the molten metal that becomes the bell. Let's assume we are in the early 1900s, one of the heydays of bellfounding. You have been sent a letter that asks if you can supply a ship's bell that has to have 'Titanic 1912' on it. It is quite possible that the letter was delivered to the wrong address, but you think it is worthwhile having a go.

A ship's bell is not very big so probably shouldn't be too difficult. A galvanized bucket is handy in this case for lining inside with stuff like clay to make the external shape mould. You need to make a hole in the bottom of the bucket first, so that when it is upside down you can pour the metal in. Get a circular metal plate for the internal shape to be built up on. This will look a bit like a sand castle made out of the same clay. You clamp the moulds together ready for pouring the metal in, and the space between the two moulds becomes the bell.

The other way is that over the internal shape you make a clay 'false' bell that has a thin coating of wax on the inside and outside with the inscription made of wax letters as well, that looks just like the outside of the bell you want to make. You pour a thick coating of runny clay all over the false bell and let it set. After reinforcing this you melt the wax by heating the moulds up, and the outside mould comes away. You destroy the false bell and clamp the two moulds together as is normal, and you have the space for the molten metal. This is fairly complicated, so you don't want to try this first time round - leave it for another day!

So the first method is best and easiest for what you want right now, and you heat a mixture of copper and tin known as 'bellmetal' to the required temperature. You can't do it on your gas cooker because a friend who knows about melting metal told you, 'Bellmetal only begins to look like mushy peas at about 900 degrees, and you need 1,100 degrees,' so a brazier with some coal and bellows is necessary. Having achieved this, you fill the mould up with the metal and go for a cup of tea or a beer, or ideally a leisurely meal. A meal stops you being impatient and asking yourself every five minutes, 'Is it okay? Have I made a bell?' When the bellmetal, a type of bronze, has cooled down you break it out of the moulds, and hopefully you have a bell, but be careful to avoid burnt fingers if it is still very hot and hasn't cooled down enough.

If you have been cute you have ignored the instruction to put 'Titanic 1912' on it, so after polishing it with a few sheets of emery paper and elbow grease you take the bell to be engraved telling the man, 'Make it look good and fill the letters in with black wax.' He tells you to shut up, and it comes back just fine.

You then have to provide a clapper inside to strike it, so you have to get someone to drill a hole in the top of the bell. The top of the iron clapper goes through this hole, and it's also useful for bolting it to a bracket on the ship. You then need a rope lanyard that goes through the hole you thoughtfully had drilled at the bottom of the clapper. The sailors grab this to sound the bell to tell everybody what 'watch' it is.

The bill goes to Cunard Lines who are not going to pay until they have the tenth reminder as they keep shuffling the bill through various departments and retired admirals. Every time you ask to be paid they say, 'Next week!' In this case, loss adjusters get involved and they complain, 'The bell didn't last very long!' You have to point out, 'This is not my fault. The bell was fine.' You get paid eventually, but a pity about the Titanic and your shiny bell!

If you get interested in making more bells and scale this activity up, you find that a number of moulds are necessary. The efficient way to do this is to have cast iron bell-shaped things called 'cases'. These are bell profile mould formers for the external shape, and a thick cast iron plate is used for building up the internal shape. A good foundry only needs about forty of these, and you have to stress to the people who are making them, 'The largest pair will weigh about twenty tons and that means twelve feet at the largest diameter'. You then need storage for these cases, and a place to make the gooey mixture of sand, clay, horse manure, and water to bind it all together, called 'loam'. The horse manure has to come from well fed horses, so you have chatted up the local fox-hunting stables which is why you didn't shout, 'Ban fox hunting,' at the rally near your house.

Completed moulds have to be carefully dried so that cracking doesn't take place, and the moulds have to have no moisture in them whatsoever otherwise the molten metal you pour in can spit back out. When this does happen one day, you say to your workers, 'Told you so! Listen to me next time!' Following the casting, you break up and regenerate the loam, so only a few bits of milling equipment needed and an extension of the foundry! The larger the bell required, the more heavy lifting equipment you need, and various expensive overhead cranes are very helpful. Unfortunately, you have to have these certified as being in good working order, along with yourself, every twelve months. 'Every twelve months?' 'Afraid so.'

You have to keep a good stock of copper and tin which is very expensive to buy, and this has to be kept in a secure locked store otherwise your insurance company won't play ball if burglars run off with it. When casting takes place, you need an area in front of the furnace where large moulds can be buried up to the top with sand packed round them. Gravity allows the molten metal to flow out of the furnace down a channel into the mould. Various sizes of ladles are handy to enable the molten metal to be transported by the overhead crane to a collection of moulds, but storage is needed for the ladles. When you break the mould open and expose the bell it is vital to check that the commemorative inscription that was indented into the external mould backwards way round says what it was meant to. If it doesn't, the men will say, 'Well, where were you with your mirror when it needed checking?' If it says, 'PRAISE BE TO DOG,' you've boobed. You need copious amounts of individual letters and special symbols as well as custom made coats of arms and logos, all kept in a special storage area so visiting school kids don't nick them. By now they are in various languages as well, so not too helpful when you are trying to find the Norwegian ones you last used fifteen years ago. It's no good asking anyone else as they just say, 'Your problem - not mine. You put them away!'

So when a bell is finished you summon a haulier and tell him, 'I've got a nice job for you,', and you write out the bill and put it in the post. Shock and horror, you find out that the vicar wanted the bell you made to sound a particular musical note, and there are already several others in their church going up and down the scale. Your new bell has to be the correct note to fit in with other bells, and he tells you, 'Two of them were cast three to four hundred years ago by two itinerant bellfounders.' You have never seen these bells, let alone heard them! If he had said, 'This is what I want,' to start with, it would have been a big help. Even hour bells for clocks have to be in tune with the quarter hour and half hour bells. This particular bell you thought you had seen the last of then comes back with a note saying, 'It's too flat, so no good!' 'Flat??' Oh, they mean in note not shape! So this bell is now useless unless you can sell it to someone else which is quite doubtful, even if you grind off the inscription. Of course, the day after you break it up as scrap metal some cleric rings you up and asks, 'Have you got a spare bell that we can have? We don't need any inscription,' and now you haven't!

So you need a tuning department, and you find that there are a variety of different notes when a bell is struck, and you can only lower them downwards by removing metal from the inside of the bell. You need to cast the bells a little bit thicker than they will finish up. A musician you know tells you, 'All these notes need to be in tune both within the bell and as regards all the other ones in the set.' A large number of tuning forks or other acoustical test equipment needs purchasing, and then you advertise for 'someone with a good ear'.

Several large and small, specially adapted vertical boring machines are needed now and a quiet location with just a few more men. You build a tuning shop and office on the bit of land you had been cultivating as a rose garden, so more expense and rotten luck about the roses!

Finally, with an efficient moulding department, several sizes of bellmetal furnaces and drying areas, ladles, mould formers, a secure metal store, a different furnace for the assorted cast iron accessories you have now found are necessary (with suitable moulding boxes of course), and all the other departments, you begin to think you have the system cracked. Bellfounders don't ever say, 'I've cracked it', as some bells get dropped when put on the lorry at your end or dropped when taken off, and they are definitely cracked and completely useless. Your main works area has a wooden block floor to try and stop this happening at your end. So back to the moulding area where you have to break any cracked bell up and put the bits back in the furnace for another try. Makes you want to weep!

Unfortunately, you get complaints that the large hole at the top of the bell tower is just a hole. You're asked, 'Can you provide a framework?' This starts off by meaning a saw mill and a large, wood seasoning store where you have to leave the enormously expensive oak beams to season for at least ten years. Your small joinery shop needs drastically extending, and the foreman says, 'More carpenters, please.' So you either make a frame of huge wooden timbers or riveted steel girders if you are starting to go modern. As cast iron frameworks on top of the girders for the bells to hang from become popular you need more patterns and another store. Some church architects, even if they know about steel and cast iron, still say, 'Wood is better,' so you can't sack any of the carpenters.

Your cast iron furnace has now needed enlarging, or another one building. For a long time you have been making wrought iron clappers that are blacksmith forged with a very noisy steam hammer. Neighbours start saying, 'Can you stop all this noise, please?' and you have to say, 'Sorry! No!' Cast iron is a different proposition, and if you try altering it with the steam hammer it shatters, so you have to get it right first time.

You have now extended your cast iron area with a fettling shop where the rough bits are smoothed over, and then the whole lot sandblasted. This has to be done in a separate area with a well-fitting door as it results in a dense fog of black dust, soon several inches deep if you don't tidy up regularly. Life expectancy of your men in the fettling shop is not good! If they come to complain, they can't cough the words out, so you get away with it. Phew, what a lot of work! Your haulier's bill is now immense, and then your customers start asking, 'Can you send one or two men to put the bells in?' What? More men, called 'bell hangers'!

You have found out that the English method of ringing bells is to ring them in a mathematical sequence called 'Change ringing.' To do this, all the bells in the tower have to be able to rotate just over 360 degrees and be very briefly balanced mouth up before they are pulled back round through another 360 degrees in the other direction. You have to make large wheels with spokes, and wood is easiest as you already have a large joiners' shop. Yokes known as 'headstocks', with axles, are fixed to the tops of the bells with straps or bolts. They have slowly changed from being big chunks of wood to cast iron over the years, so you have to cope with this as well.

The axle and pivoting arrangements have to be just right as some bright spark tells you, 'When correctly designed, one man can pull a bell that might weigh three tons completely upside down on his own, and needing two men is chicken!'

When church bell ringers have finished, all the bells are pulled mouth down again, and they may well sit there until the next Sunday unless the ringers have a practice session in between. Sometimes the bell ringers will come and ring very complex mathematical sequences for a long time. If they have to stop, they get all huffy and will tell you, 'It fired up,' perhaps when one of the ringers started to nod off. So you have to be sympathetic and say, 'Better luck next time.' When the bellringers have finished they all go off for a real ale and discuss how it all went. They use code words such as 'Stedman Cinques', and they may go really quiet and start muttering about 'the extent'; obviously a secret society.

Ropes have been needed that go round the wheel, so you have found a supplier who can also weave in the fluffy bits called 'sallies', that the ringers grab hold of, near the bottom end. You just need to supply a few wooden pulleys where the ropes connect in the bell chamber and some nicely machined cast iron rope bosses for the ropes to pass through in the various

Introduction: Making Bells is Easy Peasy!

floors on their way down, as the bell ringers are lower down the tower. When all the bells are upside down, a nifty bit of wood called a 'stay' with a 'slider' stops them going right over again in the wrong direction. Occasionally, one of these stays may have been snapped on the Sunday morning by an inexperienced learner pulling the rope too hard, so some Tuesdays you get a letter or two asking, 'Can we have a new one please, posted off for fitting before next Sunday?' At least it provides a bit of work for the joiners if it is a slow day.

You can now relax! You have a very comprehensive bellfoundry, far removed from the idea of just casting bells, with all sorts of allied trades and loads of men. The trouble is, every Friday they ask, 'Is it pay day today?' They think they deserve paying every week whether you have a slack week or a busy one, so another person in the accounts department, now up to two with a secretary, takes care of that.

Having had the weekend off, on Monday morning you get a letter saying, 'We would like you to quote for a 'carillon'.' Investigation reveals that, starting on the continent, a whole collection of bells tuned like the black and white notes on a piano are hung stationary on a frame. There might be thirty-seven or forty-nine bells, and the largest may be ten tons unless you are talking about the Riverside Church Carillon in New York at Morningside Heights (where else!). This lot cunningly moved their carillon from one church to another and then added bells at both ends with the largest one being eighteen tons. When they finally finished messing around they had seventy-two bells in all, just so they can tell everyone in earshot, 'Size really does matter'. The millionaire John D Rockefeller Jr was providing the loot. The Yanks tell everybody, 'The biggest bell weighs twenty tons,' because they weighed it in New York. It doesn't, because being Americans they think there are only 100 lbs in every hundredweight, not 112 lbs, so their tons of 2,000 lbs are called 'short tons', and English ones with 2,240 lbs are 'long tons'. You know it is eighteen English tons as it came from a bellfoundry in Croydon that has been a bit of a thorn in your side as they copy everything you have done and say, 'Look at this wonderful idea we have had!'

At least in carillons they don't expect all the bells to be turned upside down every few seconds! The framework for these bells is now immense, mostly made of huge girders all cut to size and bolted together, and higher than your semi-detached house including the chimney. You have to provide a mechanism whereby a man or woman (let's not be sexist) can sit on a thing like an organ stool and pound their fists on wooden levers called 'batons'. These are like the rounded ends of broom handles and stick out horizontally from the large contraption in front of them. As they only have two fists they want foot pedals as well for the biggest bells. Each time they hammer down on one of these batons or pedals a bell rings out. This device is called a 'clavier'.

You are now into levers near the bells, enormous and diddy clappers, counterbalances, and miles of tensioned stainless steel wire linkages. Everyone says, 'Stainless steel is best,' but it's not at all cheap. So after employing another design engineer and someone who can go off to the States or other far flung places to discuss the job with the people who you hope will pay, you have a carillon department. When you've made a carillon, your experts have to go back to supervise it being installed.

The only thing is, these bells can be pretty loud, and you find that the person playing them, called a 'carillonneur', says, 'I want to be able to produce loud sounds and quiet sounds from different bells and all at the same time!' 'What?' A complete redesign of the whole linkage system with a lot more bits helps, with polished steel rods, adjustable counterweights, and a million or so low friction ball bearings and their housings. Then they tell you that the general public up to ten miles away are not too impressed when James or Caroline plays wrong notes, so they need a quiet practice keyboard. These are made with more wooden sticking out bits and pedals, but at the top they make xylophone-type, aluminium bars strike quietly. A resonator tube helps improve the sound of these bars; just one for every bar and note, so now you are producing 'practice claviers'.

You ship one off and James tells you, 'Gee, its great!' (Why can't Americans speak decent English?) Unfortunately, Caroline says it is no good at all. A polite inquiry reveals that she is a lot shorter than James and has difficulty stretching her legs out to either end of the pedals when hammering away with her fists at the other end. The carillon curator says that when she is giving recitals she gets an appreciative audience looking through an observation window as she always wears skirts that ride up showing off her good legs. You politely suggest that she wears trousers, but she tells you she is a home spun Kansas girl who likes the wind on her legs. She comes from corn growing country where, if Buck is out on his combine harvester and you have just baked some brownies, you need good binoculars to see where he is in the fields before you saddle up the horse.

She says that another carillon she went to had pedals that curved up higher from the middle ones towards both ends and were much easier to reach. As Daddy paid for 'her' carillon she is sending the practice clavier back and asks, 'Can you alter the main one as well?' After you have got the practice one back, worked out how to do it, and shipped it off again, you have to send one of your technicians with a whole kit of new bits as there is no way the pedals on the main clavier can be dismantled unless on site; but eventually she stops griping.

By now you are producing such a large bit of kit and bells that they have to go off to their destinations on ships, and you have the haulage bills at both ends. Of course ....wait for it ...they want skilled men to erect the whole caboodle and put on a fifth coat of paint on site and adjust all the twiddly bits until the carillonneurs, including people like Caroline, are happy. Then you just hope that the various committees and benefactors pay up.

So you go off for a few days having got a bank draft that will take at least ninety days to clear and is in dollars, and you go to the Bahamas. You have gone there deliberately as the nearest thing there to bells or hemispherical gongs are halves of coconut shells. After you come back all invigorated and sunburnt you get a letter in the post from Henry Burkbank Junior III asking, 'How much is a big bell to herald the dawn over San Francisco?' You find out that a 'big' bell to him is about sixty inches in diameter, so at least he thinks in imperial

Right: *The Metropolitan Cathedral of the Transfiguration at Markham, Toronto. The three bells are in the central tower.*
Photo: George Socka

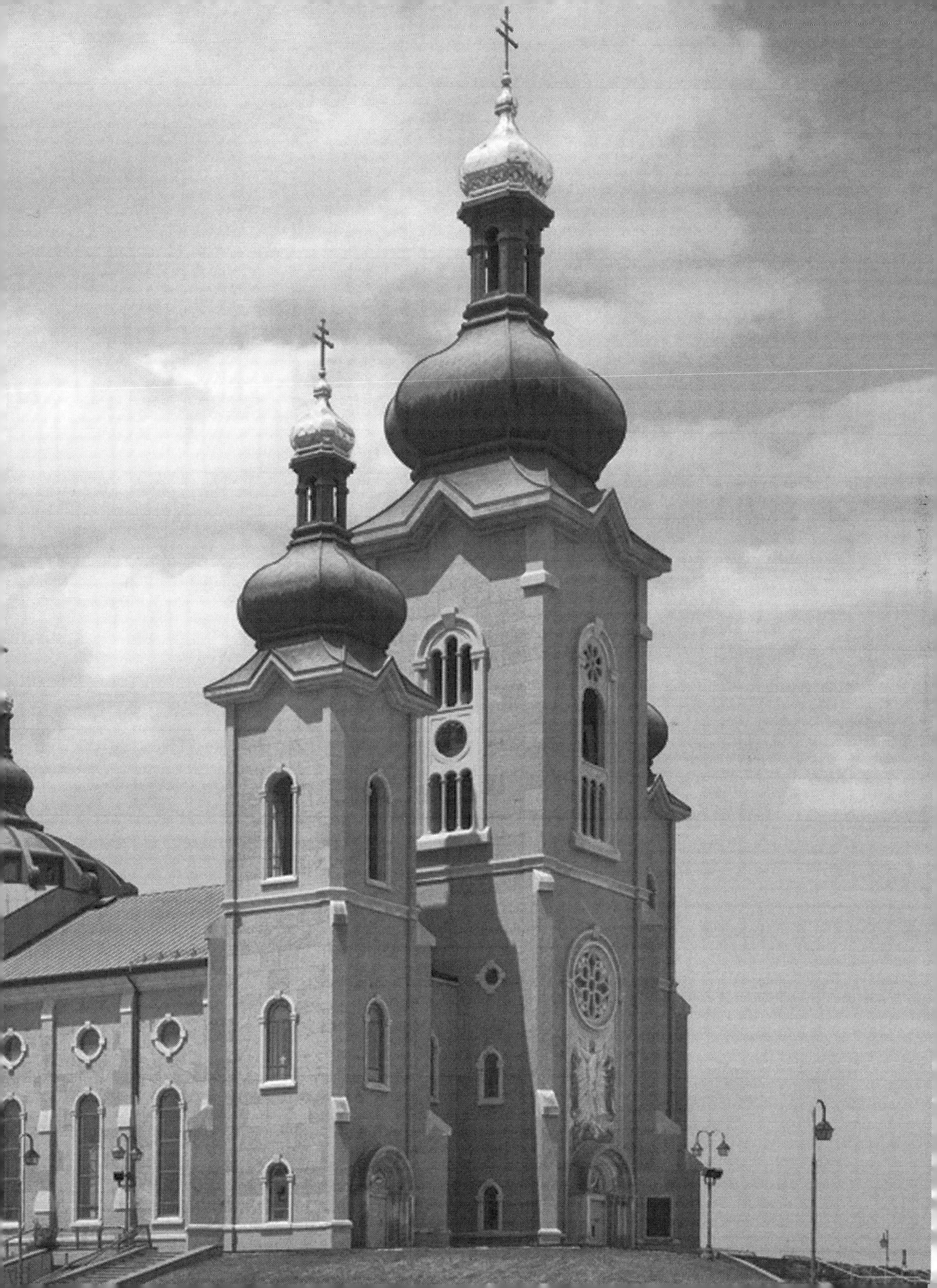

measurements even if it is another dollar deal.

Having dealt with that, the next enquiry is from Toronto from a Canadian multi-billionaire of Slovak origin who is building the Metropolitan Cathedral of the Transfiguration, with onion-style domed towers, and he wants three enormous bells. You try to work out a quote that will not bankrupt the whole company and result in the loss of your new car.

You ask your bank manager, 'Can I have a loan if I can't get a big deposit?' but of course he replies, 'Well, maybe....depending,' so not too reassuring! Meanwhile, you have sent photographs of Archbishop Makarios, with his funny hat and beard, at the foundry standing beside a big bell that you cast thirty years ago because this billionaire is presumably Greek Orthodox. Good try, but he tells you he is a personal friend of the Pope and is a dedicated Slovakian Byzantine Rite Roman Catholic. This is serious, so you have to go to Toronto (twice) to his penthouse suite of offices. This really happened when I was bellmaster at Taylor's bellfoundry at Loughborough, and we were very close to clinching the order after I had gone back the second time! Why we didn't do this job I will explain in a later chapter.

Did you think being a bellfounder was simple stuff?

1. The Origins of Bells

'Come all to church, good people, - Oh, noisy bells be dumb; I hear you, I will come.'
Bredon Hill, A Shropshire Lad - A. E. Houseman

Early bells were cup or tulip shaped, or hollow spheres with a letter-box hole and a piece of metal inside like a marble, called 'crotals'. Miniature crotals were often sewn onto clothing, and if a nobleman heard the bells tinkling that were fixed onto his wife's skirt, he could shout, 'Where are you heading off to?' and stop any illicit sorties, or her using his credit card. Bells for horses that were part of the harness, and for the funny hats that minstrels wore, were a common use for crotals. Reins for children with miniature crotals to keep them from running off into the far distance, so you have to leg it after them, have been used for centuries.

The words 'Made in China' on an item have not exactly signified high quality for a number of years. Christmas tree lights that really lit up the room when they caught fire were not uncommon. Recently, as they are building their version of the 'Airbus', they have coined a new phrase, 'Created in China'. This will look much better than having 'Made in China' stamped on the wings. The very earliest bells, as you might expect, seem to have been made and used in China. So we can say that these were certainly 'Created in China', possibly as early as 4000 BC. Accurately dated Chinese bells start about 1700 BC. Herbert Allen Giles (1845-1935) wrote a book, *China and The Chinese*, from a series of lectures given at Columbia University in 1902. He wrote another book, *Religions of Ancient China*, in 1905, that also has lots of facts. He was a diplomat in China, so he got it from the horses' mouths.

Small Chinese 'nao' bells were used as a reference for measuring grains of rice or corn, and these are shaped like a scoop fixed to a base plate, with a rod. There are three of these that would hold a decent amount of grain in the Museum of Chinese History in Peking. People leading strings of horses, ponies, or camels put a bell on each animal to keep them all together at night, or in dust storms. If the bells went quiet, you had probably lost them, so you jolly well had to find them!

An amazing discovery was made in China in 1977 when a complete royal tomb, made for Marquis Yi of Zeng, was found during excavations for a factory at Suizhou. Accurately dated to 433 BC, it contained everything needed for his journey into the afterlife, including twenty-one young ladies, thought to be virgins. The major discovery was sixty-five bronze bells, known as a 'Bianzhong', hanging on wooden racks, at three levels in groups of eight. They are designed for five musicians to play and range from 446 lbs/203 kg down to 5 lbs/2.8 kg. Each bell produces two notes depending on where it is struck, and the tuning is extremely advanced and highly accurate. Inscriptions on all the bells relate to how they should be played. This find has rewritten the history of Chinese bells and metallurgy at this period in time. How on earth did they do this? Acoustics experts are still in the dark, with various tentative theories! As regards archaeologists, most of them promptly fainted away on the spot. An assortment of over 100 musical instruments was found in the tomb, including a sophisticated xylophone with stone bars.

A booklet was published by an anonymous author in about 1866 relating to the London Whitechapel bellfoundry, but with a short history of bells. This narrates that in India, but it is not known exactly when, women and girls of important families had miniature copper bells worn as ankle bracelets or necklaces. You knew where they were and could thwart men with roving hands. This booklet also tells us that Hebrew virgins had bells sewn into their clothes. Early Hindu bells on clothes were often made of brass as it polished up to a shinier finish. As cows were often sacred they had bells, and in Ceylon it seems they used bells for elephants. If an elephant wandered off when the owner was having his supper, the family could shout, 'The elephant is going off again', and it was easier to find.

There is good evidence to suggest that bell makers from Korea went to China and Japan to cast the largest bells, mostly for religious use. These were made of bronze which had a much better sound than iron. In China, they were not at all short of tin mines, so making things out of bronze was all in a day's work. One large bell, cast in 712, is six feet in diameter, weighs fifteen tons, and was probably made by Koreans. The first emperor of the Ming Dynasty chose Nanking to be his headquarters, and a twenty ton bell cast in 1389 is still there.

The emperor Yong Le (1403-1424) started moving the capital to Peking, and he wanted several bells, with the smallest one twice as heavy as the Nanking one. He obviously wanted people to think, 'Yong Le is more important than he was'. One of these enormous bells, which are tulip shaped, can be found in Beijing. This 'Great Temple bell' is some fourteen feet in diameter and twenty-three feet high. It has a circumference of forty-four feet and a carefully estimated weight of fifty-four tons! If you very accurately measure the thickness of a bell, all the way up, you can use an abacus to work out the weight. Legend has it that this was third time lucky because the first two bells were scrap, so lots of doom and gloom.

An important Chinese calligrapher, Shen Tu, (so he was really good at joined up writing on things like parchment), was told to write a very long series of prayers and several chapters from the Chinese bible all over this bell, inside and outside, with 277,000 characters. How exactly he did this is completely unknown. Probably he borrowed a felt tip pen and wrote it out neatly and then chipped away with a small chisel for more than six months. Perhaps he just used the felt tip pen, and someone else did the chipping whilst he went off and carried on writing somewhere else.

Right: *'The Great Temple Bell' in Beijing, 14ft in diameter and 23ft high, with an estimated weight of 54 tons. It was cast during the reign of Emperor Yong Le (1403-1424).*
Photo: Sanshichiro Yamamoto

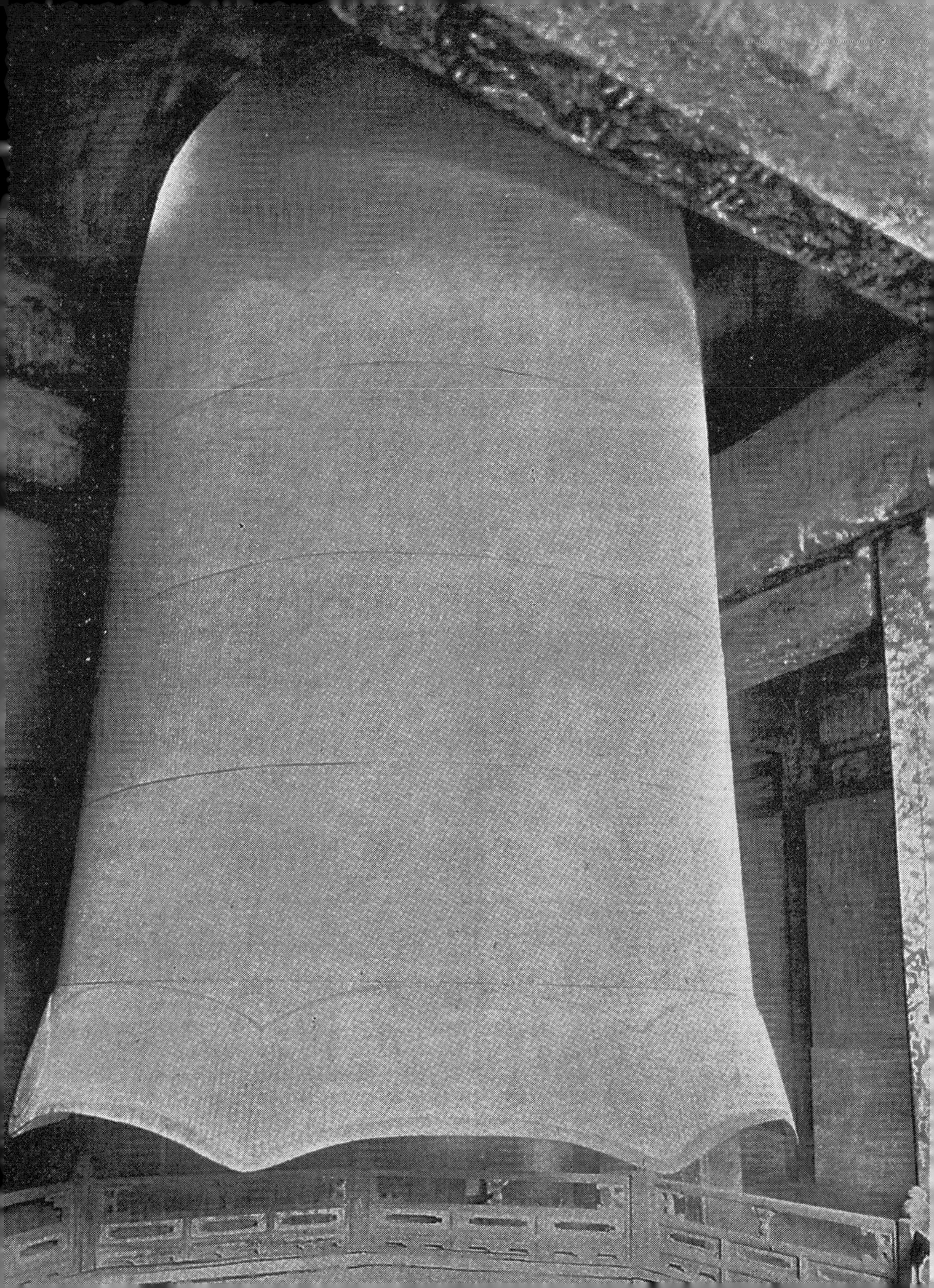

Emperors and monks were very influenced by superstition, seasons and locations. Apparently they couldn't decide where the most appropriate place was to put this bell, so they left it buried somewhere for about 100 years. Points of the compass were important: North was associated with water and West with metal. A location of Northwest was chosen as the religious high-ups said, 'Metal produces water'. They considered that striking bells and praying at the same time would bring on the rainy season, necessary for crops. Part of the reason they wanted colossal bells, apart from the kudos, was because the bigger the bell, the further away it could be heard. It is said that this bell could be heard fifty miles away if they clouted it hard enough, so more Chinese peasants quaked in their flip-flops.

The right time to cast a large bell was always carefully charted by astrologers. A Burmese bell christened 'Maha Ganda' (Great Sound) is at a pagoda in Yangon and is inscribed, 'On the eleventh day of the moon crossing Iabotwai, after the third watch, the position of the stars being good, this bell was cast'. This was in 791, two years and six months after the bell had first been ordered by the monarch, Singu Min. Were the Koreans told, 'Get on with it and finish it quickly, before he changes his mind.'?

The Japanese put bells on all the sticking out bits of pagodas, and a disk like a weather vane was glued to the bottom of the wooden clapper, so gusts of wind made the bells sound. This was considered very religious and mystical as God had made the bells sound, not a man. The oldest surviving bell in Japan was cast in 698 and is in Kyoto. Like many other very large Chinese bells, this one was probably made by the Koreans who certainly got around. Legend has it that it has been rung every day since it was first put in place, for fifteen minutes at sunset; so a lot of evenings since 698.

In countries such as Russia, a collection of stationary bells (from very large to small) were played by one or two men sitting on chairs. Ropes attached to the clappers were held in both hands, or tied to their elbows as well as their feet. For big bells, there was a piece of wood that was pressed down. Waving any part of their anatomy (well, nearly any part) gave random sounds or some sort of sequence. The main use, by monks, was for religious purposes, and the technique is called 'Zvon'. When you are close to big bells, the sound is extremely loud. In 1912, the Russian author, N. Olovyanishnikov (so he sounds Russian to me) stated that the monks often put gooseberries in their ears. This isn't a duff translation; they used gooseberries! In 1917, to get funds from foreign exchange after the Russian revolution, many large bells and thousands of smaller ones were broken up and sold as scrap.

Many bellfounders also made cannons as the metal used was almost identical to bell metal. This was very handy if you were a bit short of orders for bells. The bellfounders who produced cannons as well were often made 'official cannon makers' by the authorities. When there was a decent war being fought, cannons were the first requirement, and you couldn't say, 'I'm in the middle of making some bells, so get in the queue'.

Bells gradually became used for purposes other than religion, or to ward off evil spirits. Bells that were not destined for religious use, or were rejects, were placed near watchtowers to warn the soldiers when some cheeky, invading bandits had been spotted legging it over the plains. They were used for special events such as to summon sellers of cattle to market, or quasi-religious use, where they approximately marked the particular time of day. Agricultural workers knew when to start work or stop, by the sound of a bell, and no doubt muttered, 'Oh no! Surely it isn't time to get up!'

Bells were also rung to stop lightning or storms, or mitigate other natural disasters. I have a very old book with a section about bells, first published in English in 1740 and translated from the original French. I came across the 1749 amended edition in a bookshop and thought I paid over the odds for it. The lady in the shop said, 'Well, it was printed in 1749, so I'm not over charging you.' In all, there are eight volumes about all sorts of things, and this one is number seven. The whole set is entitled, *Nature Display'd,* and on the first page it reads: *Spectacle de la Nature or Nature Display'd. Being Discourses On such Particulars of Natural History As were thought most proper to Excite the Curiosity and Form the Minds of Youth. Containing What belongs to Man confider'd in Society.*

It has details of some interesting observations from the 1500s to 1600s. The author writes, 'The Motion of the Air agitated by the Ringing out of one or several Bells, are Causes very fit to dissipate storms, or even fitter to pierce the Clouds and determine the Fall of the Fire'. Then he adds, 'I Have, within these thirty Years, been Witness of five Storms, in which the Thunder-bolt fell upon five different Steeples where all the Bells were ringing out'. So there we have it; it must be true! The Latin inscription on 'The Great Bell' (nine tons/9.16 tonnes) at the Minster of Schaffhausen, cast in 1427, is: 'I call the living, Mourn the dead, Shatter lightening'. An Italian bell from 1843 has the inscription: 'I drive away lightning, I call the living, I weep for the dead'; so even in 1843, another allusion to lightning.

So bells were rung to warn of storms or fend off lightning, but weather forecasters often get it wrong even now, with satellites and other gizmos. Some pleasant young woman on one of the TV channels gives you a big smile and says that tomorrow it will be blisteringly hot. So women wear skimpy clothes, and men have shorts and hideous Hawaiian shirts. When they go out for a stroll, it tips it down and they get soaked. Or (still smiling) she says it will be really cruddy with ice, snow and severe floods. So, if you were going off to play golf, you cancel this, and what happens? It is quite sunny with a few clouds. If she burst into tears and sobbed when announcing terrible weather, you might feel really sorry for her when she got it wrong.

What they have all forgotten is that in 1503, Pope Pius III disbanded a society that was investigating the weather; so early meteorologists. He told them firmly, 'Storms are caused by God or by witches, so don't pretend otherwise'.

The Chinese divided sunrise to sunset into six units all with subdivided quarters, which meant the time periods varied with the seasons, but not too important if you worked in the fields. The latitude in different parts of the world also has an effect. If you had been doing a spot of looting and pillage, you may well have collared an attractive sundial. When you get back home on your ship and set it up to show your friends, it doesn't work at all because you are in a different part of the world. They say, 'Never mind, but don't bother us next time.'

In 1120, the French Cistercian monks seem to be the first people to divide the day and night into equal units. They didn't bother telling anyone else as they had taken a vow of silence, so it was about one hundred years before other people started doing the same thing.

When bells became used for marking the time, they did this initially by having a device called a 'Clepsydra' where water dripped out of a large plant pot with a very small hole in the bottom. It slowly filled another container which tipped over every hour if they got the drip right. This banged a lever down that hit the bell - very cunning. In other places, the water made metal balls drop into the sloping mouth of different shaped bells. There must have been someone who had to collect the balls and put them back at the top every so often.

In the 14th century, basic mechanical clocks were built, and in Padua in Italy in 1344 one used two weights that hung down. One was for the clock and one for triggering a bell, exactly the same as grandfather clocks. Clock bells got bigger on the principle that bigger bells were louder, and putting bells high up in a tower helped. The clock weights now hung down a long way, through various levels. This helped the man who had to wind the weights back up. He only had to say to his wife once a week, 'I'm just nipping off to wind the clock. Keep doing the housework while I'm gone.' Clocks and bells were by this time not always in churches. Despite this, the bells usually had religious inscriptions.

Francesco Cancellieri (1751-1826), who wrote oodles of books, tells us that a 14th century clock bell at Ulm town hall in Germany was inscribed: 'O merciful God, Jesus Christ, have pity on all who hear my sound who are Christians, amen, and on all believing souls, amen. O King of Glory, come to us bringing peace, amen. O Virgin Mary, pray for us. St. Luke, St. Mark, St. John, St. M'. It wasn't that the bellfounder didn't know how to spell Matthew, but because he ran out of space on the bell!

In the 16th century, dials began to be added to clocks which helped tell exactly what hour of the day it was. To start with there was just an hour hand, but there was a major disagreement as to whether the 'first hour' began at sunset, midnight or sunrise. When the Gregorian calendar was adopted in 1582, there were officially twenty-four 'Equinoctial' hours, and the numeral XII was at the top of the dial. In many places, particularly Italy, Austria, France and Spain, where there was just an hour bell, the hourly strokes were repeated twice, with a gap of about four to five minutes in case you had your head in the oven the first time.

Ships' bells were rung every half hour by a boy using sand glasses (egg timers to you), and the sailors said a quick prayer to prevent shipwrecks, or for better food and less scurvy. As ships got bigger, the largest of three bells was placed on the bridge, the next largest at the sharp end, and the smallest at the crow's nest. The lookout had to ring his bell after the bell was rung on the bridge to show he hadn't nodded off, and shout, 'All's well!'

On land, special figures known as 'Jacks' rotated out of a space under the dial, or were a permanent fixture. This is obviously the forerunner of cuckoo clocks. They either struck bells you could see or appeared to, but there were often other bells behind the clock.

Top right: *A Chinese bronze crotal, 4.8 ins/12 cms diameter, in the possession of the author. The inscription refers to the very bloody Taiping rebellion of 1851-1864.*
Photos by author
Bottom right: *A Russian monk at the Kostroma Ipatievsky monastery ringing some small bells 'Zvon' style.*
Photo: Matthias Kabel

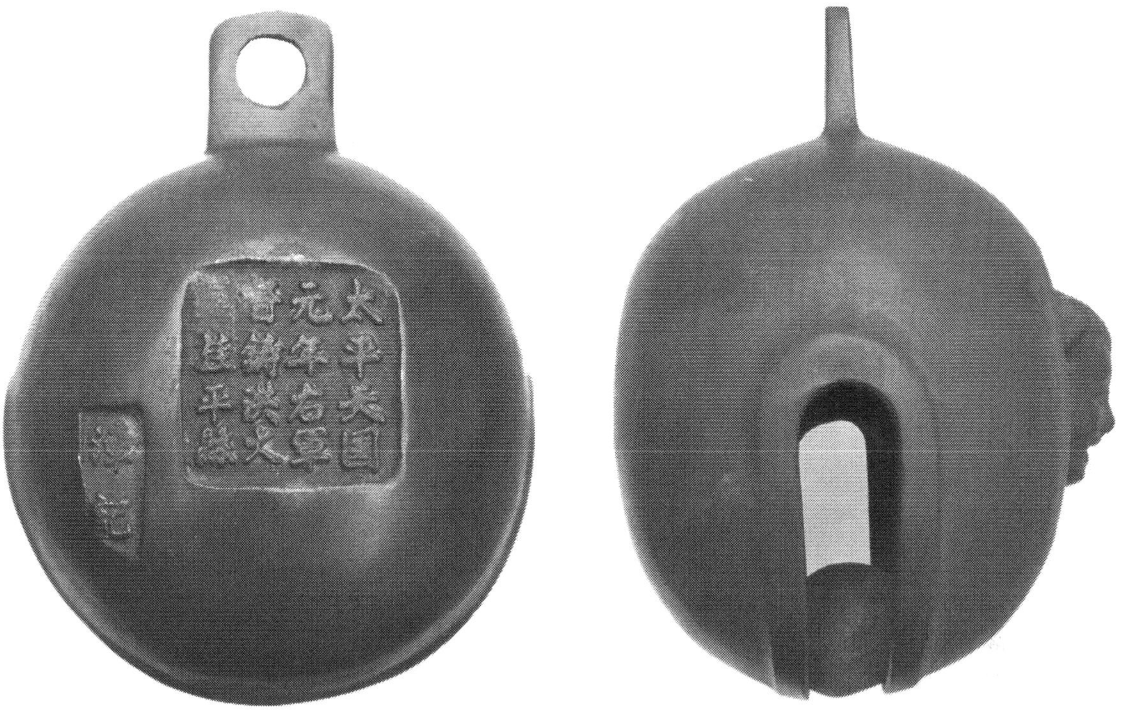
太平天国
元年右軍

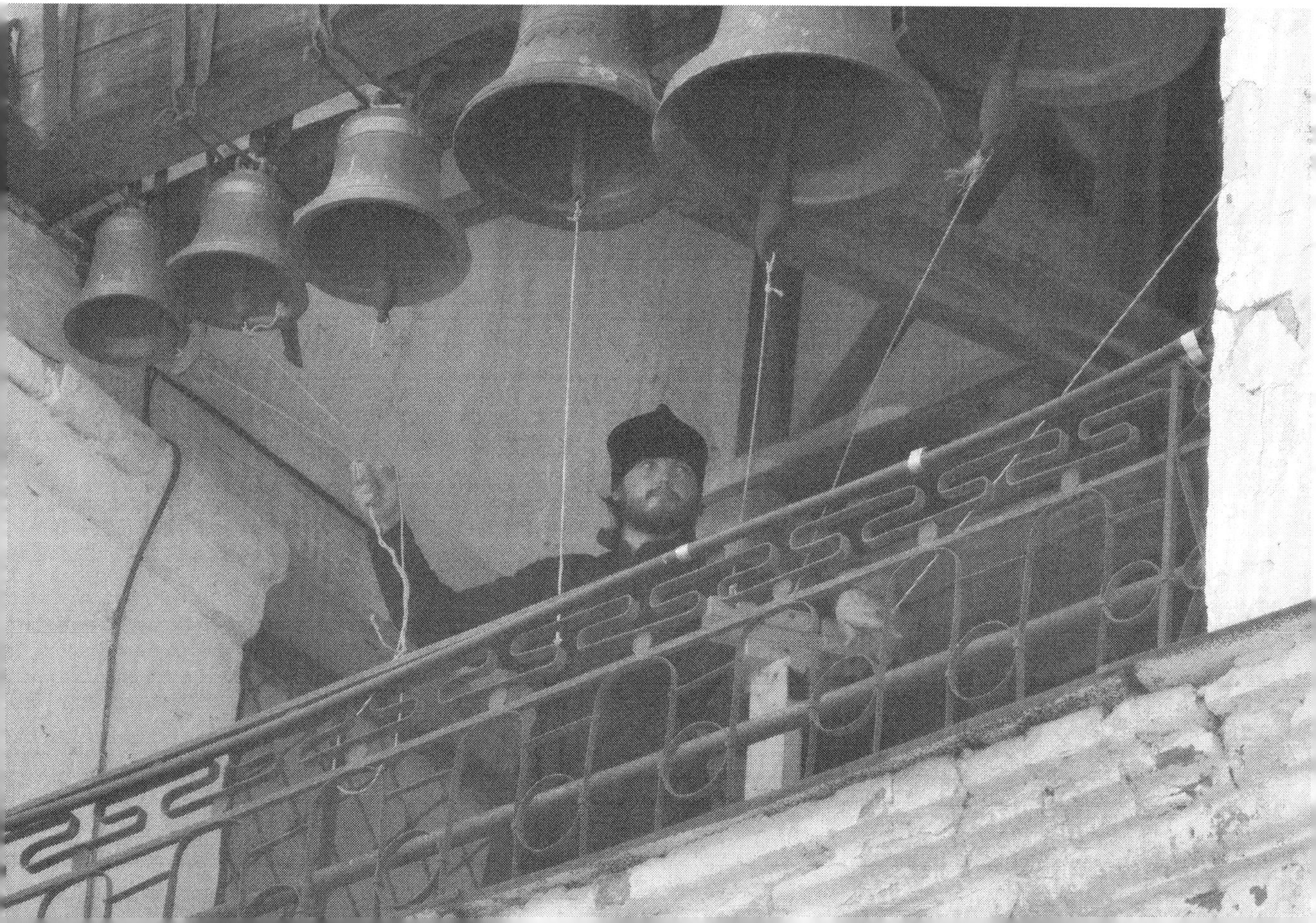

It became a good wheeze for invading troops to nick these jacks and take them back home. A French invasion force in 1382 took some mechanical figures from a church in Belgium and installed them at Dijon in France, where the mustard comes from. They are still there today. It's bad enough suffering a defeat, but to have your jacks stolen as well!

Coming back to churches and monks, the main use was to call people to church for a service and announce this for people not able to get to church. Work stopped for a moment, people knelt in the streets, workers in the fields paused, and everybody recited a prayer. Bells tolled to announce deaths, funerals, and different events in the church year, and it was considered that bells were the messengers of God's word. In the Bible it says, 'The voice of the Lord is in power'. Bells were often rung in the evening before a fast day to remind the faithful that on the next day they had to stop eating and observe the fast.

The *Liber Pontificalis,* a Vatican book, tells us that Pope Stephen II (752-757) erected a belfry with three bells (campanae) at St. Peter's in Rome. Bells were often blessed and baptised, and the Reverend Alfred Gatty's 1848 book, *The Bell: Its Origin, History, and Uses*, is full of interesting information. He tells us that no lesser person than Pope John VIII (872-882), 'Himself baptised at Rome, for the Lateran church, the largest bell which at that time had ever been cast. And he named it "John"'. We don't know how big this bell was, although it was obviously a European bell.

By the year 750, church bells in England had become sufficiently common for Egbert, Archbishop of York (732-766), to order in his *Excerptions* that all priests should toll them at the appointed hours he laid down. H. B. Walters, in his 1912 book *The Church Bells of England,* tells us that in Bury St. Edmunds, a large bell cast by a monk called Hailficus was given to the abbey about 1102-1105. It was hung in the central tower and said to be the largest bell in England at that time but was destroyed about 1210.

The main service in the Roman Catholic Church is called a Mass, and from the 6th century there was one every day. The most important moment is when the wine and bread are consecrated and blessed before communion and are then called the 'Blessed Sacrament'. A bell called a 'sanctus bell' rang to announce this moment for people not in church, so they could say a quick prayer. If someone was ill, and not just a nobody, the Blessed Sacrament would be taken to their house later. A boy rang a hand-bell in front of the priest. People stood aside so that there was no delay, and they were supposed to say another prayer. If they weren't quick enough, no doubt the boy shouted, 'Get out of the way.'

A 'Sermon bell' told the Catholic faithful that they ought to leg it up to church to be told what to believe. Another custom was a 'Wedding Bell', sometimes only used for this purpose. It was rung when the bride and groom arrived at the church entrance, which told their friends and family that they had better finish putting on their best clothes quickly and find where they had put their present.

If a Catholic was being excommunicated, so slung out of the Catholic Church for some severe misdoing, it was done using 'Bell, Book and Candle'. The bell told everybody to come to church, and a special religious ceremony was read out. When the candle was snuffed out, the unfortunate person was condemned to hell for ever; that must have been a bit rough.

A 'Passing Bell' was rung at the time when a death seemed certain. This drove away evil spirits who wanted to collar the spirit that was passing out of the body. Some people didn't die as expected but got better, so I expect they were given a good telling off. John Donne (1571-1631), the English poet and clergyman, wrote, 'Prayers ascend to heaven in troops at a good man's passing bell'. A different bell sounded the 'Death Knell' that announced an actual death. There was often a sequence to this bell which told the listening people whether a man, woman, or child had died. If it was for a woman you knew, you might say, 'I didn't think she looked at all well last week!'

If a king, queen, lord of the manor, or someone else really important died, the death knell bell might be rung every hour between the death and the funeral. The Bayeux Tapestry shows two boys ringing hand bells to protect the body of Edward the Confessor when his coffin was taken to Westminster Abbey in 1066. Various church bells were often rung along the journey if the person in the coffin was very important. If a normal burial was taking place, and the ground was really hard because of ice and snow, the coffin was kept until digging a grave was easier. I expect the gravediggers said, 'Sod this for a game of soldiers', when they saw the ground was rock hard. A bell known as a 'Moving Bell' signified that the coffin was on its way to be buried.

Patrick Lafcadio Hearn, an 18th century scholar, tells us that in 1055, the Council of Lisieux in the Duchy of Normandy in France decreed that every night at a certain time, a bell was rung. This told people that their fires had to be reduced to just glowing embers by being covered over, lights had to be put out, and that it was time for bed. This 'Covering of the fire' is 'Covre Feu' in French, and this is the origin of the 'Curfew Bell'. It wasn't a religious event, but church bells were used as they were handiest. In the 13th century, the time for this in London was 9p.m., and in Paris, 8p.m. in winter and 7p.m. in summer; so Londoners got to stay up later. The winter time of 8p.m. in Paris was because the fires needed stoking up more to stay warm longer. If they did it at 7p.m., the fires might go out, and everybody's teeth would start chattering. This is where the famous line in a poem by Thomas Gray comes from: 'The curfew tolls the knell of passing day'. The 1866-ish booklet I have tells us that William the Conqueror introduced this French custom into England. Christian armies on the warpath also called it a day and had a rest when the curfew bell sounded. They could get a bite to eat and lick their wounds.

Percival Price, in an excellent 1983 book entitled *Bells & Man,* cites a French source, Auguste Vidal in 1907, relating to the Danzig Lutheran Church in 1612. They decreed when bells had to be rung, and the first bell rang from 4a.m. to 5a.m. to wake people up for a morning service. At 7a.m. every morning, the largest 'Prayer Bell' rang to remind everybody, wherever they were, that they had to say a prayer. Special bells rang on Sundays, and if there was a funeral (I'm sure it had its own bell), the mid-morning bell was rung a bit later. At 5p.m. every day, the prayer bell rang again for evening prayer, followed by a curfew bell. Apart from this, bells rang for weddings, funerals, and special occasions such as the bishop dropping in! Phew! What an enormous amount of bells being rung all day and half the night. It was a bit tough in 1612, if you were a Lutheran follower.

The inscriptions were not always religious, and a bell cast in 1511 for Breda in the Netherlands reads: 'Those who would live happily in Breda must have the upper hand over their wives'. So what was going on in Breda in 1511?! Sounds like domestic strife to me.

The other bells I have not yet mentioned, particularly starting in Holland and Belgium, were bells rung to make music, and also, the very unique 'Change ringing' that takes place on sets of bells in England, to start with. Just be patient, and I'll come to these later.

2. Making Moulds

'Make your mould. The best flux in the world will not make a usable shape unless you have a mould to pour it in.'
Robert Collier

If you are claiming to be a bellfounder, you have to make bells if nothing else. All the other bits somebody else could make for you. I had 'Bellfounder' in my passport which sometimes impressed customs officers, but once at J.F.K. airport in New York they weren't at all amused. They couldn't find 'Bellfounders' in their list of approved occupations, and I had a temporary visa to work there that they didn't much like either. They went on about the small iron clapper I had taken along to bash some of the bells. They said it was an offensive weapon, which was probably true as I was seriously thinking of hitting the awkward customs man with it. Furnival Jones, who was one of the bosses of MI5, put 'Gentleman' as his occupation in his passport. An American customs bod queried this, and he asked, 'Don't you have any here?' It was fair enough; he couldn't put 'Master Spy'.

To make bells you need moulds, and you can't really get round this. If you remember the introduction, I explained that you can make 'false bells' as part of the moulding process, partly using wax that you melt away. This technique is called 'lost wax', or the more modern description, 'investment casting', but the general name is 'cire perdue' in French.

The lost wax process is used by sculptors for a bronze or other metal figure, but it isn't very easy. Suppose you are a sculptor, and there was a man or woman who won a couple of gold medals in the 2016 Olympic Games and lives in your town. The mayor decides they want a bronze statue to put in the square, and you are given the job.

You start with a stick-person using metal rods and coat hangers. Round that you form a plaster figure, like the dummies you see in shop windows, using bandages soaked in plaster. You get some thin wax sheets, like slices of processed cheese, and you mould these round your dummy and then start carving all the features. Your statue will reflect all the very detailed bits you carve on it, if you take your time. If you get fed up and think, 'I'll do this when I come back from the pub after drinking ten pints', it will be apparent that you did this when they unveil the statue.

At this stage you go back to mixing plaster and smear it carefully all over your wax figure. You then make a cylindrical shape of strong cardboard or something like that, and after putting your figure inside, you pour plaster all over it in a block. What you should have done is stick pins in the figure at various places, pretending you are a witch-doctor and want something nasty to happen to your mother-in-law. These locate your figure inside the outer plaster mould, so that when the heated wax runs out, the dummy is still exactly in the middle. What we are supposed to be doing is seeing how this process applies to bells, so let's summarize the remaining steps for your sculpture.

You turn your plaster cylinder upside down and stand it on two bricks inside a large saucepan in your kiln and heat it up so the wax runs out. You turn the cylinder right way up and pour in the metal. When it has set you can you break up the plaster cylinder. You piggle any remaining plaster out of crevices in your statue, and you smooth it with abrasive paste that comes in tins labelled 'coarse', 'medium' and 'fine', which takes a long time.

After you have made a few bronze statues, you probably say to your wife, 'I'm going to become a stone mason. I just need big blocks of stone or marble, a few hammers and chisels, and forget the wax and plaster.' If she is listening, she says, 'Good idea!', and if not, she just grunts. Making bells with moulds and wax does not involve some of the stages of making a statue, but there are other stages instead. You have done all this work in a nice workshop with neon lighting, and you listen to *Radio 2* or your favourite CDs. The roof is fine, with no leaks, and your better half keeps bringing you coffee, unless she is at the Oxfam shop getting you some more work clothes. After dinner you open a nice bottle of red.

If you started making bells from the 12th century up to about the middle of the 19th century, there is a major complication. To make decent size bells, you need to dig a large pit in a field near the church where they want them. This is why many towns and villages have land that may be called 'Bell Field', or there may be a 'Bell Lane' near the church. Initially, most bells were made by medieval monks who may have travelled from one monastery to another. We know that Saint Dunstan, but he wasn't a saint at the time of course, cast various bells, and he is the patron saint of bellringers. After this period, other individuals started casting bells who were not monks but thought this was an interesting occupation.

The reasons you need the pit are fairly simple. Firstly, the priest, vicar or local squire that is giving you the job wants it done on site. When you turn up, they want to see that you don't get blind drunk on the first night, and you ooze confidence. They also want to know that you are a devout Christian and a very regular church-goer. If they don't like the look of you, they say, 'We've had a meeting, and we don't think you are a suitable person, and we don't really think you know what you are doing, so get back on your horse.' As well as this, making a new bell is an important event for the town or village, and they want to watch how you do it.

From your point of view, you don't have an airy workshop - anywhere. You are an itinerant bellfounder which means you travel up and down the country, or at least in a certain area. You are touting for work when the weather is good in winter or spring. If you did manage to make a bell somewhere else, hauling it down country lanes would be a real bind, and you haven't got a white Ford Transit truck.

Once you accept that you are going to be working in a pit by the church, the only advantages are that there are local carpenters, a blacksmith, available bricks, local sand, and clay, and wood and coal for the furnace. 'What furnace?' 'Sorry!' You have to build one at the top of the pit. Lifting the bell out of the pit is possible with some ropes and pulleys, or beams and horses if it is a very large bell.

When you travel to the church or town hall you don't need an enormous amount of kit or tools. The most important thing is that you have prepared a wide wooden board that won't twist when wet, and on this board you have drawn two shapes. One is for making the inner mould, called a 'core', that is the inside shape of a finished bell when you look up it from underneath. The other one is for the external shape of the bell, and in the lost wax process, this is the shape of the outside of the false bell. Bishops and other church bosses wear 'copes' that are like posh cloaks with lots of different colours and embroidery, although poor monks only have plain ones. You need to be smarmy and keep on good terms with bishops, vicars, Catholic priests and monks as they give you most of your work, so the outer mould is called a 'cope'.

The shapes you have drawn are absolutely critical. In a European bell, the bottom edge is called the lip. The internal and external profiles both curve outwards from the lip. This thick part of the bell is called the 'sound bow' and is where the clapper is going to strike it. It needs to be thick enough for the clapper not to crack the bell. Bronze bells are fairly brittle and can be cracked quite easily. If you are breaking an old bell up, you just give it some thwacks with a sledge hammer; you don't have to try and cut it up.

Above the sound bow the bell is thinner, and this is called the 'waist'. When you get nearly to the top of the bell it curves inwards, forming the 'shoulder', and starts getting thicker again. The top of the bell is called the 'head' or 'crown'. This has to be thick enough to have things like jug handles at the top, or eventually be drilled and have bolts going through it. You have to fix the bell to whatever it hangs from.

Quite often, the bells you are making have to have certain similarities to other bells, so if you are at a church where they have three bells, and they want another one, you have to take note of the existing profiles and diameters. You make yours the same, and hopefully, this gives your new one a sound that fits in with the others. If you have been asked to cast a single bell, you use a shape that you have decided is best. The size and weight are related to how much dosh they have.

Very old bells are taller than modern bells, and the first dated bell in England is this shape, cast in 1254. If you want to see it, it's at Lisset in East Yorkshire. Other bells around this period have inscriptions that may be a saint's name, or a phrase from the bible, but dates on a bell were not all that common. When bellfounders started putting an inscription, 'Cast by Joe Blogs, from Cheapside, in London, on March 1st, 1756', these are the easiest to date.

When you are drawing out your bell shape on the board that you need to take with you, it is very complicated. A good place to start is at the bottom of the lip, with the outside diameter. You then get involved in all sorts of geometrical measurements for the profile. If you have divided the diameter into twelve or twenty-four equal measurements, you can use this distance, called a 'brim', to start forming the shape further up, or the total height. In this book I have mentioned, printed in1749, the profile is given as starting with: 'The Thickness of the brim of the Bell to be cast, or the Thickness of the Brim of the largest Bell, when he is to make many agree together with different Notes. The Brim is the fundamental Rule of the whole work'. So okay, we're following this, aren't we? He then says, 'To measure the said Thickness, he uses Compasses with bent Legs, and carries this Measurement upon a Rule, divided into Feet, Inches, and Lines'.

Then it gets complicated! The next bit is: 'Such is, for Instance, the Measure NA. The Brim GE is the same Measure as NA, which is divided into three thirds. Each third is called a "Body", in French, "Corps"'. A bit further down, he tells us, 'The Sound-bow GEA is a Triangle, whose Basis GA is the diagonal of the Square, which the Side GE multiplied by itself, or by its equal EA, would form'. Phew! There are pages and pages of this, but you get the drift. The contours of the outside and inside shapes are almost exclusively arcs of circles of some diameter, so portions of a circle. This is where compasses come in handy, but they might have two legs six feet long, so you need your apprentice to hold the end with the point.

I am going to be mentioning John Taylor & Company a lot; the bellfounders in Loughborough, where I worked. They started drawing out the shape using a quarter of an ellipse, not a circle. If you eye up a kiwi fruit, its outline is an ellipse, and you can see it is quite different to the round shape of an orange, and the taste is very different too. We will look at this new shape later on, but it was a big step forward. Drawing up these profiles has to be done when you are wide awake and alert, and at home. Apart from being very complicated, you don't really want anyone else watching to see how you do it! You consider that this is one of your 'secrets'.

So you get to the church, make sure the horses are given some food and straw, and find out where you are going to stay. I've said 'horses' because you have taken your son, nephew, or apprentice. You don't take your son-in-law in case he doesn't cut the mustard and wanders off after he has only been married for six months. If you think he is a really decent bloke, you might tell him something about making bells, but not as much as your son. He's family.

The next day they show you where they expect you to dig a pit, but some local labourers are going to do this for you. If the place you have been shown is a bit wet, you say, 'Where to next?' Damp holes are really bad news. If you are making just one bell, a square pit is fine, but if you have to provide three bells you need a much larger pit. The basic requirements are that when you are making the moulds, you have to have room to walk right round with your wooden 'sweep' or 'strickle board'. The top of the finished mould has to be below ground level so the metal can flow in as it won't go uphill. Your labourers find this hard work, but you have to keep saying, 'You need to go down a lot deeper, and the hole is not wide enough.' Eventually, you get this done to your satisfaction. Summertime is best as you don't want to be working in a downpour.

Right: *Forming the core mould in a pit with a large wooden strickle or sweep board at the French Cornille-Havard bellfoundry in 2012 for one of the eight bells destined for Notre Dame Cathedral. The date could equally be 1912 or even 1812.*
Photo: Vincent M.

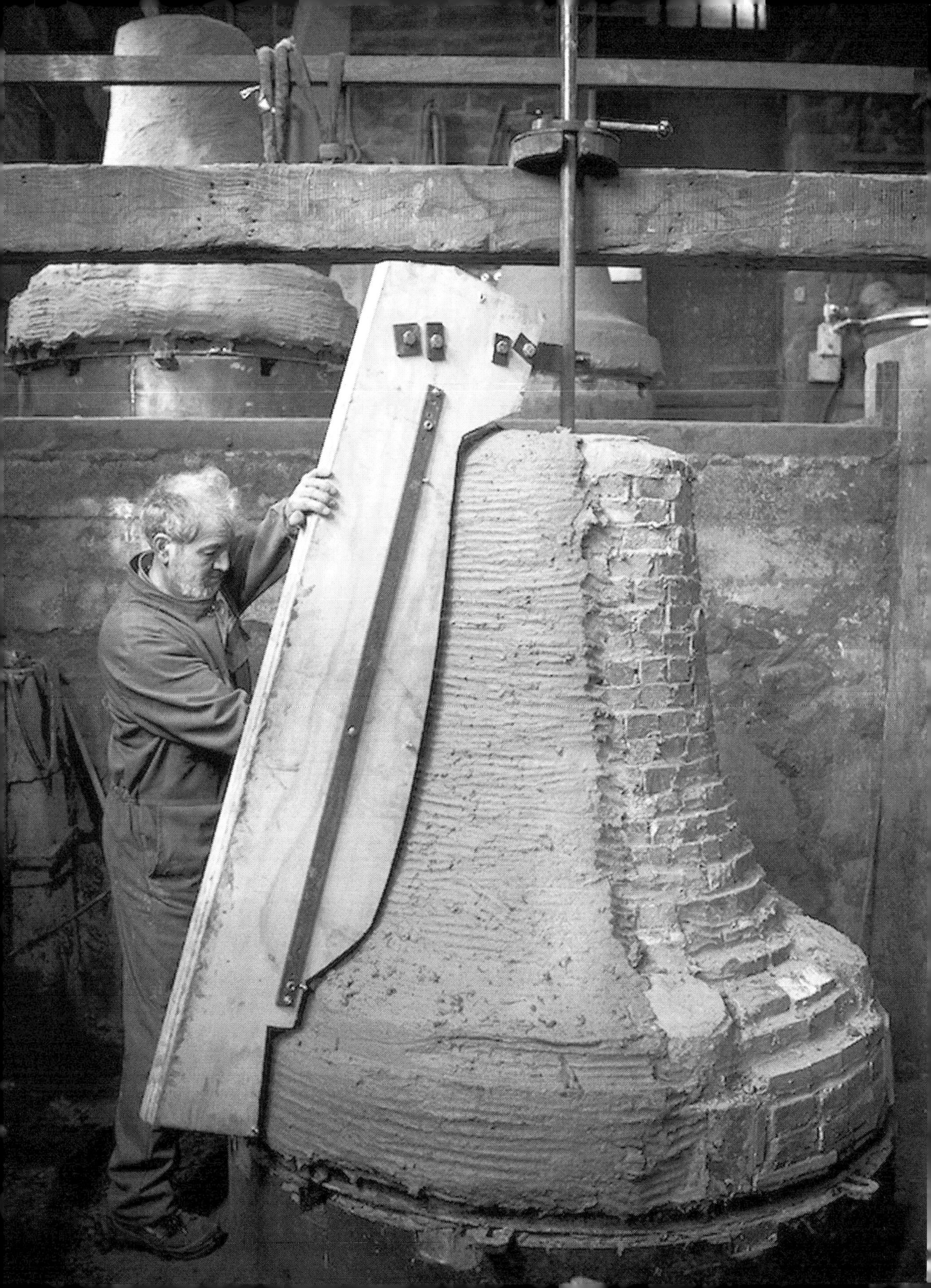

When you are happy that the outside and inside shapes on your board look okay, the local carpenter cuts the board to the inside one. This will be used to make the mould that is the inside shape of the bell, called the core.

A blacksmith has made you a strong stake which is hammered into the ground in the middle of the pit, to halfway up the core height. Another strong rod rotates in a hole at the centre of the top of this stake, and finishes above ground level. A piece of flat iron on your sweep board that fits into a slot near the top of this rod is tightened with wedges. Now I think if I had been a bellfounder a few hundred years ago (God forbid!), I would have got my local blacksmith to make the stakes and rods. They have to be precise, and you need quite a few.

Before you get round to setting the sweep up, you get some bricks and lay a flat circular disk at the bottom of the pit, a bit bigger than the lip diameter. You may need two courses, depending on the size of the bell, and this is called a 'Bellfounder's mill stone', except it is brick, not stone. Now you can start making the core. The sweep board shape, from where the bell's lip will be, extends further down to the brick base. This shape is made at the bottom of both the core and the cope, so that the two shapes will mate together, with no gap. You put your sweep board in and check the rod is vertical with a plumb-bob, (a piece of metal with a point, on a piece of string), because you don't know about spirit levels. Now, you need a lot more bricks, and if these are second-hand or rejects from the brickworks, they will be cheaper than new ones. You start laying the bricks, end on, and keep putting on more courses, checking that the sweep is a suitable distance from the bricks as you turn it round. The core is not solid; you leave a good size hole in the middle, all the way up.

When the pit was being dug, you looked at the earth to see how much clay was in it. If there isn't very much, you need some more, and sand. You also want some horse manure, so you told the man at the stables to keep collecting it along with used straw. You also need horsehair, or goat hair. With a bit of forward planning, you brought some of this with you as you want a fair bit.

You get someone to start shovelling the earth that has been dug out, without any stones, and then add clay, sand, manure, chopped straw, and the horse or goat hair, all mixed together with water. This turns into a really gooey substance like thick mud that a bellfounder calls 'loam'. You or your apprentice are going to want to rotate the sweep board, but a labourer or two slap on the loam and smooth it over roughly with their hands. They have to roll up their sleeves, otherwise their wives or mothers will go mental. It's a certainty that when they get home, the women will say, 'My God! You stink!' They keep plastering on this mud till there is only a minute gap all the way up between the loam and the sweep board. When it looks good, you lift out the board and rod. It's convenient if it is now supper time. This is because you drop wood and embers from a fire you started above the pit, into the hole in the middle of the core. You close off the top so the fire smoulders, and say, 'Goodnight, sleep tight.' By morning, the core may be dry, or if not, you keep going with more embers.

When it all looks wonderful and is dry, you use the sweep to make sure it is a very snug fit all round then lift it out again. If you were going to make the outer shape inside a big metal case that you eventually use after having abandoned the lost wax process, the core is made the same way, with bricks and loam.

While the core was baking, the carpenter cut your sweep board to the outer profile. First, you brush a mixture of wax and oil over the core, which is like greasing a cake tin and stops the false bell sticking to it. The sweep goes back in, and the false bell is started with flat loam bricks like square fish cakes, with as little loam as you can get away with to stick them together. These loam bricks were made and dried when one of the labourers had a spare moment. These steps, using several layers of runny loam, result in a shape that is exactly the same as the outside shape of the bell. Well, hopefully. When the false bell is completely dry by putting more embers into the core, you are ready to dribble hot wax all the way round it using the sweep to keep the shape. You have made a few small slots at various places in the sweep, and these make some ridges like shoelaces all round the bell that make it look a bit sexier. Bells without these look really boring! The ones you have formed at the top of the waist are really handy for getting level the wax lettering that you are going to put on it.

The bods who are paying for the bell want an inscription on it, or a coat of arms, or an impression of some medallions or coins. You have some oak boards into which a master carpenter has carved the letters of the alphabet, backwards way round. When you have put melted wax into them, they look like normal letters when you prise them out. Alternatively, you may have a set of stamps to make the letters. If they want some medallions, you press these into clay to make a mould. This is where the lost wax process is a lot easier than having to do this on the inside of an outer mould, in a big bucket-type case. Providing they pay, you can put a fancy design all round the bell near the lip or at the shoulder, with crosses, or practically anything, but it may take a very long time as it is really fiddly.

Progressing a few centuries, when you are making these bells in your own foundry, not in a field, you can put on a wax representation of saints, angels, flowers and leaves, etcetera. Any wax figures or letters are glued onto the layer of wax on the false bell, and an egg white mix is good for this. Your junior apprentice can keep knocking out the letters, and put them in a tray with compartments, just like the typeface early printers used.

When you think you have finished, before you go home for the night, you go cap in hand to whoever gave you the piece of parchment with the inscription written on it. You ask them to drop by ASAP. If the man that comes wears a thing like a dress and a big cross round his neck, there is a fair chance that he has given you something in Latin. When he comes and says, 'Bless you, my son', and makes the sign of the cross, you know everything is fine. If he says it's okay, but the letter you thought was an 'O' is actually a 'Q', you can cope with this. You get your penknife out and cut off the offending letter. Altering anything in wax is not a great problem.

In the 1880s, John William Taylor I, in Loughborough, decided he might be losing orders because his outer profiles were now all made in metal casks or cases. The detail you could imprint into these moulds was limited, with no angels with trumpets, or saints. He went to see Marcel Michiel, a Belgian bellfounder who was making carillons, to pick his brains regarding false bells and the lost wax process. This didn't help him as he complained, 'They keep this thing very close'. He also tried to tempt some skilled foreign workers to come to Loughborough, but this didn't work out either!

By 1897 he was buying sets of letter and ornamentation moulds, which totalled 101 pieces, from a company in Birmingham. He then contacted the Italian Parlanti family who had set up the 'Art Bronze Founders of Fulham' company. In 1898, he paid them twenty guineas (£21) to come and show him how to do it. He wasn't giving up! 50% of the money was paid up front and 50% after he had mastered the technique. In one of his notebooks, he detailed the complete process which was very complicated. He produced a twenty-four inch bell in 1898 that was sent to a Roman Catholic school in Kendal. It was very ornate, but still with some room for improvement. It is now in the Taylor bellfoundry museum.

By 1899 the process was sufficiently understood and mastered for the four bells that were being recast for Loughborough Parish Church to be used as a show piece. By now they had also perfected the tuning skills which they had been fervently experimenting with. This set of bells was suitably proclaimed, from both points of view, as being a triumph. So he had got there! These weren't small bells; the largest weighs 30 cwts/1.5 tons/1,527 kg.

In 1907, his son, John William II, observed, 'During the latter years of his life, my father amused himself with casting bells, moulded by the "cire perdue" process. This admits much more ornamentation, but is dreadfully slow and tedious.' The idea of regularly making a false bell with wax decoration was dropped. It remained being known as 'the continental way'. It was briefly revived in 1913 for the new four smallest bells to make a set of ten for Surfleet in Lincolnshire. The last time it was used was for the four smallest bells at Lincoln Cathedral, cast in 1928. Both these additional sets of bells were the brainchild of the Rev. H. Law James, one of England's most famous and influential bellringers. He personally paid for the additional bells at Surfleet and for considerable restoration work when he was the vicar there from 1898. He formed the Lincoln Diocesan Guild of Church Bell Ringers and subsequently published *A Collection of Methods* (different ways of ringing church bells).

So getting back to your pit in a field, you now have a false bell, suitably ornamented with wax lettering and probably some wax medallions or coins, all approved.

Right: *'Johannesglocke' (John bell) Diameter 7 ft/ 2.13 m, weight 7.7 tons/ 7.8 tonnes, cast by F. Schilling & Son in Apolda, Germany, in 1928, in the northwest tower at Meissen Cathedral. The false bell would have looked identical, but the canons would have had their own mould.*
Photo: origin unknown.

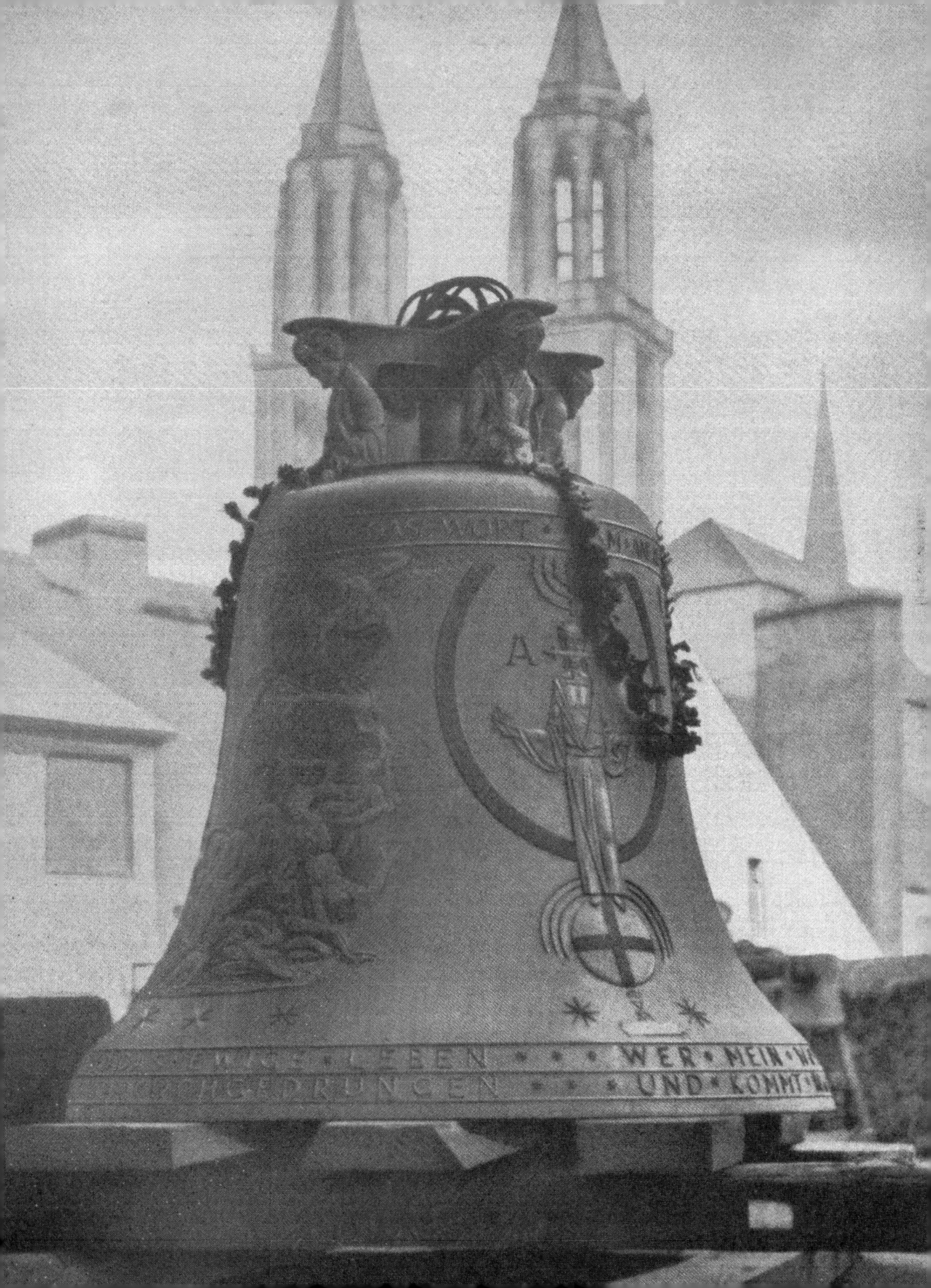
WORT
LEBEN
WER • MEIN
UND • KOMMT

3. Finishing the Moulds, Pouring the Metal

'Never was Bell-Founder so confounded, when his Mettle miscarries.'
The History of Don Quixote of Mancha and his Trusty Squire Sancho Pancha

Once your false bell is finished, with all the decoration and wording approved, you go on to the next step. The labourers start mixing up quite a sloppy loam mixture but without the chopped hay as you want this to be quite a fine mix. This is pasted onto the false bell, and you want all the wax decoration to be carefully covered. Once it is done you leave it to dry, and then you put on another layer with the normal loam mix. The idea is that the cope is reasonably solid at this stage. You make sure there is plenty of horse hair in the mix, and you probably put some iron bands round it as well. When it is dry, you put a lot more hot coals or burning wood inside the core, so it gets really hot. When the false bell is hot, the wax runs out from some slots you cut at the bottom.

If two men who had three Weetabix for breakfast can lift the cope off, you can examine the backwards way round letters and decoration. There may be one or two places where it needs the last traces of wax removing. If it is a very large cope, and there is room in the pit, you don't have to move it right out to the top. You get your bods to lift it away from the core with ropes. These go round some sticking out bits you thoughtfully made on the cope half way down, or from some slots you made right at the bottom. Be careful because the last thing you need is the cope dropping down onto your head! You position it so that you can have a look in with a candle to check the inscription. If it is fine, you then light a fire of straw under it, or if you are going modern you use bitumen. This gives the cope a reasonable coating of soot which will fill any very minor imperfections. Now the cope is removed you break up the false bell which is a bit like shelling a hard-boiled egg. Once you have started, pieces will break off. All this material from the false bell is now scrap unless you have your own foundry and you can chew it up to go in another load of loam.

To finish the core you have to close off the hole at the top. Old bells don't have a flat top. They are slightly conical inside and outside. The only thing is, there are no drilling machines within several hundred miles, if at all, and you need a clapper inside the bell. You get the blacksmith to make you a strong piece of wrought iron that is 'U' shaped. This is going to be set in below the top of the core mould, so that when the bell has been cast you can suspend your clapper from it. The two legs of the 'U' shape stick up into the space between the core and the cope moulds, and the molten metal swirls round it and locks it into the head of the bell. So you make a thing like a Chinese coolie-hat out of clay and loam with the crown staple above and below it, and you close off the core hole. The last thing you do is brush a mixture of ash and water all over the core to make it as smooth as possible.

Assuming the 'U' shaped 'crown-staple' is nice and chunky, this is really good for your grandson when he becomes a bellfounder. It starts to rust, with a good chance that it causes a crack in the head of the bell. The technical term is 'expansion and contraction of differing metals'. When this happens, this is a really good excuse for your grandson to say to his customer, 'Well, you need another bell.' When he tells them this, they ask, 'Well, why did your grandfather do this?' His reply is, 'He didn't know any better then!' So you finish the top of the core not knowing this will really please your grandson. Other bellfounders use cast-in crown staples too, so your grandson can condemn these bells as well. In about 1880, John William Taylor I from the Loughborough bellfoundry wrote to a clergyman who was whining on about his bell being cracked. He told him, 'More than 50% of all cracked bells are cracked because of the cast-in crown-staple'.

The next step is to finish the cope. This is very tricky when you thought you had nearly finished! Because there are no drilling machines, your bell needs some hefty 'jug handles' at the top. You will use these to put big metal rods through, with metal straps up to the big bit of wood which suspends the bell. If you remember, this is called a headstock and will have axles fitted to it if the bell is being swung. At the top of the cope mould you have left a big hole which is the same diameter as a disc you will use to mould the jug handles separately.

The name for these jug handles is 'canons'. You are going to make a replica of these, and on a small bell you may only need four. On bigger bells you may want six or eight. There are various methods including making these out of straw bound together to the approximate shape and then covered in wax. At a German bellfoundry they make them using flat pieces of wax to form a hollow box section. When you are happy with the shape of the canons you pack a fairly sloppy mixture of loam and clay all round them. You want to finish up with a circular shape at the bottom just a bit bigger than the hole in your cope mould. When it is fully dry you melt out the wax or set fire to the straw and wax if you have done it this way. You put this finished mould on one side for the moment.

This next stage is extremely important. You 'close' the two moulds so that they fit snugly together at the bottom. No bellfounder is going to let anyone else do this, probably not even his son, and certainly not his apprentice. The most important thing is that the cope is a perfect fit over the core. If you wrote A, B, C, and D, at the bottom of the core and cope before you lifted the cope away, this was a good forward thinking plan. This will help you to make sure the cope is in the same place in relation to the core when you lower it down. This is very nerve racking, so you take a few minutes off and have a brew before you complete this operation.

Right: *Two foundry workers at Taylor's standing beside the case and core moulds for a large bell about to be closed down; exact date not known.*
Photo: Taylor archive

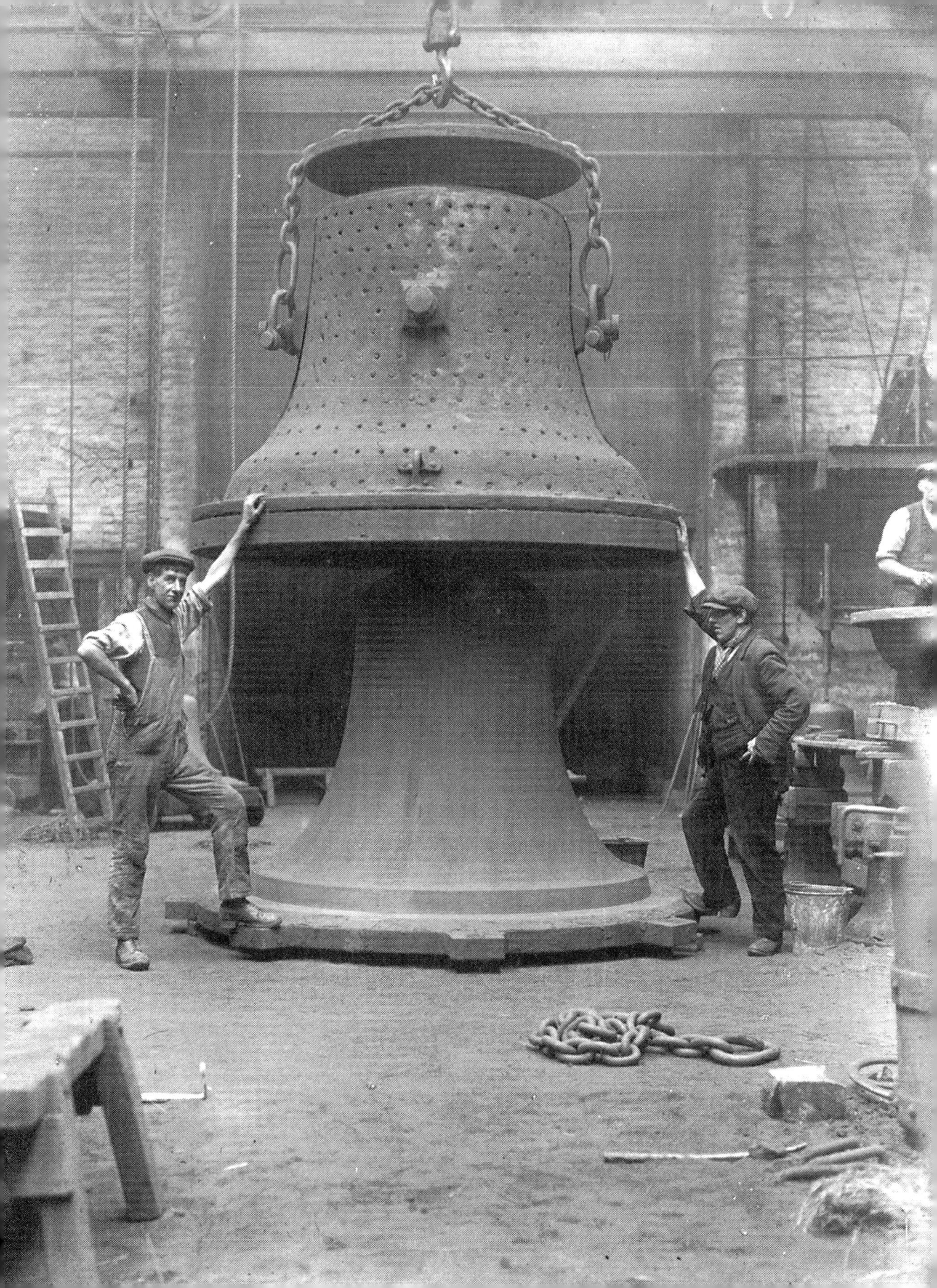

If the big hole at the top of the cope mould is about level with the sticky up bits of the crown staple you can measure all round to see if it looks central. If not, it has to be!

The 1866-ish book about the London Whitechapel foundry has an engraving showing this exactly how I have described it. Once you are happy, the coolie hat with the mould for the canons is fixed in place. You are not going to move the cope again before casting the bell, but it has to be as strong as possible. There is a lot of pressure at the lip when the metal is poured in.

The physics involved is just the same as when women teeter about on stiletto heels. To keep upright, they have to throw their shoulders back which makes their breasts stick out. Most men find this attractive, but all their weight is now on the very small end of their stiletto heels. This equates to 240 pounds per square inch for an average woman and can punch holes in vinyl flooring very easily. If they stand on your bare foot by mistake, it's definitely a hospital job.

You are extremely close to wanting some metal, and this is the next problem. If you have broken up another bell this is fine, and there may be some left over. You tell them, 'This has no value, but I will take it off your hands!' If you get away with this it's brilliant, but perhaps you need another horse and a cart. They may say, 'Do you think we are idiots?' and tell you that you have to take some money off the price. One way of deciding how much metal was needed was to weigh the false bell when it had been broken up. This weight is likely to be approximately 10% of the weight of the metal you need.

If there is no broken metal, you need copper and tin, with the tin being about 23% of the total, but if you are being mean, a bit more than 20%. There is a big difference in price if you are making a big bell as tin is expensive. In my old, 1749 book it says, 'The red Copper is undeniably the best. The Yellow, though of an inferior Quality on Account of the Calamine, may however do. But no other Kind of Copper. Mixtures of this Kind would render the Metal too brittle, and the Sound too dull. Tin of the finest Sort, is added to the Copper.' As you don't know what 23% looks like, you sort out the metal into thirteen ingots or piles of copper to every four portions of tin. This 13:4 ratio was considered the ideal metal mix to make bells at John Taylor & Co. As there are different alloys of bronze, this mix of just copper and tin in these proportions is called bellmetal.

Quite often, the vicar will have told all his flock that they are to bring him old copper kettles, pans, or anything he mistakenly thinks is useful but not made of copper or tin such as candlesticks or old pint mugs. You don't tell him these are useless and will totally disappear in the furnace. Everybody likes to say, 'A bit of the metal in the bell belonged to me.'

So you round up your labourers, but the wife of one of them says he has a bad back. As you saw him quite nimbly jigging round in the pub last night you tell his wife, 'He is faking a bad back so get him down here.' The labourers have to shovel the earth carefully back into the pit. Every so often they have to jump up and down as you want the earth compacted as much as possible. They smack it down with wrought iron rods with a big lump at the bottom called 'rammers'. If you have three completed moulds ready for the metal this is a long job.

Finishing the Moulds, Pouring the Metal

The labourers now realise why you needed such a deep hole, but they have to fill it up to the top of the moulds with a bit of a gap up to ground level. They are not all village idiots, and they think to themselves, *Looks like we're going to have to dig the moulds out again! Isn't this hard work? How about we ask for better wages?*

Meanwhile, the bricklayer has been building your furnace, shaped just like an igloo. Eskimos know that the best way to build a house is to keep slamming on blocks of ice and reducing the diameter as they go up. Bricklayers know this too, and putting a brick arch over an entrance using a former is very common. The bricks all press down, and the arch is suspended without falling down as long as the bricks keep holding hands. So your brick igloo has a part wall at ground level where the Eskimo would crawl in. You don't build the little tunnel where he has to leave his snow shoes on the way in before he puts his slippers on. You build a small chimney here, and under this chimney you have dug a small pit with a grid over it where the ashes will collect. The coal or wood to melt the metal is lobbed into the top of this chimney which has a lid. Where the back door of the igloo would be, you leave a hole in the bricks. You then need two small windows, one either side, just above where you think the level of the metal will be. These types of furnaces are known as 'igloo furnaces'. (They aren't really; I made this up). In my old, 1749 book there is a side view and plan of a furnace, and it is exactly how I have described it.

You check on the labourers who are beginning to flag, but eventually the soil is at the same level as the top of the mould including the jug handles bit. You stand an iron rod or a piece of wood in a hole you left right at the top of the canon mould and slap some more loam round it. This will become the hole for the metal to be poured in. Quite often you make another one alongside the main one that will allow the air to come out. Because of the horse manure that you couldn't do without, some methane and stannic gases are released. This could make you a bit light-headed at the crucial moment, so you light this gas as it trickles out.

When I worked at Taylor's we didn't have a hole at the top of the mould for the air to come out because there was a hole in the centre of the core plate. The air and gas went through the core, and we put pieces of coke in to help keep it porous. When we put the moulds in the pit, we used some old bits of iron drainpipe, and a 90 degree bend took this pipe from under the core plate up to ground level where we lit the gases.

So, back to the olden days, you mould a bit of a wall on all four sides where the metal is going to be slurped in, known as a runner box. This hopefully stops the metal running anywhere else when you open the furnace. The earth floor of the furnace slopes down, and you build a loam and clay channel from the back door of the igloo to the runner box.

All this work now has a purpose. The molten metal is going to come out at the back door where you chucked the metal in. Afterwards, your brickie had made this hole much smaller and you had jammed it up with clay. The wood (or coal if you can get it) is going to be dropped down the chimney. The little wall at ground level stops the fuel for the fire and the metal mixing together which would be a very bad thing. You tell all the important people when you are going to light the furnace, and the whole village decides this is a bank holiday and want to watch. If you have been trying to chat up other churches to have some bells made, you send a runner and invite their bigwigs along.

If you are using separate amounts of tin and copper you haven't put the tin in the furnace yet. This is because tin melts at about 200 degrees centigrade and copper at 1,000 degrees. You may feel the need to kneel down and say a few prayers on the morning you are going to cast the bell. Any help you can get is valuable, so a prayer such as 'Help me, God' is a good one. Your labourers start shovelling wood or coal and pump air in with large bellows. The little windows that were built in means you can watch the metal as it melts. When it starts to look about the right temperature there is some crud on the top that is partly all the rubbish things the vicar collected. This crud is called 'dross', and you pull it out with a rake. When you are thinking that there is some chance that the metal will be ready only three hours later than you said, you chuck in the tin. If you are really clever, you toss in some pieces of willow. Somebody may have told you this is customary, but the scientific reason is that willow contains salicylic acid. This helps the copper and tin fuse together and is far cheaper than a big sack of Aspirins. Potash was used to help fuse the metal as well.

When the temperature in the furnace is about 1,100 degrees, the surface of the metal has little swirly bits going round like tadpoles in a pond, and this signifies that the temperature is perfect. Sir Theodore Martin translated the poem *Das Lied von der Glocke (Song of the bell)*, written in 1800 by Friedrich von Schiller. He wrote, 'See! White bubbles now rise thickly! Good! The mass is melting fast. Stir in potash freely, quickly, Then 'twill soon be ripe to cast. From all scum, too, free, Must the mixture be; So may its voice, full clear and round, From the pure metal then resound. Yet, or ever we run the metal in, Send from the heart a fervent prayer! Now strike out the tap! God shield from mishap! Smoking, the fiery tide shoots down.'

Robert Southey (1774-1843), famous for writing the original *Goldilocks* story, tells us in *The Doctor*, 'The brethren of the monastery stood round the furnace, ranged in processional order, sang the 150th Psalm, and then, after certain prayers, blessed the molten metal, and called upon the Lord to infuse into it His grace, and overshadow it with His power, for the honour of the saint to whom the bell was to be dedicated, and whose name it was to bear.' If there aren't any monks, the vicar will do it. This is still very common on the continent, and if it is a Roman Catholic priest he probably throws some holy water about as well, and everybody bows their heads respectfully. Just a short prayer is a good idea as the noise from the furnace probably totally drowns out what he is saying anyway.

So at this stage, when everybody is getting really excited, you punch a hole in the bit of clay at the back door of your igloo with a metal spear. This gives you some control over the metal flowing out into the runner box. When it fills up, showing you that the mould is full, you jam a spade down at the igloo end where the metal is running out. If you have three bells and three channels, you keep the metal out of two of them the same way.

Right: *Casting a series of Taylor bells, about 1980. Author, third from left, and Roger Johns, foundry manager, far right.*
Photo: David Humphrey

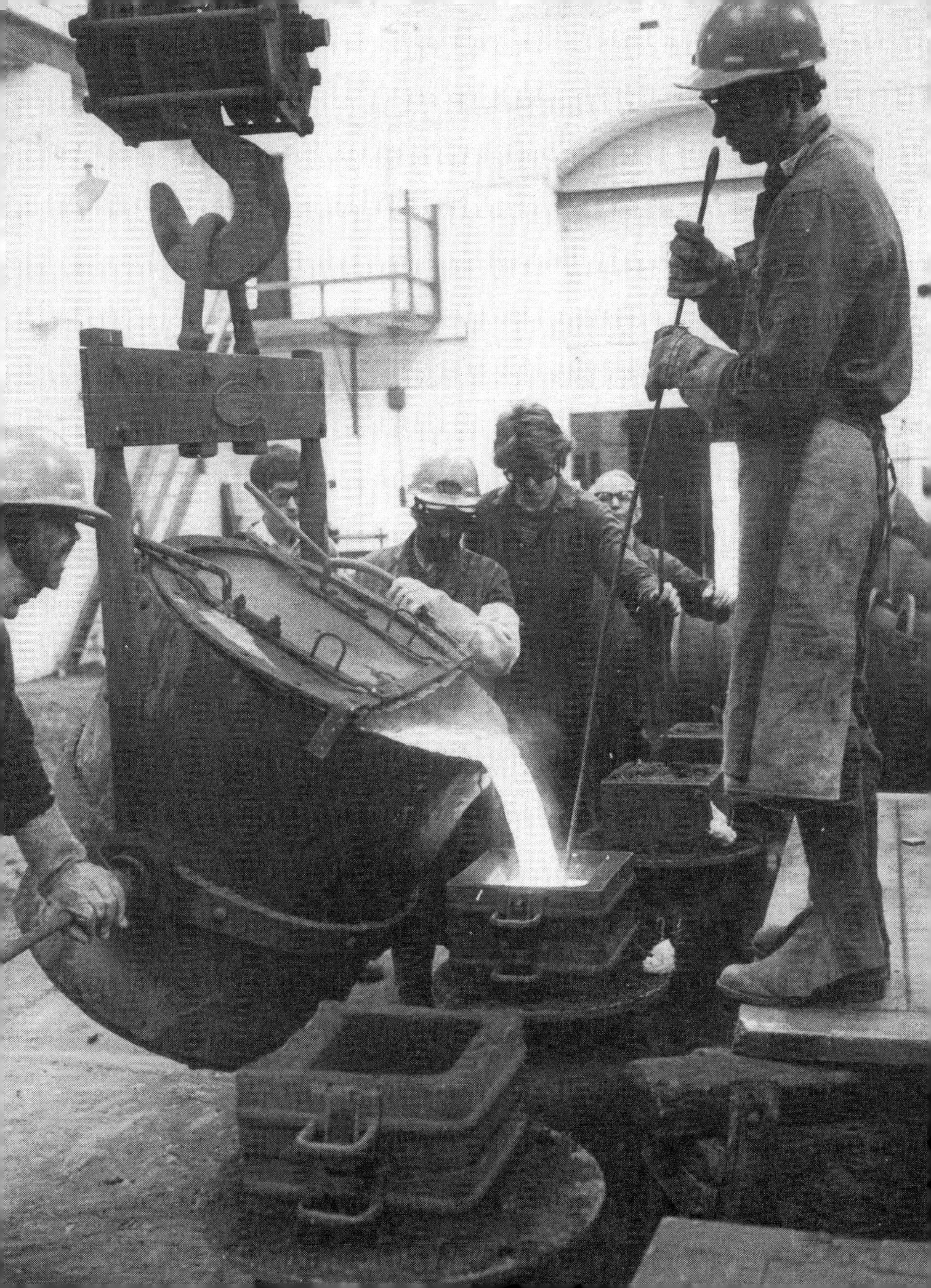

Any remaining metal (assuming there is some, and your calculations worked out fine!) is run out into another channel you have made near the bell. Watching metal melt, and then running it into a bell mould is very exciting, and it never failed to impress me. It has the basic elements 'earth and fire', and you could argue that the sound of a bell is the element 'air'. You used the fourth element, 'water', to make the moulds. You have to have an extreme respect for molten metal as it tries to do what it wants to.

At Taylor's, I could look in over the metal from the back of the furnace (after I turned off the air and oil blower for a couple of minutes), and we could check the actual temperature with a measuring gadget that had a probe. We temporarily removed a brick at the front above the level of the metal. When everything was tickety-boo we normally ran the metal into a ladle and raked off any dross. If we had just melted down old bells we put extra tin in if needed and stirred it with a thick willow branch. Visitors liked this as sparks go everywhere. I checked the temperature again with the probe, sometimes waiting five minutes or more for the temperature to drop if necessary. This can give another potential, real problem. The biggest bells are left until last as they need the lowest temperatures, so if you run out of metal the biggest bell is scrap! I didn't ever do this, luckily, but it is by no means unknown.

Spies told me years ago that one day, at the London Whitechapel foundry, the visitors were very late. The cast should have gone ahead, but they waited for them. This meant that by then some of the molten metal had oxidized, so they ran out of metal on the biggest bell. Horrendous! A 2012 'YouTube' video filmed at Whitechapel, when a bell for Inverness Cathedral was being cast, shows at the end, eight ingot moulds ready for the spare metal left over. They just manage to fill one of them; that's it! Richard Keene, a very unlucky bellfounder, ran out of metal twice in about 1678 when he was casting one big bell in Oxford.

So you stand back, and everybody is cheering and throwing their caps in the air. Hopefully, the pub landlord has provided some jugs of ale, home-made pork pies, and local cheese. Your son or apprentice has to keep going a bit longer. The metal in the runner box is starting to cool as it is open to the air and is above the hole into the bell. Bellmetal contracts as it cools, so if you walk away, the head of the bell or the canons may be porous. They want more molten metal, but there isn't any that is liquid. To stop this, a heated iron rod is put down the hole until it touches the top of the core mould, and you start to stir the metal. This allows more liquid metal to be drawn down into the canons, or the crown of the bell if it is being cast with a flat top. This part of the proceedings is called 'feeding' the bell.

When I was positioning a ladle in front of the furnace, filling it with metal, and then taking it to each bell mould and tipping some in, it was like a well-practised dance. The workers nearest the ladle, including me, wore overalls and leather aprons. We put on fire-proof spats that came up to our knees, elbow length gloves, safety glasses and hard hats. Someone you could trust used the overhead crane to move the ladle around gently. Visitors commented on how regulated it was, but we had practised it many times. Lastly, we broke out all the very hot bricks at the front of the furnace, so the whole inside was exposed, and we

Finishing the Moulds, Pouring the Metal

scraped the floor with a long piece of iron like a solid rake. This is called 'slagging' and was to remove any dross left in before it started to set hard.

I kept visitors well away, but previously they had been allowed to crowd round. In 1970, the British Government gave a very large carillon to the people of Australia. It may well have been the fiftieth anniversary of stopping sending convicts there; I don't remember. A lot of big knobs came to see the cast after their chauffeurs had found a place to park. One of the runner boxes spat back and bits of metal flew up. Paul Taylor, who was herding the visitors, had to buy a new suit and put his hand in his wallet. Another man had a hole in his suit, and two women needed new dresses.

We must never forget bellfounders Matthew Bagley and his son who were casting a large cannon at the London Royal Foundry near Cripplegate on May 10th, 1716. As they were pouring the metal into the mould, which was still damp, it exploded throwing metal everywhere. According to parish records, Matthew died from horrendous burns on May 22nd, and his son on May 26th, with a foundry boss killed as well and numerous spectators badly injured. So beware of damp moulds at all costs!

At Taylor's, when everything was under control, after we had cast all the bells, I invited any guests to feed them for a moment under strict supervision, and visitors love this. They pose for photographs and you have a moment to have a fag. After you have taken over again, you keep doing this until the rod won't go down as far as when you started, so you are above the level of the crown. This could take ten minutes or an hour or more, depending on the size of the bell and the temperature of the metal.

If a bellfounder casts a bell that is a bit porous at the top they can pour lead into any holes in the canons or crown and rub something over it to hide it. This is not a good solution unless it helps them get paid if no-one sees them do it. Your grandson has another reason now to condemn bells and says, 'The head of this old bell is very porous, and "amazingly" they poured lead into the holes. Because of this the head of the bell is not strong enough, so you need a new one!'

Everybody who pours metal into a mould wants to know instantly that the casting is okay, and they break open the moulds at the first opportunity. With bells, particularly big ones, you have to wait until they have completely cooled as premature exposure to the air can affect the sound. The longer you leave the bell buried, the better it is, as the micro-structure of the metal is different with slow cooling. The mould material has also been proven to have an effect, and a traditional loam mixture is still used at Taylor's today instead of more modern materials. Nowadays, all the moulds are buried in the sand up to the top of the cases with just the runner box above ground level. In my time, medium size moulds were not all totally buried, but bigger bell moulds always were. At the London Whitechapel foundry all the moulds are above floor level when they slurp the metal in, unless they position them lower down for ease, but they aren't buried. The Royal Eijsbouts foundry in Holland has all the moulds for whatever size bell above floor level. I think this is a mistake as cooling is greatly reduced in time. Another of the engravings in the old booklet about the London Whitechapel foundry shows four moulds completely buried. Only the channels where they ran the metal in are visible. So at some stage they stopped doing this. As the old proverb tells us, 'The proof of the pudding is in the eating'

So, going back in time, the labourers round your pit are now almost in revolt because they have to dig all the soil out – again. When they do get it all out you can break up the cope. You may be able to prise it off in the pit as the metal has contracted a bit, and then the bell is exposed. It is a fairly dark grey colour as the soot from inside the cope has become baked onto the surface of the bell. You know, but they don't yet, that the ash coating you brushed onto the core has also transferred itself to the bell. English bells are traditionally grey until metal is machined off when the golden bronze colour is revealed. Continental bells are this colour inside and out, and they polish the outside of the bell the same as a sculpture.

Now you can have a quick squint at the surface of the bell and the inscription. Does it look okay? You can't tell absolutely until any bits of loam that are left on the surface are all removed. To get the core out it is far more complicated than taking off the cope. The bell has contracted onto the core which now makes the bricks and loam not unlike good quality concrete. The labourers, if they haven't all run away, have to break it out with crowbars and pickaxes with the bell lying on its side. Eventually, the inside is brushed clean as well as the outside, and the canons have been exposed. You raise the bell from the pit, and you bang it with a lump of iron. This is the moment of truth! If everybody agrees it is first rate this is brilliant, but the other requirement may have been that it fits in with existing bells. If both are true, congratulations!

A lot could go wrong, as Doctor Raven tells us in his 1906 book, *The Bells of England*, where he refers to an account in Latin from the Cistercian monastery at Croxden, near Uttoxeter: 'Anno1313. The great bell of the house was through ill luck broken on Easter Eve (in 1313, April 22nd) and Master Henry Michel of Lichfield came to cast another and worked at it with his attendants from the Octave of Trinity (in 1313, June 11th) up to the Feast of the Nativity of the Blessed Virgin (always September 8th), and then failed in the casting and lost all his labour and expense. And again when the great quantity of copper and tin had been collected afresh, recommencing the whole business, he at length finished it as is now reported, about the Feast of All Saints (always November 1st)'. Did it really take Master Henry Michel all this time, or did he go away and come back? He was hopefully under cover, but how big was the 'great' bell? I have no idea, but it all sounds a really bad experience and extremely bad luck!

If they made you sign a contract you made sure it said, 'Any surplus material to be disposed of by the parish', or monks. There are a lot of surplus materials. There is a big pit, but soil taken out never fills the hole it came from. (It's probably Murphy's Law.) Also, you have a scrap core, false bell, the cope and the brick furnace. Igloo-shaped furnaces have the same basic design as the ovens that bakers used to make bread in the distant past. Perhaps the local baker wants it? If nobody wants to take it over this is more rubble.

Gradually over the centuries, bellfounders started setting up small workshops where it was convenient to leave their tools and the bits and pieces for hanging the bells. The logical extension was that they built furnaces and cast bells there, not just in pits by churches. Once they had done this they often worked in about a fifty mile radius.

Robert Taylor, the first member of the Taylor family to make bells, was born in 1759 at Riseley, near Bedford. About 1780, he moved eleven miles to St. Neots in Huntingdonshire. Joseph Eayre had established a bellfoundry there in the 1730s, and Robert was taken on. A plan of the site about 1757 shows a structure that has a circular base, a conical waist and a circular top, and some parts are bound together with metal hoops. There is a ground plan and elevation, and it is remarkably like an igloo furnace. In 1887, John William Taylor I wrote a letter to a historian asking for any evidence of what had been at St. Neots. The answer came back that the bell-shaped 'foundry' was close to a brewery and owned by the same landlord. I don't think that there is any doubt that the 'foundry' was an igloo type furnace.

Edward Arnold had taken over when Joseph Eayre died, and Robert went to work for him. Edward, with Robert in tow, cast ten bells for a church in Leicester in 1781 just 'outside the city walls' as they were required to have a foundry on-site to get the job. Edward stayed there, and in 1784 Robert was in charge at St. Neots, and by 1786 he owned this foundry outright. About 1818, the land owner was talking about wanting the land back, but a fire burnt down the foundry in 1821, so Robert moved to Oxford.

His first son, William, had been born in 1795 and was starting to help his father when he was eleven. What! Didn't he go to school and learn his three Rs? Another son, John, was born in 1797, and he eventually went to start a foundry in Devon. Sweeps for bells, now called 'crooks', were taken down from Oxford to Devon sometimes, but John didn't think much of his brother's bells. He did consider that William was an excellent clock-maker. He was quite rude about the bells William made; no brotherly love at all.

Taylor's published a little booklet in 1870 that they sent all over the shop to show people how much work they had done. The work completed up to 1825 is given a separate section and is riveting reading. Up to then, between them, they had cast three 'rings' (sets of bells) with ten bells each, two being for Leicester city. They had made eleven rings of eight bells, twenty-seven of six bells, thirty-one of five bells, and lots of other single bells or clock bells. The heaviest tenor bells (the largest of a set) at Grantham and Leicester city were one and a half tons each, and twelve of the largest tenor bells were over one ton. This is a considerable amount of work! They were consolidating a very good reputation and collecting in orders. The booklet was extremely impressive and very good publicity to send to all and sundry. In the 1830s John put in a letter, 'I intend going to Staffordshire to build a furnace to cast a peal of eight for the parish of Penkridge; probably I shall stay several months.' He didn't manage to get a lot of work there so he moved back.

There were a number of bellfounders with allied trades, and John was scathing about the London Whitechapel bellfoundry. 'I have seen many of his (Thomas Mears) peals cast and recast within the last few years. Some of his trebles (the smallest bell in a ringing set) are complete lumps of metal'. Not exactly a glowing tribute to their work, but they were competitors. John personally thought that bells were often unnecessarily heavy in weight.

In 1838, the churchwardens at All Saints' Parish Church in Loughborough decided to have their bells recast. A condition (still very common) was that the bells had to be cast 'in or near Loughborough'. John was given the job, and after he had gone there in 1839 he built quite a comprehensive foundry. He virtually stopped travelling round the country to cast bells locally for churches or other people. His days of digging pits in far flung places were nearly over. Although initially this foundry was a subsidiary of Oxford, everything was moved to Loughborough, and John took a twenty-year lease on his foundry land. He intended to stay and totally centralize his operation.

Loughborough was very attractive as a base. After Leicester city, it was the largest town in Leicestershire with 10,000 inhabitants. There was a good potential labour force if he needed a few workers, roads were better, and there was a canal for transport. The Midland Railway was under construction in 1839, and as there was no British Rail then the station opened on time. Allied trades were abundant, so he could farm out some of the 'fittings' needed for bells. He could say to one man, 'Joe down the lane has given me a cheaper price. Are you sure this is your best price?'

By 1853 he had built three furnaces, the largest holding over three tons. His son John William I had worked for his uncle William at Oxford and then his father in Loughborough. He officially became a partner in 1849, so it became John Taylor and Son. A son, Pryce Jemson Jones Taylor, had been born in Oxford in 1835 and moved to Loughborough and cast bells there, but died in 1862. It was absolutely common that in trades like bellfounding any sons were roped into the family business. They were told, 'Now you are old enough, you start work every morning in the foundry at 6a.m. sharp.' They weren't asked, 'What do you want to do when you grow up?'

If John was travelling about, he had a gander at any church on the way to look at the bells. He then prepared an estimate for any work that needed doing, and the vicar received a letter, often not knowing at all that he had been there! Bit sneaky, but good if it got him work. He also took advertising space in magazines such as *The Builder* or *The Church of England Magazine*. His sales line was, 'Messrs J. T. & Son are Successors to old established firms of Watts, Eayres & Arnold of Leicester & St. Neots in Huntingdonshire, and beg to be understood they confine themselves to bell work'. It wasn't true, of course. If they were a bit short of bell work they still had one or two other things up their sleeves to keep the wolf from the door.

If you have a foundry and build several furnaces and other things, there are times when you think, *Casting bells using the lost wax process is a real bind. Isn't there some other way?* The alternative, going back to the Introduction of this book, is that the external mould, the cope, is made separately; so no false bell. With this method, putting on an inscription means pressing metal letters or stamps directly into this mould in a mirror image, and this is a completely new process as well. So you're going to ask me, 'When did people start doing this?'

Finishing the Moulds, Pouring the Metal

At a large London foundry, John Warner & Sons who started casting bells from 1850, they soon patented an object in 1853, registered by Frederick Warner and John Shotton. They called it a 'shell', and it was a bell shaped, cast iron former or case. They lined it with loam to make the cope, and holes in the case gave a better key for the loam. This new technique involves using the outer sweep or crook upside down to form the cope mouth uppermost. The external bell profile is now made using the outside of the strickle or crook, not the inside.

I don't know exactly why they claimed a patent, but obviously they had been experimenting a lot before they considered they had invented the ideal former. They also dabbled with using a cast iron cone for the core as well, but apparently not for long. Warner's had an iron foundry, or part owned it, at Norton near Stockton-on-Tees, so I expect they may have cast large ones there. I will explain about them casting the sixteen ton 'Big Ben I' in 1856 at Norton, which is really interesting, in another chapter. An engraving at the time shows a cast iron case for this enormous bell.

As regards the London Whitechapel bellfoundry, *The London Illustrated News* items featuring the casting technique relating to the George Mears' 'Big Ben Mark II' hour bell, cast in 1858, states it was made with a false bell. Although undated, a booklet entitled *A History of Bells as Practised at the Bell Foundry Whitechapel* was probably printed about 1866. It refers to a ring of eight bells in their works which were sent to Port Philip in Australia for St Paul's, Geelong. These were cast in 1866, and it is quite clear from this booklet that they were still using the false bell method then. The author refers to 'the facsimile' bell being destroyed. He tells us that the Whitechapel bellfoundry is 'the oldest, largest, and best known of the kind in London, or England'. What a cheek!

John Taylor I spent a long time learning how to make bells using the lost wax process in the 1880s. He was born in 1827, so in 1842 he was fifteen and may well have been working in the foundry. If not, he would still have had first-hand knowledge of all the casting techniques. So I am sure that they had abandoned the lost wax process before 1842. This is why he knew nothing about casting bells this way and neither did his workers. They all said, 'What's all this about then? Lost wax? False bells? Never heard of 'em'.' They didn't adopt cast iron cases until about 1870 because they were still experimenting with the bell shape, so there had to be an intermediate stage.

About 1840 they started making the crooks out of wrought iron with pieces of sheet metal bolted on for both the internal and external profiles. This would only have made sense if they were now making the cope as a free standing item, mouth uppermost. Nobody is quite clear how they built up the cope mould. They may have used a stiff loam mix and broken bits of brick pushed in at every stage, inside and outside, or a similar technique. At other foundries, tarred rope was used to bind the mould together, so this is another possibility.

There must have been some iron hoops or possibly rings, that may have been bolted together to give it enough strength. The main requirement would have been that the case was rigid enough to stand up to being put on its side for the inscription to be indented, but not so heavy that it was a real problem turning it upside down to lower the completed mould over the core. Once it was placed over the core in the pit, ready for casting, it would still be compacted down.

No-one seems to know exactly how it was done, including some archivists I have asked. A lot of books about English bellfounding go straight from using a false bell to a cast iron case. So on Friday they were making a false bell, and the following Monday were using the metal cases! This may basically have applied to Whitechapel with not much gap between the two methods, but certainly not Taylor's.

The attraction of using iron cases, apart from it being quicker, was that once you did this, (although you did need a lot of cases for different sized bells that all had to be cast specially), they didn't wear out. There was no false bell to be broken up, and whilst the mould for the cope needed breaking out of the cast iron case it was considerably less work.

Manhandling the cast iron cases on their own, or with the loam lining inside, was not a problem once there were mechanical cranes. Moving core or cope moulds to be put in the drying stove, or to be closed down and then put in the pit was not a big problem either.

Top right: *Anthony Stone using metal letters to indent the inscription.*
Photo: John Taylor & Co.

Bottom right: *A conical case former for a 36 tonne bell made of circular girders at a foundry in Holland.*
Photo: Royal Eijsbouts foundry

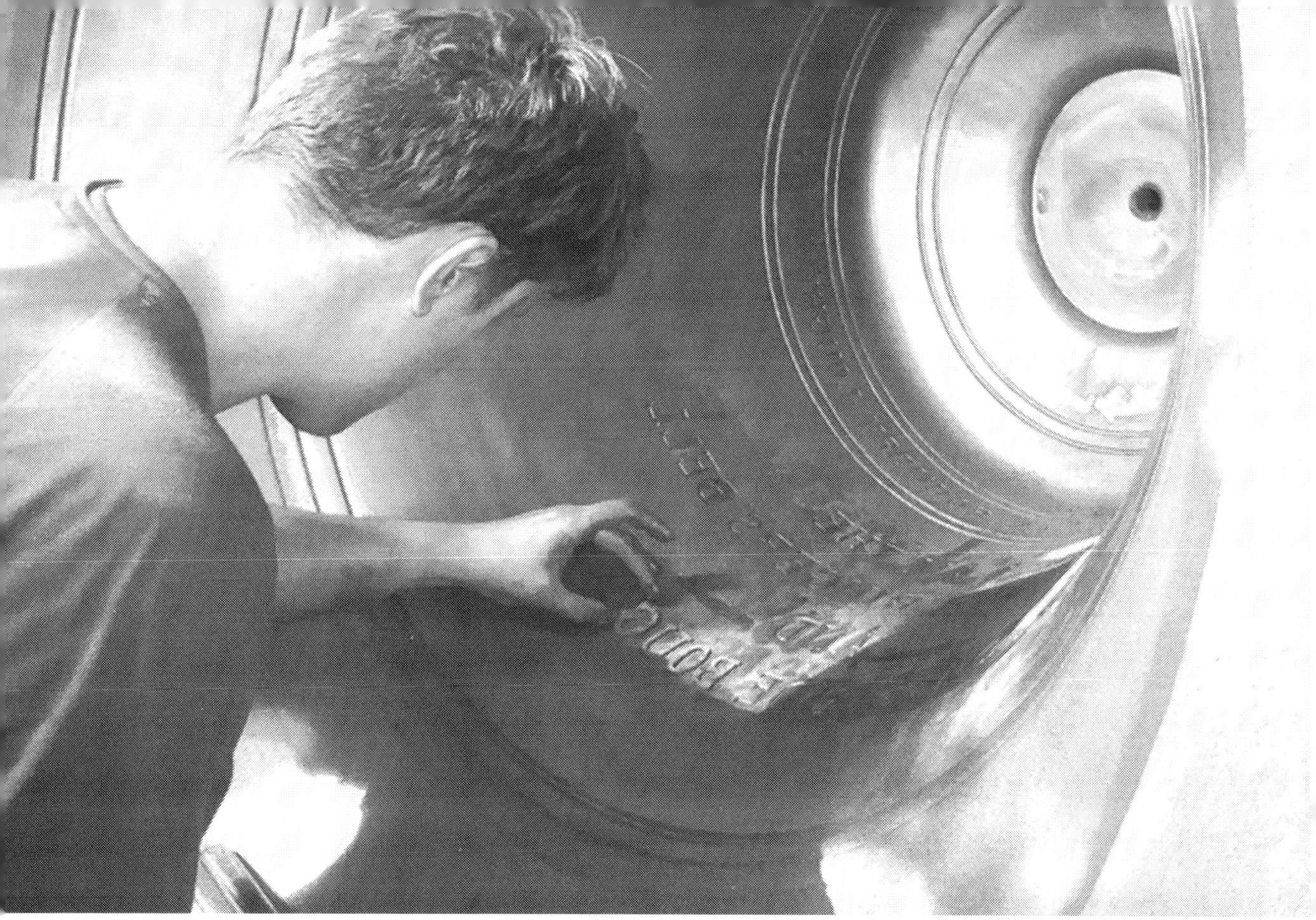

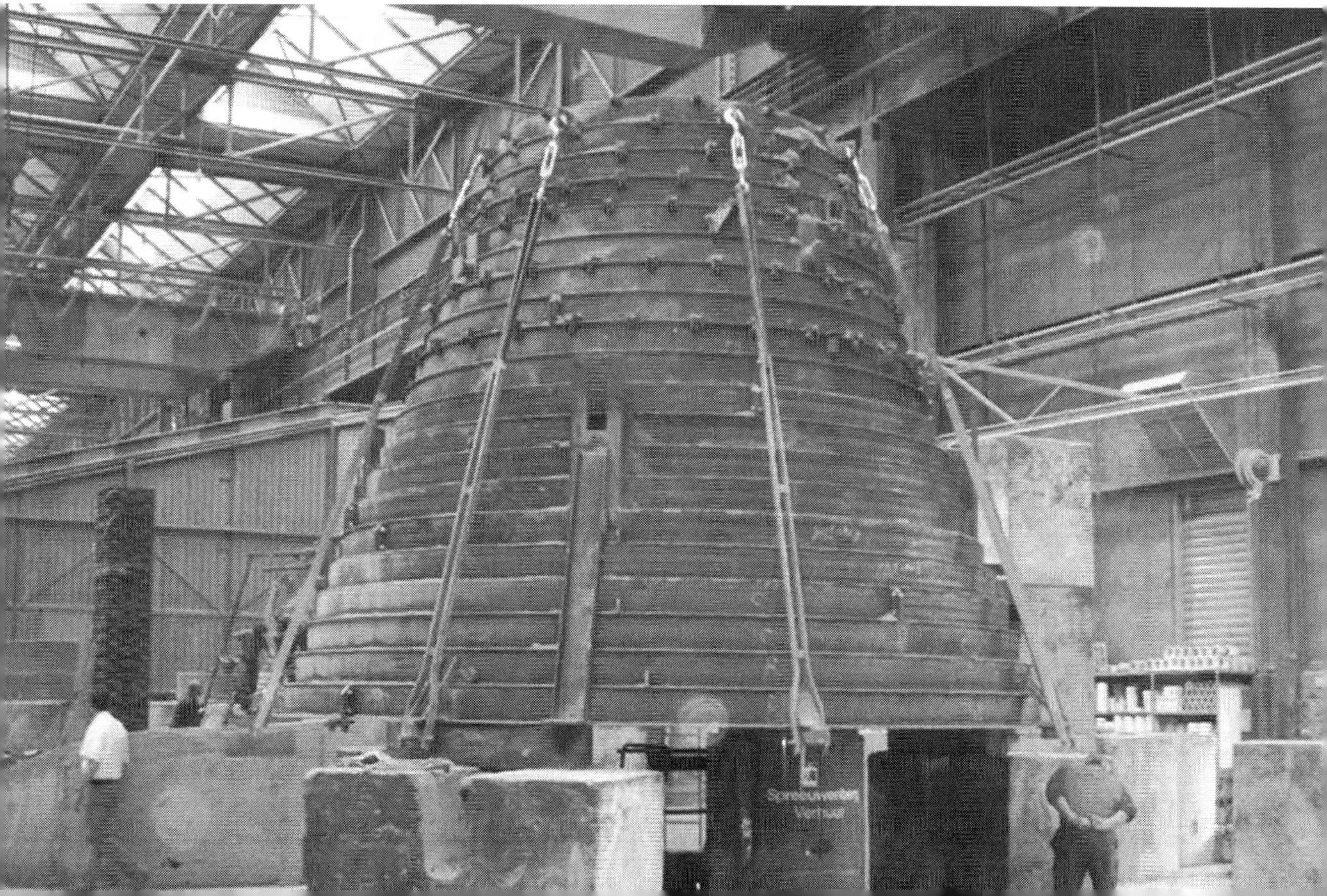

4. My Early Years

'In Quires and Places where they sing; here followeth the Anthem.'
1662 English Prayer Book. Rubric after Third Collect.

Both my mother and father were Londoners, and my maternal grandparents had progressed through 'being in service' with some landed gentry's family. My grandmother was head housekeeper, and my grandfather was eventually a chauffeur and mechanic. Practising three point turns in a quiet London cul-de-sac was out of the question, so he studied driving skills and the mysteries of repairing automobiles at the main Daimler showroom.

It all sounds very much like *Downton Abbey* but in real life! At some stage they went to work for some rich persons' property agency. It seems that they moved into the 'below stairs' accommodation when the particular titled family had decamped with their staff to foreign parts or were on safari, hunting tigers. My mother was consequently born in 1904, at 4, Ladbroke Square, Kensington; a really good address. She was christened Myrtle Violet, and her sister, my aunt, was born in 1907 and baptised Daphne Odora Marguerite. Obviously flower lovers! Typical addresses were Marble Arch, Belgravia and Hyde Park.

When my mother was the right age she went to a Pitman's Shorthand and Typing College for several months. Shorthand looks like Egyptian hieroglyphics; a complete mystery to anybody else, but it converts spoken words into symbols, and she became a skilled private secretary to some quite well known people.

My father was born in 1908, and he, five brothers and a sister were born in Camberwell, definitely considered 'the wrong side of the tracks!' My paternal grandfather was a London Metropolitan bobby, or 'peeler', stationed in Bermondsey. The house and area were a bit run down but despite my mother considering they had all been 'dragged up,' all the sons received some technical training. My father became an electrical draughtsman and a brother called Bill became an early BBC engineer. Two other brothers worked at the Harwell nuclear power station, and I don't think they were just sweeping up neutrons.

Unfortunately, my mother married my father in 1929 on the re-bound from his brother Bill, who it turned out was actually engaged to someone else! She married on the solemn vow, as significant to her as her marriage vows, that as soon as she got herself 'back together' she was off! Not a good start, and she still thought this for decades!

In 1935, after being laid off from his job at the Power Electric Company in London during the 'slump', my father got a job in Manchester at Erskine Heap & Co.; so goodbye to London! I bet my mother slumped too when she heard that she was moving to Manchester! During the Second World War my mother listened with increasing dismay to the effects of the bombing raids in London as she still considered it was 'her home town'.

As a contribution to the war effort, my mother set out to produce another child, and I was born in August, 1943. I was premature, a 'Leo', and a 'war baby' as well. I was baptised Michael John as I was a 'Gift of God' - allegedly! Events took another complete turn when in 1947 my father was set on as a senior electrical draughtsman at the Brush Electrical Engineering Company in Loughborough. He put his bike clips on in the morning and cycled to work and had a canteen lunch. When he came home, we had tea with things like sandwiches, cake, and tinned fruit. On Friday nights (pay day), he came home via the fish and chip shop and gave my mother his pay packet.

My mother could certainly be considered 'well read', as befitted her perceived status in life. She had loads of books, mostly on religion, music, and culture. You name it; she had them. From her training she was an extremely competent typist and had a typewriter. She wrote to all and sundry including the King or Queen at Buckingham Palace, the Prime Minister, various Members of Parliament, major figures in classical music, films and theatre, senior church figures and other eminent people. Her sister used to reply eventually to a letter that my mother had dashed off at the speed of light. The next day (first class post was just that in those days) my mother read it and put at the top 'r/r', that meant 'read and replied' with the date. The same day of course! Her sister groaned the next day as it was then her turn again!

The downside was that my mother was a 100% control freak! Family life was totally dominated solely by her, and she often had bilious migraine headaches that lasted about three days. First she threw up, then had blinding headaches, and then needed another day to recover. She was extremely dominant, and there were frequent rows, always initiated by my mother over inconsequential things, usually involving some disapproved of action by my father. Sadly, she also had phases of severe depression often threatening suicide when she strode out of the house. When I was diagnosed in later life as being stage one bi-polar, the 'trick-cyclist' soon pronounced that I had inherited it from my mother!

She was also a 'died-in-the-wool' fatalist. If my sister was even ten minutes late for tea having gone out on an errand, this was definitely because she had been sexually assaulted by a man in a raincoat. There was no other explanation. If I was late home by a few minutes I had certainly been killed by an errant car or drowned in a brook. She was fully prepared for the policeman who was going to come to knock on our door and say, 'Mrs Milsom? I'm afraid I have some bad news.'

Nevertheless, I mustn't make it out to be all bad. It was just a very complicated upbringing for both me and my sister. I was fascinated by and petrified of my mother alternately. I used to count slowly from one to ten at the meal table if I wanted to ask some innocuous favour like going out to play or permission to go to a friend's house. I often chickened out and started counting again!

Our front 'parlour' room was absolutely her sole domain and out of bounds to all other family members except after I had started having piano lessons and was allowed in to practise after copious hand washing. When on top form, she held soirées where people she knew were invited to listen to records and discuss books. She interviewed and discussed theology with a range of archdeacons, vicars, curates, and eventually Roman Catholic priests, monks, and nuns. Mr. Onions, the piano tuner, was allowed in but not engaged in conversation apart from being given a cup of tea in the non-posh cups.

On Saturdays, my mother sometimes suggested trips out to villages, towns, or cities, where she wanted to see the churches, guildhalls, or other historic buildings of note. Amongst my mother's collection of books were well-thumbed copies of Arthur Mee's guide books on the various counties, such as Leicestershire, Nottinghamshire, Derbyshire and Lincolnshire. These were supplemented by the famous Sir Nikolaus Pevsner guides to architecture in the same regions. Rail and bus timetables were perused and sandwiches prepared. Having changed into our Sunday best, all ready to leave the house, if there was one word said that she took exception to (particularly from my father) the trip was cancelled. We then changed out of our best clothes, and she went off to her bedroom to sulk. After an hour or so she might decide we were going after all! Bus and rail timetables had to be consulted again, and the best clothes re-donned! My parents never had a car, ever. This was obviously completely out of the question although I am sure we had the money to buy one! If my father had learnt to drive then the first time my mother sat in the passenger seat and my father let out the clutch she would have vomited straight out of the window!

As a young boy, I was a bit scared of the dark, so my very small bedroom usually had the door ajar, and I listened to my mother playing her piano or records. When I was about seven years old I was sent for piano lessons to Mrs. Green, accepted as suitable by my mother as her husband, 'Jumbo' Green, was a local headmaster. At the age of eight, I was enrolled in the local parish church choir as a boy treble and loved the escape aspect. My mother liked studio portraits of selected family members at key events in their lives, so I was sent off for photographs in my freshly washed cassock and surplice, brought home for the occasion. For the evening choir practice every Friday, my father walked me there and back. On Saturday evenings my freshly washed, wet, curly hair was 'set' in a hairnet with the latest *Amami Wave Set* chemical hairdressing treatment, and then dried with a hair-dryer. I frequently complained on these Saturday evening sessions that my head was getting frazzled, but I had to be respectable for Sunday services as I was in the choir!

A really amazing event took place just before I was ten. My elderly, primary school headmistress whom my mother regularly corresponded with, gave me a letter to take home. I was terrified I was in big trouble, but it asked my mother to go and see her. She told her that my singing voice was excellent, and I should be sent away to be in a cathedral choir. She gave my mother entry forms she had acquired for a choral scholarship at Southwell Minster Cathedral choir school, between Nottingham and Newark. This was astounding to my mother, but she decided that this was a message from God through Miss Mills, my headmistress.

She also comforted herself that it was like sending Samuel to the temple as God required and suitable training for me becoming a clergyman. If your bible studies are not exactly up to date, Samuel was the only son of Hannah. She prayed repeatedly for a son, and the Lord obliged. When he became old enough, she took him to the temple priest saying that before he was born she had vowed that he would serve the Lord at the temple for ever. She took offerings to the temple every year and a new coat for Samuel. Now, isn't that nice?!

My mother typed letters to all and sundry at the school and cathedral beforehand, and I duly learnt my test piece, *Who is Sylvia?* On the appointed day, we took three trains to get there, and I had my music and general school exam. We were told by letter that I was first reserve after the six boys they took every year were told they had a place. An anxious two weeks ensued until the letter came saying one of the six had been accepted at St Paul's Cathedral in London as well and was going there rather than Southwell Minster. I was in!

So just after my tenth birthday I began my choral scholarship at Southwell Minster Cathedral and the grammar school. The school claimed that an ancient fusion of pupils and monks dated back to 956, so I expect this was right unless they wanted to point out that the buildings hadn't just been slung up over a long weekend. All choristers, who could be as young as eight years old, were boarders and pupils at the school, and there were about sixty general boarders. The school and the cathedral choir were totally entwined, and school assembly was held in the cathedral. As it was only about 200 yards away this was really helpful if it was hissing down with rain.

To get to Southwell by train from Loughborough you had to get the train to Nottingham. You then went on a branch line to Rolleston Junction and caught the 'Paddy push & pull'. It was two carriages on a single line, so the steam engine pushed them one way and pulled them back the other way. Some Sunday afternoons, two or three of us would try to get on the only train to Rolleston Junction and back. The porter turned a blind eye if he was in a good mood, and we wangled our way on for free.

There were two boarding houses, and the large one, called Hill House, near the station, was for normal boarders and the young ones who were still being trained as choristers but not yet part of the select team. It was a longer walk to where the main group of choristers and the headmaster lived at Sacrista Prebend, opposite the cathedral. There were two dormitories of eight choristers each, and two senior sixth form prefects lived there as well, to exercise some control over us.

So I started off at Hill House with tears from my mother, and there were two days before the start of term for learning the ropes. After absorbing the situation, I decided I was in heaven! I took to boarding school like a duck to water and thought it was brilliant.

Right: *Southwell Minster Cathedral, from an old postcard.*
Photo: Frith's Series, of Reigate

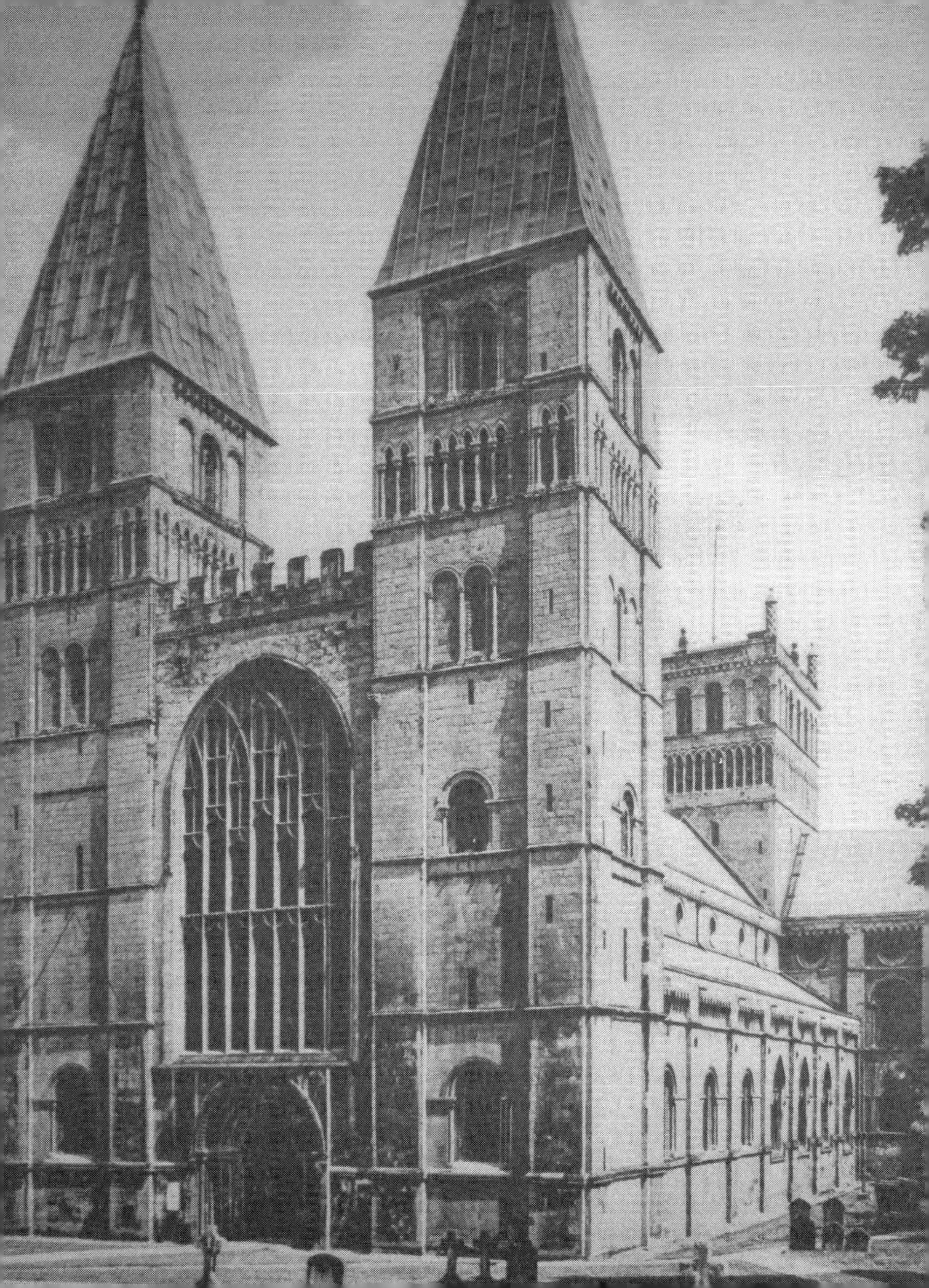

Our lives were totally regulated, and we knew exactly what was happening every day of the week. There was some time off on Saturdays and then Sunday afternoon and evening, after we had sung at morning service and had lunch.

When I arrived at Hill House, the matron there was in her early thirties. Apart from looking after our medical needs she doubled as housekeeper and sorted out the laundry and supplies for the cook. She also sewed the badges on our Boy Scout jumpers. Her name was Catherine Moakes, so we called her 'Smokey' but not to her face!

It was 'recommended' to parents (so that was what they had to do) that they only came to see their offspring twice every term. The first time my parents came to see me, my mother demanded to know why I was wearing a tatty blazer that obviously belonged to somebody else! I proved to her that it was mine by showing her the name tape, and she was not at all impressed and gave me a good telling off!

The Minster Cathedral is huge to small boys only knee high to a grasshopper, and we thought it was absolutely immense. Studying to be a full member of the choir dominated the lives of choristers totally, with lots of pomp and ceremony. In 956, the then church became owned by the Archbishops of York. The nave dates from 1100 and the choir area from about 1240, and later on they added the choir screen. This is fairly typical of large cathedrals where they built bits on when they had spare cash, or a bit of looting and pillaging had taken place.

One of the very large stained glass windows is French, from about 1575, and this is the good bit – it was reputedly found in a French pawnshop in 1818! I wonder who on earth pawned it? The minster became a cathedral in 1884, and this information is cribbed from the official guide book that my mother bequeathed me when she died. When I was there I didn't mind or care very much when they had built it. It was a bit scary when we trooped into the vestry area to change into our special gear, prior to evensong, if only a few lights were switched on. Some nasty older boy would whisper, 'Did you see that ghost?' and make moaning noises. Hardly fair when you are only little!

At a cathedral, there are a whole host of people who need feeding. Clergy, a choirmaster and organist, an assistant organist, and a verger who puts out the hymn-books, lights the candles and snuffs them out afterwards. The seats in the nave were often all moved round for an orchestral concert, or there might be a big nativity play. So the verger has a minion or two as he isn't going to drag all the chairs round on his own as well as do the hoovering. Churches need a sexton who looks after the general maintenance and cordons off an area when some of the stonework starts falling off. In a cathedral, he has at least one assistant who has to leg it over to the two stonemasons and tell them, 'We need a new statue. Another one has fallen down'. At one time at Southwell there was... a 'dog whipper'! In the olden days, the country squires brought their basset hounds to church, and he controlled and whipped them. Good job there was no R.S.P.C.A then. It says in this booklet that when he was made redundant he became a caretaker and gardener for the outside bits where the gravestones are. I expect he missed whipping the dogs and shouted, 'Lie down!' to the gravestones.

At all the church services there were twelve fully fledged choirboys on two pews facing each other, along with four probationers ready to be promoted. Six men provided the harmony; most of them teachers from the school. Every school day at 8.30a.m., prior to the school assembly in the cathedral, the choristers had a rehearsal for afternoon evensong, and another one, including on Saturdays, before evensong at 4.15p.m.

The organist and choirmaster, Dr. Robert Ashfield, entitled 'Rector Chori', was a perfectionist and drilled us in the art of singing religious music of every description. It was pure theatre when the organ boomed out over our heads followed by a silence you could almost touch or take a bite of, whilst everybody waited for a prayer or bible reading. At Christmas and Easter, all the choristers had a 'stay-over' until midday Easter Sunday or midday Christmas Day, after morning service. All the ordinary boarders had sloped off for their normal holidays, and the choristers decamped to Hill House. This meant on Christmas Day, the headmaster could admire his new, shiny cane in peace. On Christmas Eve, there was a large carol service in the nave, and bigwigs and influential people like mayors, with their chains of office, attended. After the carol service there were small presents and mince pies for the returning choristers at Hill House. Our boarding house staff and matron couldn't nip off for Christmas hols until we did! Easter Sunday and Christmas Day meant a long day of singing and then travelling. In my case, on Christmas Day when there were no trains, I shared a taxi home with another chorister who lived our side of Nottingham.

Choristers up to the age of eleven were all taught normal school lessons in one classroom called J.D. (Junior Department). The school was considered a centre of academic achievement and going on to Oxford or Cambridge Universities was not a problem. All pupils in the main school had passed the countrywide grammar school entrance examinations, known as the '11 plus' because you were aged eleven when you sat them. We had to sit this exam as well to go up to the main school, and you were out if you failed however good your voice was. So for us, it was very important.

Because my birthday was in August, I was only ten when I sat the 11 plus exam at the end of my first year. When I passed and went back, I was in the choir proper and moved to Sacrista Prebend with all the other ones. This meant that I could sing a wide range of religious music and had developed 'aural acuity', so I had really good hearing. I could also sight-read which meant that not only could I read music, but, if given a piece of music to sing that I had never seen before, I had a 99% chance of having a really good stab at it and getting it right first time! Apart from breakfast and cocoa at night at Sacrista Prebend, we had lunch at school and then, after evensong, went to Hill House for high tea, and also lunch at weekends as well. What time we arrived at Hill House for tea on a Friday was variable.

Evensong on Fridays was very nerve-racking. It was billed as 'Unaccompanied Evensong' that meant the organist hardly did anything; he was free to read a book. In reality, he was more hawk-eyed, or in this case hawk-eared, than normal. Just before we started a musical item he played a chord quietly on the organ, and off we went on our own. The main piece of music we sang was an 'anthem' by some famous composer of church choral music. There might be jumps where we went from a low note to a high note several times. When we had finished, he very quietly played the last chord to himself and compared the sound of the organ to our voices. If we had infinitesimally gone up or down by just a mere fraction, we had 'drifted' and were in big trouble.

Members of the congregation couldn't tell anything at all had happened as it sounded fine to them, but that was why Dr. Robert Ashfield was organist and choirmaster and none of them were! At the end of the service when we were hoping to nip off, he might storm down to the vestry and tell us, 'Don't bother getting changed!', and we were singing it again. This type of unaccompanied singing is called 'A Cappella' meaning 'chapel style' in Italian. The people in the kitchen at Hill House saved us some sandwiches if we were late getting back.

The younger probationers progressed into the select twelve over time because at puberty the voices of the oldest ones 'broke'. You couldn't tell by looking at them, and nothing fell out of their mouths and made a mess on the floor. What did happen was that hitting high notes became difficult, and their voices eventually resembled a strangled chicken. The ones who had the most experience were suddenly redundant, and you couldn't do anything about this unless you lived in Italy about three hundred years ago.

The Italian choirmasters had a cunning idea. The boys with the best voices were quietly told, 'Follow me', spread-eagled on the church floor one evening and had their nuts crushed with a big hammer. It was probably more of a surgical nature, but it meant that whatever age they attained, they still had the pure and high voices of a young boy! It also meant they didn't have to shave. The Italian word for a person subject to this castration practice is 'Castrato' and the last such 'man' came to London in 1902, gave a concert and made a record. People flocked to see this strange 'choirboy'. Being Italian, he was called Allessandro Moreschi (1858-1922). Amazingly, you can still order the CD of his record on amazon.com after all this time! About 4-5,000 boys in Italy were given this treatment over the years.

After the morning service on Sundays and lunch at Hill House, we had to write a letter home in our best handwriting before we could do anything else. The letters were censored to see if we had complained about the food or one of the teachers! If so, we wrote it out again, and I think my record was three times as I had put some forbidden comment in the second one that wasn't in the first one! In the boarding school hand book that I still have, detailing the rules for the parents and pupils, there is a short bit about letters. It states, 'Letters are an index of progress and a free expression of a boy's own interest and feelings.' What a whopping great lie! It isn't dated, but it must have been fairly old, and they had obviously printed too many (or perhaps they got a discount for quantity) as amounts of money had been changed by being crossed out over the years and updated in ink. They hadn't changed the pocket money from the printed amount of one shilling a week. How mean! Prefects got two shillings and sixpence.

Very rarely, a couple of coaches were hired, and we were taken to the cinema in nearby Newark. I remember being taken to see *The Dam Busters*, a suitably uplifting film with no sex. We had to leave before the supporting film that was probably *Shoot-out at Tombstone Creek*.

At Sacrista Prebend we played pontoon on Sunday evenings, hurriedly changing the called out bets to 'snap' if anyone in authority came in. We were by no means perfect angels, and I was the one who became the court jester. They had christened me 'Milly' which I didn't mind. We sent off for packets of 'Foreign' or 'Empire' postage stamps and other items such as assorted magic tricks 'on approval'. This meant that when they arrived, you paid for the ones you wanted with a postal order and sent it back with the others that you didn't want. Matron would always sneak us a few stamps meant for Sundays if asked nicely. We never returned any of the items or sent any money!

Another good trick was that we bought a small bag of Sharp's toffees. We put them on a radiator in winter or left them in the sun until they went soft and misshapen. We then sent then back to Sharp's with a letter of complaint. We were always promptly sent a nice, big tin with a printed apology. There was a large grocery shop in the village called Kirby & Sons that sold us broken biscuits for one penny a bag which was dark blue and made of stiff paper. One of the assistants took a shine to me, and if I was cadging broken biscuits and they hadn't got any, she went in the back and broke a few up! The affectionate term for the BBC by their staff is 'The Broken Biscuit Company!'

The school was very strict in every respect. The teachers wrote things on a blackboard and at the end of the lesson, it was rubbed out with a blackboard duster like a large wooden shoe brush with felt underneath. If you had nodded off or were reading a comic under the desk, the blackboard duster would come hurtling through the air. Now you couldn't do that nowadays, could you?! Parents wouldn't allow it! If Mr. Fletcher hadn't got his duster handy, he yelled, 'Milsom! Stop slouching and sit up straight!' We were all addressed by our surnames.

There were various punishments depending on the severity of the crime. There was detention where you wrote out one hundred times phrases such as *Manners maketh man*. Detention was normally after school, but not possible if you were a choirboy as you were legging it over to the cathedral. For us, it was part of our lunchtime. Being sent to the headmaster's study usually meant you were going to get the cane! It was a very flexible thin stick with a curved handle. There was not much point saying, 'No sir! Not me, sir!' He already had his black handkerchief on his head. For reasonably serious misdeeds the cane came swishing down on your outstretched palm. If you were told to bend over and touch your toes, you were usually given 'six of the best'.

In the boarding houses there was a points system. You could achieve plus points from one to three for being helpful or smarmy, or minus points from one to three. If I had done well, in my case I finished up at the end of the week with no more than minus two. If, by the Saturday, you had clocked up minus three, some serious task was allocated. Every Tuesday night, three of these boys were chosen and sent off after the evening meal down to the station. The Paddy push and pull had dropped off two boxes of fish cakes from Grimsby. As there were about sixty boarders at Hill house, and we got two fish cakes each on the Wednesday, the wooden boxes, with two rope handles, were fairly heavy. This was a regular journey for me and, because of the hill, it was hard work carrying the bigger box between two of us, so we swapped over at strategic points. The smaller box for Sacrista Prebend was much lighter.

One punishment for naughty boys at Hill House was that we had to get up early and walk to Sacrista Prebend through the village streets in pyjamas and dressing gowns, clutching our sponge bags. Once there, we had a cold shower and walked back. Imagine this now! The school would be shut down with the school masters all put in prison, and Social Services and the media would have a field day!

On two occasions whilst I was there, the BBC *Choral Evensong* programme on Wednesday afternoons went out live from Southwell Minster. Outside broadcasting vans and generators were allowed onto the cathedral grounds, and a host of BBC people arrived with clip boards. The relevant minutes and seconds were written down carefully as evensong had to finish on the time it said in the *Radio Times*.

The 'reverberation time' in any cathedral is a real problem for a live broadcast. It was measured in several places down the nave with a stop watch after a loud chord from the organ. The reverberation time is the time it takes for a sound to become inaudible after the sound source stops. At Southwell Minster the reverberation time is about three seconds because the organ and choir are in the middle, otherwise it would have been much longer. At King's College, Cambridge, it is nearly five seconds, and at Grace Cathedral in San Francisco the distance from the large pipe organ is 150ft to the west door and the height to the roof is 90ft. The reverberation time there is an amazing seven seconds! This was exploited in 1971 when a superb record called *Gandarva* was recorded there. Side two has the pipe organ, a baritone and alto sax, and an electric bass, all entwined in this enormous cavern. (The CD, as often happens, isn't as good. Probably the engineer was having a really bad hair day.) This LP was the last one I played when I was dismantling my Hi-Fi equipment if I was moving house and the first one when it was set up again. So you can tell it's outstanding!

Back to 'Smokey', our matron. I was completely besotted with her, and she was lovely to me as well. I suffered from chronic hay fever, said to be hereditary because my mother had severe migraines, so she was particularly nice to me in the summer months when I was streaming. I was excused swimming lessons as the outdoor pool was about 50% chlorine, and playing cricket was also out if they had mowed the grass the day before. She made sure the local doctor prescribed me anti-histamine medication and eye drops.

One end of term, when everybody was getting ready to go home for the holiday I must have seemed less excited than I should have been. She gently extracted from me what my home life was like and suggested that in school holidays I should write to her if my mother said I could, and she gave me her address. I did write to her, and she always replied. No doubt my mother had previously sized Cathy up as a suitable matron to look after her prodigal son!

Top photo: *Southwell Minster choirboys during a BBC broadcast of choral evensong.*
Photo: Diocese of Southwell & Nottingham

Bottom photo: *Southwell Minster choir area showing the elaborately carved choir screen and organ.*
Photo: Mattana

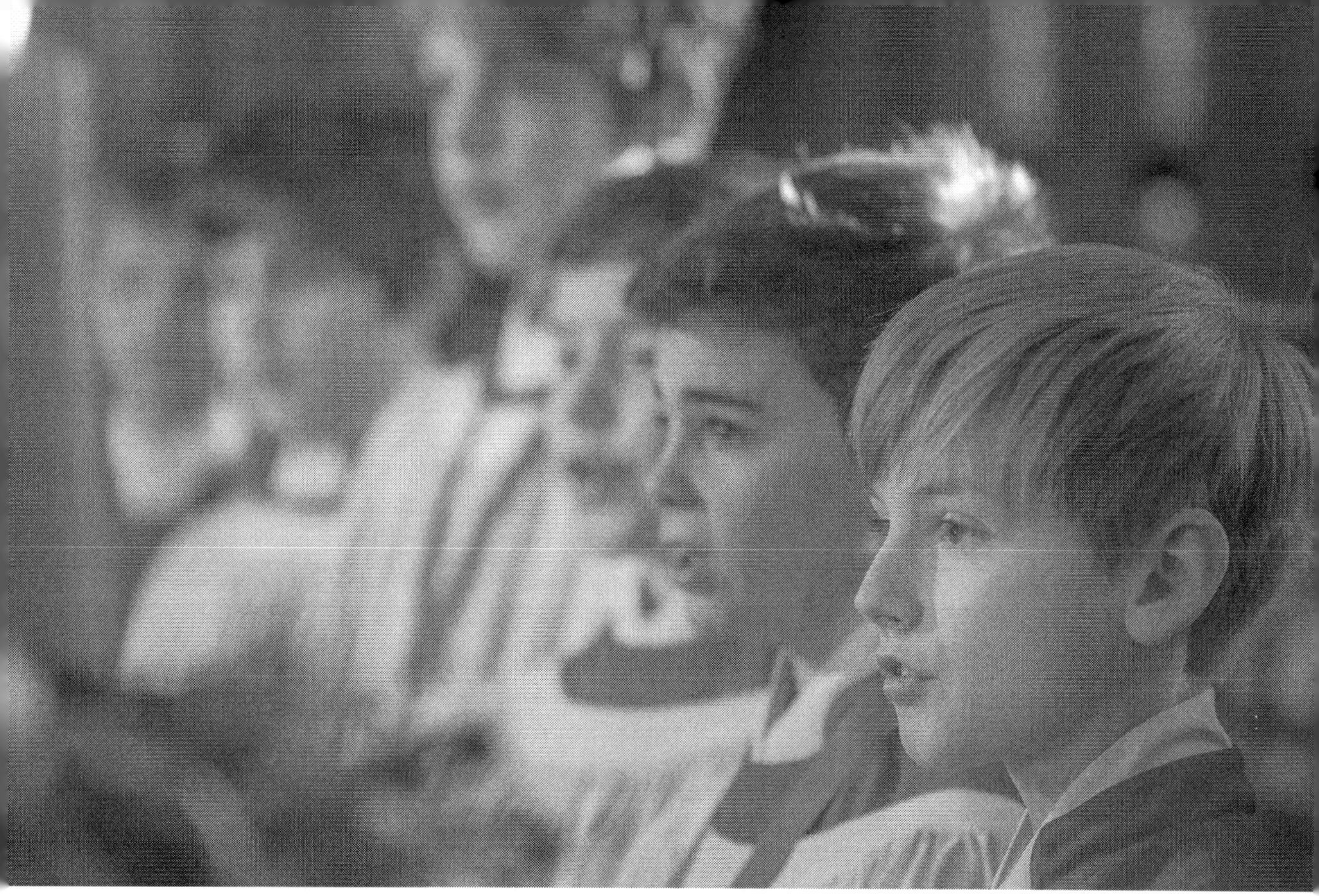

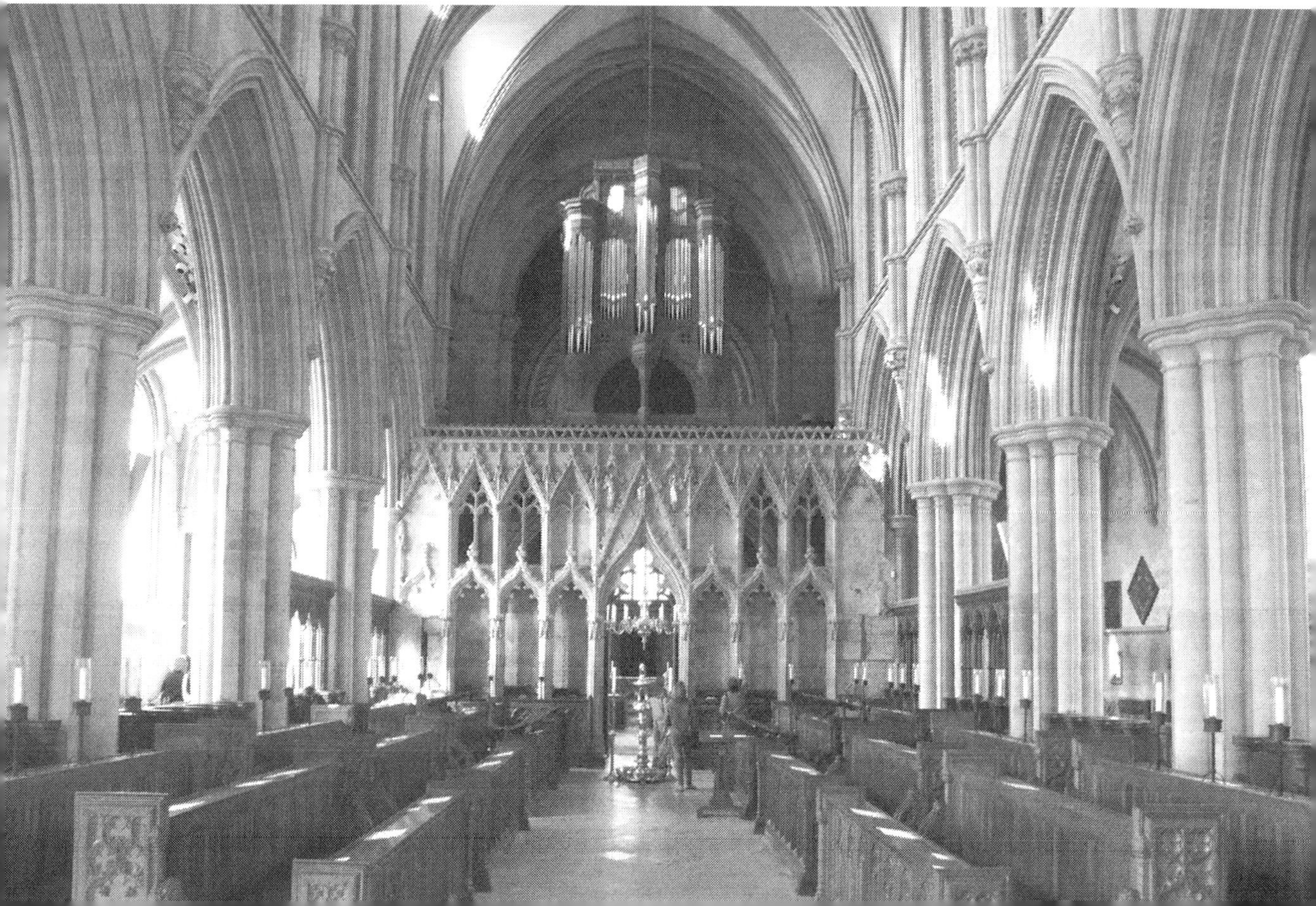

I could forge Cathy's name perfectly in her distinctive handwriting, out of sheer adulation and a lot of practice on sheets of paper. When I wrote to her I put her name on the envelope exactly as she signed it in curly writing: *Catherine E. Moakes.*

When I was aged twelve, my mother embraced Roman Catholicism and was 'received' into the Catholic Church. She liked the way Catholic priests told it straight and narrow, right down the line, and sermons were instructions and dictates on what to believe without any airy-fairy ideas.

Very sadly, one of the rules of joining the Catholic Church club was that attendance at church services of any other denomination was banned. My mother explained to me in a letter that she could sit in the back of the cathedral, a million miles away from where I was, but not in the choir area along with normal evensong faithful or other proud visiting parents. My father had to toe the line as well of course, although he was still Church of England. I thought this was extremely harsh and unloving and never forgave her. Why didn't she write to the Pope?

Many years later I wrote her a letter detailing some of my hurtful childhood memories, and I castigated her for not coming to see and listen to me in the choir stalls. It was still fresh in my memory, and I accused her of being 'so unchristian a Catholic that you could not come and watch your own son sing – which was the one thing he had been proudest to have done up to then in his whole life.' I still have a copy of this letter as I typed it up twice, and it still brings a lump to my throat after all this time. Just talk amongst yourselves for a moment while I wipe away a tear. Why is it that childhood memories can remain so strong?

5. Setting down Roots

'The man who builds a factory builds a temple, that the man who works there worships there, and to each is due, not scorn and blame, but reverence and praise.'
Calvin Coolidge

In the nineteenth century, bellfounders began working from central locations with workshops where they built furnaces and cast bells. John Taylor signed a lease in 1839 for their first premises in Loughborough which allowed him to stay there until 1860. In 1842 they cast their first set, or ring, of ten bells for Newark Parish Church. They also started getting work from an important Irish architect who was designing and building Roman Catholic churches.

In 1851 they held up production slightly and cast two bells of thirty and fifty inches in diameter for 'The Great Exhibition' at Hyde Park in London, under Royal Patronage. These bells were to be judged by a skilled committee, and the two bells were highly acclaimed as being 'superb' with the largest bell rung at opening and closing times. Various bellfounders from several nations exhibited over one hundred bells, and John was delighted to receive a 'Certificate of Special Approbation' and a 'Prize Medal'. He lost no time in publishing this prestigious achievement, but he had to get back to all his customers who were saying, 'Never mind the exhibition and junkets in London, where the hell are my bells?' He was so chuffed that a bell at Pilton in Devon from 1853 is inscribed, 'Recast by John Taylor and Son, Who the best prize for Church-bells won, At the Great Ex hi bi ti on, In London 1. 8. 5. and 1.' Not too good as regards poetry but never mind.

In 1854, Taylor's were given the order to recast the fifteen bells at The Royal Exchange in London, a very famous centre of commerce dating back to 1751. The London foundry, Mears, at Whitechapel, had cast the bells in 1845 for a new building following a severe fire in 1838. It was considered however that the bells were badly cast and inharmonious. The Taylor family realized that this was a golden opportunity to get work in the capital and were really bucked to be given the order. Apart from getting the job, it rubbed the noses of the Mears foundry in the dirt. The contract had a completion time of eight months, with a total weight of eight tons of bells, new fittings and a new frame, so he was going flat out. He fired up his furnaces twenty-two times throughout 1854 but not at all in February. The weather may have been really rotten then.

In 1858, John William put in a letter, 'I flatter myself that I have at length come to the full knowledge of bell casting. Master, I say, of my Art'. This was a true statement regarding the skills of English bellfounders at that time, but there was still a long way to go. He died a few months later, and his son John William I took over the foundry with his brother Pryce, for the two years before they had to move. Trevor Jennings, in a book I will refer to later, has calculated that before they moved they had fired the various furnaces up 165 times since 1844.

A list of bells published in 1858 shows that their work since 1825 included three rings (sets) of ten bells, eleven rings of eight, twenty-seven rings of six, thirty-one rings of five, and an incredible fifty-five of rings with less than five bells, as well as clock bells and single bells. At least twelve of these rings, according to my own calculations, had the largest bell weighing between one and one and a half tons. A big job for Dunham Massey in Cheshire was for a ring of ten bells with an additional ten bells to sound the hour and quarters and play tunes. He was still 'cooking on gas'.

In 1860, the lease on their bellfoundry land, owned by a clergyman, was due to expire. Bellfounders were not at all popular because they lit fires to dry the moulds and then slopped molten metal in. Fires spreading elsewhere were common. If you had applied for planning permission in the High Street, the owners of other properties would have definitely got up petitions. They would have paraded in front of the town hall waving assorted placards such as, 'No bellfoundry here!' or 'Bellfounders go away!' In 1859, John William I started building on a very large plot of land in a fairly undeveloped area of Loughborough called *The Cherry Orchard*. In just a few years it was to become the largest bellfoundry in the world.

In the 1980s, it was decided to open a Taylor bellfoundry museum. This was a good plan as there were lots of things lying around, and two old codgers who were prime exhibits. Trevor Jennings, a retired headmaster, became the museum curator, and he was asked to do some research and write a history of the foundry. It was published in 1987, entitled *Master of My Art, The Taylor Bellfoundries, 1784-1987*, and all employees were given a free copy. To give Trevor his due, he researched a host of facts. He tells us exactly how many bricks were purchased in 1876 to build an extension, and he found out what tonnage of bells were cast in practically every year. I had previously copiously researched the period 1895-1905 when the tuning process was substantially improved. I found out where the tuning forks came from, when the tuning machines were bought and where from, and things like this that were of particular interest to me. Trevor wasn't technical so some of his conclusions and inferences in his book are not in my opinion correct or (sorry, Trevor) are plainly wrong. He didn't consult as many people at the foundry as he should have done. Actually talking to people will often result in information culled from dusty tomes being reinterpreted.

When John Warner & Son in London had started using cast iron cases in 1853 and taken out a patent, this had doubtful value at the time. Any interested people could read the patent application. Trying to stop someone making anything similar was very difficult, with going to court the only remedy. Trevor Jennings writes that the first Taylor order for a cast iron case that he found (and was importantly being made elsewhere) was in 1868. Thirty were acquired from1869-1871 for bells from twelve inches to seventy two inches in diameter. In November 1871, John William I wrote to Edmund Beckett Denison, a very important London figure extremely interested in bells and clocks, and I'll come to him in detail later on. He told him, 'Upon being favoured by the hint from you, Sir, some time ago, I at once went in for iron shells, all my bells are moulded that way. I have a complete set of shells for bells up to four tons. I moulded them at my own foundry and carried the moulds to be cast at the iron foundry with which I am connected'. About 1875 he ordered more to increase the range. In 1869 he had told Edmund Denison that he was making a whole set of new iron crooks, 'based on shapes he had experimented with for over twenty years'. I think the 1869-1971 set of cases were needed then because the future Taylor bell profile had been fixed just prior to this.

Jed Flatters, a very important Taylor employee, started out as a bellhanger and then progressed to carrying out inspection of bells in towers and often went abroad doing the same thing. He wrote comprehensive reports with the appropriate quotations for work to be done. He is a mine of information and has pointed out that there were some cases at the foundry that had been made with wrought iron trunions (the sticky-out bits used when they lift the cases up with the crane) riveted on, not cast. This implies Taylor's were making at least some of them, and also there were core plates that were rough on one side. Casting them in the Taylor foundry in sand moulds would have meant the top surface was rough to some extent. Cases are very similar to bells in profile so making cases in the foundry would not have presented too many problems.

In foundries with a lot of tackle, heavy items could be picked up and moved with jib cranes and eventually overhead cranes. Making moulds in cast iron cases was not normally a problem weight-wise, and the cores were made on thick, cast iron plates. Cores were still hollow in the middle to help the air and gas escape, but lighting fires inside them was no longer necessary as they went into a drying stove.

The only time completed moulds were totally put in a pit was when you were ready to cast the bells. The cases had flanges, top and bottom, so you could stand the cases on the ground, or upside down, or on a trolley. Before casting the bell, the bottom flange was held tight against the core plate with heavy, 'C' shaped clips, tightened up with wedges.

To make the external shape, the cast iron case is set mouth up. The strickle or crook is upside down as well. As I have mentioned before, the crooks are thin metal plates bolted to pieces of wrought iron. The word 'Crook' is almost certainly because the shape looked like a bishop's crook, an elaborate version of the shepherd's crook that Jesus shepherded his human flock with. If the bishop was elderly, it handily doubled as a posh walking stick. The crook is fixed above the mouth of the case by an adjustable horizontal bar, and the bottom of the crook rod is located in a hole at the bottom. Then you start lining the case with loam. There are fewer canons needed as you have drilling machines, so the top of the bell is normally flat. Cases have a lot of holes all over them which means less weight, and the loam lining is stronger as it protrudes into the holes. Major changes!

There is no false bell, no wax letters, decorative shields or medallions made in wax, or elaborate figures of saints. As you build up the loam inside the case it goes in the drying stove overnight. These stoves are like your living room but six times as big with a coal fire and a chimney. The large drying stove at Taylor's was eventually heated by oil, and in the morning, the workers pulled the chains that made the big door lift up to get at the 'work in progress'. In winter, the foundry was very cold, so they had their tea and bacon-butties sitting just inside the stove. If they came and complained, 'The stove is cold,' you replied, 'Why weren't you keeping an eye on the level of oil in the tank? I'll ring up for more oil, but don't let this happen again!' It did, of course.

When your case is fully lined and dry, you turn it on its side. If it is not too big it goes on a table, or if it is extremely big it sits on the foundry floor. You paint the mould with plumbago which is a mixture of graphite and water. More graphite in a muslin bag allows you to sprinkle it onto the mould, and with a metal thing shaped like a mushroom you keep working it in until it gets all shiny and smooth.

The outer mould is beginning to look good, but then there is a snag; you are back to the inscription. All Taylor bells have *John Taylor & Co * Loughborough * Date ** all round, below the shoulder, and * *England* * as well, for exported bells. On very small bells where you can't get your hands in you use a Taylor shield instead. So you cut a groove in the mould, fill it with fine, damp loam, and press all the letters in one by one. These metal letters are easy to read when laid out on your table because they are just like normal letters.

It's a pain to put even the foundry inscription on every bell, but your crib sheet may also list the names of the vicar and three churchwardens or coats of arms. This means more slots in the mould to be filled up and impressed with the lettering backwards way round, so you have to check it with a mirror. It isn't as easy as when all the inscriptions were in wax, but this is the price you pay for the ease of the new method in other respects. If the clergy or donors start asking for tall angels all round the bell, you have to tell them, 'Sorry, we can't do that'. This is why John William I got worried as some cheeky bellfounders from Belgium and Holland were selling bells in England. They were still using the lost wax process and told the people who might want their bells, 'We'll put on it whatever you want. Angels? How many? The Lord's Prayer? Latin on one side? English on the other? No problem!'

If it is an enormous bell you put your prayer mat inside the mould because you need all the help you can get. You kneel on this mat and keep turning the mould round. The last crucial stage is that your boss checks the inscription with a mirror. If he agrees it is fine, get him to sign it off. If there is a complaint later on, you can say, 'I just did it how you told me to, and you signed my bit of paper. If it's wrong, you wrote it down wrong!' This gets you off the hook.

Right: *Roger Johns, foundry manager, lettering a cope mould by tapping metal letters into the loam for the largest bell of a ring destined for Wellington Cathedral, New Zealand.*
Photo: David Humphrey

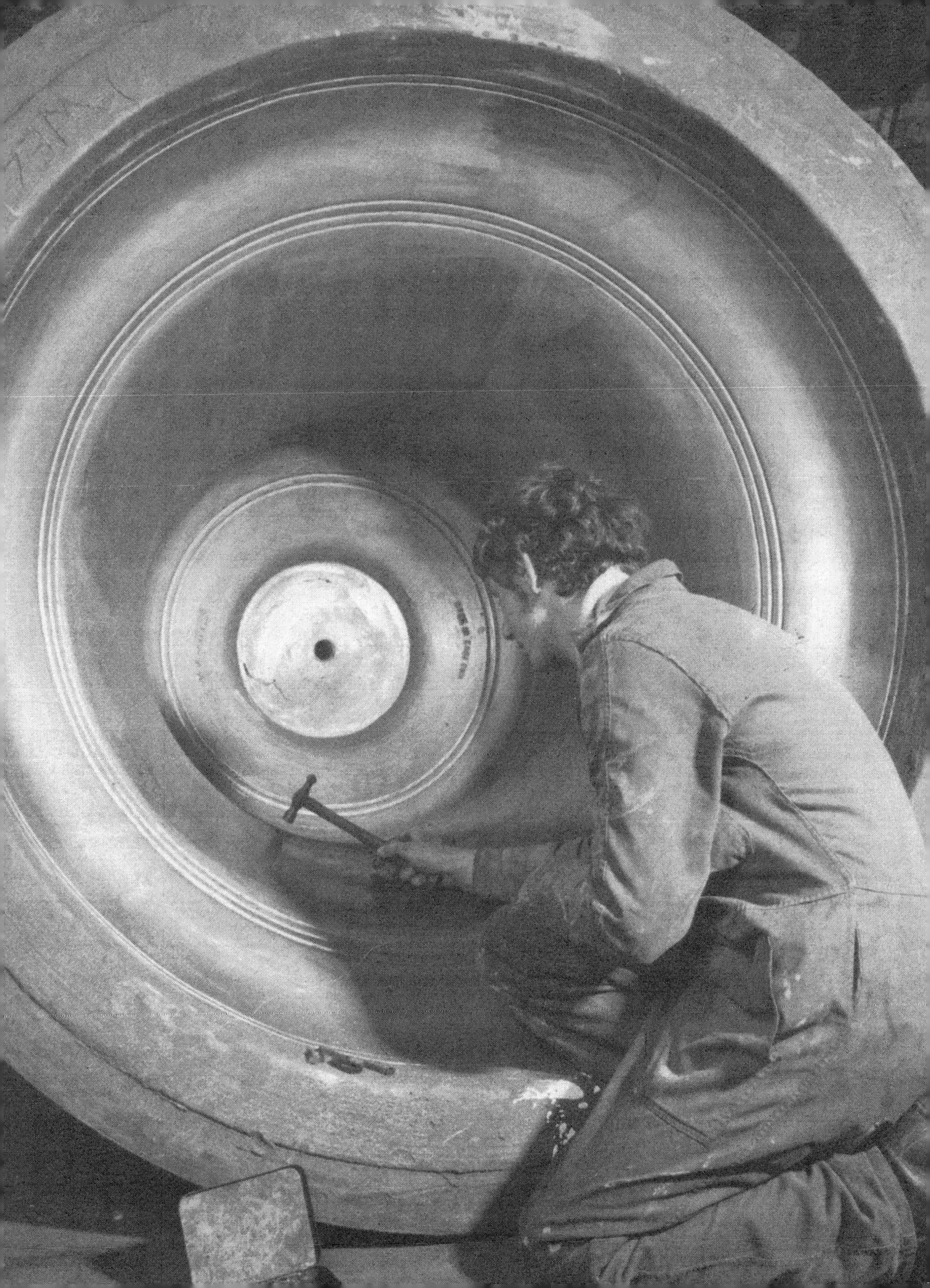

'Closing the moulds' can still be extremely hairy. The cast iron case allows for the taper on the cope that mates with the taper on the core with a thin bit of loam just underneath the flange. When you lower the case over the core, the flange is not quite resting on the core plate but the loam band is. The two tapers need to be a perfect fit, not just to stop any molten metal escaping but to get the musical note you need. A case and core that close down perfectly should guarantee that the note of the bell is as designed, with some metal to be machined off the inside during the tuning. If you lower a case over the core and it does not come right down, the taper on the case is probably slightly smaller than the core taper. If it is minimal, you rotate the case round the core which rubs off some of the dry loam, so you get a good fit. If the case comes right down very easily, it may be that the tapers have not aligned correctly. To check this, you either try to push the case over towards the core by hand with the weight taken by the crane, or see if it moves over with crowbars if it is a big bell. If you can shift the case, the taper is too big; or is the core taper too small? A conundrum! If it turns out that the cope is a fraction too big, you put a few bits of thin metal at various places round the core taper, held there with chewing gum (but silicone out of a gun is better). Does it fit now? The bell will be a little thicker than normal or than how you wanted it to be. If you are closing the moulds for a ten-ton bell, it is important that you do it with all due thought and your full attention. If somebody comes to ask you something you say, 'Go away!'

Cases are very durable. At Taylor's today they still use all the ones bought since 1868. Enormous ones don't get used too often, but they still have them. You keep using the appropriate cases and core plates for every order you get. Storage is a problem, but you can put one inside the other like Russian dolls. They stored some in a large brick-lined pit they had built between the foundry and the timber/girder store, and the largest ones were kept in the open yard.

To give you an idea of the size and weights of the cases and plates, I am going to introduce you to a few musical terms. Don't glaze over. I will try and keep it simple. If you have an Aunt Mable and she has a piano, go and see her and look at the keys. If you sit on a chair in the middle of the keyboard, the white and black keys are in groups. Straight in front of you, there should be three white keys with two black keys between them. (Ignore the groups of white keys to the right or the left from where you are supposed to be looking which have four white keys with three black keys between them.) The white key to the left of the first of the two black ones is note 'C'. Because it is in the middle of the keyboard, it is called 'Middle C'. The notes on a piano, other musical instruments, and written music are named A, B, C, D, E, F, & G which are repeated as you go up the scale. The white note two down to the left of Middle C is A. Put a coin on Middle C, but not one of the stupid, tiny ones that even shops don't want, in case it falls down the gap.

Right: Making the outer cope inside the cast iron case for the bourdon bell 'Great Peter' at York Minster in 1927. This bell is 8 ft 8 ins in diameter with a finished weight of nearly eleven tons.
Photo: Taylor archives

PREPARING MOULDING CASE FOR
GREAT PETER OF YORK MINSTER
1927
TAYLORS, BELLFOUNDERS, LOUGHBOROUGH

Middle C is also called C4 because if Aunt Mable has a decent piano with eighty-eight black and white keys there are a lot more C's. The one that is two notes up from the extreme left is C1, then C2, C3, and then Middle C4 where your coin is. Going to the right you have C5, C6, C7 and C8, the last one before you run out of keys. You can get the idea if your mate has an electronic keyboard, but he won't have eighty-eight keys. All these notes called C are eight white notes apart, and this is called an octave. Octaves occur in music in almost any part of the world, not just the Western world. I expect Eskimos sing gleefully in octaves when they have harpooned a very large whale. If you sing the word 'Somewhere' from the start of the song 'Over the Rainbow' from the musical *The Wizard of Oz*, these first two notes are an octave apart. X-Factor contestants often choose this song, so you probably know it already.

You sing in octaves that sound very natural quite often. I can hear you saying, 'I don't', but you do. At the birthday party for the precocious teenage brat that is the son of your boss eventually the cake is brought out. Bert who works in dispatch and has had three beers has a very low voice and starts to sing, *Happy Birthday to You*. If you are a woman or a man with a higher speaking voice, you join in but an octave higher. 'Thug' (that's the son's nickname) has a sweet, much younger sister called Mary who has a really high voice. When she joins in you are all singing two octaves apart.

So from your Middle C (you didn't take the coin off, did you?) you can go up to the note A which is five white keys to the right. In 1939-1940 there was an international committee of acoustical scientists and musicians. They eventually agreed that the A above middle C was a very precise 440Hz because every sound has a frequency that can be expressed as a number. It took them ages because first of all they didn't speak a common language, and this note A was a very different number in loads of different countries. The Hz stands for Hertz but nothing to do with car hire so ignore it. An octave is a doubling or a halving of any of the scientific frequencies. The A below Middle C is 220Hz, and the one below that is 110Hz. The next one up after 440Hz is 880Hz and then 1,760Hz and so on. The A that is the very bottom note on an eighty-eight note piano is 27.5Hz.

Coming back to bells, there is the doubling or halving of the octaves as well. Taylor's supply as standard a 30 ins/75 cm C bell that weighs 5 cwts/560 lbs/254 kg. If you had asked the price of this bell and then said you wanted to know about a C bell but an octave up, this is a 15 ins/37.5 cm bell weighing only 70 lbs/31.8 kg. A big difference for two bells an octave apart in frequency or 'pitch' (another name for high and low sounds). The Taylor bell that is a C bell an octave below the first one clocks in at a diameter of 60 ins/150 cm, weighing 40 cwts/2 tons/4,480lbs/2,038 kg. This is a decent size bell! So go for gold; the next octave bell down from the two ton one is 120 ins (10 ft in diameter)/300 cm, weighing 320 cwts/16 tons/16,290 kg. I agree with you that this is a really big bell.

Right: *A diagram of an 88 note piano keyboard starting with A0 at the extreme left, with middle C marked, and going up to C8 at the extreme right. The frequencies in Hz are shown above each note.*

Middle C

Note	Freq (Hz)	Note	Freq (Hz)
A0	27.5	A0#	29.135
B0	30.868		
C1	32.703	C1#	34.648
D1	36.708	D1#	38.891
E1	41.203		
F1	43.654	F1#	46.249
G1	48.999	G1#	51.913
A1	55.000	A1#	58.270
B1	61.735		
C2	65.406	C2#	69.296
D2	73.416	D2#	77.782
E2	82.407		
F2	87.307	F2#	92.499
G2	97.999	G2#	103.83
A2	110.00	A2#	116.54
B2	123.47		
C3	130.81	C3#	138.59
D3	146.83	D3#	155.56
E3	164.81		
F3	174.61	F3#	185.00
G3	196.00	G3#	207.65
A3	220.00	A3#	233.08
B3	246.94		
C4	261.63	C4#	277.18
D4	293.66	D4#	311.13
E4	329.63		
F4	349.23	F4#	369.99
G4	392.00	G4#	415.30
A4	440.00	A4#	466.16
B4	493.88		
C5	523.25	C5#	554.37
D5	587.33	D5#	622.25
E5	659.25		
F5	698.46	F5#	739.99
G5	783.99	G5#	830.61
A5	880.00	A5#	932.33
B5	987.77		
C6	1046.5	C6#	1108.7
D6	1174.7	D6#	1244.5
E6	1318.5		
F6	1396.9	F6#	1480.0
G6	1568.0	G6#	1661.2
A6	1760.0	A6#	1864.7
B6	1979.5		
C7	2093.0	C7#	2217.5
D7	2349.3	D7#	2489.0
E7	2637.0		
F7	2793.8	F7#	2960.0
G7	3136.0	G7#	3322.4
A7	3520.0	A7#	3729.3
B7	3951.1		
C8	4186.0		

PIANO KEYBOARD

The number beside each key is the fundamental frequency in units of cycles per seconds, or Hertz.

OCTAVES

For example, the A4 key has a frequency of 440 Hz.

Note that A5 has a frequency of 880 Hz. The A5 key is thus one octave higher than A4 since it has twice the frequency.

So with bells, the diameter of bells an octave apart is either twice going down or a half going up, and you may have twigged that the weight is increasing or decreasing by a factor of eight. In every octave on a piano, there are thirteen white and black notes. The four C bells we have mentioned span four octaves which is forty-nine notes in total. Now you can see the range in size of bells over four octaves, and the weights of the bells that all need heavy cases and core plates.

What I have said regarding the sizes and weights is correct, but on very small bells for a carillon the diameters and the weights are different otherwise they may well be inaudible. Sets of church bells, known as a 'ring', also have some of the bells heavier than normal, partly to make them easier for the bellringers.

The largest bell ever made at Taylor's is usually quoted to be 9 ft 6 ins in diameter but actually it is just less than 9 ft 7 ins. Before it started its long journey to London, it was accurately weighed in the foundry as being sixteen and three quarter tons. (Work out the metric equivalent yourself. It's getting boring, and I have supplied some conversion figures at the back of the book). The cast iron case for this bell was two inches thick all over and was designed to stand a pressure of 200 tons. It weighed just over fourteen tons, and the core plate weighed seven tons. When the moulds were finished, the total weight of the case, core plate and moulds was approximately thirty tons. Into this very heavy bit of kit, seventeen tons of metal was poured in to make the splendid bell called 'Great Paul' at St Paul's Cathedral in London. We'll come back to 'Great Paul' in a bit, and I have a really good story to tell you about this bell.

I am slightly getting ahead of myself, so we need to see what happened when the bellfoundry moved to the new location.

6. The Cherry Orchard

'Great God in Heaven, the Cherry Orchard is now mine.'
The Cherry Orchard - Anton Chekhov

John Taylor died in 1858 aged sixty-one, but the end of the lease on their first premises in Loughborough in March 1860 had obviously been discussed with his sons, John William I, Robert Edward and Pryce Jemson Jones. The premises they were in were fairly dilapidated and had served their purposes but were becoming too small anyway. They all started drawing out plans for a new foundry in a part of town where the neighbours weren't going to be bolshie.

In 1859, John William I was thirty-two years old, and his brother Pryce was twenty-four. They knew that their reputation as bellfounders was being increasingly respected, and orders would come in, or they could go out and get them. Robert had died in 1856 at the age of twenty-six, and Pryce died in 1862. Assuming he was not incapacitated or very ill before he died, he would have helped with the plans and the move. John William I found land on a site known as *The Cherry Orchard* a little way out of town and bought his first 1,179 sq yds. Adjoining land was available if he needed it, and within only a few months he increased his land area to 6,682 sq yds (about three-quarters the size of a football pitch).

A local builder, William Moss, had built various hosiery factories, and the plan for the new, custom designed bellfoundry was basically an open yard with high walls and various buildings round the inside of the walls. William Moss wanted the work and put in a lean price that would still give him some profit, thinking that extensions were going to be built and hoping he would get this work at a better price. The trouble was, John William was in a big hurry. He had to leave his rented premises and not interrupt his work schedules, and he cast five bells right at the last minute.

When nothing seemed to be happening, he went and found the builder and basically told him, 'The starting date we agreed was last week, and I need you to get started. If you don't, I will find another builder and tell everybody you are completely unreliable!' This threat had the desired result and work started very quickly. In the original contract there was only one furnace, one casting pit and a very large saw pit for wood. Coal for the furnace came in at a door where a 'railway-type' track was laid which had hand trolleys. Later on these trolley-ways were extended.

Whilst at the first foundry, they had been experimenting with a different type of furnace.

These were named 'Reverberatory furnaces', but the igloo types they had been using still came in this category. The word 'reverberatory' referred to the flame being reflected back onto the metal by the arched roof. (Nothing to do with large cathedrals and the time it takes for sounds to become inaudible). The whole caboodle was lifted up off the ground with solid brickwork. It was like a miniature railway tunnel built in the yard against the foundry building wall.

One of the first ones was 7ft long by 3ft wide and 3ft up to the arch internally. Where the back door of our igloo was, it was now carried on into the foundry, through the foundry wall. They loaded the metal in from the opening inside before bricking it up. This opening was above floor level, so a ladle could be put below it if required, or the metal run down a gutter. These types of furnaces were described as 'wall furnaces.' Where the arched roof met the foundry wall there was a gap with a high chimney to draw the flame over the metal, so no bellows anymore.

The design of the chimney was critical as this sucked the flame over the metal. If it was 'efficient' the metal didn't take too long to melt, and metal loss was about 3%. If it was a bad design, or too much metal was put in, it could take hours and hours to melt, and losses might be double or more. The Taylor family constantly played around with the dimensions to try and improve things. Was it better to have a hump in the roof over the pier that separated the fire and metal? Or did the flame have more strength if there was no hump?

If the flame was very fierce, the brickwork was scoured, and if the roof was not strong enough, brickwork could fall into the metal, so a complete disaster! Where the flame started to go up the chimney, this could collapse as well if it couldn't cope with the heat. Any new furnace was 'run-in' as gently as possible. Was this a really good design or not? Until a new furnace had been properly commissioned, no-one was sure the design was the best, how much metal could be loaded into it, and the time needed to get the metal to the right temperature. 'Suck it and see' was the order of the day.

Each new furnace had a larger capacity of metal than the one before to cope with larger bells, so this was also a voyage into the unknown. The other problem was when the walls and roof in the furnace started to be damaged by the intense heat. The lid had to be taken off and the furnace re-lined with new fireproof bricks, so the furnace was out of action. Local builders did this, so the boss would say to his workers, 'Nip down to the bellfoundry and reline the furnace quick as you can.' They replied, 'Not again! Which furnace is it this time?'

Continual improvements took place, and by 1862 they had covered areas for the joinery shop, a wood store, a shed where the blacksmith worked, and a special area for making the loam and chewing up the used loam. Sand and other materials were stored there as well. They had an area for casting small bells for town criers, railway stations, and other uses, along with hemispherical gongs. Orders for items like this were a good addition to their church bell work and continued to be a major string to their bow.

Right: *A sketch of the bellfoundry that is post-1867 as the 67 ft steam engine chimney can be seen, and before 1875, when the new foundry to cast iron & bronze was built where the tree trunks are, at bottom left.*
Sketch: Taylor archive

BELL FOUNDRY, LOUGHBOROUGH.

J. TAYLOR & CO.

In 1862, John William I exhibited a three ton bell at the London International Exhibition, but he found that bells were relegated to a 'hardware' category, and no-one was interested in the sound. He was proposing to sell this bell and put up a 'for sale' sign at the exhibition, but one of his patrons said, 'Just hang on a bit!' It went eventually to Halifax town hall for a decent amount of money to be a clock hour bell with four new quarter bells. His bell had been seen by many international visitors, and he did get some orders for, 'The Colonies, and other places abroad'. He sent a bell to New Zealand, but the ship, the *William Brown*, sank with all hands after a fire at sea! I expect he got the order to make another one though.

In his first year at his new foundry, he cast just less than eleven tons of bells, and this went up steadily each year. He continually improved his premises that were now a factory. By 1863, all this work had cost £1,200, so a considerable amount of money! John William I was getting strict about churches paying promptly for the work he had done, and sometimes he asked people such as architects to put pressure on the churchwardens to get the money in! Occasionally, he got landed with the dreaded 'warranty bonds' that were a form of a guarantee, meaning he wasn't due for his money for a year and a day! Not good news at all.

In 1866, he invested in a steam engine that drove various machines. The chimney was sixty-seven feet high, so became a distinctive landmark. If someone asked, 'Can you tell me how to get to the bellfoundry?', the reply was, 'See that very tall chimney? That's where it is!'

The same year, he took the unusual step of publishing his prices. If a customer asked for time to pay, they were told, 'Strictly cash'. He justified this by telling them, 'Bells are entirely a retail item, and there are no wholesale buyers!' This didn't always work, and sometimes he was strapped for cash.

He got married in 1852, and of his various children, the most important as regards the bellfoundry were his sons, John William II, born in 1853, and Edmund Denison, born in 1864. When he had a spare moment from adding bits onto the foundry, he wanted to have a decent house as businessmen were often gauged to be successful if they had a posh house. Charles Hansom, an architect from Bristol, was supplying a lot of work, so he wrote a smarmy letter to him. He put in his letter, 'I remember how cordially you gratuitously proffered your professional assistance....and I enclose a rough sketch'. Really smarmy! The architect normally only designed churches and large buildings, but he forwarded a design. John William had covered his bets by putting in his letter, 'I have no idea what a house of that size would cost, and if it is too expensive I shall be compelled to curtail my notions.' In other words, don't make it too expensive! The house was built with space for his growing family, and it had enough twiddly bits to show his peers what an upstanding member of the community he was.

Since 1858 John William I had been keeping good records of how much money he was spending, or borrowing from his obliging or cross bank manager. Also, how often he was casting bells and the total weights at each year end. In 1865 he started compiling a 'crook book' that recorded the thickness of the crooks (so the bell profile inside and out) and the weights of the bells that were being cast from each one.

He was still experimenting with the profile, in common with most bellfounders. Up to then, all continental and most English bellfounders were basing their profile on arcs of a circle. Find some plant pots and turn them upside down on a piece of paper, and draw a little way round each one. What you have are arcs of different circles. Eventually you forget the plant pots and use a long bit of string with a drawing pin at one end. I think that about 1866 or 1867, John William came across an ellipsograph. To explain what an ellipse is, get two eggs out of the fridge and hard boil them, otherwise it gets messy. Put one into an eggcup with the bottom at the top, so the rounded not the pointy end, and cut this half off with a bread knife, but mind your fingers! Do the same with the other one and put these two halves together. The shape of the cross-section of this is an ellipse, not a circle, and I have mentioned kiwi fruit if you haven't got any eggs.

Playing with mechanical gadgets was very popular with Victorians in the 19th century, and when John William discovered the mechanical device called an ellipsograph it made drawing out an ellipse much simpler. The old way of doing it was by using a piece of string with both ends tied together at a very precise length. You then used two drawing pins and a pencil to trace out the shape. It was a bit of a bind doing it this way and required a lot of patience. If he was the same as some other members of the Taylor family in later years, patience may not have been one of his strong points! Getting technical, the distance from the top to the bottom of your special egg is called the 'major axis', and the width of the egg is the 'minor axis'. By adjusting the position of pegs on his mechanical aid, he could make an ellipse that was fat or thin. If you have a rubber egg and squeeze it between your palms, the minor axis of the ellipse is smaller, and the major axis is a bit taller. Okay?

John William liked this gadget, and after playing around with it he decided it was perfect for drawing out the external and internal profile. The one he acquired was a very small one made of brass in a nice little case; very nice, but no good for bells. His men in the foundry made him a bigger one, and he cast a bell using this to draw out the profile. The ellipse gave him a very flowing shape, much better than messing around with arcs of a circle. You could ask, 'Did he wake up one day and decide to make his profiles elliptical, and then needed to find out how to do it?' I don't think so. I believe he came across this ellipsograph first and then started experimenting.

Once he decided it was fine, he started with bigger ellipsographs, all courtesy of his foundry. These lived in the 'crook room' at Taylor's when I was there, and the biggest ones were very heavy. Neither Paul Taylor nor I knew exactly how they were used as we didn't have the basic geometric construction details. You know, 'Draw from A to E, and then two brims upwards.' If a person had said to us, 'Here is a nice big bit of paper, and here is an ellipsograph so draw out the standard Taylor profile', we couldn't have done it!

Paul Taylor wasn't too bothered because we had all the crooks we needed, but when I was searching through old Taylor papers one day I found the construction drawing. With a bit of sucking my pencil (well, quite a long time to be truthful), I saw how it worked and dusted off one of the ellipsographs. The internal profile, from the level of the inscription band, is an exact quarter of an ellipse all the way down to the lip. Externally, an exact quarter of an ellipse comes from the inscription band down to the thickest part of the soundbow. A small arc of a circle takes this down to the lip. This makes a very simple flowing design, and each curve takes about five seconds to draw out. Trevor Jennings was pleased to put a profile I had drawn out in his museum. We always said to visitors, 'Taylor bells are best because the shape is based on an ellipse.' We knew it was, although we didn't have a clue then as to how it had first been drawn out. We didn't tell them that, of course!

So certainly by 1869, John William was making crooks for all the bells to the new shape that he said was the result of experiments over twenty years. Trevor Jennings found the orders for a whole set of cast iron cases made to match. There is no evidence that another complete set of cases was ever ordered, and we know that by 1871 he had a large number of them. In 1869, John William and his son-in-law took over a small iron foundry in Loughborough, so the cost of cases and core plates would have been minimal, but very large ones were farmed out to an iron foundry in Derby.

There is an engraving of the Taylor foundry between 1867 and 1875, showing more areas covered over, with two reverberatory furnaces for bells and a drying stove. Some of the buildings were two storeys to give more storage space, but it was still at a premium. And now there were a load of cast iron cases and core plates as well. The biggest ones were buried in the furnace area to get rid of them, but John William decided he had to expand again! Across the road on another bit of land he built a custom designed 'casting hall' (because that sounded posh). All the bell and iron casting and mould making, and all the cases and core plates went into this one hundred by forty-feet new building. It had two new furnaces for bells, one for iron, and a very large drying stove. He could now demolish the furnaces in his main yard, but he kept a small one in use for a short period. His bell factory was now extremely impressive.

Between 1860 and 1875, he cast 506 tons of bells, and from 1870 to 1875 the annual average was forty-six tons. He was buying most of his clappers from a company in Derby, but he wasn't totally satisfied with them. In 1874, apart from all the other expenditure, he bought his own steam hammer to forge better clappers. He still sometimes suffered from not getting paid promptly, and once or twice resorted to a debt collection company. He tried to be accommodating as he didn't want to get a bad reputation for squeezing clients to pay up, but in some cases he had no option.

If he had a set of bells come in that were going to be boiled up to cast new ones, he stopped paying for the old ones as scrap metal when they came in. He advised clients, 'Payment made for the purchase of old bells to be recast or a surplus in weight is calculated at the end of the work carried out'. A much more satisfactory idea. Was he running a charity? He was a businessman with a factory and men to pay! He had sometimes found that much smaller companies, or amateur bellhangers, used bits that were being taken out of a church when he was doing new work. He stopped that! 'All old materials, in place of which new ones are supplied, to become the property of the contractors.' So there, get your sticky mitts off it.

In 1877, Taylor's received the prestigious order to provide a ring of twelve bells for St. Paul's Cathedral in London, where there had never been a ring of bells. John William II, who was only twenty-five years old, was dealing with a very influential man, Edmund Beckett Denison Q.C., Chairman of the Bell Committee. This man commanded intense respect, but he had extremely strong and rigid opinions about bells and clocks which were his passion. You went against his advice and stipulations at your own peril, so I need to explain how he became so influential.

Edmund Beckett Denison was born in 1816, the son of Sir Edmund Beckett, 4th Baronet of Grimthorpe, M.P. for the West Ridings in Yorkshire. After going to Eton and Cambridge, the son started practising law in 1841, rapidly becoming very famous in the legal profession. In 1854, he became a 'Q.C.' These initials stand for 'Queen's Council', signifying he was qualified to give legal advice to the English state, supposing someone silly was trying to sue it. He became Leader of the Parliamentary Bar in the House of Commons as well, so you didn't mess with Edmund. He became Baron Grimthorpe in 1874 and Lord Grimthorpe in 1886. His passion for clocks (enormous clocks, not the ones you put on your mantelpiece) resulted in him becoming president to his death of the Horological Society. His wife was the daughter of the Bishop of Lichfield, and he was earning oodles of money from his fees in court cases. If you were going up against him in court, you had better get up really early to lay your stall out.

He paid for a big chunk of St. Albans Cathedral when the West front needed re-building, and one of the new statues had his face carved on it. Well, it would have! Some people thought this design was not very sympathetic, and one person who wasn't too scared of him coined the verb 'to Grimthorpe'. This meant to alter totally the character of some ancient building! In 1868, he worked closely with the architect on the building of St. Chad's church in Leeds. 'Working closely' meant you did what he said! Officially he retired in 1881, but that just meant he had more time for clocks and bells and writing forthright letters to *The Times* on various subjects. He was often very rude about other important people he considered idiots. To curry some favour, John William I had called one of his sons, Edmund Denison. The only thing was, the father of Edmund Beckett had added Denison to his name at some stage. When his father died, the son dropped the Denison. Oh well! Good idea at the time!

So I have set the scene, but let's go back to about 1840-1850. The Houses of Parliament had suffered a severe fire in 1834, so a new tower with 'a noble clock' was planned. The architect, Sir Charles Barry, approached The Queen's Clockmaker in 1844. He didn't rush to come up with a design so another clockmaker volunteered. The Astronomer Royal, George Airy, then decided that he would get involved, with conditions such as, 'The first stroke of the hour must be accurate to one second.' Edmund Beckett took over this squabble, and the clock was ordered in 1854.

They wanted a big hour bell and four quarter bells, and there are two stories why the hour bell was christened 'Big Ben'. The most likely one is that Benjamin Caunt, a famous bare knuckle prize-fighter at the time who weighed eighteen stone (252 lbs), had the nickname 'Big Ben'. Originally, the bell was to be christened either 'Royal Victoria' or just 'Victoria'.

Edmund Beckett was pally with the London bellfoundry of John Warner & Sons who had started making bells again in 1850. Early in 1856 they were awarded a 'Royal Warrant', so were the official suppliers of bells to the English monarchy.

Apart from working at various sites in central London where a variety of other products were made, there was an iron foundry, Warner, Lucas, & Barrett, at Norton Furnaces, near Stockton on Tees. George Mears, who owned the Whitechapel bellfoundry, wasn't too friendly with Edmund Beckett due to a previous dispute, so they declined to quote. Taylor's put in a quote without too much enthusiasm. They weren't then using cast iron cases and had stopped making false bells, so they thought casting a bell this big was very dicey indeed. They also wanted money up front for the metal! This ruled them out from getting the job, but I'm sure they weren't too bothered.

Warner's were given the order, and apparently Edmund Beckett drew out the bell profile personally on the floor in their works! From an engraving at the time, they made a cast iron case (of the sort patented in 1853) and cast the sixteen ton hour bell at Norton on August 6th, 1856. One account, from *The Illustrated London News* of August 23rd, states that when the furnaces had 'attained the requisite heat …. the operation of charging or putting in the metal commenced occupying about one hour' (loading up the tin?), and 'in less than two and a half hours the whole of the metal (eighteen tons) was in a state of perfect fusion'. They then slurped the metal in, 'which in five minutes completed the casting of the bell'. Five minutes sounds absolutely right.

They took the bell to West Hartlepool by rail and then transferred it to the boat *Wave*. At the crucial moment, the bell dropped suddenly onto the deck. The bell was okay, but the ship didn't like it at all. It was still just about seaworthy, so they took the bell to the port of London. A team of sixteen white horses pulled a cart over the Westminster Bridge to the yard by the tower. The bell was suspended from some very large beams, like a huge gallows suitable for a public execution, mainly because the tower was far from finished.

Through most of 1857 it was struck with a large external hammer for fifteen minutes every Saturday until a crack four feet long appeared! There was a big fight over this with various theories. 'The hammer designed by Edmund Beckett is far too big,' or 'The bell is too thick in the wrong place,' and 'The mixture of copper and tin is not right.' All experts had their own idea, and the only agreement was that it was cracked. These arguments were achieving nothing so Warner's were asked to have another go. They obviously thought, *Once is enough. How can we be sure this won't happen again?* So they put in a ridiculous quote as a good way of getting out of this mess. They later claimed that the proportion of seven parts of tin to twenty-two of copper (so 24% tin) had been dictated by Edmund Beckett, and they would never have used such a high proportion of tin on a very big bell themselves.

Right: *'Big Ben I' cast by John Warner & Son in 1856 for the clock tower of Westminster Palace, at the Houses of Parliament, London. This sketch appeared in their catalogue of bells sent out to clients.*
Origin of sketch unknown.

The LARGEST BELL in ENGLAND, cast by JOHN WARNER & SONS for the Clock Tower of the NEW PALACE AT WESTMINSTER, 1856, by order of HER MOST GRACIOUS MAJESTY QUEEN VICTORIA.

They stated that left to their own devices the bell would not have cracked! They went on to say that the clock hammer should have been five to six hundredweight, not 'nearly a half ton weight' (ten hundredweight). So there!

There is a very interesting observation about the Warner 'Big Ben I', as it seems quite likely it wouldn't have been able to be lifted up the tower as the shaft was too small! George Mears, who owned the Whitechapel foundry, then decided they would put in a quote as, all things considered, it was a prestigious bell. It seems that their quote for a smaller bell was just over half of the new Warner quote, and they were given the order. After flagging down a large number of horses and carts, they broke up the Warner bell in the traditional way by laying it on its side and smacking it with a very large weight suspended from a jib crane.

After moulding a false bell, they cast their smaller version, 'Big Ben II', in April 1858. The diameter of their bell is stated to have been designed so that it was able to be lifted up the hole in the tower! A newspaper account states that the metal in the largest furnace was melted down over twenty-two hours using wood as the fuel, and over ten hours in a second furnace. They then took a very slow twenty minutes to fill the mould. Part of the inscription reads, 'Under the direction of Edmund Beckett Denison, Q.C.' This was quite accurate as he had again specified the same high tin content. George Mears warned him that the bell would be too brittle, and he would take no responsibility if there were any problems.

In October 1858, it was hauled 200 feet up the tower sideways, because the hole wasn't big enough to lift it straight up. (The height of a modern English bell is about 80% of the diameter). Unfortunately, it cracked in September 1859! It had only been striking the hour since July 11th when the clock striking mechanism was installed and operational.

Wow! Another cracked bell, and it couldn't be lowered down the tower as the new clock was in the way! Fierce accusations again, with Edmund Beckett being criticised over the size of the clock hammer. He blamed George Mears, saying it was a cruddy casting. He claimed, 'Porous holes had been filled up by Mears, as a dentist fills teeth with amalgam, and then covered up with a coloured wash.' Mears went to court because although there were many blow-holes (with some of them half an inch deep), they had been filled in with lead on the instruction of the Clerk of Works, not Mears. A chemical 'patina', or wash, that was often used on bronze statues, was also applied in the tower, but not by them. Edmund Beckett withdrew all his accusations in court and agreed to pay all the court fees and expenses from engineers who came to look at the bell. The court decided the case was resolved, and the jury was discharged without being asked to rule on the dispute. A report on the court case and judgement was subsequently published in the magazine *The Engineer,* in 1860.

In the 1903 eighth edition of Denison's book *Clocks Watches and Bells,* first published in 1860, he strongly criticises the twenty minutes they took to pour the metal. 'I have no doubt that slow running contributed to its unsoundness' (as opposed to the time taken pouring the first 'Big Ben', from Warner's, which was just five minutes). He also criticises Mears melting bellmetal using wood as the fuel as at the Woolwich Arsenal they had given up using wood for melting gun-metal, which is very similar to bellmetal, as they thought it took far too long and was bad for the metal. Both Warner's and Taylor's had switched to coal fired furnaces before 1858.

In the House of Commons, at question time on June 4th, 1860, Mr Crowther, the First Commissioner, recommended that the largest Warner quarter bell, which weighed nearly four tons, was used for striking the hours. He announced that if this was done, 'The House would be spared the loud and dismal strokes of the great bell which they must all remember, and which occasionally drowned the voices of honourable Members and diverted attention from the business before the House.' So forget Big Ben!

The hour strokes were then struck on the largest Westminster quarter bell, and in 1862, the Astronomer Royal was asked for his advice to try and solve the stalemate. The main question was, 'Is it safe?' He proposed three things. Firstly, the bell was turned round so the hammer could strike on an undamaged part of the bell. Secondly, the weight of the hammer was reduced from 6.5 cwt/728 lbs to 4 cwt/448 lbs. Thirdly, a piece should be cut out of the bell just above the crack. Mears did all of this, and a platform was built under the bell to protect the clock and tower just in case it came adrift. Dr. John Percy, a famous metallurgist, carried out tests on the chunk cut out and is said to have reported that the metal was 'Inhomogeneous' (not well fused). So cheers from Sir Edmund who could jump up and down with a clear conscience and shout, 'Told you so!' He criticised the specific gravity (a posh name for relative density) of the part cut out as being far too low. Dr. Percy was asked to inspect the bell again in 1865 to see if the crack had spread.

I puzzled over the inscription on 'Big Ben II' for a long time because it has normal raised lettering and partly reads, 'This bell weighing 13 tons 10 cwts 3 qrs 15 lbs (13.7 tonnes) was cast by George Mears of Whitechapel....'. But hang on, how can the weight be in raised up lettering when they hadn't then cast the bell? Even Winnie the Pooh, created by A. A. Milne, who said, 'For I am a bear of very little brain and long words bother me,' could have seen that this didn't make sense. I found the answer eventually from *The Illustrated London News* at the time. Mears (for some reason and I don't know why) wanted the finished weight to be on the bell, so on the false bell they left some blank bits in relief where the weight was going to be put. 'Big Ben II' was subsequently weighed by Messrs. Stewart & Co. at a steel yard. After this they carved the weight on it.

'Big Ben', now the general name for the complete tower, clock and bell, has become synonymous with London and is famous throughout the world. Since the Diamond Jubilee of Queen Elizabeth in 2012, the tower is now officially called the 'Elizabeth Tower', but in reality, the whole caboodle will always be known as 'Big Ben'. This bell is the third largest bell in England apart from the two bigger ones which Taylor's cast, but being mean, it is 'The largest cracked bell in England' and apparently a bad casting to boot! In 2015, when it was revealed that 'Big Ben' would be out of action for a long time, the chiefs in Nottingham City said, 'On behalf of our city, our superb, ten ton Taylor hour bell, "Little John", and quarter bells could be used instead.' They would certainly be oodles better, but why don't they just let Taylor's cast a replacement? 'Big Ben II' could be hoiked out and put on a plinth at ground level for the tourists to gape at and throw coins into to pay for the new Taylor bell, 'Big Ben III'. Since

August 21st, 2017 Big Ben is out of action until 2021 for 'Elf n safety' reasons to stop workers at the tower becoming deaf or falling off the scaffolding! It's a very long time!

Coming back to St. Paul's Cathedral, there was a large group of people involved in the project for a ring of bells. The Lord Mayor of London became President of the bells committee, and the Dean of St Paul's was very keen. The Cathedral organist, Dr. Stainer, was very influential and a fan of Taylor's, and the cathedral architect was well disposed to Taylor's.

Another man who was very influential in a negative manner was the Rev. H. R. Haweis. He thought English rings of bells were rubbish and wanted a carillon installed instead because he said the Belgians made better bells. He had travelled on the continent listening to carillons, and he put these thoughts in a booklet published in 1875, entitled *Music & Morals*. Sir Edmund (now) wrote to *The Times*, '(He is) a musical amateur with no experience of bell making.' To shut this person up, it was said at the committee stage that there would be a carillon as well, but no-one actually thought this was going to happen! Canon Cattley, the senior religious bod from Worcester Cathedral, was on the committee and was oozing good will to Taylor's. In 1868 they had supplied a heavy ring of twelve bells, along with three extra semitone bells, and a four and a half ton hour bell that was just over six feet in diameter. If they were all used together, they made a chime of sixteen bells. Edmund Beckett had been involved in the design, and it was agreed that this set of bells was almost perfect. He was now heavily involved in the new plans for St. Paul's.

The Lord Mayor of London had been very good at twisting the arms of various Livery companies (guilds). The Worshipful Companies of the Drapers, Salters, Merchant Tailors, Fishmongers, Grocers, Turners, and Cloth Workers donated bells or money, and the Corporation of London sponsored the largest bell. All the money was promised by the end of 1876, so Sir Edmund gave the job to Taylor's. He specified how much the bells were to weigh, the diameters, and the 'key' (the musical note). He was convinced the specifications were right, and this is what had to be done! At Taylor's, they privately decided he was wrong! Wow! So they made them the weight he wanted, but with different diameters and key note. When the balloon went up, they told Sir Edmund, 'Sorry! We made a mistake.' He wasn't at all impressed, so being a lawyer, he stated, 'The bells were not according to (my) contract, and would be thrown back on the founder's hands.'

Eventually common sense prevailed because they were still a very heavy-profile set of bells, with the tenor bell weighing 62 cwt/3.1 tons. The total weight of all twelve bells is thirteen and a half tons. Everybody agreed they were splendid, so he eventually stopped griping and wrote off to *The Times* for about the one-thousandth time. 'On the whole, these are unquestionably the Grandest Ringing Peal in England, and therefore in the world.' So he had backed down and everything was forgiven. A really good ring of bells, in the very centre of London! Good propaganda for Taylor's, and George Mears was really cut up about it.

Right: *The West front of St. Paul's Cathedral, London, circa 1890-1900. The Taylor ring of twelve bells is in the left hand tower and 'Gt. Paul' in the right hand tower.*
Photo: Photochrom

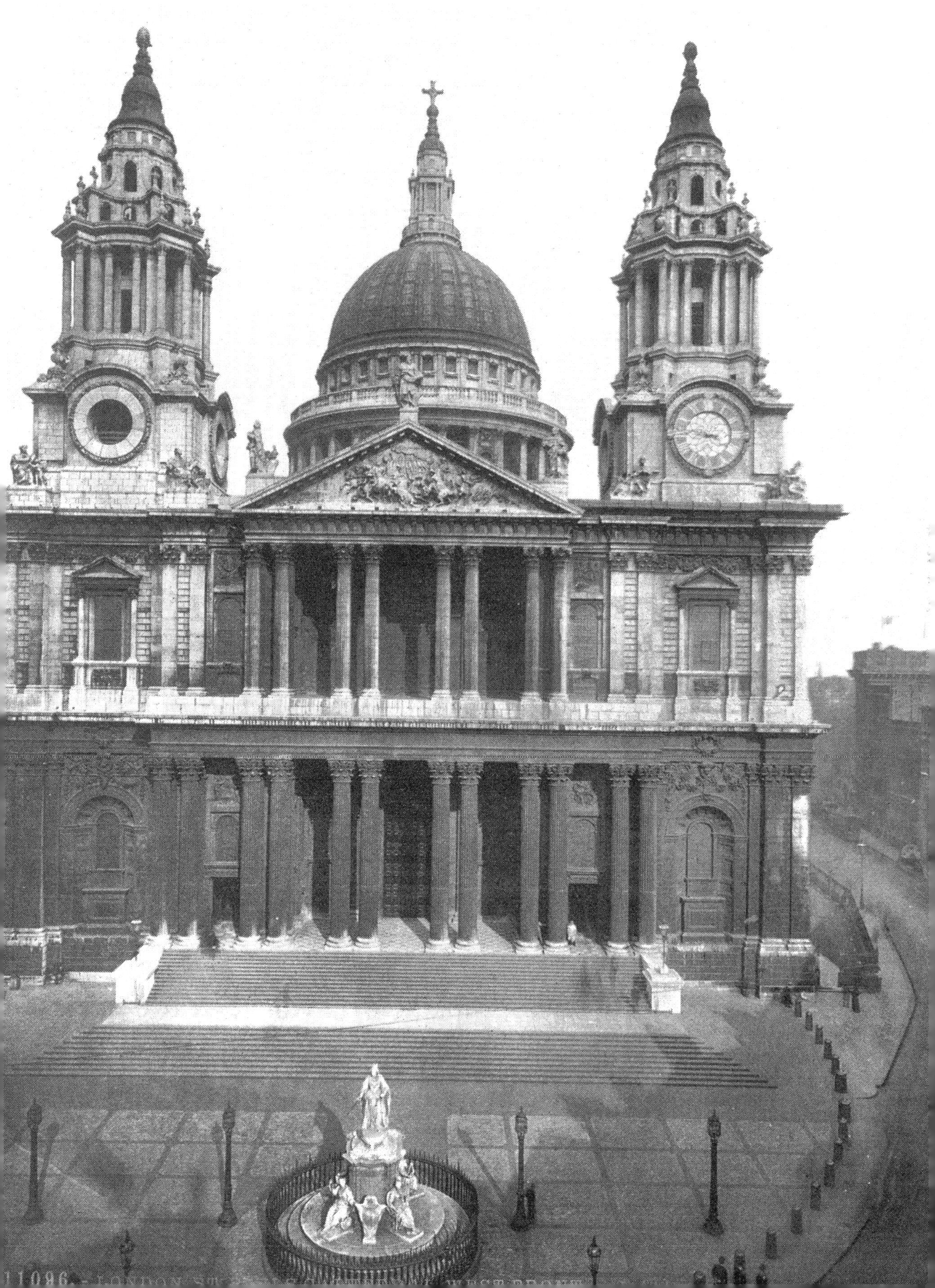
11096

They still ring out today and are accepted as being absolutely the best of their kind from this period in bellfounding history, and they do produce a glorious sound.

Rejoicing at Taylor's was slightly curtailed when word came down the line that the bell committee were going to suggest they had an enormous 'Bourdon bell' cast. These bells in England are called 'slow-swingers', purely because they swing slowly, at least up to the horizontal. They are either rung by hand or with the aid of a motor. If they are properly hung and not a pain to ring by hand, or the electric motors are fine, they can be taken up even higher but not right up to the top. They are rung either on their own, or when all the other tower bells are being rung at the same time. To sound 'in tune' they have to be a musical note that is five notes lower down than the note of the tenor, (largest bell of the ring), and they are only installed alongside a ring of twelve bells. (The largest bell in a carillon is also called a bourdon bell). If you want to know where this word comes from, I will tell you. It's the French word for 'bumblebee'!

John Stainer, the organist, was given the job of negotiating, and he decided this bourdon bell would weigh nine tons. Taylor's said, 'More likely fifteen tons.' Sir Edmund was involved again and made chairman of the new bell committee! John William enlisted the help of his mate Canon Cattley from Worcester Cathedral and asked him to write to the Dean of St. Paul's and try to dissuade him 'in the matter of the Baronet's heretic notions as regards the big bell for St. Paul's Cathedral.' I expect he did, but everybody London way (except George Mears & Warner's) thought this was a really good wheeze.

John William knew he would have to have a special cast iron case and core plate made, and he would need another large ten or twelve ton furnace in addition to the five and seven ton ones they had already. He asked himself, 'How on earth are we going to be able to manoeuvre this bell and the closed moulds in the foundry?' Eventually, it was decided they had to bite the bullet in case other bellfounders were approached. John Stainer had been told to get a variety of quotes, but he was only talking to John William. So the stage was set, with a lot of worries and mutterings at Loughborough!

7. The Ringing Isle

'Disturbers of the human race, your bells are always ringing – I wish the ropes were round your necks and you upon them swinging.'
Anon.

I have started mentioning 'rings' or 'peals' for churches with a set of bells, so I need to explain what these are. If we summarize the ways that bells can be rung, the simplest way is that bells don't move and are 'hung dead' from wooden, wrought iron or steel girders and struck with a clapper or some sort of hammer. They go up in size from ships' bells to small ones for churches or schools, or bells that go with a clock to strike the quarters and hours. The Russian 'Zvon' way of pulling clappers inside the bells to ring a set sequence is typical of this fixing method, and Russians could never understand why anyone would hang bells differently. Bells to play Western-style music so they qualify as being a musical instrument are hung dead and either called a 'chime' (just a few bells) or (if there are loads of bells) called a 'carillon'.

Bells that move start with the simple school or small church bells which are swung with a rope going down over a pulley. The bells don't swing very far, but pulling the rope allows a person to keep ringing the bell for however long they want to. Originally, big bells could be swung by changing the large fixed beams to a headstock or yoke that had strong axles. These headstocks not only held up the bell, they also enabled them to swing. Big bells could be swung if you had the corresponding amount of men. In one case, thirty men were struggling to swing a big bell, so a lot of puff needed. Eventually everybody agreed, 'This bell is not ring-able, so get the bellfounder (Mears) back that supplied the bell and tell him the whole set-up is rubbish!' So they did, and the bell was then used stationary with an outside hammer.

In churches they started to fix a wooden half wheel or three-quarter wheel with spokes to the headstock. A rope round the rim of the wheel went down so someone could haul on it. These wheels gave more leverage, so the bells swung easier. Less puff, less men. On the continent they hang bells with a wooden headstock and axles, but they keep slamming on heavy bits of wood above the headstock. Eventually the bell and headstock are 'balanced', so they can spin the whole lot through 360 degrees and keep going. Two men or more stand in openings in the tower beside the bells. One pulls, one pushes, or everybody joins in, and eventually the bell is completely rotating as long as they keep going. This is quite dangerous unless you are strong and don't mind heights, and I am sure some men fall out of the openings and go splat on the ground.

The way bells became rung in English churches was completely different to any of these methods and enabled a 'pattern' of ringing the bells known as 'Change Ringing'. The origins of change ringing started during the 17th century when full wheels were used. A person could then totally control the bell by pulling on the rope and turning the bell just over 360 degrees. Pulling the rope again meant the bell came back round another 360 degrees. There is a wooden square section piece of ash that sticks up above the headstock, and when the bell is slightly over the 360 degrees this 'stay' comes in contact with a wooden 'slider' on the frame under the bell. The slider has a limited movement that stops the bell going any further unless you pull really hard and break the stay. Budding bellringers may occasionally do this if they are very inexperienced, but skilled ringers stop the rotation of the bell before the stay has actually gone to the stop on the slider.

Assuming you have controlled the swing of the bell, and it is now upside down with the stay resting on the slider, nothing else happens until you pull the rope again. You can let go of the rope and go for a walk in the churchyard, nip in the pub, or go home. The bell you have pulled up just over 360 degrees stays there for good, but it would slowly fill up with pigeon shit politely called 'guano', assuming pigeons can get in. When there is a set or a ring of bells of any number they are numbered downwards from 1, the smallest with the highest note, called the 'Treble', to the largest one, called the 'Tenor'. The simplest way of ringing the bells is in this order, called 'rounds', from the highest note to the lowest. To make it more interesting, bellringers ring 'changes'.

Now this is the cunning bit! Find three egg cups and turn them upside down so they look vaguely like bells and stick labels on with the numbers 1, 2, and 3. Bellringers would never ring changes on only three bells but if they did they would change the order of 1 and 2 and leave number 3. (2:1:3). Then, leaving the first one in place and changing the other two, the next sequence would be 2:3:1. Next, changing the first two and leaving the last one in the same place it would become 3:2:1. Leaving the first one in place and changing the others it becomes 3:1:2 and then changing the first two gives 1:3:2. Finally, swapping the last two takes you back to the start, 1:2:3. So if you have done this you probably realize that there are six different ways to arrange the three egg cups and no more. If you did write this down you will see that egg cup number 1 goes on each line of three from being first then second then third. It stays there and then goes back to being second and then first again, and ringers learn the pattern of their bell. This complete set of changes is called the 'Extent' 'cos there aren't any more ways of doing it. With four bells it is more complicated. If I told you how to do it you would end up with twenty-four different sets or permutations. With five bells it works out at 120 sets or changes, but don't even think of going next door and borrowing another egg cup!

Right: A ringing bell assembled for testing with a cast iron headstock, wooden wheel, and axle bearings. The stay (not fitted) goes into the socket at the left of the headstock.
Photo: David Humphrey

THE
PEOPLE'S
BELL

Incidentally, bellringers do not consider themselves 'campanologists'; this is a name only used in books. All people who ring bells in churches are 'bellringers'. If someone chatting you up in the pub says, 'I'm a campanologist,' they don't ring church bells, so they may be fibbing about everything! The group of bellringers at a church is called a 'band' or a team.

In his 1848 book, *The Bell: Its Origin, History and Uses,* the Reverend Alfred Gatty narrates that in 1456, a 'Peal of five bells (so a set) was presented to King's College, Cambridge, by Pope Calixtus III, and the largest bell weighed fifty-seven hundredweight (so nearly three tons). For some time the largest bells in the Kingdom,' but we don't know exactly what they did with these bells. A man called Fabian Stedman was born in Cambridge in 1631 and had time on his hands, so he started working out the permutations on five or six bells about 1666. He was a printer, so he printed it out and showed all his friends and sent them all over the place. He and Richard Duckworh published a book in 1667, *Tintinnalogia,* sub-titled: *A plain and easie Rules for Ringing all sorts of Plain Changes. Together with Directions for Pricking and Ringing all Cross Peals; with a full Discovery of the Mystery and Grounds of each Peal.* It gave him work as a printer, and in 1677 he published another book entitled *Campanalogia.* This was obviously a smart move because it had gone through three editions by 1680, so his printing press was humming along nicely.

Groups of ringers started springing up and formed societies. The *Lincoln Cathedral Guild* claim they started in 1612, and the *Society of Ringers of St. Stephen* in Bristol started in 1620. In the summer of 1657, the *Society of College Youths* from London, who had six bells at St. Martin's, College Hill, came to Cambridge. Stedman gave them a copy of his changes on five bells that they seem to have rung at St. Bene't's church in Cambridge, according to Alfred Gatty. This society can be traced back to the 16th century, so there was some idea of messing around with a sequence on bells then. Bellringers didn't always go to church, and apparently they often became quite rowdy, starting the tradition that bellringers adjourn to the pub afterwards and (disgracefully) get drunk. Alfred Gatty tells us, 'They may sometimes revive their exhausted strength in the belfry by poations of ale immoderately deep'. Tut-tut.

Bellringers have to know what each of the others is doing, so they stand in a circle with the ropes coming through the 'ringing chamber' ceiling. Bells are positioned on the frame so that the ropes going down through pulleys are in the best approximation to a circle. The position of the bells and ropes is therefore fixed when the framework, which started off being huge timber beams, is designed. The headstocks were wood as well with metal straps that went down to the canons. Eventually the frame work where the bells rotate was made of heavy cast iron resting on girders.

The place where all the bells are is called a 'bell-chamber', and the gizmos that go with all the bells are called 'fittings'. A bellfoundry will supply all of these: headstocks, bearings and housings, wheels, clappers, stays and sliders, pulleys, ropes, and ceiling bosses that guide the ropes between floors or just the ringing chamber ceiling. One of the most important items for change ringing is the clapper. This hangs down inside from the top of the bell and has a round ball, which hits the sound-bow at the thickest part, and a 'flight', a cone that sticks below the bell from the ball. Clappers have to be very carefully designed so that as the ringers turn the bell up to the top of the 360 degree circle the clapper is driven by centrifugal force to hit the sound-bow exactly at this time. This is termed a 'rising clapper' and is an extremely important element. If the clapper hits the bell at the bottom of the swing, not the top, it can crack the bell and also kill the sound. Continental bellfounders don't know too much about rising clappers as they are not designing bells and clappers for change ringing. They probably say, 'Thank the Lord for that.' When the clapper meets up with the bell there is a quick moment of bouncing off and back before it rests on the sound bow ready for the next swing down. To a very small extent this mutes the sound and means that all the bells are easy to pick out when they are ringing, and the overall sound is cleaner. If you hit the same bell hanging downwards with the same clapper, the sound is slightly different.

The rope length is made so that it falls close to the floor or has a coil on the floor, depending on the size of the bell and wheel. There is a furry bit called a 'salley' part way up the rope, and you can order these in different colours to make them more interesting. The end of the rope that the ringer holds is doubled back to make an easily held 'tail-end'. The first pull is called the 'handstroke'. The salley is pulled down and then disappears up through the rope bosses unless the ceiling of the ringing chamber is high. The ringer keeps hold of the tail-end to control the bell as it reaches its balance point. When the tail-end is pulled down on the 'backstroke', the bell comes round the other way to the starting position, and the salley miraculously comes down again, so you grab it. Bellringers have to control the momentum of their bell and fit in with the whole set of differing weights. They may be pulling it back just before it is at the top or holding it at the top.

The amount of possible changes increases dramatically with the number of bells, and we have seen how the permutations are a mathematical sequence and not a melody or a tune. The simple pattern explained above is called "Plain Hunt". Different patterns of sequences are called 'methods'. This probably comes from the saying, 'There is a method in their madness.' If you see it all written down in columns, you can see how any bell keeps changing place with another one as long as you put a wet towel round your head. Methods have to be worked out by skilled bellringers, or nowadays on a computer that does it in two nanoseconds. I have mentioned that the 'extent' is the name given to the full set of mathematical permutations for any number of bells. The extent on six bells is 720 permutations and on eight bells is 40,320. On ten bells it is 3,628,800 and on twelve bells an eye-watering 479,001,600. Ringers call ringing at least 5,000 permutations, a 'peal'. When a peal has been rung for a very special occasion a plaque may be put up on the bell chamber wall recording this.

Ringing the extent on eight bells at a normal strike rate (how quickly each bell is struck in turn) of about once every 200 milliseconds (so five bells are struck every second) would normally take 22 hours and 24 minutes. On ten bells it would take 84 days and on 12 bells 30 years and 138 days. In 1963, a band of male ringers completed the extent on a light (in weight) ring of eight bells in the tower at Taylor's bellfoundry. The ringing started on July 27th at 6.52a.m. and finished on July 28th at 12.50a.m., so the 40,320 changes took 17 hours 58 minutes of continuous ringing. There had been various attempts over the years that were unsuccessful. Wow! Now you are convinced bellringers are totally bonkers. I know exactly what you are thinking. Did the men all wear nappies or have a short piece of hosepipe sticking out and a bucket?

If bellringers are attempting a peal or a quarter peal they only achieve this if they get to the end without making mistakes, and they have to keep going from start to finish with no short breaks to have a *Kit-Kat*. If, during the successful extent on eight bells at Taylor's bellfoundry, it had ground to a halt because of a mistake after 17 hours 50 minutes that was that! They can't go back a few changes and finish it off. The same ringers that start have to finish, so there are no substitutes that say, 'I'll take over for a bit while you have a nice rest.' If someone starts to feel faint they have to grit their teeth, but if they do keel over, the peal has as well. All the ringers will have memorized the pattern called a method that all the bells follow, and there is a conductor (nothing to do with the person waving a stick in front of an orchestra) who is one of the ringers and gives verbal instructions when the method pattern is to be changed.

If there is a failure, and it has 'fired-up', the bellringers' wives, husbands, or partners know they have to make soothing noises when they come home. They learn to say, 'You put your feet up, and I will make a nice cup of tea and put the telly on.' Or a stiff gin and tonic.

The various methods all have names that finish with words such as *Minimus, Minor, Major, Royal,* and *Maximus* for rings of even numbers of four bells up to twelve. Odd numbers of bells are rung as *Singles, Doubles, Triples, Caters* and *Cinques* for rings of three bells to eleven. In *Stedman Cinques* the changes are rung on eleven of the bells, and the tenor stays as the last bell like a foundation stone. I think this sounds excellent. 'Caters' is pronounced as in 'Cater-ing' and comes from the French word 'Quatres'. How did they get in on the act? Similarly, 'Cinques' comes from a French word as well but is pronounced 'sinks' as in kitchen.

The simplest method on four bells is called *Plain Bob Minimus,* and on six bells *Plain Bob Minor.* Some of the names for methods are very exotic such as *Reverse Grandsire Place, Cambridge Surprise Major,* or *Double Birmingham European Summit Bob.* That's sound like a good one! When a band rings a method for a short period of time, this is known as a 'touch'. Don't bellringers use strange words?

The band of ringers at St. Paul's Cathedral in London is an example of a very skilled group of dedicated people. We have seen how Taylor's put in the first ring of twelve bells in 1878. When Sir Christopher Wren designed the cathedral, the two towers at the front were strong enough to withstand a nuclear bomb, so there were no problems putting in a ring of bells.

Top right: *The bellmetal plaque in the ringing room at Taylor's bellfoundry, recording the extent of 40,320 changes rung on July 27th-28th, 1963.*
Photo: Taylor archive

Bottom right: *Bellringers in action at the Bury St. Edmunds Norman tower.*
Photo: John Hughes

THE LEICESTER DIOCESAN GUILD OF CHURCH BELL RINGERS
BELLFOUNDRY TOWER
ON 27TH & 28TH JULY 1963
THE EXTENT OF PLAIN BOB MAJOR 40,320 CHANGES
WAS RUNG ON THESE BELLS IN 17 HOURS & 58 MINUTES

BRIAN J. WOODRUFFE	FAIRFIELD	TREBLE
JOHN M. JELLEY	LEICESTER	2
NEIL BENNETT	ASHTON UNDER LYNE	3
FREDERICK SHALLCROSS	ASHTON UNDER LYNE	4
JOHN C. EISEL	STOURBRIDGE	5
JOHN ROBINSON	STOCKPORT	6
BRIAN HARRIS	PETERBOROUGH	7
ROBERT B. SMITH	MARPLE	TENOR

COMPOSED BY C. K. LEWIS   CONDUCTED BY R. B. SMITH
UMPIRES:
JOHN A. ACRES   JOHN F. BARLOW
DEREK OGDEN   PETER J. STANIFORTH

The *Guardian* newspaper reported on December 11th, 1893, that 'the Ancient Society of College Youths rang a peal in four hours seventeen minutes', a very respectable time on these bells. As these bells are so heavy, the strike rate is about every 230 milliseconds. Loads of important peals have been rung, and when there was no room for any more plaques on the walls they sensibly bought a nice book and wrote them down in joined-up handwriting.

William Cook, a member of the cathedral guild of ringers, published a booklet, *The Bells of St. Paul's*, in 1981 following the centenary of the bells being dedicated. He tells us that ringing a peal to celebrate the Coronation of King George VI was only successful on May 29th, 1937, two weeks after the coronation, as the first try on May 12th fired up. Another peal to celebrate the Coronation of Queen Elizabeth on June 2nd, 1953, wasn't successful, but they achieved one on June 20th. It's just the way it happens, not that they don't know how to do it. The tenor bell of the twelve weighs 3.1 tons/62 cwts/6944 lbs/3,156 kg. Totalling thirteen and a half tons, they were the heaviest ring of bells in the world for seventy-three years. They rang a peal on July 29th, 1981, after Prince Charles conned Lady Diana Spencer (bless her!) into marrying him as they didn't know he was a bit of a baddie and lusting after Camilla. In 2012, during the men's and women's Olympic marathon, peals were rung and to show that the men didn't all think women should stay at home and cook, when the women's marathon was being raced, an all-female band rang the peal.

The Reverend George Tyack, in his 1898 *A Book About Bells*, tells us that at Leeds Parish church in Kent there is a headstone that reads:

'In memory of James Barham, of this parish, who departed this life Jan. 14, 1818, aged 93 years: who from the year 1744 to the year 1804 rung in Kent and elsewhere 112 peals, not less than 5,040 changes in each peal, and called Bobs, etc., (the conductor) for most of the peals; and on April 7th and 8th, 1761, assisted in ringing 40,320 Bob Major in 27 hours.'

What? Twenty seven hours! There were thirteen men, and one of them rang for eleven hours and another for nine hours and all the others took it in turns. So strictly speaking this doesn't count as a world record with thirteen men between eight bells, but a very long time to keep ringing. At this time there were not the strict rules that were introduced later. James Barham was thirty-six at the time so did he ring the eleven hour stint? The front six of the ten bells (but they only rang the back eight) had been cast by Robert Catlin in 1751, and the tenor was cast in 1617 weighing seventeen and a half hundredweight, so probably difficult to ring as the strike rate was a lot more than 200 milliseconds.

In 1909, Taylor's published a special memorial booklet celebrating 'The amazing feat performed upon the bells of All Saint's, Loughborough, on Easter Monday, April 12th'. Ten bellringers set out to achieve a world record, and the rounds went into changes at 7.30a.m. The ringers kept going until they had rung 18,027 changes of *Stedman Caters* in twelve hours and eighteen minutes, so they finished at 7.48p.m. It was stressed that 'In most feats of skill and endurance the participants are usually fed and refreshed at regular intervals. Not so in the records of the ringing world'.

The booklet explained, in case anyone had missed the relevance, 'This is the longest peal ever rung in any method by one set of men without food and rest'. So this was serious stuff.

It was also pointed out that any other peals even close in the number of changes were done on bells much lighter in weight than the ten bells at Loughborough Parish Church where the tenor weighs 30 cwts/1.5 tons. A very famous ringer, William Pye, rang the tenor bell and was the conductor. The booklet went on to point out that 'It demonstrates beyond a doubt the superiority of the modern over the mediaeval. It is a triumph for the iron frame and modern high quality bearings, and points unmistakeably to Messrs. Taylor's workmanship in the Loughborough tower as reaching the acme of the art of bell-hanging'. So buy bells, fittings, and a new cast iron frame from Taylor's if you want to reach the acme of the art.

A crack band at South Petherton in Somerset successfully rang the longest peal on twelve bells taking fourteen and a half hours on October 17th, 2015. This was given due prominence in the *Ringing World* which is a weekly publication for bellringers. Taylor's had recast all the bells in 1998 with the tenor bell just over one ton. David Hull composed the 21,216 changes of a method known as *Cambridge Surprise Maximus*. The event took two years to plan, and one ringer, Dave Purnell, one of the local organizers, had already rung the previous longest peal on twelve bells at Birmingham Cathedral in 1965. In 1980, he and a handpicked team of ringers set out to beat the previous record of *Stedman Cinques* at Midsomer Norton near Bath. The bells had been augmented from eight to twelve in 1976 by Whitechapel. Unfortunately, after nine hours one of the clappers decided it was too much like hard work and snapped in two. It wasn't a Taylor clapper, so nothing to do with them, but it was really bad luck and back to the drawing board and the pub!

At South Petherton, as with other special attempts, there were umpires that have a stint of ninety minutes each checking they aren't ringing the same pattern twice or cheating, but no ringers would do that; goes without saying. The band checked the ropes on the Friday night, had a quick touch, went to bed early and the next day they started ringing at 6a.m. There were some stools in the ringing chamber with items of food such as flapjacks, bananas, mini scotch eggs, and chocolate. If any ringer thought they could grab something without wrecking the peal they did. For the ringers on the heaviest bells who were expected to suffer from dehydration there were plastic cups half-filled with water or cartons of fruit juice, but the cups were not easy to grab and more trouble than they were worth. As regards needing to pee, incontinence pants were pressed into service and 'more sophisticated solutions had been used elsewhere'. Like what?

One ringer commented, 'There is some comfort in knowing that if you ache all over and can't feel your feet, then the rest of the band is probably suffering with you.' Almost the whole village turned up to watch a large TV screen in the church showing the ringers in the ringing chamber. There were long cheers when the successful attempt finally came back into 'rounds'. I have already mentioned that this is when all the bells are rung from the treble down to the tenor in the natural order. Ringers do this before they start the chosen method and again at the end. Ringing rounds to start with shows that there are no problems with the bells otherwise someone has to go up to the belfry and see why. This event was like local people coming to see a bell cast in the churchyard. Not only was this a world record, it was something happening in 'their' church, so it was a really important event for the churchgoers at the village as well.

There is a *Central Council of Church Bell Ringers* in England, founded in 1891, and they say, 'Bell ringing is an activity that stimulates the brain and helps keep you fit. It also makes a glorious sound. Many consider ringing to be their contribution to church life, others do it for the pure pleasure and the company it brings'. So sounds like you can be an atheist or a Muslim. They ask, 'Could I become a ringer?' The answer is, 'If you can ride a bicycle (so this is why I never became a ringer) you can ring.' A bit further on they say, 'Being able to count is all the maths you need to know, and you can become a very good ringer without knowing anything about music.' So if you can ride a bike and count - go for it! It could change your life totally and get you out of the house if your partner keeps whining on about something. You have to go to the pub afterwards because it is very traditional.

This council states, 'As of September 2015, there are 7,140 "English style" rings. The Netherlands, Pakistan, India, and Spain have one each. The Windward Isles and the Isle of Man have two each. Canada and New Zealand eight each, and there are ten in the Channel Isles. Africa as a continent has thirteen, Scotland twenty-four, Ireland thirty-seven, the USA forty-eight, and Australia fifty-nine.' Somehow Wales clocks in at the end with two hundred and twenty-seven. They obligingly work out that 95% are in England totalling 6,798. Some towers don't have bands because there is nobody interested, or the bells cannot be rung because they need fixing or are derelict.

Dedicated bellringers go 'tower grabbing' which means they go to a tower because they have never been to it before. It might have special bells or a very interesting ringing chamber or may not be generally open for ringing. After ringing the bells, they mark this tower off in a special book they keep under their pillow. Some of them try to combine their visit with a trip to a nearby steam railway and a pub that sells real ale. Sounds good sense to me; do it all at once.

Loads of churches only have five or six bells, but whatever the number, when they are rung in rounds they go from the highest note down to the lowest. If there are eight, and you remember the music lesson, this is the same as from one C on the piano down to the next C on the left. A 'scale' such as from one C to the lower octave C using all the white notes is called a 'major scale'. Starting on a different white note on the piano needs some black notes.

Top right: *The Taylor 1936 ring of fourteen bells and the 7.5 ton 'Hosanna' bourdon bell at Buckfast Abbey, Devon, assembled in the works.*
Photo: Taylor archive

Bottom right: *The ring of eight bells after restoration with four new bells at St. Mary's, North Creake in Norfolk. The bells are mouth up ready for ringing.*
Photo: John Taylor & Company

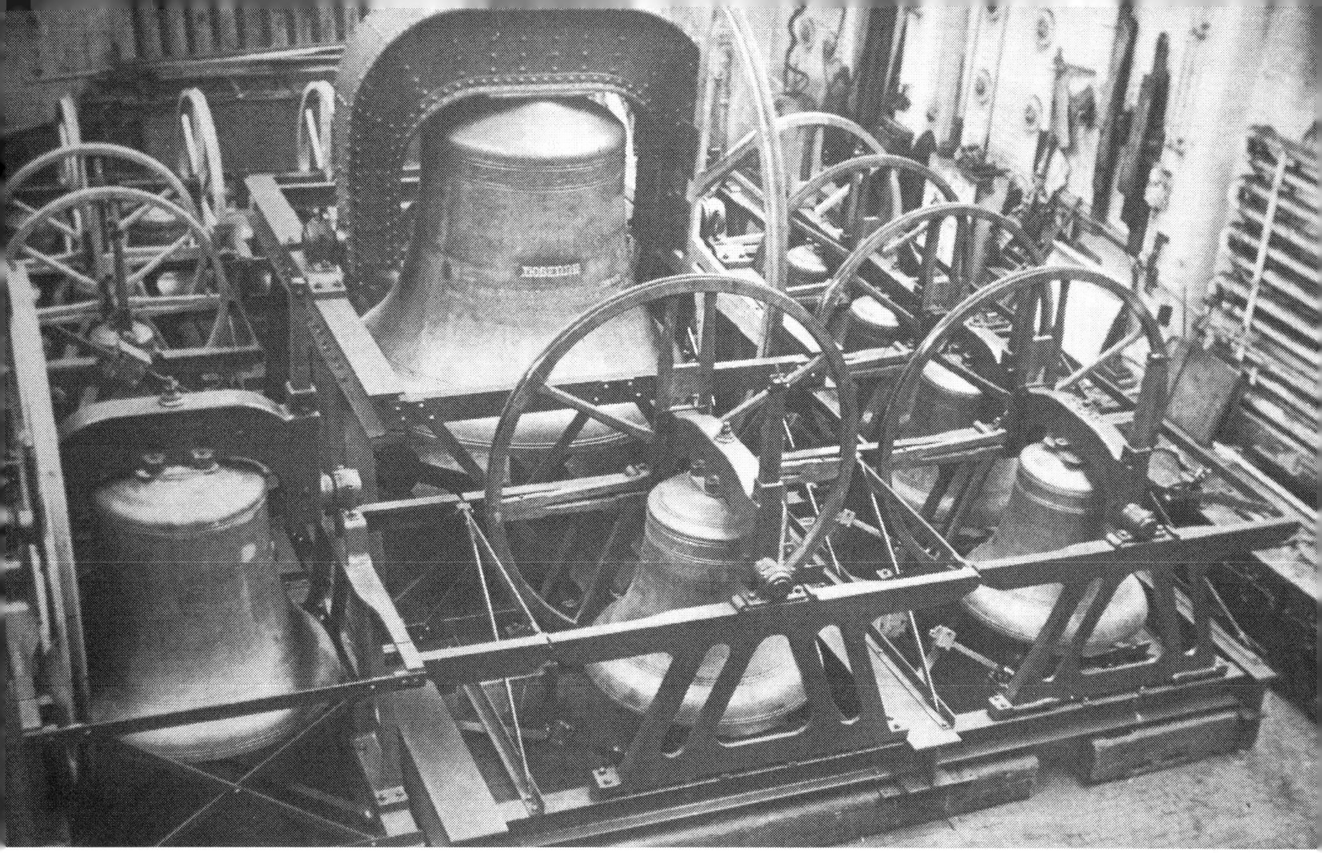

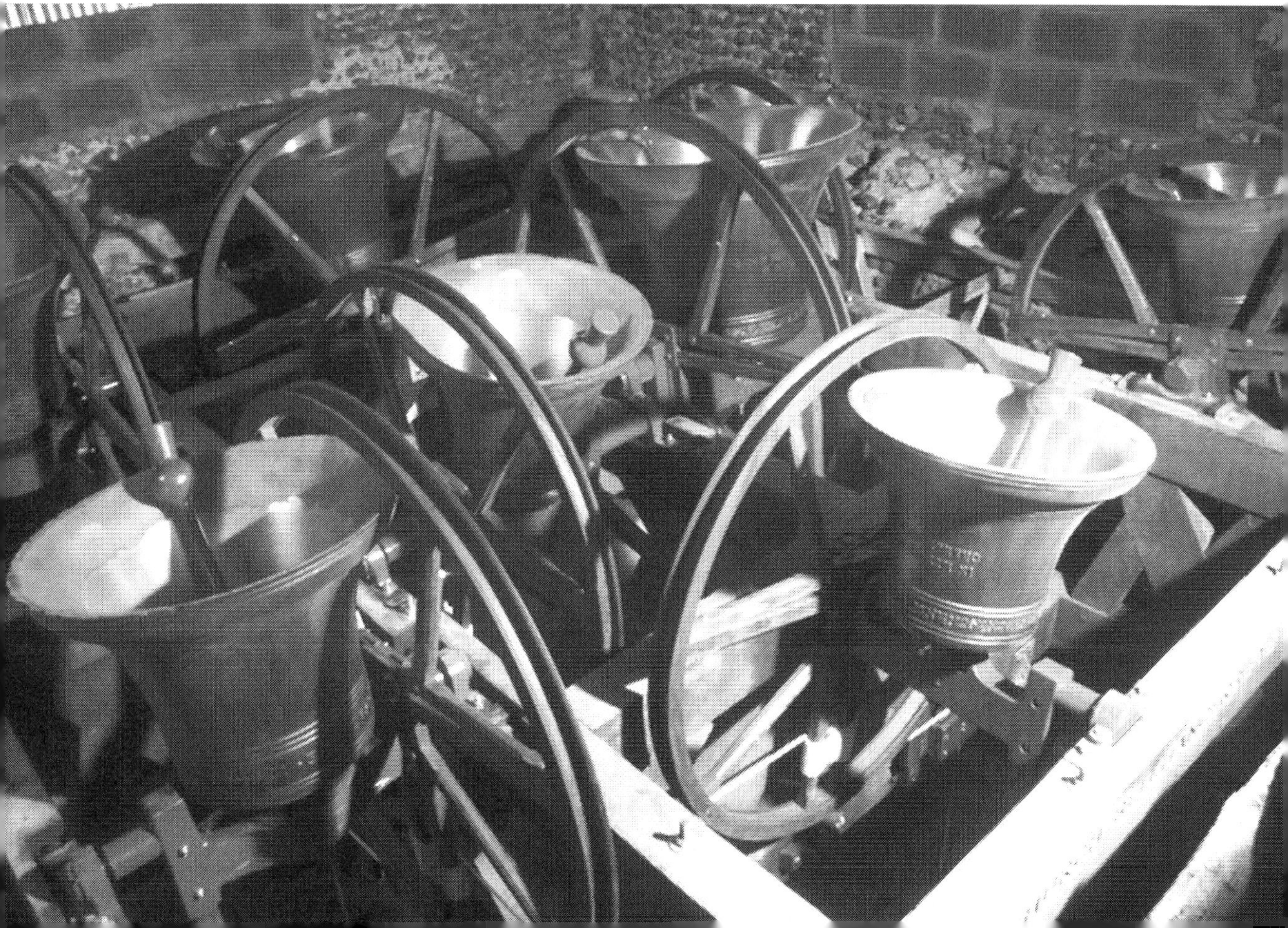

If there are ten bells, they start from the note two up from the octave, so note E in the scale of C, and they still finish at the next C down. If twelve bells are being rung, they start five notes up from C, which is G, and also come down to the lower C. Twelve bells is considered the sensible maximum that are rung in rounds or changes, but some churches with a ring of twelve have thirteen or fourteen bells, but not just to show off. If they only have eight ringers, and the others have sloped off somewhere, they can still ring the eight bell octave down to the tenor bell. The lowest of these bells including the tenor may be extremely heavy, and experienced ringers normally handle these. I have mentioned that you can get another major scale starting on another note apart from starting on C, but you need at least one black note. If there are thirteen bells, a 'light eight' can be rung as an octave using a black-note bell, so it still sounds fine. You can do this differently if you have a fourteenth bell.

Rings of bells over the centuries have been the bread and butter for bellfounders, and the icing on the cake if they produce a ring of new bells that are tip-top. Churches often want bells re-hung with a new frame and fittings, or cracked or duff bells replaced, or they want to 'augment' from six to eight or ten or twelve or more. Churches sometimes have a ring of bells that are pigs to ring because they are poorly hung, or they may sound atrocious. If they are very heavy, the bells can all be broken up and some lighter ones substituted. The surplus metal bought as scrap by the bellfounder helps defray the cost. Of course, the bellfounder may say, 'The cost of copper and tin is at an all-time low but I will give you something off the price'.

But don't just sell the bells for scrap metal! Coming back to George Tyack, he reports that according to Sir Henry Spelman, 'In the year of our Lord 1541, Arthur Bulkley, Bishop of Bangor, sacrilegiously sold the five fair bells belonging to his cathedral, and went to the sea-side to see them shipped away; but at that instant was stricken blind, and so continued to the day of his death.'

In 1987, David Potter, an authority on bells and the then Ringing Master at York Minster (he's now the President), wrote a comprehensive booklet entitled *The Bells and Bellringers of York Minster*, and he followed this with another comprehensive booklet entitled *The Bells of York Minster* in 2015. It appears that four bells were moved there from another church and added to the existing eight in 1655, and this made the first ring of twelve. They obviously weren't a very good combination because Abraham Smith and William Cuerdon, who were local bellfounders, recast two of them in 1657. In 1671, Samuel Smith recast the eighth bell, and in 1681 he recast the top four trebles. In 1765, the whole ring of twelve was recast into a ring of ten by Lester & Pack from Whitechapel, but there were still various complaints. 'Why have we only got a new peal of ten worse bells when before there were twelve?' The Dean was criticised for 'meddling with them' and damned by the claim, 'The old bells were much better as well as the former Dean'. Oh dear!

The whole lot were destroyed by fire in 1840 when a workman forgot to snuff out a candle after adjusting the clock. A kindly man left money in his will in 1843 for a new set of twelve that were cast by Messrs. Mears who had taken over the Whitechapel bellfoundry. Edmund Beckett Denison promptly said they were worse than the previous ten! There was one bell (the tenor) left over from the fire and that was recast in 1849. In 1913, Warner's re-hung them with all new fittings, but the ringers were still muttering.

After a report in 1924, the whole lot were boiled up in 1925 by Taylor's who made a superb job of course, and a new frame was installed as well. The tenor is slightly under 3 tons/60 cwts/3,048 kg, and they are the fourth heaviest ring of twelve bells in the world with the whole lot weighing eight tons. One man can ring the tenor bell on his own, so job done, and York bellringers say they are absolutely the bee's knees! They should have gone to Taylor's well before this, but it gives a good idea of the work done at just one place over centuries. Many bellfounders fed their wives and children from work done at York Minster and probably their horses as well, or put petrol in their cars.

A ringer, Bill Thow, published a booklet in about 1986 giving comprehensive information on all the places where there was a ring of twelve bells or more. He asked me to check loads of details, and as I thought it a worthwhile exercise I did. He listed thirty-two towers where the complete set of bells had been cast all at the same time. It worked out that twenty-one had been cast by Taylor's, seven by Mears & Stainbank (Whitechapel), three by Gillett & Johnston from Croydon, and one by John Warner & Sons from London. So I had loads more details to check than Whitechapel! One of the complete rings of twelve by Gillett & Johnston, cast in 1936, is at Croydon where their bellfoundry was, so as you might expect, Taylor's weren't asked to quote for these bells!

Every year in June, bands of twelve-bell ringers meet up at a particular tower. Some are weeded out straight away, but the ones who are left have a 'striking competition' to see who makes the best job over a twenty minute period. Umpires listen from a suitable place, ideally a pub window, and the bands draw lots to determine the order they ring in. The umpires don't know which band is ringing, but they may guess who it is. Paul Taylor provided the *National 12 Bell Contest Trophy* about forty years ago.

One interesting thing that bellringers do is to put on a temporary leather pad that straps round the clapper ball on one side to give a quieter sound. This is known as being 'half-muffled', but ringers don't do this every week, they save it up for when someone dies. This may be a person who has special links to the tower or church, or some famous figure. When Winston Churchill died, a half-muffled peal was rung at St. Paul's cathedral.

But is bellringing just a skilled art or a sport? This question was posed after a High Court decision in February 2016 that playing bridge is not a sport as 'no physical training' takes place. Some pundits then argued that bellringers engaged in physical activity that includes improved agility and muscle development, cardiovascular benefits, stamina, and regarding the competitive issue, there are striking competitions. The organization 'Sport England' gives grants for sporting activity and media campaigns to raise the profile. Various letters were sent to *The Ringing World* underlining these views. The editor, Robert Lewis, came out in favour and stated that for the 40,000 bellringers it was a healthy activity and a mental workout. The *Central Council of Church Bell Ringers* said this was nonsense and the 'Primary object of the council is to promote and foster the ringing of bells for Christian prayer, worship and celebration'. Their president asked, 'Where is the glamour of the sports field and where are the David Beckhams of the belfry?' Well, I'm sure ringers could nominate someone with the necessary tattoos!

George Frideric Handel, a very famous German composer, settled in London in 1712 and became the official court musician and composer. One of his most famous compositions is the oratorio 'Handel's Messiah'. He took British nationality in 1727 and died in 1759. He was amazed to hear church bells being rung 'English style' all over the shop, so he christened England, 'The Ringing Isle'. I bet you thought I had forgotten to explain where this name came from.

In February 2017, a restoration appeal was launched at St. Paul's Cathedral in London to carry out vital work necessary to the bells, fittings and frame, after 140 years of use. A target of £360,000 was announced, and the total money, donated by October 2017, will enable 'Great Paul' to be put back in action as well. The appeal was for £30,000 per bell, and the City of London Corporation and some of the Livery companies agreed to donate this amount for 'their bells'. Other amounts of £30,000 came from the St. Paul's Cathedral Guild of Ringers, the Ancient Society of College Youths, and three individual ringers at St. Paul's. A number of smaller donations from various organizations were received as well. The bells will go back to Taylor's in January 2018 to be cleaned to remove the London grime, a new set of fittings will be supplied, and the wooden frame strengthened. The ringing chamber will be refurbished at the same time. The work is scheduled to be completed by November 1st, 2018, to commemorate the 140th anniversary of the installation of the bells, and the 100th anniversary of the end of World War I on November 11th.

There is a special affection for St. Paul's Cathedral as it is considered the "City of London" cathedral. Built on Ludgate Hill, the highest point in London, it is truly iconic. Nowadays, all sorts of things are called 'iconic', but 99% aren't. Apart from being designed by Sir Christopher Wren, this was the first English cathedral built since the reformation.

During World War II, Winston Churchill decreed that the London fire fighters had to save St. Paul's 'at all cost'. One bomb came through the dome in October 1940, badly damaging the high altar, but with no resultant fire. The St. Paul's Fire Watch Team, working with the London Fire Brigade, successfully smothered an incendiary bomb during the night of December 29th/30th, 1940. Major fires were engulfing nearly every other building nearby, and an American journalist looking at all the smoke and flames described it as 'the second Great Fire of London'.

8. 'Great Paul'

'Laborious work it was to maintain the brazen giant in continuous speech.'
Illustrated London News - June 1882

When it was agreed in May 1881 that Taylor's were casting this enormous bell there was a lot of huffing and puffing as the recent history of casting big bells was not good. I think Taylor's thought that the Warner foundry was competent, but 'Big Ben I' promptly cracked although Edmund Beckett had upped the tin content. The Whitechapel foundry under George Mears probably commanded less respect, and their attempt at making the replacement, 'Big Ben II', was also a disaster with the composition of the metal being criticised by Dr. Percy. The Manchester town hall hour bell, 'Great Abel', cast by Taylor's in 1877, a mere six tons, had cracked in 1880. An oversize clock hammer was blamed for this again, not a cruddy casting, but it was the largest bell Taylor's had cast.

It wasn't as if they could just make any old large bell. Because it was designed to be a bourdon bell, it had to be in tune with the tenor of the ring, five notes lower down. There was no way this bell could be tuned, so it was going to be a 'maiden bell' which meant that however it came out of the moulds, that was it! John William I covered his bets and refused to guarantee it would be the right note, but he was of course going to do everything he could to make it the right note, out of professional pride.

He moulded and cast a bell that was half-size, so an octave up in pitch. After he had tuned this bell as much as his basic tuning machine allowed he could then weigh this bell and also measure the thickness all the way up. Trevor Jennings states that the test bell was then broken up, but he wouldn't automatically have done this. I am sure it would have been cast with the normal inscription, 'John Taylor & Co, Loughborough, 1881'. He did have some chance of selling it, so there was no point breaking it up for the sake of it, and it weighed a touch over thirty-nine hundredweight, just under two tons, so a fairly useful size and weight. He had eventually sold his 1862 exhibition bell to Halifax town hall as the hour bell with four new quarter bells.

With the test bell carefully measured, the next step was to draw out the crook for this nine feet six inches diameter bell. The foundry would have been promptly told, 'Make me a much bigger ellipsograph.' Once this was done he could then draw out the case shape, designed to be two inches thick all the way up, and the ironworks he dealt with in Derby were given the green light. At Taylor's there was always a rule of thumb if you were working out girder sizes or the thickness of cast iron. You would do this and then add on at least 50% to give a good safety margin! So, back to the pressure at the lip when you poured the metal in, and taking into account the stiletto heel effect, he concluded that the case and core plate would need to stand a pressure of 200 tons. The iron works quickly said that they were going to cast the case in three sections, but John William said, 'Fine!' It made road transport easier as well.

The next thing that was needed was a new furnace! They already had two furnaces for just over five and seven tons, so the new one was designed to hold twelve. It would have been a copy of whichever of them was best as regards metal losses and the time it took to melt the metal. Furnaces are rarely filled to their full capacity as this can cause problems, so he decided the combined amount of metal he could melt was just over twenty tons. He hoped the twelve ton furnace would be a useful addition as he didn't want to fire it up for this bell only.

A big pit was dug out fourteen feet deep, and they built a room with brick walls all round the sides and a solid base. This was a sensible way of making a pit as picking up the core to go in the drying stove was out of the question. I expect there was space for a couple of chairs for when the workers needed a rest! Once the seven ton core plate arrived, they could start making the core. At the bottom, they started with three bricks laid end to end, so this was nearly three feet from front to back, and they switched to two bricks laid end to end as they went up. Two bits of the case arrived in August with the last bit delivered in early September, and the whole case weighed nearly fourteen tons! The iron foundry would have weighed the case and core plate as they would have been charging according to the weight. Making the mould inside the case was then possible.

As the case diameter at the bottom was over twelve feet, John William wrote, 'The bulky case already monopolised an extensive working area in the foundry and interfered with the ordinary sized work.' I bet it did! Enormous bells need a ladder providing so the workers can climb down into the case whilst pasting on the loam. After it was fully moulded it was time for an inscription. They put their normal foundry name, and the year in Roman numerals, and on the waist of the bell in Latin, 'Woe unto to me if I preach not the Gospel' which came from the bible. This was a brilliant idea! If the bell stopped being rung, Taylor's could go and see why not and have a moan. Work done to the bell in 1971 was a direct result of this inscription being pointed out to the church authorities. After the bell had arrived at St. Paul's, some misery complained that the bell was very plain! What was he expecting? Hordes of angels and twiddly bits? I'm sure he was, and this person may well have seen some large continental bells covered in decoration. Taylor's just replied, 'Simple is best!'

On November 15th, the case was closed down over the core and clamped together. They immediately slung in sand and earth and let it all settle before the minions rammed it tightly down. Meanwhile, they had been fabricating the big box to go at the top of the case where the three gutters would shoot the metal in. It was now getting really exciting, or in actual fact, probably really scary! Copper and tin ingots arrived, together with some bronze ingots, and twelve bells they had acquired were broken up. Trevor Jennings, in a pamphlet he wrote about 'Great Paul', described this as being an 'indiscriminate and un-assayed alloy', but it wasn't. When bells are being broken up to go in the furnace as part metal, the person deciding on the copper and tin mix has a good squint at the broken bits. When I was doing this, the workers in the foundry always came to fetch me when they had broken up any bells and left them in their respective heaps, and they knew this was important. When you hit a bell lying on its side with a large sledgehammer it breaks fairly easily, but don't ever hit it at the top or the sledgehammer may bounce back and crack your head open. The broken bits have a sort of 'grain', a bit like when you cut a slice of bread from a very dense wholemeal loaf that is not much good for making soldiers with your boiled eggs. The density of the grain is a good indication of the composition of the metal, along with the colour, and good bellmetal is verging on being a silver colour. Less tin than normal results in a more golden colour. So the composition of all the broken bells would have been inspected and an allowance made for extra tin if needed. Over the years, a bellfounder gets to know the likely composition of bells cast by other bellfounders. Some are good, and some are not so good. Trevor goes on to say that when tested 'years later' it was exactly the right Taylor mix.

The twenty tons of metal were put in all three furnaces over several days and at 2p.m. on Wednesday, November 23rd they lit the blue touch paper. The normal times it took to melt metal in the two smaller furnaces would have been known, but the twelve ton furnace was an entirely unknown venture. John William and his foundry manager would have been juggling to get all the metal ready at the same time, and I expect every member of the workforce shovelled coal, but it took eight and a half hours. His son John William II was twenty-eight in 1881, so no doubt he held his father's hand. Denison, his other son, was only seventeen, so he may have been wherever he was sent to serve an apprenticeship. No visitors were invited to see the casting taking place as that was the last thing they wanted!

A very long slog, and I bet the workers were only given a few sandwiches (if at all). At 10.30p.m. the metal from all three furnaces ran down the gutters into the mould which took four minutes to fill up! Four minutes, after months of work. This is about right. You have to shoot the metal in quickly to get it down to the bottom. When the Paccard bellfoundry in France cast a thirty-three ton Millennium bell for the US in 1999, they teamed up with a foundry at Nantes that cast propellers. They took just under six minutes to shoot the metal in, and they knew what they were doing as I bet casting bronze propellers is not simple. Although the first 'Big Ben' cracked, we have seen how Warner's had only taken five minutes to slurp the metal in, but Mears took twenty minutes to fill their 'Big Ben Mark II' mould.

So this was it. Job done! Well, everybody hoped it was. I expect the men had to come in at their normal time next morning and didn't get a lie-in. If they had cast the bell on a Saturday it would have been better for the men, but they may have been due for some overtime payment if they were still there in the early hours of Sunday morning. The bell should have stayed in the pit for ages, but they managed to hoik it out on November 29th. I'm sure nobody could stand the suspense any longer. The outside of the bell looked fine, and then they started breaking the core out. I think six to eight men would have taken a full day to do this. Eventually all the crud was cleaned off and the bell was ready to be hit with a big lump of something. A critical moment! Good casting.... how did it sound? It was fine. John Stainer the organist and Canon Cattley arrived, and they both said it was wonderful. Dr. Stainer promptly wrote off to *The Times*, 'The casting proved to be as smooth and delicate in surface....as a little treble of five hundredweight'. More importantly, 'A musical note boomed out that was impressive beyond description.'

The cathedral chiefs had been told that the bell was going to be a lot heavier than they had at first thought, and a weight of fourteen tons had been suggested. They just multiplied this up by the amount John William was charging them per ton. After he made the half-size bell he worked out it would be much heavier, but he kept quiet. I imagine he thought, *let's get the bell cast and worry about the weight later*. Of the twenty tons put in the furnaces, there was some left over (good job), and they calculated the likely losses in the melting. John William thought the bell might be just over seventeen tons, but the losses from the big furnace were unknown. There was no way Taylor's could determine the actual weight, so the cathedral architect said he would go halves if they hired some extremely large bathroom scales.

'Great Paul' weighed sixteen and three quarter tons, and the initial payment due once the bell had been cast was quickly paid over. John William had a lot of bills to settle! No mention was made that the bell was nearly three tons heavier than the fourteen tons that had been previously suggested, so that was all right, and they paid for the extra weight without a murmur! It was left on view until Christmas, and hundreds of people turned up to see it, but other work in the foundry was getting well behind. A couple of churches cancelled their orders, and John William realized the sooner he got rid of 'Great Paul' the better!

The joiners made an enormous wooden headstock with boiler plates built in, and because of this the bell had been cast with stubby canons. Very strong iron straps went up to the top of the headstock, and a clapper was made that bolted right through the whole lot. This idea of a wooden headstock was something John William had been pointing out as being a bad idea for ages in order to sell his steel box-section or cast iron headstocks, so this raised a few eyebrows. Eventually the bell was hoisted two feet off the ground ready to be rung. Two spars were fixed to the headstock, but there was hardly any room to pull the ropes down. They did manage it somewhat, but the clapper that had been made at another foundry was not exactly right. Everyone from the bell committee who had come to listen to the bell, including Sir Edmund, agreed that when it was hung properly everything would be fine.

When they had gone, John William ordered another clapper that was a bit lighter. Part of the testing was to see how it swung because it had not actually been decided where it was going to be put! No bell this big had ever been cast and hung for swinging in the UK before now. As everything looked kosher it was agreed that it would be hung for swinging in the front tower where the clock was.

There are amazing stories as to how it got to London, but finally it went by road on a specially made low truck pulled by a steam traction engine. The bell was extremely well fastened down, so there was no chance of it falling off. Been there.... done that.....read the book...... seen the film and got the T-shirt!

Right: *'Great Paul' assembled for testing in the foundry with a very substantial wooden framework. Sir Edmund Beckett, John Stainer and Canon Cattley came to see if the bell was suitable to be installed as a swinging bell. The ropes fixed to the spars that only gave a very limited movement can be clearly seen at the top.*
Photo: Taylor archive

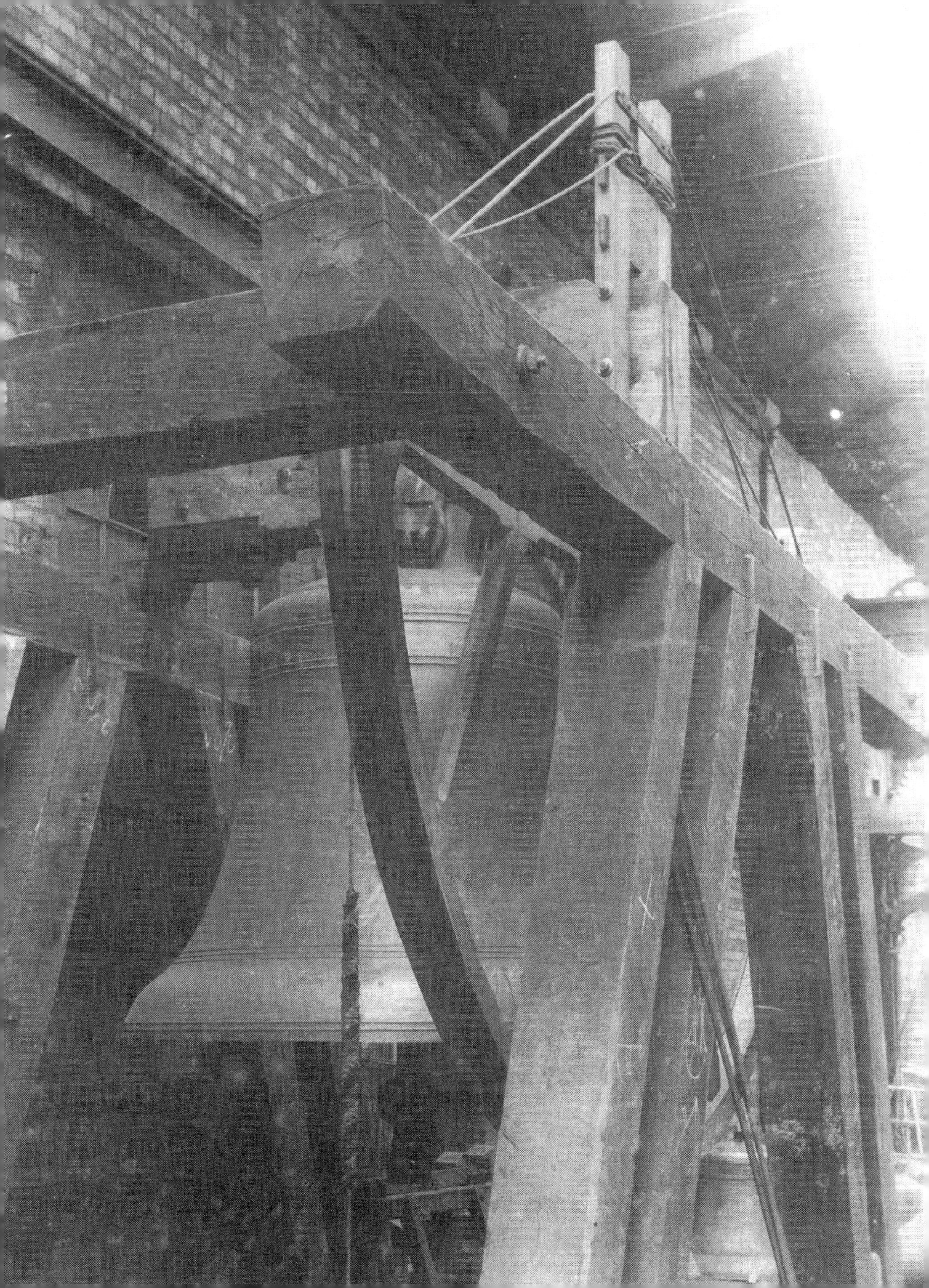

People made themselves packed lunches and walked along beside the bell for a whole day if they had nothing else that was pressing. The cathedral architect had realised it wouldn't go through the door nearest the tower, so a lot of masonry had to be removed. There was a circular hole in the ceiling that was too small as well! I expect Sir Christopher Wren was looking down from heaven and not impressed at all with the wholesale demolition going on in his cathedral!

'Great Paul' arrived at Highgate in London on Saturday, May 20th, but local byelaws prevented it leaving Highgate for St. Paul's until Monday morning, so they started early at 3a.m. and got it there at 8a.m. John William had carefully stated that once it got to the cathedral someone else had to take over, except that Taylor's would put the headstock on when it was in place after somebody else lifted it up into the tower. Lots of 'somebody elses', but very sensible! It was slowly winched through the wrecked door into the cathedral on greased planks by the following Saturday! Finally, it was under the defaced hole in the ceiling, and the 'somebody else' who was going to hoist it up were Royal Artillery engineers. They were used to hauling around thirty-five ton gun carriages, so I expect their boss in chief, who was called Captain English, said, 'About seventeen tons? Do it before breakfast!' They did manage it in fifteen hours, and then the headstock was fitted and the clapper put in. The final cost was £3,000 including the hoisting up. What? Did the Royal Engineers put in a bill?

On June 3rd, the bell was dedicated during a special service, and everybody who was anybody legged it up as far as they could to where it was suspended. *The Illustrated London News* stated, 'When the solemn notes of "Great Paul" boomed through the tower doorway....... there was universal admiration of the quality and musical perfection of its tones.' So they liked it as well. Regarding the eight men who were pulling on the ropes, they reported 'Laborious work it was to maintain the brazen giant in continuous speech.'

In a pamphlet about 'Great Paul', Trevor Jennings gets to this stage but then put, 'Subsequent alterations to Great Paul's frame and fittings became necessary, but these belong properly to the cathedral history and not to the initial story of the bell'. He shouldn't have stopped there as there were important changes made a few years later and also in 1971.

Two iron spars were fitted at right angles either side of the headstock, and eight men pulled on ropes tied to the spars. What Taylor's should have done was to fit one wheel, if not two, as it was difficult to swing the bell up far enough because the spars got in the way. It was also surrounded by Christopher's substantial masonry with no holes in the tower at that level.

Top right: *'Great Paul' securely fixed to the truck pulled by a Fowler agricultural steam engine ready to leave Loughborough. The tricycle belonged to Robert Coles from the Birmingham engineering company who cycled the whole journey down to London.*
Photo: Taylor archive

Bottom right: *The 14 ton case used for 'Gt. Paul' in 1881 and 'Gt. George' in 1940 on display beside Loughborough War Memorial carillon.*
Photo: John Taylor & Co.

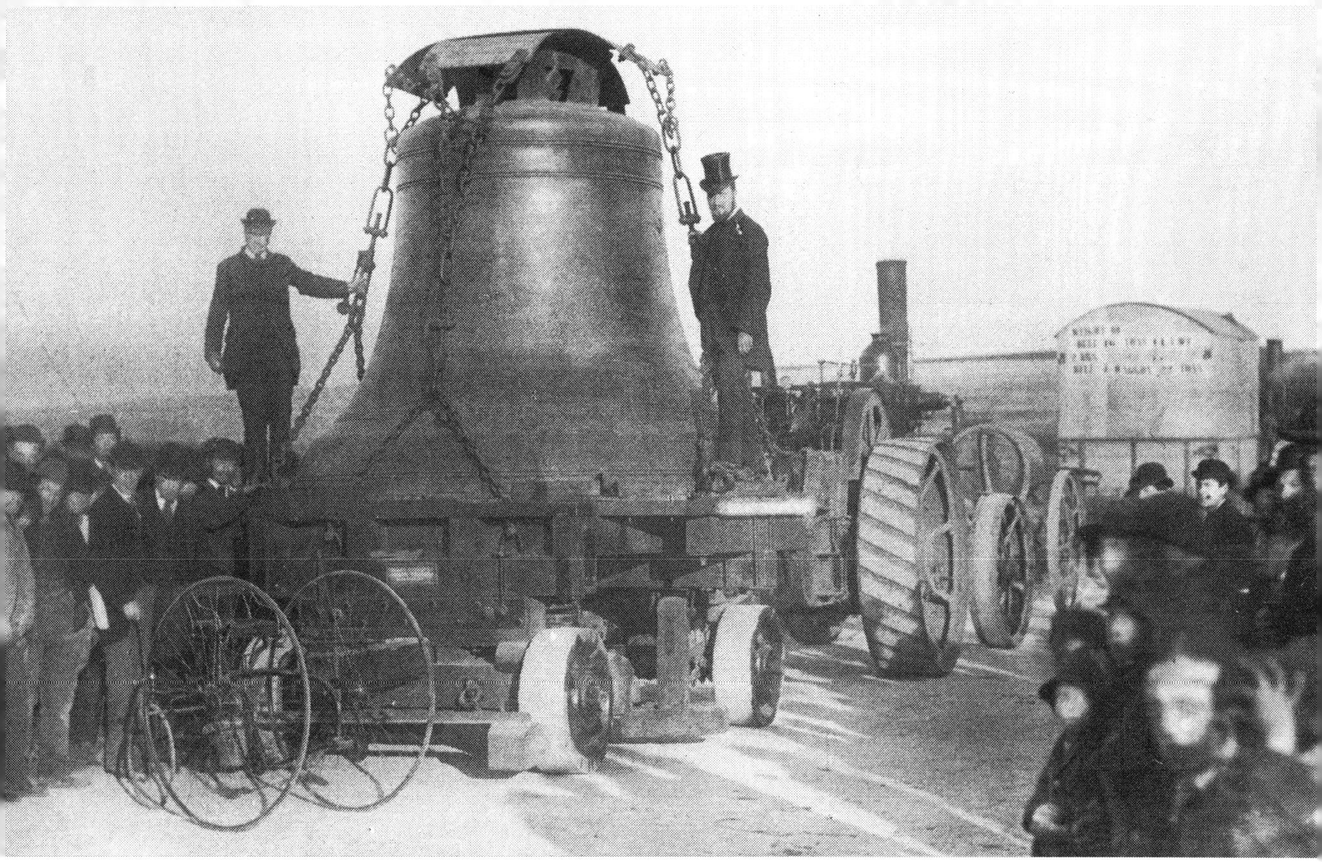

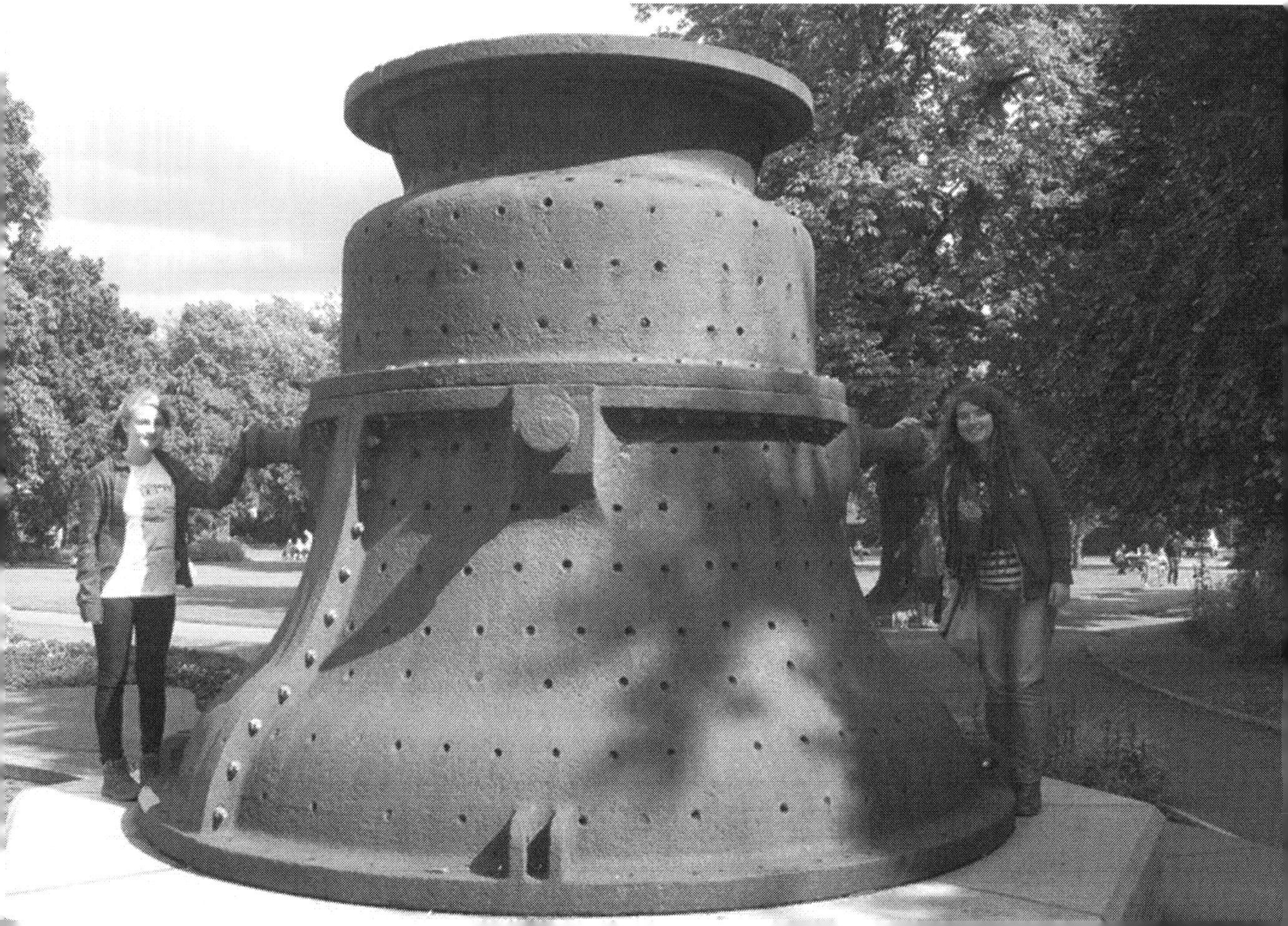

Someone wrote off to *The Times*, 'The papers tell us that for some time past "Great Paul" has been knolled every morning. To have so big a bell and not to notice that you have heard it makes it a very valuable acquisition indeed!' In November, another person wrote a small pamphlet entitled *Great Paul Tongue-tied: Why Don't He Speak Out?* So the location was a problem although it was being rung twice every day for morning and afternoon services. Taylor's messed around with it in 1883, but it was not much better.

In 1891, the Dean and Chapter at the cathedral decided a new clock was needed as the old one from 1709 was on its last legs. Sir Edmund, now Lord Grimthorpe, was asked for his advice, and a contract was awarded and work started. It then emerged that he and the cathedral authorities were at cross purposes. His plan was that 'Great Paul' would be put much higher in the tower and hung dead to be the new hour bell with a rope on the clapper if it needed to be tolled. The Dean politely said, 'Excuse me my Lord, but we still want the bell to be swung not hung dead!' After a bit of argy-bargy this was agreed, so the bell was moved up just sixteen feet, and Taylor's equipped it with a new box-section steel headstock that they should have provided at day one, and a new wheel and clapper.

This new 'yoke' headstock altered the centre of gravity of the whole caboodle making it much easier to ring. The centre of gravity of something is not too difficult a concept. Get your bike (you can't borrow mine because I've never owned one), stand it upside down and spin the wheel at the front. It goes round for a long time because the centre of gravity is exactly in the middle of the wheel. All the way round the weight is the same. Okay?

So switch to two identical twin girls dressed the same and with pigtails, on a see-saw that is quite long and heavy. As the twins weigh exactly the same they can both push off and come down quite easily. If Anna at one end then holds her baby brother it doesn't make much difference, but if her much older brother gets on with Anna, Mary at the other end doesn't have enough weight. Pushing off is really tricky and coming back down with her own weight is impossible as the centre of gravity has shifted towards Anna and her brother. If the see-saw could be pivoted nearer to Anna, eventually by trial and error the extra weight of the swing on Mary's side would counterbalance Anna's end with her brother and would be the new centre of gravity.

Think of a bell with a curved yoke headstock which is an upside down 'U' shape, so the axles are not level with the top of the bell but some way down. When the bell is being swung there is not too much difference in the weight on either side. We don't want the weight exactly equal like a bike wheel but bringing the centre of gravity towards the lip of the bell means it will swing easier with less puff for the men on the ropes. At Taylor's, we always knew almost exactly where the centre of gravity was on a standard Taylor shape bell. Fitting a straight headstock moved this point slightly towards the head of the bell, but a curved headstock made the bell 'tucked up', so the centre of gravity of the whole lot was further down.

Only four men were needed to swing the bell now, and the wheel helped them a lot. It was now being rung every weekday at 1p.m. as they found out there used to be a bell called 'The apprentice bell' that rang then. The four men all came from the maintenance team and were very skilful, so before the hour bell had struck one o'clock they started swinging 'Great

Paul'. It reached the height where the clapper started to hit the bell just after the time the clock struck the hour and boomed out afterwards. They pulled a few more times and then collapsed in a heap. It took several minutes (about five) before the weight of the bell slowed the swing down so that the clapper then stopped hitting it. On Sundays, the normal bellringers rang it for morning service and everything was fine until 1963. The whole front end of the cathedral was being cleaned, so they stopped ringing 'Great Paul'. I imagine they thought the workers might have a heart attack every day at 1p.m. or fall off the scaffolding. When the work had been finished, the maintenance men complained it was really hard climbing all the stairs, pulling 'Great Paul' up, and then having to climb down again, and they weren't going to do it anymore. Remember the inscription? It reads, 'Woe is unto me if I preach not the Gospel.'

Elizabeth the Queen Mother was eighty in 1970, and it seemed a good excuse to do all sorts of things. 'Son et Lumière' was a sound and light show that was becoming very popular, and this was going to be installed at St. Paul's. I think Paul Taylor wrote to the Dean pointing out what the inscription in Latin meant (he would have known that anyway being a man of God). The 'Friends of St. Paul's Cathedral' decided to have a whip-round to raise the £4,000 that was needed to put a motorized drive system in. With a time clock, 'Great Paul' would ring automatically at 1p.m. or when a push button set it in motion. I went down to St. Paul's with Paul, and we met up with Pierre from the French company Beviet-Mamias who had a lot of experience in putting motors and chain drives on big swinging bells. About twelve years later, I was buying reversing motors and chunks of chain, and we were motorizing the bells ourselves, but in 1970 our experience was limited. So we had a site meeting standing on the top of the bell, as Paul had previously worked out the swinging forces.

When it was time to install all this tackle, I was nominated to go and help the two French workers including Pierre. He had come along because it was a really good thing to put on his C.V. I seemed to know the most about motors at Taylor's and had already had some experience of putting motors on smaller bells. Apart from this, I spoke fluent French. Of course I didn't! Pierre spoke pidgin English. There was an initial snag. When we had all got our boiler suits on, I asked the Clerk of Works (he dished out orders for work and made sure it was done) when there was going to be electricity taken up to the bell. I needed a temporary cable if they weren't going to do it until the next day as our drills and things worked much better plugged in. He said all his electricians were clocking up absurd amounts of overtime with Son et Lumière and he had looked at our contract and we hadn't said it was their job. Of course it was! Very special, fire-proof, flexible copper pipe has a powdered mineral inside, surrounding the actual wires, called 'Pyro' for short. He said, 'I'll send a man to show you how to make the complicated joints at junction boxes, lend you a couple of spanners, supply coils and coils of this Pyro, and good luck.' He wouldn't budge even after I got Paul Taylor to talk to him, so we had to put it in ourselves and then get it all inspected and signed off. What a pain! Luckily, Pierre and his right-hand man took it in their stride, but they weren't planning to do this either. A few days later, the two wheels, two motors (one for each wheel), chains, and control unit were all put in. The counterbalanced clapper had to be fitted with a new bit, where the pin went through at the top, on site, as the Clerk of Works baulked at lowering it right the way down. For clappers shaped like this we used a very sticky wood called 'lignum vitae' that is very exotic and extremely dense and full of resin, and lasts for just about ever. After a hole was drilled in the middle of this piece of wood for the pin, the clapper was refitted. Everybody reckoned the clapper weighed at least 15 cwts, so three quarters of a ton/1,700 lbs.

There was a special reason why we could test and adjust the motor drive as much as we liked but not ring the bell! The 7th Duke of Wellington, Sir Gerald Wellesley, was very poorly and was expected to peg it during 1971 but held on until January 1972. There was a five ton bell high up in the tower where 'Great Paul' was that they tolled for one hour on the death of someone who was famous. This bell, known as 'Great Tom', fell off a carriage and cracked in 1699 on its way to St. Paul's from the Palace of Westminster. It was a gift from King William III. Philip Wightman cast a new one in 1700 and recast it in 1708, but it was still a duff casting. Richard Phelps, who came from the Whitechapel foundry, cast a new one in 1709 that wasn't much good either, so it was recast by him in 1716. What a lot of recasting!

This 1716 bell is tolled when the Sovereign, Consort or the Prince of Wales dies or another senior member of the Royal Family after they have had a chat about it. This included Princess Diana (at least they got this right!), the Queen Mother and Princess Margaret. It is also rung for other important people such as the Archbishop of Canterbury, the Dean of St. Paul's, the Bishop of London, or the Lord Mayor of London, provided they die on the job. The Duke of Wellington was on this list as well as Sir Winston Churchill who had meticulously planned his own funeral. There was a dress rehearsal late one night after he broke his hip. He wasn't there of course, as he was in hospital.

So before 'Great Paul' was tested properly by being rung, hordes of people were going to have to be told, 'The bell that will start tolling at 3p.m. on Wednesday fortnight is nothing to do with the Duke of Wellington kicking the bucket! Don't start organizing the funeral, fire off canons in a twenty-one gun salute, and do not get on the phone to order floral bouquets.' This was a real bind as we had to tie the clapper in the middle of the bell with ropes round the flight up to the headstock to stop it sounding. One motor pulled the bell one way and the other one the opposite way, for the right amount of time. Really tricky! When the bell was about horizontal, and bear in mind it was nearly a seventeen ton bell, the motor had to keep giving it a little nudge. We had to play with this time period for a very long time watching what the motors were doing, and I cleverly put light bulbs across the motor terminals so we could see when they were going on and off. By this time, it was the day before the important Wednesday, except it may have been a Tuesday.

Right: *The French engineer, Pierre, on the left, and Paul Taylor on the right, precariously standing on the top of 'Great Paul' just prior to the dedication service on May 27th, 1971, after the motorization. Pierre is perched on top of the headstock, and Paul has one foot on the bell and the other on the top of one of the canons. He is holding onto one of the fastening nuts of the six enormous straps either side of the headstock.*
Photo: Unknown London press agency

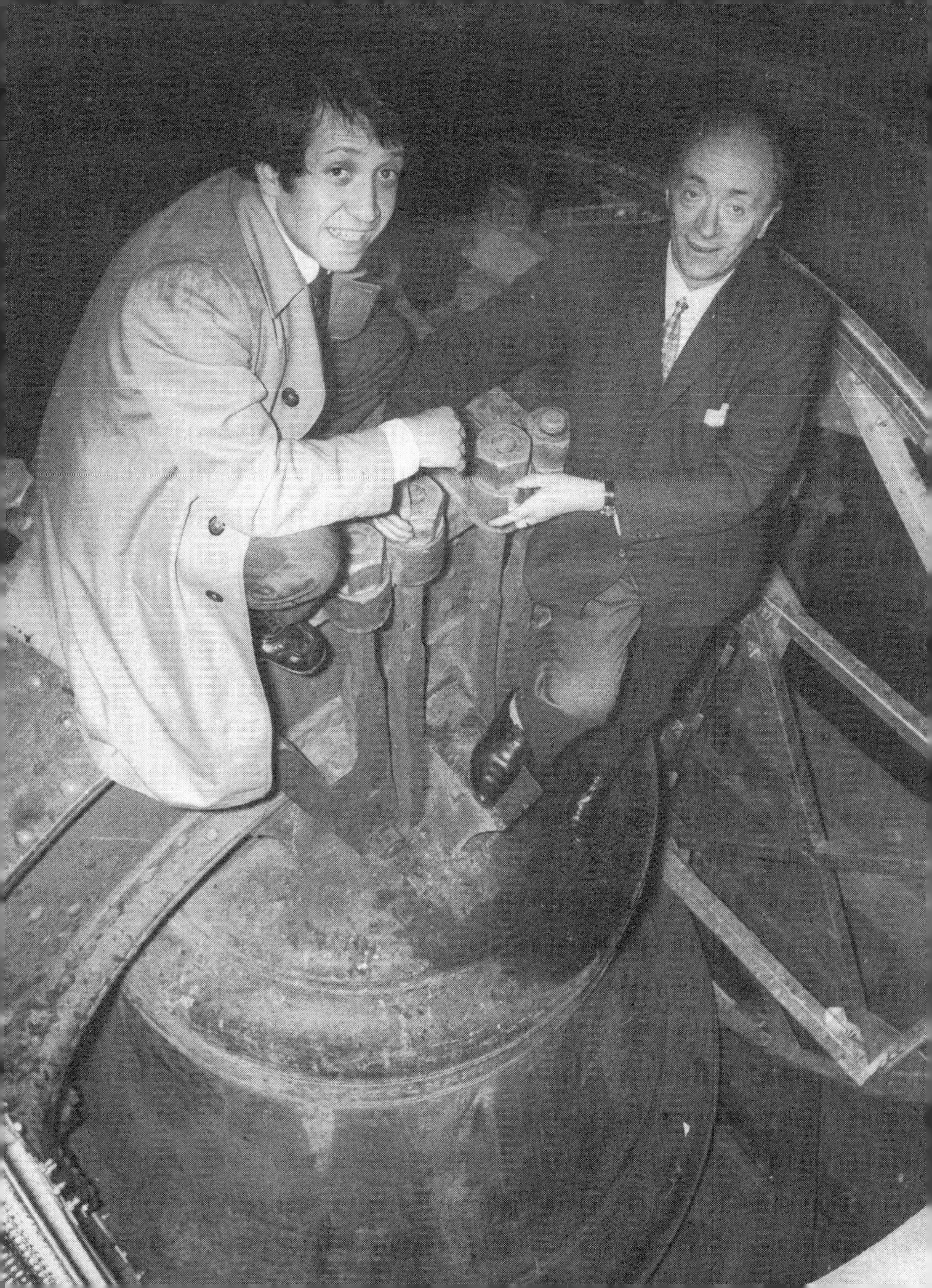

Pierre and his worker, who was probably called Henri, were having the day off to go sightseeing, so I told them not to bother going to hear 'Big Ben II'. They were coming back to listen to 'Great Paul' from outside the cathedral. No problem, what could go wrong? Feeling a touch dramatic I sent a telegram to Taylor's that read, 'Great Paul swings well, tomorrow he will sing!' In those days, I think it had to have a 'stop' after the last word like with walkie-talkies when everyone is supposed to say 'over' or 'over and out.' Paul Taylor and Peter, the works manager, were coming down to watch the final test, but it got closer and closer to 3p.m. and just before 3p.m. I was on my own. Peter had boiled up Paul's car on the M1, but I didn't know that then. So as the hour bell struck three, I pressed the 'go' button but the counterbalanced clapper stayed in the middle of the bell as the lignum vitae bush was well glued onto the pin! A moment of panic, but then I had the solution. I sat on a large beam just underneath the bottom of the bell and after the mouth swooped past my head on the way up I reached out and grabbed the bottom of the clapper! I managed to hold onto it for about ten seconds as the bell got to the top and then started down, and after doing this three times the clapper then started moving on its own. When it hit the bell, the sound was deliriously deafening! Phew! There was only this agreed fifteen minute slot to test the actual ringing, and there was no way I could go and ask, 'Can we try again tomorrow?'

In retrospect, this was a really silly thing to have done as I could have had various parts of my anatomy mangled! Perhaps they would have given me an honourable mention in the cathedral. Some sort of plaque that read, 'In memory of Mike, crushed to death by "Great Paul".' What I should have done when we untied the ropes was to push the clapper back and forth a few times. Never occurred to me! So all's well that ends well, and isn't it a good story? 'Great Paul' was first used properly on May 27th, 1971, at the annual service of 'The Friends of St. Paul's' and then every day afterwards by remote control. It does sound phenomenally loud when you have your head stuck under it. John William knew full well it was going to be the heaviest bell in England after he had weighed his test bell, and it certainly finished up the heaviest. Apart from it also being the heaviest swinging bell in England it is also one of the heaviest in Europe.

9. Mine is Bigger than Yours!

'The bigger they come, the harder they fall' (and crack)
Robert Fitzsimmons

Enormous bells are often 'curiosities' or cast to achieve some record. In Korea in 771 their skilled bellfounders cast a bell that is stated to weigh seventy-two tons and is oriental in shape like a tulip. This claimed the record of the largest oriental-style bell in the world at that time and now lives in a museum.

The 'Great Bell of Dhammazedi' gets the biggest prize. It was cast in 1484 by King Dhammazedi of Burma and said to be approximately 300 tons in old money. It was hung at the Shwedagon Pagoda in Rangoon. How they cast this bell and then lifted it up is a complete mystery, but perhaps hordes of Burmese labourers did it in exchange for a lot more rice. The diameter was reputedly fourteen feet, and a drawing that exists shows it was shaped like a beehive and suspended on a cross beam from massive pillars. It remained in use until 1608 when the Portuguese warlord, Felipe de Brito, decided to confiscate it. He apparently used a team of elephants to get it to the Yangton River and managed to lower it onto a special wooden raft to be taken further down the river. He fixed ropes from one of his ships to the raft so he could tow it, but this wasn't a good idea at all! The raft was affected by strong currents and it and the bell sank. It is stated to be in forty-feet of sediment below thirty-five feet of water. Attempts over the centuries to locate its exact place and retrieve it have all failed, and a claim in August 2014 that native divers had located it 'by supernatural assistance' proved false. So it seems to qualify as the largest bell in the world, probably in one piece, under water.

The British army nicked another bell from the same temple in 1826, but this one sank in the river as well. After they had gone away, the locals managed to recover it and take it back to the temple. They had a cunning plan and used loads of big bits of bamboo closed off at both ends so the air was sealed in. When divers had lashed the right quantity under the bell it floated up to the surface. Brilliant!

The Burmese King Bodawpaya (1782-1819) ordered another big bell that was cast in April 1808. This bell, known as the 'Mingun' bell after the pagoda of the same name, is at Mandalay in the centre of Burma, accessible only by river. It weighs ninety tons, and it became the largest bell in Asia and the world. An earthquake badly damaged the temple in 1839, and the bell was out of action until 1896 but is still there and regularly rung. It then became the largest working bell in the world again until 1902, and then from 1942 until 2000. The 500 foot high pagoda was never finished because a nasty astrologer told the King that when it was finished he would die! In case you don't know this, the word pagoda comes from 'dagaba' which is a sacred relic chamber.

The largest bell that you can go and see is in Moscow and is the 'Tsar Kolokol III', known as 'King of the bells'. Russian bells are shaped like European bells today, and as you may deduce they had two previous bells. The 'Tsar I' bell was cast in 1599 supposedly weighing eighteen tons and was hung dead with twenty-four very fit Russians pulling its clapper across so it struck. It was hung in the Ivan the Great Bell Tower, built in 1508 but increased to a height of 266 ft in 1600. It was forbidden to build a taller tower in Moscow, so the architect said, 'My tower is the biggest, and nobody can build one taller. So there!'

About 1650 there was a fire, and the bell crashed down and broke into pieces so became scrap metal. A very ambitious bell founder cast the second one in 1655 using the old metal and a lot more. It reputedly weighed one hundred tons. Sometimes bellfounders decide they have melted down a certain amount of metal and that becomes the published weight. They ignore furnace losses and sometimes the metal left over. In 1701, a fire put paid to the framework for Mark II and it was destroyed. The next one became Mark III.

The Empress Anna Ivanovna (1693-1740) was very ambitious and decided a new bell was needed that weighed an additional hundred tons. She sent her main man, the son of Field Marshal Münnich, to ask various European founders if they fancied an all-expenses-paid trip to Moscow, but they all said, 'No way!' He couldn't find anybody that took the idea seriously, so in 1733, Anna decided that the Russian founder Ivan Motorin was the perfect choice, and he roped in his son Mikhail. They were used to casting bronze cannons as well as bells. Perhaps she threatened them with losing their cannon trade, so in 1734, lots and lots of Russian peasants dug a pit thirty-three feet deep, and they started making the moulds. Anna wanted gold and silver added to the bellmetal, so she decided which jewellery she would part with. This was a false bell job, and we know that they back-filled the pit and rammed the earth down with lots of reinforcing.

The first bell was scrap, so probably the moulds came adrift or split, and Ivan Motorin may have had a heart attack because he died nine months later. Mikhail had another go and was successful in 1736. He then carved some more ornamentation on it whilst it was still in the pit, but eventually Anna asked, 'When are you going to get this bell up and ring it?' 200 soldiers hauling on ropes round capstans got it up to a wooden trestle-type platform. This had a large wooden shed over it whilst the bell was being cleaned and polished. When this shed was well alight in a fire in 1738, palace guards poured water on the very hot bell in case it melted. It cracked in several places with a piece breaking off that weighed eleven tons, and the whole lot crashed down into the pit. I expect the guards were beheaded or at least sent to Siberia, and Anna must have been really vexed about her jewellery.

Right: *An 1884 photograph of the 'Tsar Kolokol' bell outside the Kremlin in Red Square. The calculated total weight is approximately 200 tons, and the broken piece weighs 11 tons.*
Photographer: N.A. Naidenov

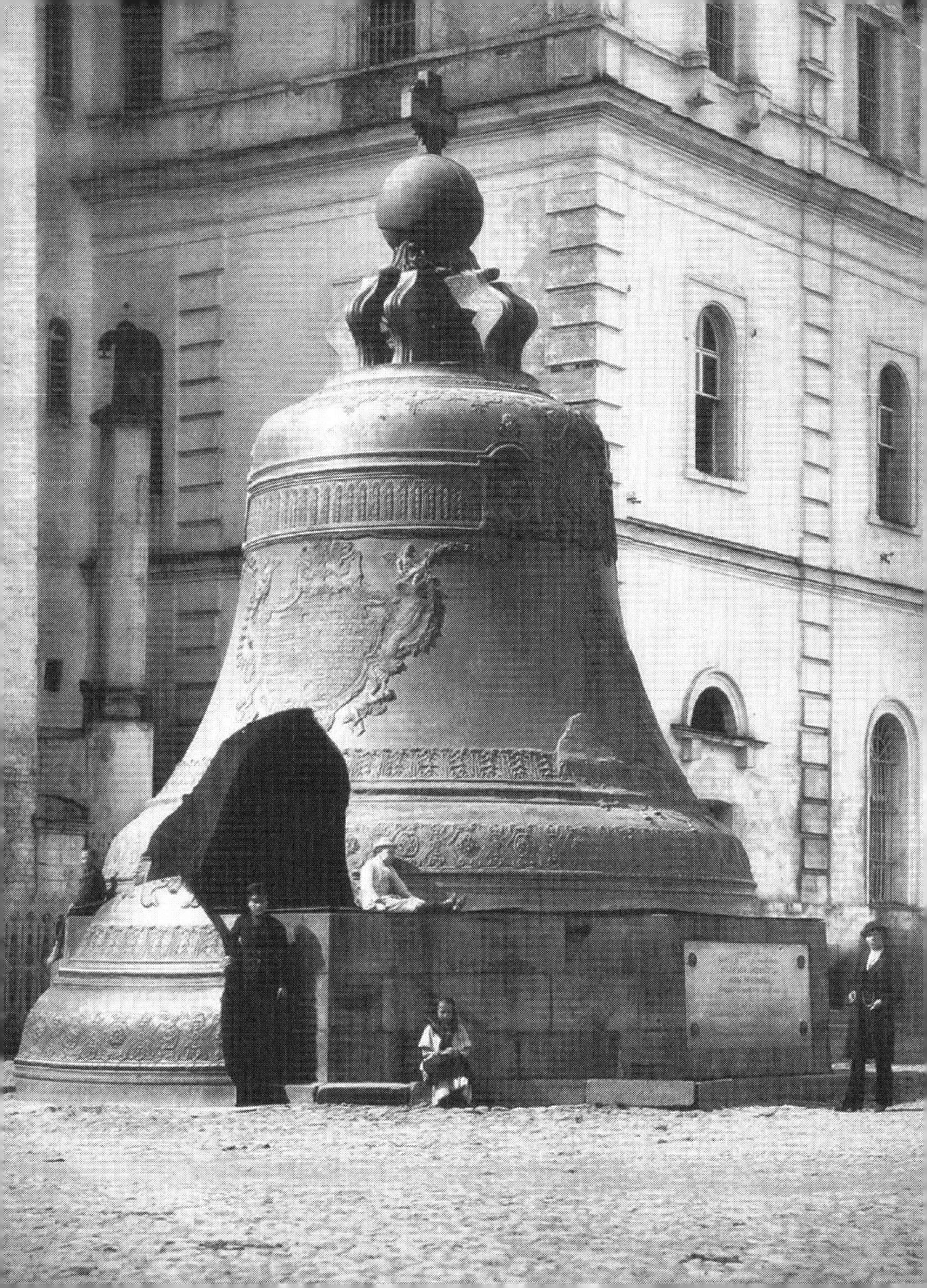

It stayed there for almost one hundred years, and an attempt to raise it in 1792 failed. Napoleon Bonaparte had a look at it in 1812 after he occupied Russia. He wanted to take it back to show his wife, Marie Louise Duchess of Palma, now Empress of France, but it was too big and too heavy so this didn't work.

In 1836, a French architect, Auguste de Montferrand, was much more scientific, and being optimistic he built a large round stone plinth beside the pit. The vast army of horses he whipped got it up and onto the plinth. The diameter was measured as being just over twenty-two feet, and the thickest part of the soundbow is twenty-two inches. It has the eleven ton chunk alongside it. It had never been rung, so no-one had any idea what it would have sounded like, but for a while they used it as a chapel. So does it qualify as being a bell? Some unkind people say it is just a large 200 ton bronze sculpture.

The 'Tsarsky Kolokol' or 'Trotzkoi' bell was the lowest bass bell of a twenty-four bell Zvon chime at the Trinity-Sergius Lavra monastery not far from Moscow. It was cast about 1715 but destroyed in 1737 (another fire!) and recast in 1746. It is stated to have weighed sixty-four tons. Like so many Russian bells, it was melted down in 1930 to obtain some roubles instead. In 2002, a replacement bell was cast at a Baltic foundry in St. Petersburg, with a finished weight of seventy-one tons. So it became.......the heaviest working bell in Russia.

The 'Great Uspensky', in the Assumption Tower beside the Kremlin, is the next largest, and is also called 'The Assumption Bell'. Cast in 1817 by two Russian bellfounders, it weighs sixty-four tons, with the four ton clapper set in motion by manpower again. It was not used after the 1917 Russian revolution until 1992 when the tower was done up. It is said that when rung it has a 'tremulous effect which is felt all over the city', so it may be thicker on one side than the other which would account for a pulsing sound.

Another tower alongside holds three Zvon bells, with related musical notes, known as the Roskov Chime. The 'Sysoy' bell, cast in 1689, is the largest, weighing thirty-two tons. The 'Polieleiny' bell at sixteen tons was cast in 1683, and the eight ton 'Swan' bell was cast in 1682. So although hung dead they are the three heaviest bells that go together musically as a set.

In 2003, a new bell was cast to replace the 'Balgovestnik' bell that had been considered the best Russian bell for 350 years and was also from the Trinity-Sergius Lavra monastery chime. In 1941, when the Nazis were approaching Moscow, they decided to hide it in the Moskva River which seemed a good plan but failed when it fell off the trailer and broke. The Russian bellfounder Mikael Maschin had only cast one weighing six tons before, so he must have been a bit bothered about this, and the new bell had to be an exact replacement in weight and note, so thirty-five tons. He melted forty-five tons of metal to be on the safe side, and the casting, with lots of decoration, was fine, after they had dried the moulds by setting fire to huge amounts of alcohol! What a waste! The diameter is a tad over twelve feet, and it weighs just over thirty-five tons as planned, so they borrowed a ballistic missile truck to get it to the monastery in time for Christmas.

Meanwhile, the Japanese or their Korean friends were busy again, and in 1633 they had cast the seventy-four ton 'Chion-in Temple' bell in Kyoto. It was rung regularly, and the 'mine is bigger than yours' idea made it the heaviest functioning bell in Japan. In 1902 however, the

124 ton 'Shitenno-ji Temple Bell' was cast, so definitely became the biggest in the world, and the monks said forget about the rest. In World War II, the Japanese army were short of metal, so in 1942 the monks were told, 'Sorry about this but we need your bell to melt down,' which they did. The 'Chion-in' bell was then the heaviest again, so they dusted off the postcards of the bell that had written on them 'the largest Japanese working bell in the world' to sell to the tourists.

Back in China, they had been miffed for centuries that they didn't have any really big bells that were in *The Guinness Book of Records*. They set about to rectify this by moulding the 'Bell of Good Luck' in 1999. This bell was cast in December 2000 and first rung on New Year's Eve at midnight (not the Chinese New Year). It is at the Foquan Temple in Pingdingshan and weighs 128 tons with a diameter of twenty-six feet. It is the traditional Chinese shape so is almost the same diameter right up to the top, and it is seventeen feet tall with a wavy lip. It is rung the traditional way with a thing like a very large log suspended by chains. To make the bell sound, the log is pushed onto the outside of the bell where there is an 'aim here' circle. So this bell is now........the heaviest functioning bell in the world!

Before this, the largest Chinese bell was the fifty-four ton Great Temple Bell, 'Dazhong Si', now in Beijing, and cast about 1415 for the Ming Dynasty Emperor Yong Le who was moving the Chinese capital to Peking. After he died it seems to have been forgotten and had never been installed or rung. In 1577, Emperor Shen Dong put it in a different temple, and it was rung for the first time. With the next new emperor in charge, it was then buried for approximately 100 years as he didn't consider the location was suitable for metal objects. A new location in Peking was chosen when it was considered the right time to take it on a new journey.

A familiar story here! In 1743, this temple caught fire, but as the bell was intact it was taken to Beijing by dragging it on a large sled after they had drilled wells and made the equivalent of a canal that then froze hard. As it was only about fifty-four tons in weight, it was nothing to make a fuss about although it is twenty-two feet from top to bottom and fourteen feet in diameter! It is claimed that on a quiet night with the wind in the right direction it can be heard at a distance of thirty miles. There is now a large bell museum at this temple, and I imagine the Chinese now claim, 'This is the largest bell museum in all of China.'

In Europe there are some very big bells but not on the scale of Russian bells. The French are always gung-ho, and they planned a bell to end all bells for the Paris Exhibition of 1889. It was to be much bigger than 'Tsar Kolokol', to be a symbol of Paris and France and an enormous hour bell. When the French government started punting round for quotes bellfounders said, 'You must be joking!' or, 'Are you completely mad?', so they built the Eiffel Tower instead. A bell called 'The Emperor Bell' or 'Gloriosa Bell' was cast in August 1873 for Cologne Cathedral by Andreas Hamm who recast it in November and then again in October 1874 after which he went bust! He had melted down twenty-two French cannons, and it finally weighed twenty-six tons, but there were always people moaning that the sound quality was terrible. They complained, 'We can hardly hear it even a short distance away.' As it was so often out of action being fixed they re-christened it 'Big Silence'. In 1918, the German army decided that the best thing to do was to scrap it and reclaim the metal, but in 1922 the

Cathedral authorities got up a petition and the necessary metal was provided by the German Chancellor. Heinrich Ulrich was given the order, so in 1923 he cast a bell weighing twenty-three tons with a diameter of about eleven feet. He was extremely worried about casting this big bell which apparently ruined his health, and he died before it was installed! It was christened St. Petersglocke (St. Peter's bell) but the uneducated Germans called it 'The thick Pitter'.

This was the largest bell at the cathedral and was fixed to an enormous wooden headstock. It became the heaviest bell in the world hung for swinging and had a very large clapper. In 1951 a one metre crack appeared, so lots of bad German words were exchanged. It is possible to weld bronze, so a German company came and did this in 1956, but welding can affect the tone, and it did. The bell was turned round slightly like 'Big Ben II', and a much lighter clapper struck it on a different place. This solved the problem until 2011 when the clapper broke! Metallurgists decided the 1956 clapper was cruddy, so a new one was made, and an electric motor now swings the bell. It is only rung on special occasions in the church calendar, apart from events such as the death of the Archbishop of Cologne and the Pope, the end of World War II, and the re-unification of Germany. So not very often!

The French Paccard Fonderie is a large bellfoundry in Annecy that can trace its roots back to 1796. Like Taylor's, it has been owned by several generations of the same family. In 1891, Georges Paccard and his two sons cast the 'La Savoyarde' bell, christened 'Francoise MargueRite de Sacre Couer' in 1895, for the Sacred Heart Cathedral in Montmartre, Paris. This bell weighs eighteen tons and was then the largest bell in France. It was re-hung in 1947 when it was decided that the belfry needed reinforcing but is still rung. The Paccard foundry are very proud of this bell and feature it in their publicity material.

In 1914, a twenty ton bell was cast by them for Rouen Cathedral in France. It was the 'Jeanne d'Arc' (Joan of Arc) bell, but because of the war it remained in storage until 1922. By then, Joan of Arc had been made a saint, so there was double cause for a good knees up. Roman Catholic bells are traditionally blessed at ground level after being on display, and in *The Illustrated London News* of April 20th, 1922, there was a report with a sketch of the bell draped in lace. It was struck in the church suspended from metal beams, before being hoisted into the North tower. It then became the largest bell in France but only for twenty-eight years.

During World War II, there was a 'gentlemen's agreement' between countries that cathedrals were not to be bombed. In 1942, an Allied air raid with US planes was being directed at industrial targets in Rouen, but a stray bomb landed in the North tower and set alight the wooden framework totally destroying this and other bells. From records compiled after the war, the 'Jeanne d'Arc' bell and four others not only melted in the intense heat, but the molten metal vaporized. All that was left was ash! This also happened in Holland.

Paradoxically, there was a carillon in the South tower, which was undamaged, that was hardly ever played because of the poor tone of the bells. The 'Francoise MargueRite' Sacred Heart bell then became the heaviest in France again.

In Toronto in 1984, work started on The Cathedral of the Transfiguration to serve Slovak Byzantine Rite Roman Catholics throughout the Greater Toronto Area. It was the personal project of a Slovak immigrant (Stevan) Stephen Boleslav Roman who came to

Canada aged sixteen. He had made a considerable fortune and was modelling the structure of the cathedral on the church in Velky Ruskov, the Slovak village where he was raised. He only wanted the best, and a central tower at the front rises sixty-three metres (about twenty storeys) topped by a gold onion dome with two smaller towers alongside. The design was by Donald Buttress, a renowned architect who overhauled Westminster Abbey. Stephen Roman decided that he wanted three enormous bells and approached various bellfounders including Paccard's and Taylor's.

When the initial enquiry came in, I assumed that this Byzantine Rite was an offshoot of the Greek Orthodox Church and sent him a picture of Archbishop Makarios at the foundry when we cast some big bells for Cyprus. Got that wrong! We were promptly informed that he was a personal friend of the Pope and was in regular contact with him. He obviously wasn't telling porkies as in 1984, the cornerstone of his cathedral became the first church in North America to be consecrated by a Pope (in this case, Pope John Paul II) who was on a trip to Canada. The three bells he wanted were to be somewhere in the region of eighteen tons, twelve tons, and eight tons and all slow swingers. As this looked serious, I went to Toronto with a cassette tape on which I had cunningly recorded the sound these bells would make by continually dropping the sound of another large bell until I had built up the right sounds for these three monsters. This cassette was an 'endless loop' one, so once you pressed the play button the sound kept going for as long as you wanted, until you pressed stop! I sussed out where his offices were in a sky-scraper that has gold-tinted windows in the Royal Bank Plaza. In the reception area there was an enormous photo of one of his several bulk ore carriers on the high seas. Very impressive.

Once the reception staff decided I really did have an appointment, a lift took me up to his penthouse offices where Barbie-type secretaries and assistants were evident, and what they lacked in height was compensated for by their chest measurement. It turned out that he was very short in height, wore platform shoes, and none of his female staff could be taller than he was! When they applied for the jobs I bet the first question was, 'How tall are you?' He wanted to know when Taylor's had previously cast a bell the same weight as the largest one he wanted, so I told him it was in 1881 but not a problem! He promised to study our quote and then got rid of me. Before I came back to Blighty, Andrea McCrady, who was a skilled carillonneur at the Gillett & Johnston 1926 Peace Tower carillon in Ottawa, took me on a quick tour. She had previously visited Taylor's, so this was how I knew her. She took me to see 'her' carillon in Ottawa, and we went to Montreal where there is an enormous church, St. Joseph's Oratory, run by monks, with a 1955 Paccard carillon. Their practice clavier was falling to bits, so I took loads of photos, and Peter worked out a price, and we got the job! Pats on the back all round so not a wasted trip.

The Toronto project was going to be a very large job, with minor considerations such as completely re-lining three furnaces not used for yonks, and converting them to oil, and the mechanical handling without any cranes that even approached being able to lift these weights. Just minor details! I must have seemed convincing because he sent a man to see us who stayed two days and ran a long way before breakfast. He appeared to be his ex-S.A.S. bodyguard and henchman, but I don't know who was looking after Stephen whilst he was away. He had a tour round the works, took photos with what was obviously a spy-camera and shook hands. My right hand was not too painful by the next day.

Various questions came, and then I was asked to go back. This time our General Manager came with me. At this meeting, Stephen had an assistant architect, various construction chiefs, other important people, and lawyers and accountants. He asked me when we had last made a bell the size of the biggest one he wanted, although we had already played this game. I told him again, 'It was in 1881, but we still have a lot of the men!' There was a very long silence and I thought, *looks like you are not supposed to make jokes with Stephen*. Then he laughed, and after he laughed everybody else did, because it was then alright.

In due course, a draft contract was sent over to us with a lot of very rigid and nasty conditions, and on about page thirty-six it detailed that we had to come up with a 'performance bond'. This is a surety bond issued by a bank or insurance company that guarantees a job is done, so that if we cocked it up, or breached the contract conditions, the client (Stephen) was paid up to 10% of the contract price, and he could then order the work from choice number two. These bonds are not good news, and the only way we could obtain one was if all the directors took out sizeable mortgages on their houses, so not popular! As I wasn't a director it didn't apply to my little pile of bricks. The technical challenges were also very complicated, so after a serious pow-wow we politely told Stephen we would not be going ahead and signing the contract in blood. Big disappointment to me but good sense, and I think we told him he could keep the cassette tape.

So then he gave the job to the Paccard foundry. Stephen had very definite ideas, and the biggest bell was to be called 'Stephen' and was now going to weigh 36,000 lbs/eighteen US tons because he had come to Canada in 1936. The middle bell was to be called 'Anne' and be 22,000 lbs/eleven US tons because Anne, his wife, was born in 1922. The smallest bell was to be called 'Daniel' and be 13,000 lbs/six and a half US tons because his son, Daniel, was very superstitious. Poor Daniel, not fair!

All of the bells had to be highly decorated, but as Paccard used a type of lost wax process, not impossible. When 'Stephen' was first cast the moulds parted company. Pierre Paccard had another go and reputedly said he didn't like the tone of this bell so broke it up! There was obviously a big problem with it. Eventually the three bells were cast and shipped to Toronto, and a photograph taken at their works shows the bells and substantial frame with the metal headstocks ready to be sent off. They do look impressive, and these bells would claim the record as being the heaviest set of three slow swinging bells in the world.

My understanding (and it has been confirmed by Alan Hughes, the former owner of the Whitechapel Bellfoundry) is that this job just about put the Paccard foundry into bankruptcy. They moved from their present location to another one seemingly to collect some money in.

Top right: *The three slow swinging bells cast at the French Fonderie Paccard in 1986 for the Cathedral of The Transfiguration in Toronto, outside their works. Pierre Paccard is in the white shirt.*
Photo: Fonderie Paccard

Bottom right: *The Fonderie Paccard 'Jeanne d'Arc' twenty ton bell arriving at Rouen Cathedral in 1922.*
Photo: Fonderie Paccard

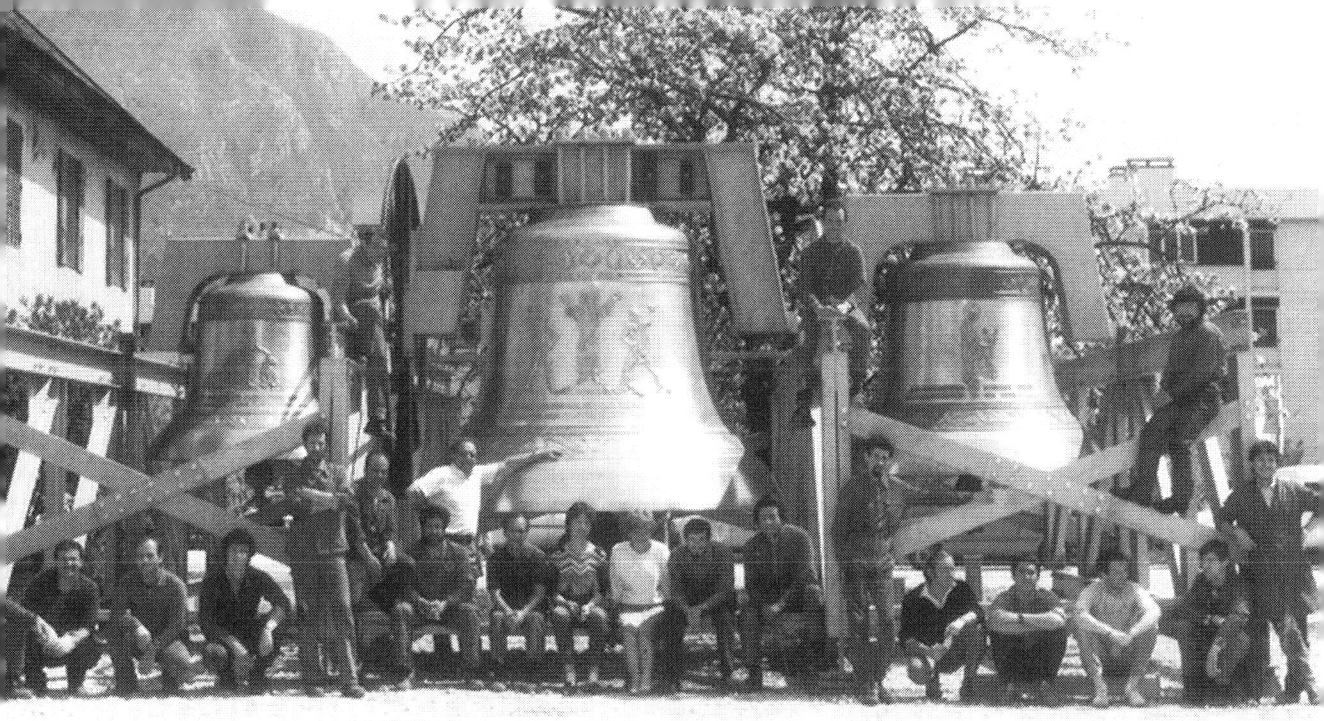

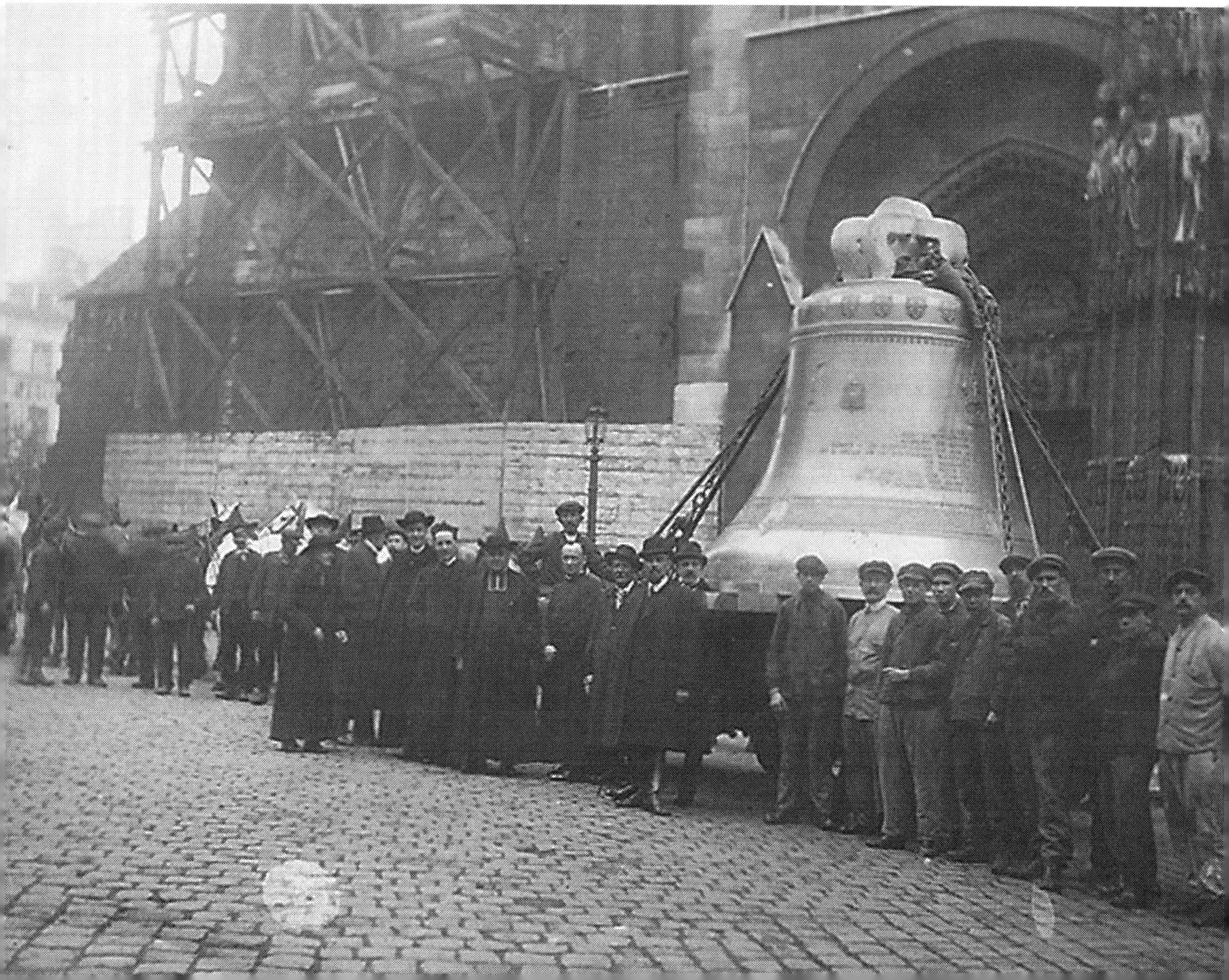

Paul Taylor told me that if the Paccard foundry were in any sort of financial problems the French government usually stepped in to preserve such an old craft industry but not in this case. Stephen Roman died of a heart attack in 1988, and his cathedral was not finished despite pouring in twenty-two million Canadian dollars.

In 2006, there was a dispute with other Byzantine Rite authorities in Toronto, and the cathedral was deconsecrated (so no more services) and the doors shut. It was estimated that there was probably another ten years work before it was properly finished.

Stephen's daughter, Helen Roman-Barber, is building 1,200 executive houses on the Roman estate called 'Cathedraltown' alongside the cathedral to try and raise funds. A large complex of apartments is scheduled to be completed in 2018. At present, these bells are the heaviest three of their type but not in use. A really sad story.

In 1997, a project was unveiled to cast an enormous bell to be called 'The World Peace Bell' to celebrate the forthcoming millennium. It was being commissioned by the Millennium Monument Company at Newport in Kentucky. This bell was to be the swinging bell to end all swinging bells weighing approximately thirty tonnes, so this was going to be an extremely large bell. Paccard went for help to the 'Fonderie Atlantique' in Nantes, who made enormous bronze propellers for ships, with a furnace capacity of fifty tonnes. A four tonne bell for another customer was moulded and cast at this foundry to make sure everyone understood how to amalgamate making a bell with moulding and casting propellers. I think this was a very smart move! Who was going to foot the bill if this thirty tonne bell was a disaster when it was being cast? At least they might have been able to go fifty-fifty, or they could just tell the propeller people, 'It's all your fault. Get out your chequebook.'

In September 1998, workers from the Paccard foundry started making the core and the false bell at Nantes. It was cast in mid-December and left to cool until mid-January, after their Christmas hols, when it was broken out of the mould. I bet you could hear a pin drop! Or several! It was a good casting, and in March the boss men from the US came to inspect it. It was then shipped off with all the fittings and put on display. It actually weighs just under thirty-three tonnes, with a diameter of twelve feet, and it was installed in a specially built tower and rung on December 31st at midnight, 1999. It is used as a clock hour bell at midday and rung with the motor drive on special occasions. No doubt the Paccard foundry were suitably impressed with their new friends in Nantes as they stated it had been cast by 'Paccard and Affiliates', so they obviously thought they were extremely useful contacts. There was no way it could be tuned as it was far too big, but it was the largest swinging bell until 2006!

In the US, the five next largest bells, after the Millennium Monument bell, are Gillett & Johnston carillon bells from the John D. Rockefeller Jr carillons at the Riverside church, New York City, and the Memorial Chapel carillon in Chicago. Both of these carillons are also called the 'Laura Spelman Rockefeller Memorial Carillons' in memory of John D. Rockefeller's mother. The largest bell is the bourdon bell of the 1929 Riverside carillon that weighs just over eighteen and a quarter English tons. Regarding the bourdon bell at the Riverside carillon, if for some strange reason you are reading this book standing up, sit down straight away. This bell was designed to be a US and European monster with nice round numbers. It was going to be ten feet in diameter, twenty US tons, so 40,000 lbs, and a 'C' bell, the lowest note ever of any carillon. It was absolutely 'mine is bigger than yours!'

A bell that was cast in December 1927 was rejected by the consultant in June 1928. Nothing wrong with the casting, but it had a pronounced 'rogue note', almost a feature of enormous bells, so it became 'Riverside I'. It was left on display for people to gawk at and 'Riverside II' was cast slightly heavier. Even Cyril Johnston from Gillett & Johnston, along with the consultant, thought this bell was worse, so they broke it up! 'Riverside III', a much heavier twenty-one and a half ton bell was then cast, and it was the worst of the three! In February 1930, the 'Riverside I' bell was chosen by the consultant to be sent to New York. Absolutely amazing! Three bells cast, all over eighteen tons, to get one good one, so Cyril Johnston had been tearing his hair out. The 'Riverside I' bell is often quoted as being the heaviest tuned bell cast in England, but it isn't! The scrap 'Riverside III' is the heaviest. The next largest is the 1932 Chicago bourdon bell weighing sixteen and a half English tons, and I will comment on these two bells in following chapters.

There is also the Gillett and Johnston 'Wanamaker Founder's bell', a single clock bell cast in 1926 weighing fifteen and a half UK tons, deliberately designed to be heavier than 'Big Ben II'. The 1963 Taylor Washington Cathedral bourdon bell is the next heaviest, followed by the 1936 Taylor bourdon bell at Ann Arbor, and then the Taylor 'Bok tower' bourdon bell, all over ten tons. So including the Millennium 'World Peace bell', this lot are the heaviest ten bells in the US.

In 2006, the Royal Eijsbouts foundry in Holland cast a swinging bell for monks at Gotemba City in Japan, not far from Mount Fuji. It weighs just under thirty-six tonnes and is twelve feet six inches in diameter. Along with other large bells it was moulded and cast at a Dutch propeller foundry at Drunen. The monks ring it in the traditional manner by hand in a free-standing frame just off the ground. They have two very long ropes in front and behind the bell and pull the wheel from both directions like a tug of war. I expect they're dedicated pacifists though. It became...........the world's largest swinging tuned bell! But guess what? The clapper hits the bell at the bottom of the swing not the top!

Unfortunately for Eijsbouts, their bell became the second biggest in 2017 when a fourteen feet nine inches diameter fifty tonne bell, christened 'Vox Patris' (Voice of the father), was cast in Poland for an enormous Catholic Basilica at Trinidade in Brazil. This bellfoundry at Przemysl, the only one in Poland, started up in 1808 but stopped producing bells in 1939 during the war. In 1948 it opened again, and Piotr Olszewski, the great-grandson of the first bellfounder, moulded and cast this bell at the large Metalodlew foundry in Krakow. A photograph of the false bell with decoration being applied shows it in a deep pit. Silesian University of Technology gave him a helping hand with technical advice, and when installed it will become the world's largest swinging bell. Probably for a very long time!

Turning to the UK, we have dealt with 'Great Paul', still the heaviest bell. Of the twelve largest bells, ten of them are from Taylor's. The second largest is 'Great George' at the Liverpool Anglican cathedral, cast in 1940 and weighing just over fourteen and a half tons. The case and core plate made for 'Great Paul' were used for the second time since 1881! The cracked 'Big Ben II' is the next heaviest, followed by a glorious bell, 'Great Peter' at York

Minster. This bell weighs nearly eleven tons and is another slow swinging bell rung manually. If you want to go and hear it, it swings for five minutes every day at noon but probably not on Sundays. So don't go then, in case I'm right! For years Taylor's were angling to recast the original 'Great Peter' which was an 1845 bell cast by Mears. They got into a great deal of trouble with this bell as it was three-quarters of an inch thicker on one side of the soundbow than the opposite side. Remember the vital importance of closing down the moulds? Sounds like a really bodged job to me, and Taylor's recast it in 1927.

In 1928, Taylor's cast 'Little John' for the Nottingham City Council building in the heart of the city. This ten ton bell is the hour bell for the clock and has the lowest note of any clock bell in England. Bristol University's 'Great George', another fine swinging bell cast in 1925, is next in the list at nine and a half tons. A bell for Wigton in Cumbria was cast in 1884 weighing nearly nine tons. Wigton? Is there a big cathedral? Has it got an enormous town hall? Neither of these, it was cast along with a small carillon for a private house! The cotton and hosiery industry was bringing in serious amounts of money, and Highmoor House was built in 1810 by a wealthy cotton and linen manufacturer. It passed to his business partner who set about making large extensions and a landscaped garden. He built a very large tower in the style of an Italian bell tower and wanted a big bell, so the nine ton 'Big Joe' was installed there. In 1920 it seems to have been lost or scrapped. How can you lose a nine ton bell? So unless it was buried in the garden, Chinese style, it doesn't appear to exist now.

An hour bell, 'Great Abel', at Manchester Town Hall was originally cast by Taylor's in 1877 and weighed six and a half tons but cracked in 1880 with doubts about the weight of the clock hammer. As soon as 'Great Paul' had been dispatched, 'Great Abel' was recast in 1882 to be a little over eight tons. Buckfast Abbey has a superb slow swinging bourdon bell, 'Hosanna', tolled alongside the ring of fourteen bells or rung on its own. It weighs just under seven and a half tons, and all fifteen bells were cast in 1935. 'Great John' at Beverley Minster lays claim to be the next heaviest Taylor bell, cast in 1901 at seven tons.

'Great Tom', also called 'Mighty Tom', at Oxford University was cast by Christopher Hodson in 1680, and this bell has a very chequered history! A previous bell, 'Mary', was moved from one Oxford church to another in 1545 and re-christened 'Mighty Tom'. It seems to have been pretty ropey and was recast in 1626 and 1654, but this bell was condemned because of the sound. Richard Keene, a bellfounder from nearby Woodstock, attempted to recast it three times from 1678-1679. In his 1898 book, *A Book About Bells,* by the Rev. George Tyak, he narrates that Richard Keene ran out of metal twice, and the third time the moulds split. What rotten luck! Tyak narrates that the authorities took pity on him and 'made him amends', so sounds like they paid him something as a consolation prize!

The London bellfounder Christopher Hodson was then summoned and cast the present bell in 1680 which reputedly weighed seven and a half tons. It was put in the 'Tom' tower and

Right: *'Great George' cast in 1940 weighing just over fourteen and a half tons in the foundry yard where it stayed until 1951. It is 9 ft 6 ins in diameter and after 'Great Paul' is the 2nd heaviest bell in England.*
Photo from Taylor archive

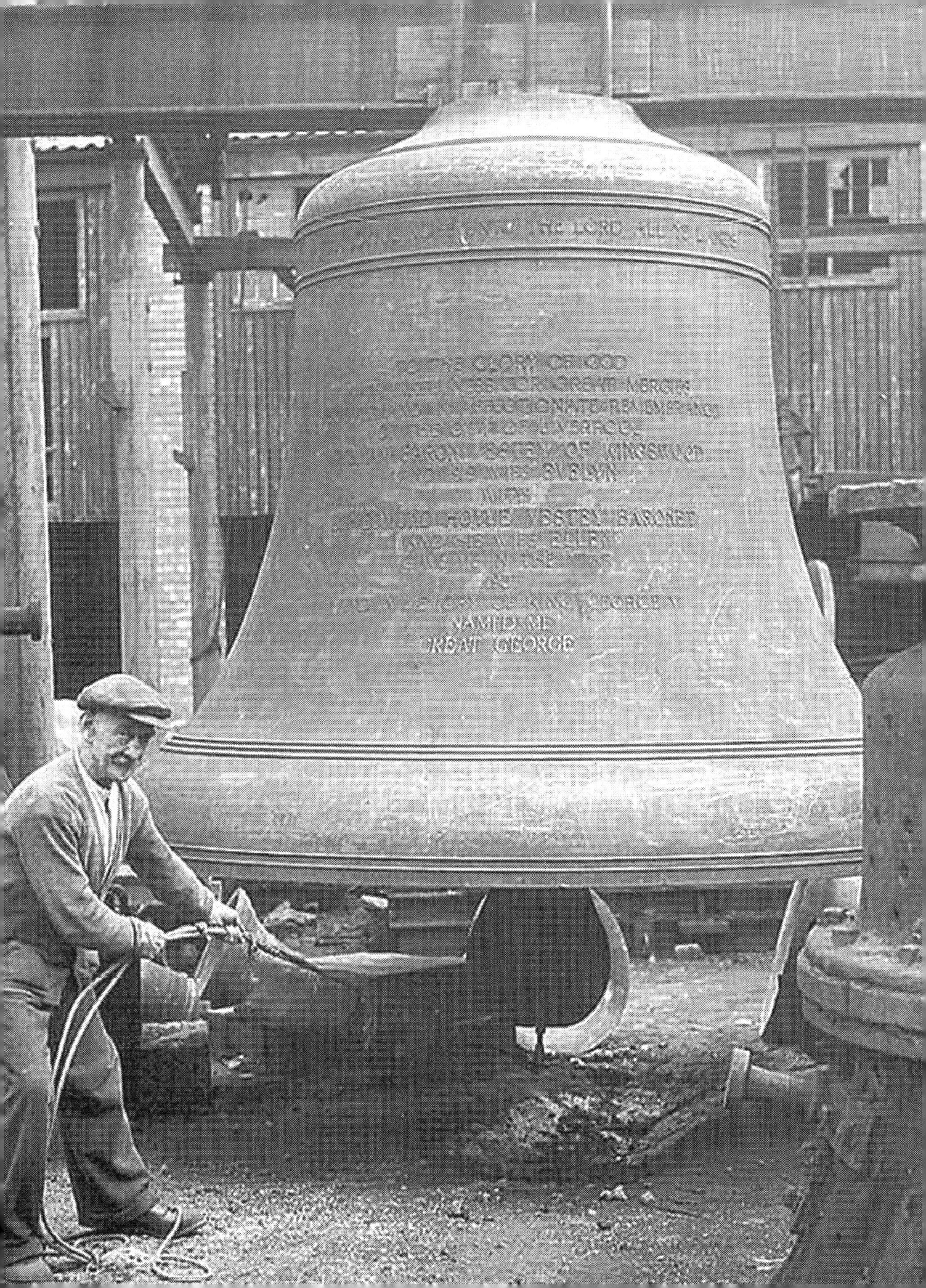
THE LORD
GLORY OF GOD
BARONET
GREAT GEORGE

rehung with new fittings in 1953 when the weight was found to be just over six tons! 'Oxford time' used to be five minutes later than Greenwich Meantime for some obscure reason, and it strikes 101 times every evening at 9.05p.m. It's like a curfew bell, and the scholars are supposed to leg it back to their rooms. Don't suppose they do nowadays!

So we are back to Taylor's and Birmingham University where the 1908 six ton 'Big Joe' or 'Big Brum' hour bell lives. In 1891, the Newcastle upon Tyne Cathedral 'Major' hour bell was cast and tipped the scales at very slightly over five and a half tons. Another bell called 'Great Tom' was cast by Mears at Whitechapel in 1835 and weighing just over five tons is at Lincoln Cathedral. It was originally supposed to be hung for ringing, but the tower didn't like it one bit. It is now an hour bell with four Taylor quarter bells. The slow swinger 'Great Bede' at Downside Abbey, cast in 1900, is just a touch lighter at over five tons. So lots of Taylor bells! The heaviest bell cast at Whitechapel in recent history seems to be 'Gregory John' at Ampleforth College, cast in 1961 and weighing just over four and a half tons.

Looking at the worldwide situation, in 1992 an almost carbon copy of 'Great Peter' was cast at Taylor's and sent to Valletta in Malta to overlook the large harbour. It is known as the 'Memorial Siege bell' and is a present and memorial from the UK to the 7,000 Maltese who lost their lives in World War II. In 1942, the George Cross bravery medal was given to Malta. The 1992 bell marked the fiftieth anniversary, and Queenie went over and unveiled it. This is another fine example of the amazing slow swinging bells and it weighs nearly eleven tons. It is swung and tolled every day at noon by a motor, and tourists can see signs in different lingos warning them it is very loud! Well, it will be, won't it?

Before too long, Jed Flatters had the unenviable task of going to Malta and removing the bell with the help of the largest crane on the island. The wooden headstock specified by the designer of the monument had shrunk by two inches in the Mediterranean sun. When Taylor's first saw this, they suspected the wood was not well seasoned, which proved to be the case. Jed rehung this bell with the tried and tested Taylor cast iron headstock.

A lot of the big Taylor bells are the largest bells in various carillons mostly in North America, and I will deal with carillons next. A carillon comprises a large number of bells, and the largest bell is traditionally called a bourdon bell again. A flagship carillon at the Bok tower at Lake Wales, Florida, cast in 1927 tipped the scales at over ten tons for the bourdon bell. The 1936 Ann Arbor carillon was a carbon copy of the Bok tower installation with another bourdon bell over ten tons, and the Washington National Cathedral carillon installed in 1963 is a sister one with the heaviest bell of the three. In 1947, Taylor's supplied a carillon for Niagara Falls where the largest bell is nearly nine tons. The largest hour bell of the five bells supplied to the Shanghai customs house in 1927 is six tons, and the Yale University carillon bottom ten bells cast in 1921 has a six ton bourdon. The 1970 Canberra carillon is a very similar copy.

Right: *Cyril Johnston from Gillett & Johnston, Croydon, standing beside the 18 ton 'Riverside' New York bourdon bell for the 72 bell carillon in 1928.*
Photographer unknown

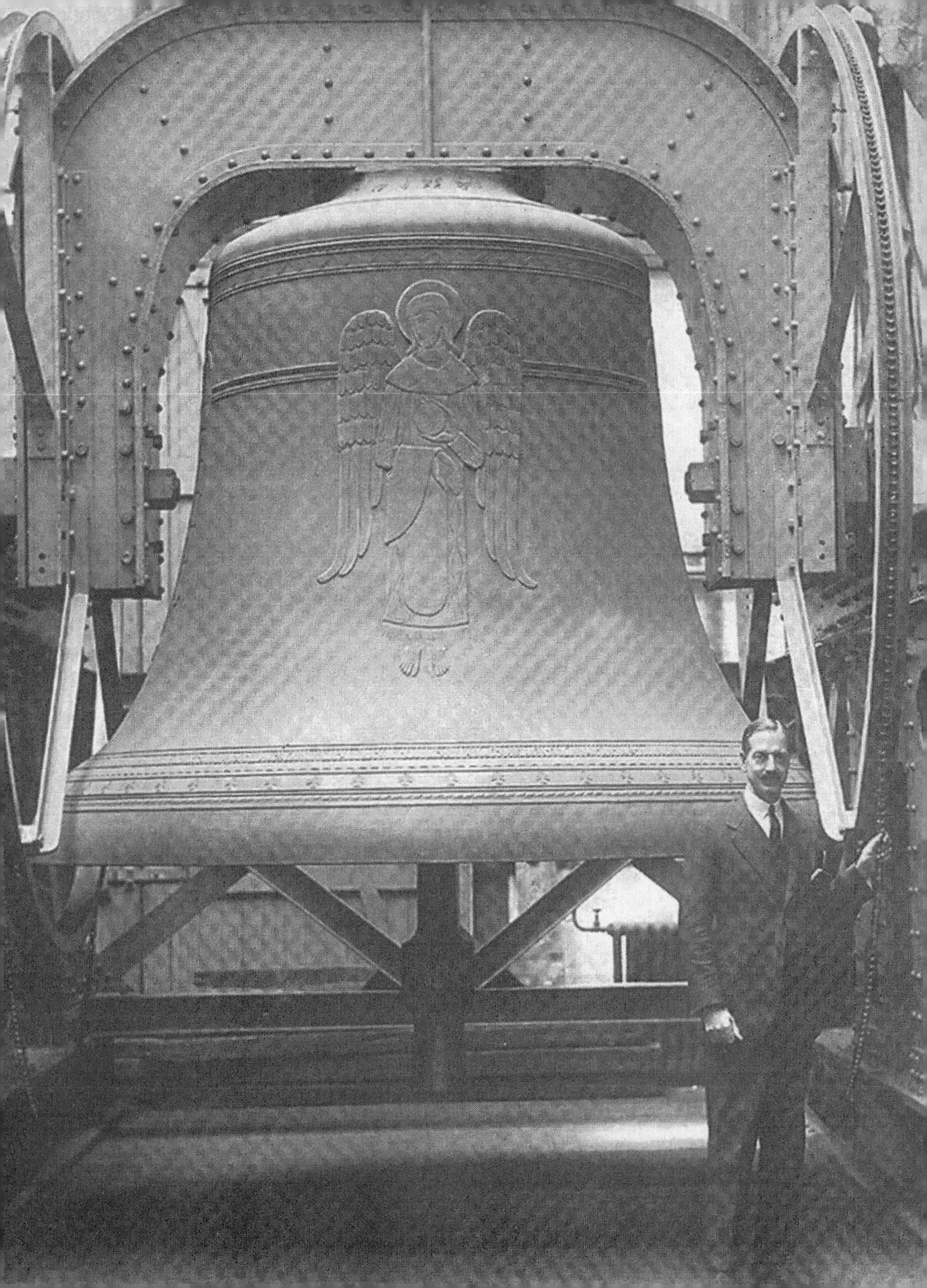

Of the ten carillons in the US with the heaviest bourdon bells, six out of the bottom eight are Taylor bells. The two heaviest ones come into the 'mine is bigger than yours' category, cast to achieve record weights and number of bells.

The home and origin of carillons is Holland and Belgium, and tremendous strides forward in tuning bells in 1894-1896 resulted in Taylor's supplying a carillon to Holland in 1897 with a seven ton bourdon, a real feather in their cap. Making bells destined for Holland was the equivalent of selling tea in China or ice to Eskimos! The heaviest carillon in Holland for 100 years was supplied by Taylor's for Rotterdam in 1921 with a bourdon bell of four tons. The hour bell of a set for Sydney, Australia, in 1891 was nearly five tons, and another set of clock bells at Brisbane in 1928 had a four ton hour bell. Malta became a good market for Taylor bells, and there are several bells over four tons there.

In all fairness, except being fair hardly comes into it, there is a bell I have not mentioned that is in London. When the pageant was being planned for the opening ceremony of the 2012 Olympic Games in London, the emphasis was on the historical legacy of England. The organizers decided they wanted a big bell, and Taylor's quoted for something really big, but the Whitechapel Foundry was given the order for a bell weighing twenty-two and a half tons. So did they build an enormous extension on their foundry? They didn't do this because they sub-contracted the order to the Royal Eijsbouts foundry in Holland. It had 'Whitechapel' in big letters round the top when it was shipped over here, but the moulds were made in Holland where they cast the bell (at their friendly propeller foundry) and subsequently tuned it. There was a lot of criticism in *The Ringing World,* the bellringer's weekly comic, and some of the national press. Isn't this cheating? A bell imported from Holland supposed to depict the English heritage? Hardly cricket is it? I think Whitechapel should have said, 'Better go to Taylor's if you want a big bell because the biggest one ever made here by one of our predecessors, called 'Big Ben II', cracked after only two months of use.' The Olympic Bell is now relegated to being a large ornamental Dutch bronze sculpture just outside the stadium and is no longer a working bell.

Lists of bells are very interesting, particularly old ones. The 1866-ish booklet has a list, as does a German book I have from 1884, but some of these bells do not exist now, of course. Taylor's website has a comprehensive list of Taylor bells, and the excellent 1963 book, *Bells and Man,* by Percival Price has a long list.

What intrigues me is that if a bell has been cast that has the right metal composition it can exist for hundreds of years. Bells don't suffer from woodworm, or go rusty, or suffer from metal fatigue like clappers do. If a bell frame collapses or burns down it probably isn't good news for the bells, but they don't wear out on their own. What else comes into this category? 'Old masters' get dirty and need restoration, Stradivarius violins need special protection against the varnish cracking, and bits fall off Gothic cathedrals.

Right: *A "bird's eye" representation of the John Murphy bellfoundry in Dublin, which first started casting bells in 1843. As can be seen, the company also made copper and brass goods.*
Artist and exact date unknown

J. MURPHY.

Copper Works Brass & Bell Foundry.

19 THOMAS STREET DUBLIN.

In 1980 we were re-hanging the bells at a cathedral in Dublin, and we had all the bells at Loughborough. Their old tenor bell was too light for the diameter, and the head was quite porous. The Irish bellfounder John Murphy, whose bells were sometimes not as good as at other times and were always a bit light in weight, had told them it weighed thirty-nine hundredweight in 1877. When we weighed it, it was only thirty-six hundredweight.

I condemned it and suggested that they had a new one just over two tons. In subsequent letters they asked what our normal guarantee was for a bell and how long the bell would last. I replied that a correctly profiled Taylor bell, if properly maintained, should last 300-400 years. I told them that in the first 100 years it might need turning through ninety degrees as over time the clapper impacts the bellmetal and starts to put a dent in the soundbow. If the dent gets very deep the bell may crack, but turning the bell is something that can be easily done in the tower. I told them that in the next 100 years it would probably need turning through forty-five degrees at some stage, but still not difficult. I finished by telling them, 'There does not seem to be much point in issuing a guarantee for 200-300 years but in effect, this is what we are saying'.

They ordered the new bell, and I cast them one that was, and still is, superb. The bellhanger from Taylor's who was putting the bells back in the tower was retiring and this was his last job. He made a point of coming to see me and said the sound of this bell was one of the best he had ever installed. I was really chuffed about that.

They also needed a new frame, but the architect was a keen yachtsman and thought wood was better than steel. He designed his own frame in Iroko, an African tropical hardwood that hardly has any knots, but we had nothing to do with it. So we lost out on the frame order but recast their biggest bell.

So bells can easily last for centuries, and I really like this. It's some sort of epitaph to whoever makes a bell that is first-rate, and me in particular for the ones I made!

10. Carillons and Singing Towers

'The crazy old church clock and the bewildering chimes.'
Charles Lamb

The word 'carillon' is pronounced 'karilon' or 'kariyon' if you are trying to impress people with your French pronunciation. It has a modern day meaning quite different from in olden times when it meant additional bells that mechanically played tunes where there was a clock. Bellfounders nowadays consider less than two octaves, so twenty-five bells, is a 'chime' even if played by a human. If you remember, the black and white notes on a piano total thirteen when you go from middle C up to the next C. If you go up to the C above this it is twenty-five in total, known as a 'range' of two octaves.

Once you start having notes or bells making up a third octave this comes to thirty-seven, and for four octaves forty-nine. Any set of bells over two octaves is called a 'carillon'. These can be played purely mechanically but usually have a mechanism so that a person can play tunes or melodies. Purists may say that without human involvement it doesn't qualify as a carillon, but they are just being picky!

I am going to limit my storytelling to countries such as Holland, Belgium and France. The period 1400-1600 is called the 'Renaissance' (rebirth) after the Middle Ages and before the Baroque period, starting in 1600. This is when there was considerable discovery, innovation, exploration, and changes in music, with extremely famous painters, novelists, and philosophers trying to explain how things worked, along with scientists and mathematicians.

It was an era in the Netherlands and French Flanders (Belgium hadn't properly been invented then) when people-power commenced, and Pieter Bruegel the Elder began painting everyday scenes with people, not just saints and angels, and he was able to flog them to somebody when he finished. The architect Cornelis Floris de Vriendt started designing buildings of a different style from churches, and people writing books were re-exploring Roman and Greek ideas and getting all excited. There was a lot of interest in folk songs, nursery rhymes and traditional dance music. Everybody liked a good knees-up, and it was no longer a reason why you would go straight to hell. It probably depended on how high you hitched your skirt up though. Too much leg and forget about heaven! Civic pride in buildings resulted in many towers being constructed to hold clocks that didn't just strike the hour.

We have mentioned jacks where figures popped out of clocks and hit bells, and having an interesting set of jacks was greeted with delight. Where these figures were cavorting alongside just two bells the next step up was four bells. The Latin word 'quatrinio' means a group of four, and the Italian word 'quadriglio' is four dancers. The similar French word for four bells was 'carillon' but being French it soon applied to more than four bells.

Originating in the UK, when a clock reaches the fifteen minute intervals and before the hour, a sequence known as 'Westminster quarters' is usually the one struck on bells. In the Netherlands and Flanders, a tune announced this instead to tell people, 'Listen up, the clock is going to strike the hour!' Bells were soon playing a longer series between the hours striking, but then it got really silly! A set of eight, ten, or twelve bells were incorporated that played tunes between the clock quarter bells, so there were bells sounding out every five minutes. At some of these towers, there was a very basic addition to the clock mechanism so a person could press down keys like those on a piano or organ to strike the bells.

Mechlin was a large city in the middle of what was called the centre of the Belgic Netherlands, and it was decided to demolish the church tower and build 'the greatest tower in Christendom.' They were keen on this as a famous saint called Saint Rombold was buried there, and six large bells were put in to start with. Antwerp decided they wanted two bell towers but chickened out over the second one, and they built the first stock exchange instead. In Ghent, they had the same idea. This big city had 250,000 inhabitants when London still had only 50,000. The wool trade with England was bringing in serious amounts of money, and everybody who was anybody wanted towers with chimes. Tuning bells so that they were more musical became more skilled which made the tunes sound better, and Joe public could recognize them. In Amsterdam, several towers were built and another stock exchange, whilst at Rotterdam, a gate tower and a town hall tower were slung up, with clocks and bells.

By the early 1600s, great painters such as Rembrandt, Vermeer, Rubens and Van Dyke were busy daubing paint everywhere. Visscher was famous for his engravings, and trade was brisk. Two brothers who were fed up with a thirty-year war turned up from the French town of Levecourt in Lorraine, and Holland seemed a good career move. Frans Hemony (1609-1667) was thirty-one in 1640, and his brother Pieter (1619-1680) was twenty-one. They had been casting bells with their father, so they weren't just starting out to see what they could do for a living. Pieter was really called Pierre but changed his name, and his brother was really François.

Bellfounders were often cannon makers as well, and they settled in Zutphen to make cannons and bells and were given the order to cast twenty-six bells for the Winehouse tower there. They cast the first bell in 1644 then Frans cast another twelve. Van Eyck, a blind organist (1590-1657) who was also a skilled carillon player and a noted musician, came with another organist to determine if they were all right.

Right: *A 2004 photograph of St. Rombold's Cathedral, Mechlin in Belgium, showing the market square in the foreground.*
Photo: Donar Reiskofler

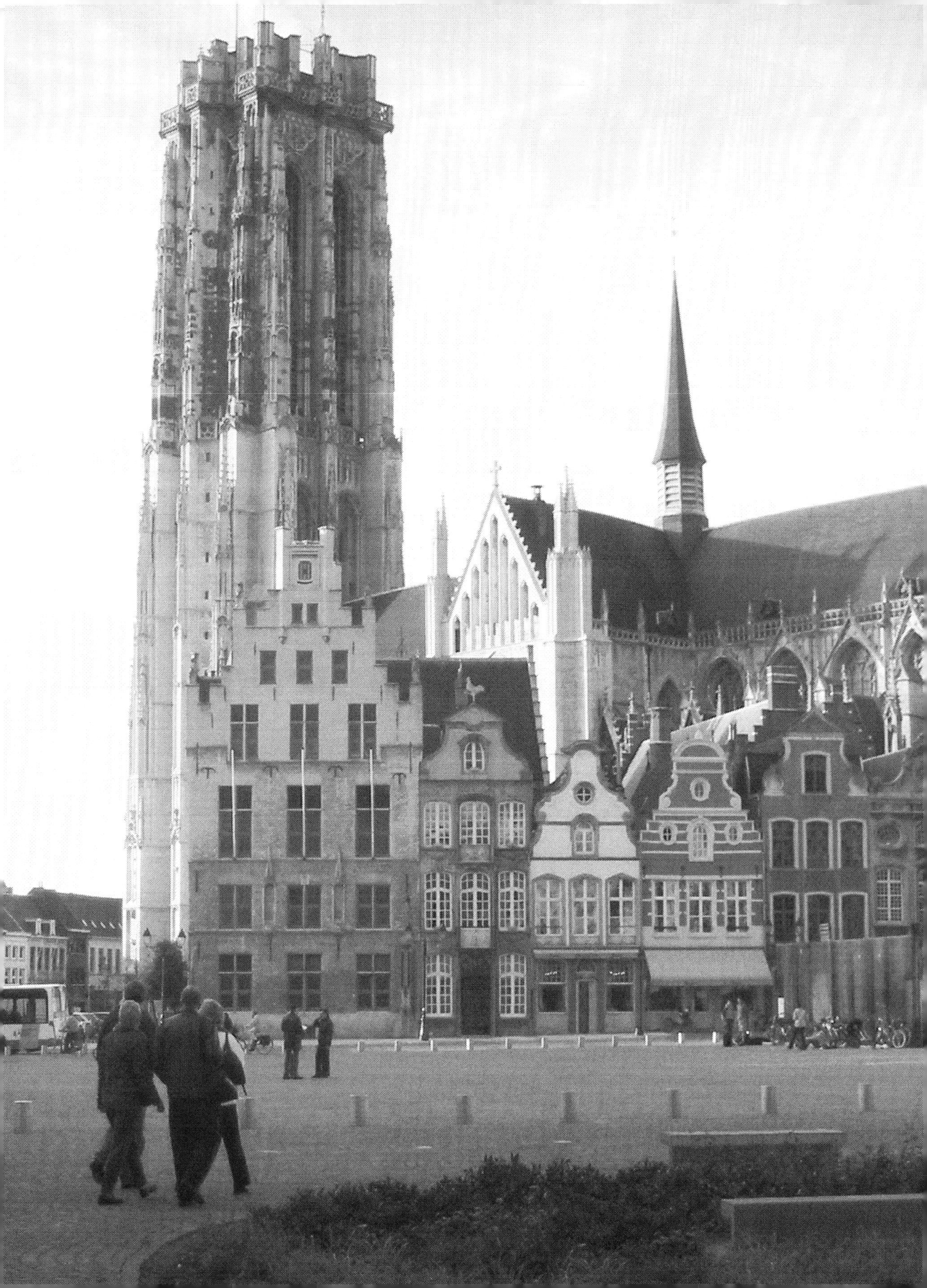

They said, 'Absolutely first rate', probably in Flemish, and Pieter was told to make the others. It took them two years to complete all twenty-six bells as well as making cannons. Van Eyck, who came from an important family, had decided which were the main notes within a bell in 1633 and was very keen to see how bells could be improved. The French mathematician and scientist René Descartes had moved to Utrecht and was very interested in the ideas about the acoustics of bells that Van Eyck was formulating. It seems that Van Eyck advised and encouraged the Hemony brothers to keep working towards producing highly accurately tuned bells, becoming something of a consultant.

The largest bell for the Winehouse tower was slightly less than two tons, and the authorities gave them a good reference describing the carillon as 'surpassing in tone and resonance all other carillons in the vicinity, so we are well pleased therewith'. I bet the two brothers quickly had it framed and put up on the wall.

Why some blind people have really good hearing is very interesting. A person blind at birth or within two years of being born is still developing brain activity, and a study of these people was made at McGill University in Canada. It seems they can 'hard wire' parts of the auditory cortex to develop improved hearing, and Van Eyck was born blind. People who become blind in later life do not appear to be able to do this to anything like the same extent. Many of these blind people do learn to become piano tuners but probably because they are taught to listen more acutely rather than it being a development in their brain. Really interesting; still more research needed!

With Van Eyck helping the Hemony brothers, their bells were considered so good that everybody from round about or elsewhere ordered bells. They were highly decorated so a good sales ploy. A cease to hostilities in 1648 when the sovereignty of the Dutch Republic was recognized meant that everything settled down in neighbouring states. They quickly got orders for two sets of fifteen bells followed by nineteen bells for Amsterdam. Twenty more were ordered for a hospital tower that probably took patients' minds off feeling really poorly. If they couldn't stand them I expect they asked, 'When can I go home and get away from these bells?' Twenty-five bells were ordered for the renovated Arnhem Cathedral, and Van Eyck persuaded his church to place an order. The brothers had hit the jackpot! Quite often the tunes from the mechanical drums went on all day and night, but the way the city towers were placed meant that as you wandered round you could hear the tunes from each tower separately. They didn't make a hideous noise unless you really hated them!

In 1654, Antwerp Cathedral ordered a new chime, but there was a slight problem. The town hall had paid for the first set of bells which were to be scrapped so considered them theirs. The church lot said, 'No way! They belong to the church.' Eventually two sets of bells were ordered to go in the same tower, one above the other! The church had twenty-six new bells and the town hall had thirty-six which included some of the old ones that weren't scrapped. Bellfounders like customers like these. Sort out the dispute, let us know when you have done it and we'll start work on the second set! So these numbers of bells qualify them as being true carillons.

The city of Amsterdam had become an important cultural centre and they welcomed refugees from other provinces where fighting had been going on. The finest talents in various artistic endeavours flocked in, nearly doubling the population, but no-one minded as they thought it was fab. The authorities in Amsterdam told Frans that if he moved there he could have land to build a foundry and be 'Cannon maker by Royal Command', but mainly they wanted bells. So he left Pieter at Zutphen in 1654 and made the long canal journey to Amsterdam.

One account is that he took with him some chipping hammers (I'll explain what these are later) to remove metal from the inside of his bells to make them sound better and 'a small set of bells to give the pitch (note)'. He started work on two carillons for the two largest churches, and then the stock exchange tower and another one for a royal residence cum city hall while Pieter was still churning out bells for places near Ghent. One story is that if it was a chime or carillon where the biggest bell was fairly small they tried to cast them all at the same time. If the metal they were buying, or cannons they were melting down, were non-standard mixtures this would have made sense.

The mechanical side for playing bells now had large revolving drums like horizontal 'Heinz 57' tins. Initially made of wood, they then became drums covered in copper. Holes went across from one side to the other all the way round the drum, with one set for each bell. Pegs were put into the holes which tripped hammers that struck the bells and played a tune as the drum rotated. Sometimes six bells rang at once. If there was an organist or musician involved, part of his job was to move the peg positions regularly to give different tunes. When they found that playing quick notes on the same bell was impossible because the hammers needed time to flip back, they dramatically increased the number of holes and pegs and had up to five hammers for each bell!

Eventually, some of these drums were about eight feet long and six feet in diameter. The largest ones only needed to revolve a short amount to play one tune, so one revolution could last all week. These were nothing more than giant music boxes, but there were no ballerinas that danced round when you opened the lid. When a considerable number of pegs needed changing this could take several hours, and they used a thing like a long ruler. Instead of it measuring anything it indicated which hole was for which note. If they made a mistake they found this out when the tune first played! If so, they had to leg it up the tower and change the peg positions. Special series of tunes were set up for Mardi Gras (carnival time), Lent, special Saints' days, and carols for Christmas. A drum installed at Mechlin in 1733/4 played 6,000 strokes on bells over a twenty-four hour period!

The other way of playing tunes was that the organist or musician had their own set of wires and hammers, and they could make bells sound loud or soft and play different tunes. Early keyboards like on a piano or organ did not allow enough control, so they started having sets of levers they pushed down, with some foot pedals as well, called 'claviers'. These musicians became known as 'carillonneurs', and many of them became very skilled.

Charles Burnley published a book in 1773 entitled *The Present State of Music in Germany, the Netherlands and United Provinces*. He went to Ghent and saw a carillonneur at work on an early basic clavier with batons. He was amazed how much force was necessary to sound the bells and wrote, 'The Carilhneur was literally at work, and hard work indeed it muft be; he was in his fhirt with the collar unbuttoned and inf a violent fweat. The player has a thick leather covering for the little finger of each hand, other- wife it would be impoffible for him to fupport the pain which the violence of the ftroke neceffary to be given to each key, in order to its being diftin&ly heard throughout a very large town, requires'. So not a job for weaklings at this 1659 Pieter Hemony carillon with fifty-two bells in Ghent!

Charles Burnley also went to the Amsterdam city carillon and watched the blind carillonneur J. Potholt playing. It was very hard work again, and a modern translation of his observations tells us, 'He could not have perspired more violently than he did after a quarter of an hour of this furious exercise; he stripped to his shirt, put on his nightcap, and trussed up his sleeves for this execution: and he said he was forced to go to bed the instant it is over, in order to prevent his catching cold, as well as to recover himself; he being usually so much exhausted as to be utterly unable to speak.'

On weekdays in the cities there were markets just about every day. There was a fish market, bread market, butter and egg market, cheese market, and days when you bought cloth, cattle and horses. The market place was the central attraction, and if you had finished buying a horse and were waiting for your wife to do the rounds and stop chatting you had a beer in one of the taverns and listened to the bells. At Mechlin, there was a rhyme about when the carillon was played by hand: 'Saturday for the country folk, and Monday for the city (council meetings). Sunday for girls who charm the men, and make themselves so pretty.' Another translation of this rhyme implies that some of the Sunday girls may have been of ill-repute! Surely not! On a Sunday?

One church had a super idea! Lent, from Ash Wednesday to Easter Thursday, is when Jesus went walkabout in the wilderness, and to remember this people had to stop eating fillet steaks, rich food in general, Jaffa cakes, and butter. This church sold vouchers that you could exchange for butter during Lent, and sales of the vouchers paid for a set of bells! No doubt the church elder that came up with this plan had a butter factory. Merchants with plenty of loot wanted bells, and one carillon is inscribed on the largest bell, 'Mr. Middelstum and his wife ordered it cast.' Any existing bells were often used as metal for new bells, with just one old bell used to sound an alarm left in place. The Spanish, who were rampaging round the Netherlands, ordered thirty-three bells for the royal palace in Spain and one for Salzburg in the Austrian Netherlands that was occupied by Spain until they went away.

In 1664, Pieter Hemony had moved to Amsterdam as well, but Frans died in 1667. He had been recognized as 'The Emperor of Bell-Founding', so Pieter carried on. If there was any pause in the orders, he cast bells to put in stock, and they often had two small sets. These were really handy when they got another order because they could either flog the whole lot or just add a few more bells.

In the 600 feet tower at Mechlin there were no Hemony bells, so Pieter chatted up the town hall magistrate who had a whip round of his wealthy friends, and they sold some of the existing bells to a church in the sticks. Pieter did really well and flogged them thirty-three bells that he cast in 1674, weighing from 10.6 cwt/540 kg down to 16 lbs/7.5kg. They kept the twelve largest of the existing bells by assorted bellfounders, with the oldest cast in 1480. The finished job, if all of them were used together, was by far the largest carillon around and was completed in 1679. It was officially opened in 1680, and everyone said it was tip-top, so the magistrate was happy and told all his friends their money had been well spent.

In a letter giving a quote for some bells, Pieter told the potential client, 'To reach me it suffices to place upon the letter: To Pieter Hemony, City Founder of Bells and of Cannons, Amsterdam.' Pieter was offering a choice of three stock carillons of different prices, the largest one with thirty-two bells but a total weight of less than four tons. He had written in 1677, 'I am resolved to dismiss my workmen and live in peace, having worked forty-four years at founding with my own hands', but he kept going a bit longer. The thing was, neither brother had ever revealed to anyone else exactly how they made their bells so musical and in tune. Nobody nowadays is certain how they did it either, but there are a lot of theories and possibilities. Just before Pieter died, he wrote a letter stating he was in poor health ready to meet his maker and now only carrying out some tuning. Frans Hemony had a wife, but Pieter never married, and there is no record that Frans had any sons to take over. An abbot at St. Salvator Abbey in Ename, where Pieter had supplied a carillon, apparently wrote to him several times asking how the tuning was done. Pieter was very vague, and in a letter to the abbot in 1677 he wrote that he was like a doctor who feels the patient's pulse and prescribes something. If it worked he continued to prescribe the same thing. Not a very comprehensive explanation about tuning bells!

Hardly any other bellfounders got a look in whilst the Hemony brothers were knocking out chimes and carillons, but Melchior de Haze had worked for them at one stage and undercut their prices on a few occasions to get work. He said he knew how to tune bells, but later admitted they hadn't shown him 'exactly' how they did it! Meanwhile, a grandnephew of the Hemony's, Mammertus Freme, who had come from Lorraine, was having a go himself and added eight bells to a Hemony carillon that had been left uncompleted, but everybody said, 'Sorry, no good!' He worked with Pieter before he died, but Pieter was still doing the tuning himself. He tried again with a new carillon for The Hague, but the musicians who tested it in his works said it was dire and they weren't buying it! Imagine! A whole set of bells that he couldn't sell. Another set for Alkmaar was rejected, unless they were the same bells and he was still trying to flog them off. De Haze had better luck, but not the acclaim that the Hemony brothers had achieved.

Guilmos Witlockx had been apprenticed to de Haze who had died by now. He made quite a few chimes or small carillons that weren't completely atrocious and rejected by the ones with the money. King John V of Portugal was trying to compete with his French cousin, King Louis XV at Versailles, who was expanding the exotic palace that King Louis XIV had started. John V had some loot from nicking Brazilian gold and was building a palace at Mafra near Lisbon, and he saw a carillon in Belgium in 1730. Witlockx was asked to supply one for the royal palace, but the King's chief accountant suggested that a carillon was too expensive.

This was red rag to a bull! John V said, 'I did not think it would be so cheap; I wish for two!' So he did have two with the second one from the bellfounder N. La Vache from Antwerp, both cast about the same time. He finished up with forty-six bells in his North tower and forty-seven in the South tower! I expect he soon let Louis XV know.

The thing was, none of them were as good as the Hemony chimes or carillons by a long chalk. The total number of large chimes or carillons made by each brother individually or together was about forty-seven. In 1677, Pieter said that this total weighed 790,000 lbs so three hundred and fifty tons! Witlockx supplied a carillon to a place called Ath, but they said it was no good. Referees were summoned and they said, 'Well, it's not too bad,' but it took him three years to get paid! In a quote for one job, he told them he was the ideal choice and had twenty-five workmen (making cannons as well). He was quoting for thirty-five bells, a drum with 2,000 pins, and a keyboard. He didn't get the job so was really miffed, and the order was given to de Haze.

Making cannons and bells at the same foundry was still very common. Van Noord was the first Dutchman to circumnavigate the world, and after he came back his ship was not very ship-shape having suffered badly on the voyage. His cannons were used to make a carillon, and the inscription on the largest bell reads, 'The heavy sound of this gun of Van Noord, Long after disuse, now gives sweeter accord.' Now, isn't that nice?

The French revolution was very bad news for chimes and carillons. The 'Goddess of Reason' was an attempt to replace religious superstition with supreme knowledge and facts. The war was carried into the Austrian Netherlands that later became Belgium, and all abbeys and monasteries were closed and property seized. They saw carillons as very handy gun-metal. One large bell was allowed to be kept in the metropolitan city in each province, but they weren't just being kind. The idea was that if they needed more gun-metal they knew where to come. Belgium had forty carillons confiscated, but at Ghent they managed to keep the best one, and the Mechlin Cathedral carillon was saved. The carillonneur Gérald Gommaire Haversals was very clever and smarmy and asked, 'How can we celebrate the glory of the republic otherwise?' but when the war was over he got a severe bollocking for playing republican songs!

The bells from Liége Cathedral were taken down by the townsfolk and hidden in the cellar of another church. A carillon at Nykerk made by Van den Gheyn, one of the best founders after the Hemonys, was saved after the merchants had a whip-round and paid over the value of the bells as scrap metal. Various church buildings were converted into 'Temples of reason' and some bells were left there. All in all, it was a really rough time for bells.

Top right: *A clock with jacks in Gloucester, England, where the four figures, left to right, portray Ireland, England, Scotland, and Wales, and strike the quarters. Old Father Time strikes the hour.*
Photo: Jongleur100

Bottom right: *The mechanical drum dated 1855 and built by Charles Nolet, at the belfry tower in Ghent, where Pieter Hemony installed the carillon in 1659.*
Photo: simonly

PRACTICAL WATCHMAKER **BAKER** JEWELLER & OPTICIAN

I don't expect you know this; well, you might not. In England in 1549, the Protestant *Common Book of Prayer* was introduced, and the Latin version banned. This caused a rebellion in Devon and Cornwall where churchgoers decided they didn't like it at all. The 1st Duke of Somerset, 'Lord Protector of Somerset', sent his head soldier, Edward Seymour, to quell the riots, mainly with mercenary soldiers. All bells except very small ones were removed from churches as the bells were allegedly used 'to summon and call in the disaffected unto their arms'. Lots of battles took place before the rebellion was over, with 5,000 deaths, but they didn't get their bells back!

In 2007, the Bishop of Truro said that the massacres during the rebellion were 'an enormous mistake.' Bit late to say that though! So the confiscating of bells in the Netherlands and Belgium wasn't the first time this had happened, but was on a much lesser scale in Devon and Cornwall.

Back in Holland and Belgium, so many bells had been looted it was difficult to find good ones. The skilled carillonneurs were having a tough time as the extremely complicated mechanical drums, wires, and hammers were neglected, and if there were any bells that could be played manually recitals were sparse. Quite often, fires destroyed bells and playing devices, and in 1821, the one at the palace in Spain was destroyed. This happened to a carillon in Holland in 1838, and a big one at Hamburg in 1842, along with one at an abbey in Belgium in 1859.

The carillon given by the Middelstum family was unplayable after 1855, and at Salzburg, only basic tunes could be played from the clock drum. Inferior carillons were still being installed in some places in France, and the founder Bollée, who lacked experience, put in fifty-six bells at Notre Dame de Chalons-sur-Marne in 1860. The editor of a French music magazine, *Caecilia* (Saint Cecilia is the patron saint of music), put a footnote on an article about carillons. He stated carillons were only of historical interest, and his music magazine should not have published the article! Music written for carillons by the Dutchman Matthias Van den Gheyn was arranged in 1862 for the piano. On the first page it read, 'Artists of our time no longer know how to execute these on a carillon.' Sad but true.

Paris decided they needed to have a carillon, and a Parisian founder had a go, but this was his first carillon and it wasn't very good. The piano-type keyboard was very difficult to play with any degree of loud or soft sounds. The mechanical playing mechanism was so complicated that the whole caboodle and the keyboard linkages took up three floors! After a few years continual maintenance was considered a waste of time. In 1862 at Cattistock in Dorset, it was decided that bells playing music was a good idea, and the Belgian foundry Van Aerschodt supplied a small chime. The church wanted the largest eight bells to be hung for ringing, so they did this but with an expected lack of skill in hanging bells for change ringing. Despite this, in 1895 they increased the number of bells to thirty-six.

Twenty-eight bells were put in at Eaton Hall in Cheshire where the Duke of Westminster officially had his residence. In 1867, they put thirty-six bells in the Boston Stump church in Lincolnshire, which were subsequently recast into four quarter bells by Gillett & Johnston in 1897. In 1932, Taylor's put in a ring of ten, and in 1951 they supplied a new chime of fifteen bells including recasting three of the clock bells. Thirty-seven bells were installed by Van Aerschodt in Aberdeen in 1885, but the same thing transpired with Gillett & Johnston recasting the bells and putting in a thirty-seven bell carillon in 1952. In 1954, it was increased to forty-eight bells, and this was the last Gillett & Johnston carillon before they stopped making bells.

Van Aerschodt replaced some carillons in Belgium, but most of them, like the ones in England and Scotland, were considered second rate. He wrote to a customer, 'I cast a dozen small bells for a particular pitch I desire and choose the best one'. One way of doing it!

In 1880, a 16th century chime of bells was moved to a new building in Amsterdam from another church, and the Dutch bellfoundry Petit and Fritsen added another ten bells, all played mechanically. The residents complained, 'The sound of this carillon is terrible and is just a big nuisance,' so it was disconnected! It wasn't one where listening in the market place was at all popular even on Sunday afternoons when the young ladies were strutting about.

Back at Mechlin in 1849, a carillonneur, Adolf Denyn (1823-1894), was appointed who took a keen interest in developing the best use of the carillon as a real musical instrument. He became blind in 1881, and they needed someone to take over. Other carillonneurs were going to be invited to come for auditions, but when they heard his son Jef (Josef) play there was no point in looking elsewhere. Jef Denyn (1862-1941) was not only a wizard player but he also dramatically improved the mechanism, linkages, and the clapper placement as he had studied to be an engineer. He wrote, 'A carillon to give satisfaction, however played, must have as a minimum, twenty-eight bells with the bass bell not less than 550 lbs (just under five hundredweight so not a very big bell). It should have bells hung in right lines, the big ones if possible somewhat enclosed rather than the smallest, with the bell loft 200 or 300 feet high'

By 1892 he was giving stunning recitals in the evening once a week. Curious visitors from Brussels and Antwerp came to see if he was as good as he was cracked up to be, and he was. The city of Mechlin started printing programmes of his forthcoming recitals, and posters were put up in nearby railway stations. He became the greatest exponent of playing the carillon of all time, and one night, just as he was about to climb the tower, he was told that Queen Elizabeth and members of the royal family from Brussels were dropping in. They could have given him time to go home and change! The American William Gorham Rice (1856-1945) had been the American ambassador to Belgium. He had written a book entitled *Carillons of Belgium and Holland; Tower Music in the Low Countries* in 1914, and he happened to be there at the time. He was very taken with a fifteen year old princess and wrote, 'A tall girl with an abundance of wonderful hair tied in a loose knot down her back.' Obviously very tasty.

In 1910, the King of Belgium came to Mechlin for a carillon competition with prizes he provided for the best performers. The competition was on August 21st and 22nd, and traffic was stopped in the surrounding streets. A report in the *London Musical Standard* stated that according to the police, 30,000 people turned up to listen. It must have been a nightmare redirecting all the traffic! In 1912, Jef Denyn had been the carillonneur for twenty-five years, so there was an enormous jamboree on July 1st and the King came again with Queen

Elizabeth. The Belgian foundry Van Aerschodt supplied a new bell to replace one of the Hemony bells that was not as good as the rest, and it was paraded through the streets. The inscription in Flemish reads, 'To the great carillonneur Jef Denyn, from an admiring public.' Other carillonneurs performed, and Jef gave the final recital. The London *Musical Times* claimed the crowds went from 20,000 to 40,000 when Jef was playing.

William Wooding Starmer, a famous English musician and composer, was extremely interested in carillons and very friendly with the Taylor family. He gave a speech telling all the important visitors, 'Our English change ringing, clever as it is, possesses none of the artistic merits of carillon playing of which Jef is the consummate master.' So William thought it was absolutely spiffing as well. Mechlin is an equal distance between Brussels and Antwerp and a thirty-minute distance by train from both cities, so a lot of extra trains were laid on. The King and Queen came in a flash car of course.

Right: *The Jef Denyn commemorative bell cast by Felix van Aerschodt in 1912. It was paraded through the streets and presented to Mechlin by the King and Queen of Belgium on July 1st, 1912, at the time of Jef's 25th year anniversary of his being carilloneur. It replaced one of the Hemony bells and is about 30ins/75cms in diameter and weighs 4.5 cwt/230 kg.*
Photographer unknown.

GEGOTEN DOOR FELIX VAN AERSCHODT LEUV

GROOTEN ... HET ...
...RDIER VOL...

JEF DENYN

11. Paradise Lost

'Lost Angel of a ruin'd Paradise.'
The Quick Dreams - Percy Bysshe Shelley

Having passed the 11 plus, which I knew was very important, I then had no interest in school work at all and achieved marks such as 4% in Latin at term end exams. This was partly because I often used this hour to make French knitting using a cotton reel. I considered I was only there to sing and have a really good time! Before the Easter when I would have been thirteen in the following August, the headmaster wrote to my mother and asked her to come and see him. He explained, 'Michael is a much liked boy by teachers and other pupils even if somewhat unruly, but his academic progress is abysmal. I have no choice but to have him sit the 13 plus exams at the end of the summer term, and he will fail'.

These exams were designed both to weed out the non-performers at a grammar school and promote any other bright pupils at a non-grammar school. He advised my mother to take me out of Southwell Minster School at Easter and enrol me in a local grammar school. He told her that if I had just started at a new school it was unlikely that I would be made to sit the 13 plus exams, so this was agreed.

In my last school assembly, the head master was droning on about some pupil who was leaving. I wasn't really listening. I was wondering what Easter eggs we would be given at Hill House. He then said something like, 'When he first came here, it was as if he had been let out of a cage,' and one of my friends was digging me in the ribs. He was talking about me! A pretty accurate observation. So I left the cathedral school and choir before my voice had broken. I said lots of goodbyes to all my friends including Bill Jewry who played the guitar quite well. He was a fellow boarder but not a chorister and later became Shane Fenton and then Alvin Stardust!

On Easter Sunday morning, after the stay-over and my last time singing in the choir, I had to have a taxi home again. When it came up to the front door at Hill House, Cathy knelt down and hugged me. I was crying of course, and she shed a few tears as well, but I didn't think matrons were allowed to cry! In the taxi the other chorister who shared it gave me his grubby handkerchief to wipe my eyes. He said, 'Cheer up, Milly!' and off we went. My Southwell days were over and had come to an abrupt end unfortunately. I do fully accept, and looked at in the cold light of reality etcetera etcetera, it was a fairly astute move to transfer me to a local school. As it was the Southwell headmaster's advice, my mother had little choice.

I obtained a place at another school termed a Community College. Stewart Mason was a very avant-garde Director of Education in Leicestershire and was setting these up for bright pupils. These were enormous schools with every department you could think of, and the whole idea was that in the evenings and weekends the local community could come for courses, improve their hobbies or acquire new skills, or form a theatre group or a choir. I started to get stuck into lessons with the encouragement of my mother who made sure I was not slacking, frequently asking, 'Have you done your homework?'

The most embarrassing episode in my entire life took place at Christmas in my second term at the school. The school carol service was held in a nearby Baptist church, and I was asked to sing the opening solo verse of *Once in Royal David's City* as my treble voice had still not broken. At the very famous King's College, Cambridge, carol service this solo performance of a boy chorister singing the first verse of the carol had become a tradition and was broadcast on the *BBC Third Programme* which later became *Radio 3*. The audience figures were minimal as it was considered quite 'high-brow', but my mother was a regular listener. (Incidentally, there is a very nice story about the evening announcers on the *BBC Third Programme* who always played the national anthem before shutting down. It was rumoured that they had to wear a dinner jacket and bow tie whilst standing to attention. One night, the national anthem was all over the place and only just recognizable. After a pregnant pause the announcer apologized and explained that one spool on his tape recorder had stopped going round, and he was pulling the tape through by hand! How admirable, and in the best BBC tradition.)

This carol service was originally called *A Festival of Nine Lessons and Carols* and was broadcast from 1928 and then extended and re-titled *Carols from King's*. In 1954, the very new BBC Television department was told that the service was being televised live. This was a bold endeavour, and no doubt the chosen TV producer had a pink fit! Looking at the recording of this service, filmed in black and white, it is mostly grey and white with the choirboys looking like Andy Pandy with pasty faces under the very bright TV lights. The sound levels are fairly patchy, and one TV camera occasionally pans across the pews to one of the breathtaking, beautiful stained glass windows, but not very spectacular in black and white! What it did do though was to introduce the carol service to a much larger audience on *BBC 1* television.

I suppose that I was an obvious choice to sing the opening solo and practised a couple of times standing beside the organist. There was some mention of the balcony area, but that seemed all right until the dreaded day! I was put in the middle of the front row of the balcony surrounded by about a hundred girls, mostly emerging into womanhood! I was still quite nervy, and on this occasion I was petrified! I froze completely with terrible stage fright and made a complete hash of the whole thing. It was a nightmare!

I have mentioned how my mother was a total fatalist, and just into November when I was thirteen, I woke up with a high fever and a very stiff neck. My mother whipped out her handy thermometer, took my temperature, and told my father, 'Go to the 'phone box on your way to work and tell the doctor Michael has poliomyelitis.' The doctor turned up after his surgery and diagnosed cerebral meningitis or just possibly polio! At the large Leicester Royal city hospital I was subjected to a lumbar puncture. This is extremely unpleasant, so avoid it like the plague if you can! Whilst you are curled up in a ball, a very large needle borrowed from a horse vet extracts spinal fluid, and this is sent to the lab, marked 'priority'. When the results came back, they weren't going to drill a hole in my head as I did have polio and was then rushed to another Leicester hospital that had isolation wards.

Unbeknown to me, total panic ensued because I was at this very large school. The Salk polio vaccine was still being perfected using unhappy monkeys, so an epidemic was a distinct possibility. My parents could visit me but only look through a glass window in the corridor as if you had polio you could spread it by coughs and sneezes.

Being a good Catholic, my mother acquired some Lourdes water from a nun she knew, and the hospital Roman Catholic chaplain was told, 'Make sure you baptise him before he has the last rites'. He knew this as Catholic priests always assume that if someone has already been baptised, the person doing it probably didn't say the right words, or they used contaminated water.

My mother packed my clothes up to go to the Oxfam shop and said prayers for my soul. I did begin to get better as polio comes in various guises, and I had the type that is non-paralytic, although the only real treatment is bed rest, good nutrition, and plenty of fluids. Several more dreaded lumbar punctures showed the disease was on the wane, but they wouldn't let me home until Christmas Eve with my bed put downstairs. No-one else in the whole of Leicestershire, during the rest of the year or New Year, went down with polio to the intense relief but puzzlement of the health authorities and the school. My family members and a few close friends, including my girlfriend and her parents, had all tested negative and were not carriers who could infect other people. District nurses kept track of pupils that went off sick for more than a couple of days.

One Monday, I counted up to about a thousand in tens and suggested that on Saturday I went to visit Southwell Minster boarding house as I was missing my friends. In actual fact, I was only going to see Smokey the matron and introduce my girlfriend to her. My mother only knew I had a girlfriend after a public health bloke rushed round to ask her who she was! The school obligingly told him her name. I explained that she would come with me 'to keep me company' and amazingly my mother agreed, so money for the trains was supplied and off we went. Smokey had bought a Messerschmitt one-seater 'bubble car' whilst I was there, so-called because it had a Perspex dome at the front, probably war surplus from their fighter planes.

When we got there she was not in her office, and her car was not outside. A large runaway lorry with brake failure had crushed her stupid little car and killed her about three weeks before on the hill. The tearful cook made us a meal, and we trudged back. I had never before had anyone die who I considered was close to me, so I was devastated. I was sure Cathy would have liked my girlfriend and teased me with big smiles and hugs.

Forty-five years later and in another country a woman came to see my wife and they got talking. It turned out that she came from Southwell, and so the Minster school and Cathy were mentioned. Our visitor said, 'I am her goddaughter, and my father was a teacher at the school'. Now, isn't that spooky?

My school music teacher, who was Welsh, told me that I should go to university and study music, ideally for a Bachelor of Music degree. He told me, 'Your first choice is Cardiff, and your second choice should be one of the other Welsh Universities'. In these ancient times there was no University Clearing Department, and no-one to contact via an email that hadn't been invented. You sent a letter to any university you fancied and travelled there for an interview. I was accepted at Aberystwyth though not for a pure music degree, and the same at Reading and Manchester, but for a Bachelor of Music (B. Mus) degree course at Cardiff. My music teacher told me to go to Cardiff, so I accepted the place on offer.

My girlfriend was becoming a talented painter, and one of her interviews was at the Royal Academy of Art in London. They drooled over the sample paintings and charcoal sketches she had taken down and made her an unconditional offer of a place there on the spot. Her immediate future was quite clear and sorted. On the appointed day in September I took the various trains that were necessary to get to Cardiff and started my life as an undergraduate there in the music department, for some reason called a 'Faculty'. A whole new experience was before me.

I went to Cardiff University with high hopes as my mother had prepared me for university life. She told me about undergraduate students studying for a degree living in a boarding house called a Hall of Residence, but at Cardiff only available for second year students. She told me you cycled to the various lectures, but it was not essential. This was probably because I couldn't ride a bike as I had never learnt how to! As the Community College was only a twenty-five minute walk I did not merit a bike as in her mind this would have been a sure prelude to my death after being crushed under a milk float! She told me that the lecturers lived in quaint university buildings, and you discussed theoretical topics such as, 'If God came down to earth what clothes would he be wearing? A nifty suit or a kaftan?' or 'If the moon is really made of cheese, is it English Cheddar or Dutch Edam?' Undergraduates, so she told me, were often plied with sherry while you stoked up the lecturer's coal fire and ran errands for them to make sure they had plenty of Earl Grey tea and pipe tobacco. On sunny afternoons you punted down the river, so she exhorted me to take great care else when the policeman came it would now be because I had drowned!

The first night I had to stay at the Y.M.C.A. as 'registration' started the next day. Having found the appropriate building I was given a lecture timetable, an address where I would be staying for the first year, a map, and a bus timetable. I found the right bus and was told where to get off after about a thirty minute ride from the city centre. The house belonged to an old lady, and she had somehow got on the university list of approved lodgings, but I'm sure had never been vetted! She was a widow, and two older men doing advanced courses in electrical engineering at the Cardiff College of Advanced Technology stayed there during the week. I think any old lady who said she had spare rooms was promptly signed up! We were given minuscule amounts of food, but the weekly lodgers gorged themselves at home at weekends.

She considered her income was not intended to supply decent food or heat the rooms. One night I tried to raid her larder when she had nipped off to Bingo, but there was hardly any food at all. If I had nicked one of the two slices of bread she would have noticed.

The next morning I went to a fairly new, large lecture hall along with all the other new students. The Chancellor of the University (he was the boss and head man) briefly welcomed us and explained that for every student they had accepted they had turned down six others. This seemed reasonable as you could apply to any university you liked and as many as you liked. He said they only had a hazy idea whether they had picked the right ones! He then asked us to look at the person on our left and our right and said, 'One of you three will not be here next year!' which sounded very harsh to me. The University of Wales had a bit of an inferiority complex, so they took 33% more students in the first year than they had places for in the second year and fired the ones who didn't measure up. So this idea did not seem to be the same lazy, idyllic existence that my mother had described!

At the first meeting in the Music Department the subjects we had to study, which were all 100% theoretical, were explained. It was a requirement that new students had to make 'progress' in playing a musical instrument of their choice. For some students this made playing the piano, or anything else, an entirely new experience never undertaken before! Incredible! We had to have a couple of hours a week studying another subject and in my case, as I had passed A-level English, it was Anglo Saxon. Probably not too useful when you left!

There was one highlight every week for me. A fellow student was a very competent organist, and after he obtained his degree he intended to go to the Royal Academy of Music for another two years. This is what you did if you were interested in practical music qualifications, so it took several years from start to finish. He had lessons at Llandaff Cathedral just up the road, so after the cathedral was shut to the gawking public he had his lesson and then practised, twice a week. I went with him to his practice sessions and either stayed up in the organ loft or wandered round the cathedral. It is practically impossible to be a really good pianist and organist unless you are a certifiable schizophrenic. You would have to wake up each morning and say, 'I've half a mind to play the piano or the organ today.' When you play a pipe organ you blast air through an amazing amount of pipes, and when you take your finger off the key the sound stops. Organists use a strategy similar to crabs. To keep the sound going they swap fingers on the same key, so they may start off holding one down with their index finger, and then, still keeping the key down, they slide another finger over. Their index finger or thumb can then press down on another key. You also have pedals that you press down with your feet, and you need to do the same thing which is called 'toe and heel'.

There are several keyboards, one above the other. The organist can set their 'stops' (things with a knob that you pull out to give different sounds) to the various keyboards, and there are words on the knob to tell you what will happen when you pull it out. One keyboard can be quiet, another can have very different sounds such as a trumpet, and another one can boom out. The more air you blast through the whole collections of pipes, known as 'ranks', the louder the sound. This organ wasn't particularly famous, but I thought the sound was really good! When the organ was very loud it reminded me of Southwell and it filled the cathedral. I often encouraged my friend to 'pull out all the stops' which is where the expression comes from. It means you are doing everything you can, and in this case producing extremely loud music. I think pipe organs are amazing, but very large bells can be louder. I have an excellent 2006 book entitled *This Is Your Brain On Music* written by Daniel Levitin, nicely subtitled *The Science of a Human Obsession*. He starts off explaining how he became an expert recording engineer, then deals with all the nuts and bolts of music, and finally explores in great detail how musical sound is processed through the ear and brain.

Music is processed through many different parts of the brain, and he comments on people who like really loud music like I do. It makes a whole lot more neurons fire that then triggers neurotransmitters and causes chemical changes in the brain. Research studies show that for some people, the more neurons that fire off the more 'excitement' this gives, but they don't understand exactly how this works. I like music reproduced or live to be really loud, and big bells satisfy my craving in spades!

In 2007, Llandaff Cathedral was struck by lightning, and the organ was severely damaged. A new one was ordered in 2008 at the amazing cost of £1.5 million. It was inaugurated in 2010 but not fully finished until 2013, and has a total of 4,870 pipes. This was the first new, really cool cathedral organ in the UK since 1962, when the new Coventry Cathedral bought one. Well, for £1.5 million it had better be good!

Unfortunately, my very theoretical Bachelor of Music degree course did not seem to be of much use for what I hoped to do afterwards. My English lecturer suggested that I changed my degree course to a Bachelor of Arts degree, a 50% joint course of English and Music that included some drama lessons, so I said, 'Yes. That sounds good. How do I do it?' The English department said, 'Shouldn't be too difficult. Leave it with us; no problems at our end'. The music professor said tersely, 'No way!' so the English department had to go above his head to the boss man called the Dean of the Music Faculty, who might be more sympathetic. The problem was, they found out that the Dean of the Music Faculty was the same professor who had said, 'No!' I expect he got double pay. Bad news, bad idea! I had to stick the course right through to the end.

During my last year at the Community College, I often went down to a large house with a conservatory where my friend Jimmy lived, and we sat in the conservatory reading back copies of *Country Life* magazine that were stored there. I think his mother was a bit horsey. The attraction of the conservatory for Jimmy was that he could smoke a furtive Woodbine cigarette! One time I was there, the most incredible organ music was drifting across the garden from a set of French doors, and after Jimmy had reluctantly stubbed out his Woodbine I was introduced to his father.

Top right: *The £1.5 million organ at Llandaff Cathedral built by Nicholson & Company from Malvern in 2010-2013 with 4.870 pipes, showing one of the two units installed both sides of the nave.*

Bottom right: *The organ keyboard and stops.*
Photos: The Dean & Chapter of Llandaff Cathedral

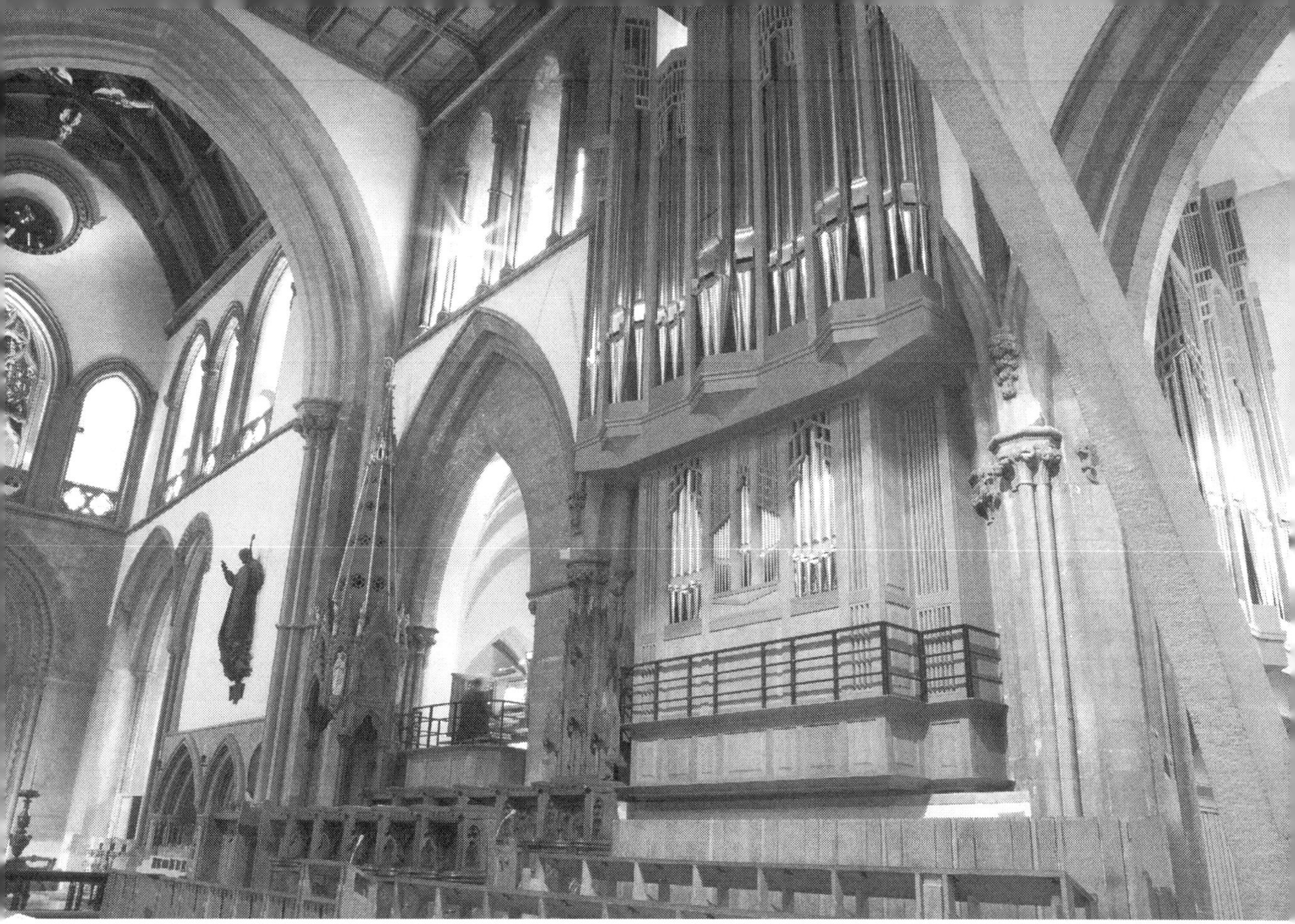

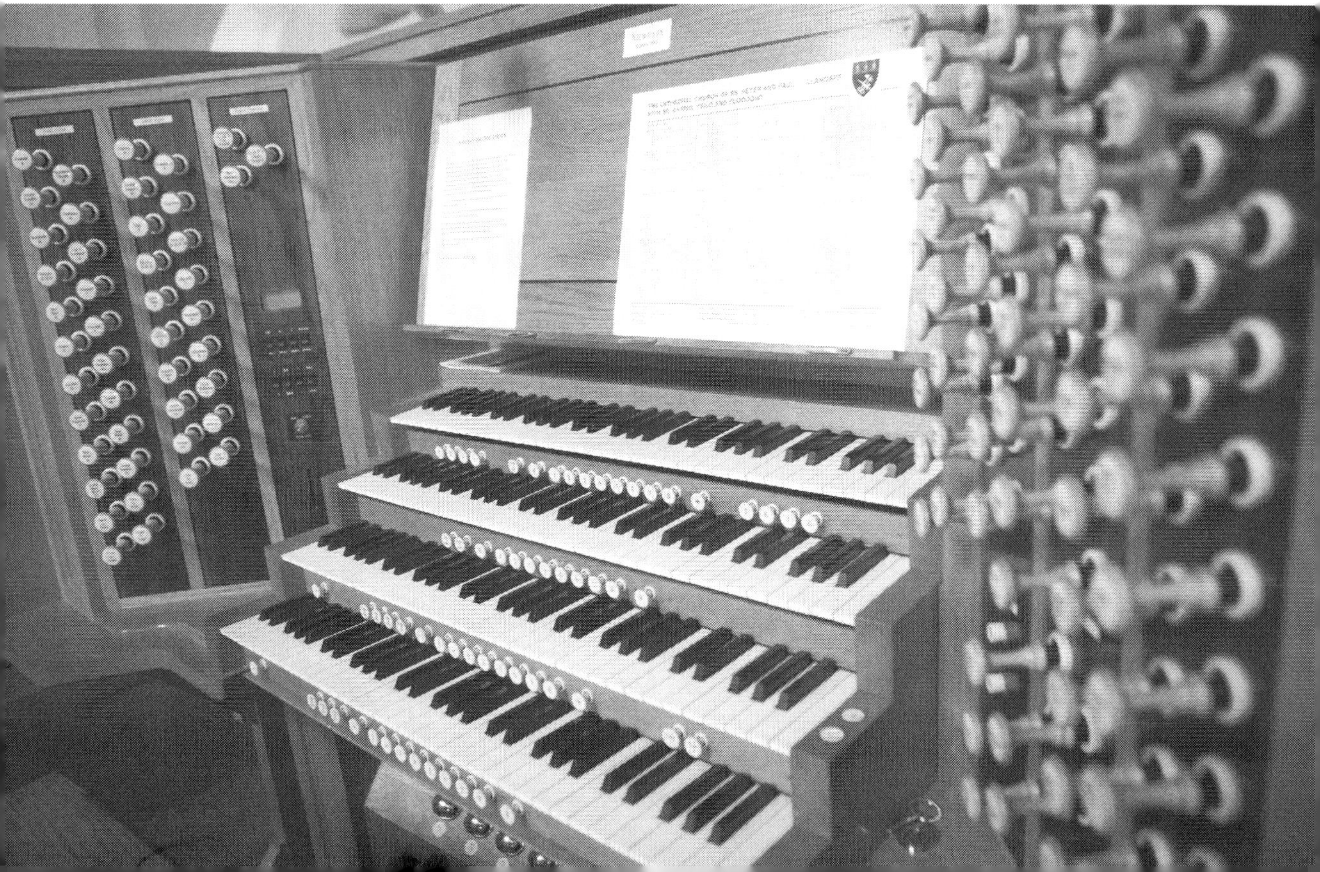

He was one of the growing numbers of hi-fi fanatics who bought the best equipment available to replay music and obviously could afford to indulge his hobby. He was very interested in the fact that I had been to Cathedral Choir School and decided I wasn't a complete dumbo. His collection of stereo LPs was mostly of classical or religious music, and over several visits on Saturday afternoons he explained the intricacies of getting the best information from the record grooves. He liked the fact that I could hear subtle changes in the sound that neither his wife nor Jimmy could hear.

One day, his brother who worked for the BBC came to stay for a few days. He mentioned that if I was qualified in music and had an interest and some knowledge of the reproduction of music there were jobs available, and he would send me some information. I didn't know whether he would or not, but he did! He thought the Trainee Studio Manager jobs where they took so many every year (a bit like choir school) might interest me most. A studio manager had a foot in both camps. They tried to get a sound recording of a performance that the artistes approved of by going to the technical bods and discussing with them how it could be achieved. The technical bods suggested how microphone placement might contribute to a better sound over the air waves. This made the performers happier, and they thought you were a really nice bloke. It sounded just like my sort of job! He wrote down the name of a BBC engineering handbook that would have to be studied, and I bought one from a bookshop.

I studied my BBC handbook at Cardiff, but there was no-one there that seemed to be able to tell me anything about sound engineering. At first, some sections of the BBC handbook were all Greek to me. Why do people say 'all Greek' if they can't understand something technical? Why not say, 'It was all Russian to me'? Apparently there was a Latin saying, 'It's Greek to me. It cannot be read'. Bet you didn't know that.

I took the momentous decision that at the end of the final term of my first year I would send in a series of blank examination papers! What? I had decided that I would be chucked out anyway so would try to seek my fortune elsewhere. I could have just not turned up for every exam, but I thought that was chicken. I had made friends with a girl doing a Psychology course who was very worried about her forthcoming year end exams, so I said I would help her revise hard for all her exams as I wasn't going to, and she would hold my hand. She met me out of every exam and took me off for a coffee to unwind. She passed her exams and was delirious as she had been really worried and was sure that my help with her revision had paid off. At least I had been doing something really worthwhile!

The music prof was not at all amused. After I had finished all the exams and sent in the blank papers I had to go and see him, with me sat at one end of a long table and him at the other end. The exams were spread over ten days, and no-one came along and asked, 'Are you okay, Milly?' He said things like, 'A personal insult! An entire waste of the lecturers' time'. And then he gave me my punishment for not being a good boy. It was not six strokes of the cane like at Southwell. He said, 'I will contact Leicestershire Education Department and recommend you have to pay your grant money back!' He really didn't approve!' I thought it would be easy for him as I was top of the list to throw out, so another person could go through to the second year. My English lecturer, when told of this latest twist, said he had a plan. 'I can get you into the ward at Whitchurch hospital where every year at exam time they have students who have cracked up! Then you may be able to come back next year and do the new course on medical grounds!' I declined this advice as Whitchurch was a Mental Hospital, and I thought my plan was not at all a lunatic idea but reasonably well thought out.

My parents took my return home quite well, and as far as my mother was concerned at least I hadn't drowned as she had feared, but I dare not mention the grant money. If I hadn't been under this threat I would have gone to see the friendly headmaster at the Community College and told him I had cocked everything up and now what?

So after two or three days, I hot-footed it down to the labour exchange to get any job going to earn some money. They sent me to a job bagging seed that came from farmers in enormous Hessian sacks and went out in much smaller paper sacks after being treated with coloured insecticide. There were three different colours so idiots could tell the difference.

Then I got a job as a ward orderly at the local hospital that lasted quite a long time. One of my jobs was shaving the men (they didn't let me near the women) prior to operations. After I had told my father at breakfast one morning to go and see his doctor because he had pains below his stomach he was quickly admitted to the hospital needing his appendix out! The nursing sister, who looked after the two men's wards, knew my surname but to everybody else I was just 'Mike'. She wanted to check this out, but whilst I was collecting my shaving kit and walking in one direction, she missed me coming up the ward the other way. We got it sorted out. I just said to my father, 'Well, who do you want to do this? It's me or a female nurse!' As he was in pain, I did it.

I had written about one hundred letters to the BBC trying to get on their training courses that they held in Worcestershire. They all replied politely, 'No degree, no dice!' They were passing my letters through various people, and I wrote back to whoever had signed the latest letter, telling them how suitable I was. In the end they got fed up and stopped replying. I expect the postage stamp bill was bothering them.

The next job with more money again (I was always looking for jobs with more money) was at the Brush Electrical Engineering Co. where my father worked. There must have been some hand of fate in this as the office job I was given was two floors above my father! I found out he was greatly respected, and people knocked on his private office door when they went to see him. A secretary looked after his every need (well, probably not every need taking into account my mother and father slept in different rooms as soon as my sister left home). A whole new perspective! He wasn't just this person who came home and took his bike-clips off, and he qualified to have lunch in a dining room with other people considered important, where they had stainless-steel cutlery and napkins, not like the canteen in the works.

One day, a man who was the service engineer at a large electrical retailer stopped my father in the street. They got talking as he had worked with my father some years before. He suggested I would be a good candidate for a job as a salesman that was going begging. I got the job (more money I might need for Cardiff) and apart from all the radio and television stuff they had a record department. This was much more to my liking. A large record department? Wonderful! The stock of LPs was quite comprehensive, and I could buy them at trade price including ones I ordered. Every Saturday we were bombed out as the weekly charts of the most popular 45s and the 'DJs' on radio stations kept sales really buoyant. If you were young and hadn't bought the latest rave single you lost all credibility, and girls looked straight through you!

It was interesting working there, and there was a very experienced manager. There is one good story; well, several actually! The electrical chain that owned the shop was doing a stock check, only they were in their warm offices in Birmingham, and we were on the dusty third floor. We had thirty-six nice convector heaters all in boxes. This was relayed down the line but they said, 'No, you should only have thirty-three. Count them again!' We did, and there were thirty-six. They said, 'We know you only have thirty-three. You can't count!' So the manager had a cup of tea and then rang them back. He said, 'You're right! You're the clever ones! We only have thirty-three.' He took one of them home, gave one to me, and Joan in the record department had one. You can't argue with head office! Now we had the right number, and the heater was very useful and lasted me for ages.

Since I had come back from Cardiff I had opened a Building Society savings account and steadily salted money away in case I did have to pay my grant back. I had to pay my mother board but not a lot of money. Gradually I relaxed and started buying tip-top hi-fi equipment bit by bit. Speakers came in all shapes and sizes, and the ones that were the best were heavily debated in the hi-fi journals. There wasn't a particular manufacturer that outshone all the others, and the two I had were fairly basic. I began to be aware of the difference between record producers such as Decca, HMV, EMI, and Deutsche Grammophon. This company is German (bet you guessed that!) and made superb recordings. Other companies could be a bit gimmicky, but they had progressed to putting two microphones in the ears of a dummy head. Their repertoire was almost exclusively first rate classical music with famous orchestras, performers and conductors.

One day, a woman I knew invited me to babysit with her while her friends went out, and in their front room there were several speakers. It turned out that the husband was just about to set up a small workshop in his cellar to make speakers. He had two partners, and one was a boffin who worked at Brush Electrical Engineering. In conversation it emerged what equipment I had (hi-fi wise), and there was a respectful pause in the conversation. I was asked to try out these prototype loudspeakers, and I made comments such as, 'The cellos are a bit muddy', so the boffin asked, 'What are cellos, and what frequency range do they have?' In case you don't know, cellos resemble enormous violins that the cello player grips between their knees, with a spike at the bottom that rests on the floor. Women cellists have to wear voluminous skirts because otherwise a normal skirt would just finish up wrapped round their waists.

Eventually, when they decided they were going into production they asked me to be their travelling salesman. They had found a workshop to rent with some decent woodworking machinery. I often organized demonstrations with hi-fi dealers, and they would hire a room in a hotel and bring along about six to eight makes of speakers. I took my equipment along with a switching unit with bulbs that lit up when each speaker was in use, courtesy of the boffin. If I was playing something like an organ recording with long sustained notes, I could switch through most of the speakers. It wasn't the most expensive ones that sounded the best, and our mid-price ones were pretty good.

One night I got a 'phone call from the Equipment Sales Manager of a large electronics company in Leicester who asked me to go and see him. The entrepreneur Charlie Clore had bought this company and came up now and then for a directors' meeting. One day, as he was getting into the door of his posh Bentley that his chauffeur was politely holding open, he paused and said, 'I want you to start making this double stuff!' They said, 'Yes sir, of course sir', and off he went. The managing director rang his secretary and asked her to find out what this 'double stuff' was, and the answer came back, 'Stereo equipment!'

After they had gone into production, the Equipment Sales Manager went on the road trying to sell these to the same hi-fi dealers I was going to. He noticed how many of our speakers were being stocked and sold, so that was why he rang me up. He was a bit out of his depth and decided they needed an experienced Audio Products sales person. He offered me a good salary, a brand new Vauxhall car (they had to be Vauxhall as Charlie owned a big dealership in Luton) and an expense account. I told my colleagues what had happened, and the one who was stuck indoors making the speakers said he was quite interested in going round dealers himself now and then. So no problem and good luck!

I'd also finally left home the weekend before. I had previously met a student at Loughborough College of Art & Design who came into the record department quite often, and he and two friends lived on a houseboat moored on the Grand Union Canal. It was a long way down a tow path that was a cul-de-sac at an old lock-keeper's house. It was a 'pontoon houseboat', so it was built on a flat wooden base and only fitted in canal locks that were double the width of a narrow boat. It didn't go anywhere, mostly because there was no engine, so it just sat beside the tow-path with electricity connected. So I bought it when they finished their course at the end of the summer, and the main attraction after several visits was that you could play music very loudly. The ducks and swans didn't seem to mind at all. I told my mother I was going to stay there for a weekend to see if I liked it, but I didn't tell her I now owned it! I slowly moved my meagre possessions in during the next few weeks, and she eventually cottoned on to the general idea that I had flown the coop.

By this time I was going out with the private secretary of the Company Secretary where I worked. A Company Secretary's job is to handle overall finance, discuss new ventures with the directors, and make sure published accounts went to Companies House and the Inland Revenue on time. His secretary was therefore privy to very sensitive information, and they didn't approve much of our liaison. We still kept going out as we decided our private lives were our own business, but they were thinking of knocking the unit audio side on the head as it wasn't the success they had hoped. They did appreciate that they were completely sailing in uncharted waters, and I had to go all over the country to see specialized dealers. Eventually they broke the news to me that they were stopping the unit audio, and with a generous pay off I was redundant!

On the basis that a good salesman could sell any product that was decent, I went to work for another company on commission only, nothing to do with audio. If a product is rubbish this is much harder work, but what I was selling was expensive but good. After about nine months, a man who lived along the street from my mother went to see her. He knew about me having been in a cathedral choir and going to university, and he was retiring from his job that was tuning bells at Taylor's bellfoundry. He suggested that I might like to learn this black art and become a bellfounder's apprentice in the tuning shop, so I went for an interview. They decided I was a good bet with the right background, and I was set on. Audio and acoustics but of a very different kind. Tuning bells? How did you do that? I was soon to find out.

12. After 'Great Paul'

'Older men declare war. But it is youth that must fight and die.'
President Herbert Hoover

When 'Great Paul' had been successfully cast and installed, John William I was taking stock of his situation. Considerable expenditure had been necessary, and he knew it would be a long time, if ever, before the enormous case and core plate would be used again. He wasn't wrong thinking this as it was pressed into service for the second time in 1940 when 'Great George' was cast! He had built a twelve ton furnace, but his five ton and seven ton furnaces each held a bit more so were able to cope with most requirements. It doesn't look as if he rushed to the bank when 'Great Paul' had been paid for and probably made hardly any profit at all, but his fame had spread, and he was certain orders would come in, which they did, but not immediately.

In 1882, he published a booklet with a list of his achievements to date and his capabilities. He had an engraving of his works inside the front cover and a blurb that started, 'John Taylor & Co. respectfully invite the attention of the Nobility, Clergy, Gentry, Church Patrons, Architects, and others interested in Bells, to the subjoined information respecting their Works.' He advertised the fact that apart from church bells he could produce 'Bells for every other use – Clocks, Ships, Houses, Sheep, Cattle etc.' He also detailed his use of 'Appliances of Steam Power for both Wood and Iron.' Two pages were devoted to his ring of bells at St. Paul's, and 'Great Paul', and two more pages to the sixteen bells for Worcester Cathedral cast in 1868. These were a ring of twelve bells with three additional semitone bells and a four and a half ton hour bell. Used together they made a chime of sixteen bells.

Christchurch Cathedral in New Zealand merited another two pages as, before getting heavily involved in 'Great Paul', he had supplied a ring of ten with the tenor just over one and a half tons. He then listed his major achievements in various places since 1858. He had not yet moved to his new works in 1858, but his previous little booklet listing work and bells cast stopped that year. He told his readers that he had a vast number of testimonials far too long to list! I'm sure this was true, and he had achieved an enormous amount of work.

St. Paul's Cathedral and Worcester Cathedral bells were his two flagship rings of twelve, and he had cast four rings of ten including the one for Christchurch, New Zealand, the first ring of ten bells in that country. In 1866, Preston Town Hall had taken delivery of a four ton hour bell with quarter bells, and in 1873 a set of bells for Bradford Town Hall had an hour bell over four tons with a thirteen bell chime. Work from the industrial centres in northern England kept coming in, and a very similar job for Manchester Town Hall listed twenty-one bells, the largest over six tons. The bell he had cast that was just over three tons for the London exhibition in 1862 had gone to Halifax Town Hall. He had recast the two largest change ringing bells at Wells Cathedral in 1877, with the tenor over two and a half tons. Rochdale Town Hall took thirteen clock and chime bells in 1871, with a two and a half ton hour bell. The same year that he dispatched the New Zealand bells, before 'Great Paul' caused such a backlog in normal work, he had shipped a heavy set of bells to Bombay University. What a lot of bells! Wasn't he getting a tremendous amount of work?

Apart from all this, he had supplied thirteen rings of eight, sixty-five rings of six, thirty-five rings of five, and carried out fifty-five re-hanging jobs where no new bells were involved!! These included eight bells at Chichester Cathedral, thirteen at Halifax, and ten bells each at Lichfield and Manchester Cathedrals. Did he ever sleep? Most of his workers were clocking up the normal working week of seventy-two hours, except when the metal was slow in melting and they stayed until it had been slurped in. We can see why he had needed to build an entirely new foundry building for casting bronze and iron in 1875, and it's amazing he lasted until then. When he first moved to the Cherry Orchard, the single furnace he had built was for five tons, but metal losses were high, and he had to re-design the chimney. A second furnace, built within twelve months, was christened 'the little furnace' and this helped. In September 1861, the metal was ready at 1.30a.m., but he had lit the furnace at 1.30p.m., so twelve hours to melt the metal! Ridiculous! For the Preston Town Hall hour bell he unwisely put just over five tons of assorted metal into his five ton furnace. This was a very bad idea, and the metal didn't get to the right temperature, and the bell was scrap. Lots of work down the drain for a big bell. In 1868, he rebuilt his little furnace with another half-ton capacity, as he had the order for the Worcester Cathedral hour bell. To do this he used both of the furnaces together, something he had never done before, but it worked! He also started loading up the furnace to have another cast when it was still white hot from one earlier in the day! This is not at all easy!

By the time a new foundry building and new furnaces could be put off no longer, he had used the various furnaces on 260 occasions from 1860-1875! He had a few disasters but only to be expected, and he made some notes in his diary, including his explanations in brackets: 1866 'a nugget of metal got thro' the core'. In 1869 'metal got out of the pit (poor ramming up)'. In 1871 the same thing happened again, but he described it this time as 'metal got out of the mould (poor closing down)'. His last listed disaster was in 1873: 'Case gave way and let metal out (insufficient loam lining)'. When there is a lot of work it is possible to line a case with the loam thinner than normal to obtain a larger bell, but you have to be careful. No doubt this had worked on many occasions but not this time! The first bells cast in the new building in April 1876 were fine, and he had put slightly under five tons of metal in the new five ton plus furnace. He soon started using the seven ton plus furnace, but for reasons we will never know, at the time of one of the casts, they poured the metal at 4a.m. 4a.m.? How did they all stay awake? Slurping metal into a ladle and then into various moulds when everyone is completely knackered is a very bad idea. Good job there wasn't a bellfoundry workers union! It wasn't until 1919 that a national strike of foundry moulders happened because they wanted fifteen shillings a week! Denison Taylor wrote to a customer telling him that the casting of his bells would be delayed as 'all our wretched moulders are out on strike, and there is only John Smith left in the foundry today.' Who was John Smith? Why wasn't he out on strike as well? Taylor's weren't unsympathetic to their workers, and Trevor Jennings writes that about 1838 a young lad named John Cook was caught trespassing on a member of the gentry's land. Was he going after rabbits? They told the big knob that John was very contrite, and he was released from prison without going to court. This was a good move, as John Cook put in forty-seven years working at the foundry, and his last fifteen years as a foreman! A commemorative half-muffled peal was rung on the Loughborough Parish Church bells when he died in 1885. Well done, John Cook, a stalwart worker if ever there was one.

In 1881, John William was pushing for the adoption of cast iron frames. When a frame for a ring of bells was installed at the Cornish town of Camborne in 1882, the *Western News* reported, 'This is the first cast iron framework for a complete ring of bells that has been installed in England. ……the frame will be much more durable and not require such constant attention as a wooden one'. John William was boasting that his cast iron frames 'are more massive than those made by any London firm……but consequently the price may be a little higher'. So go for it! Well worth the extra money.

George Dawson, the very well respected archivist who is now jointly in charge of the Taylor archive, found a reference to 'possibly the first cast iron frame' in inspection notes from 1934, when an important Taylor employee, Jack Fidler, went to Saxby church in Leicestershire. He commented on a not very substantial cast iron frame, 'too light for their job', that was almost certainly supplied by Robert Taylor in 1801 when he recast the three bells. Jack Fidler, recognizing the significance, recommended that the cast iron frames should be removed without breaking them. Subsequently, one of these frameworks was found and is now in the Taylor bellfoundry museum. This is certainly the earliest reference to a cast iron frame that exists anywhere. A Taylor cast iron frame from 1801? Absolutely amazing!

John William was still investing in plant and machinery and had to talk nicely to his bank manager in 1884. Queen Victoria celebrated her golden jubilee in 1887 when Taylor's obtained a plum job at the Imperial Institute in London to provide a ring of ten bells with the tenor just under two tons. Another big London job! When it was officially declared open in 1893 John William put his best suit on and went to meet the Queen. Unfortunately, he didn't get introduced, so he was really cut up about it.

Copper and tin were very cheap during this period, and in 1887 Taylor's cast seventy-five tons of bells. Patriotism was the order of the day! A foundry tower was built that had a height of eighty feet and a clock, but after this surge in activity the tonnage cast went down to forty-nine tons in 1888 and forty-three tons in 1889. Disaster struck in June 1891 when there was a substantial fire. The newly built clock tower was reduced to just four walls, and an area of the works measuring sixty feet by thirty feet was completely wrecked. John William rushed into the office area and was able to save many of the important record books, but the insurance had not been increased as additional extensions were made, and only £1,400 was paid out.

Repairs and extensions started immediately, with the builder William Moss involved again, who knew he had to get on with the work straight away! The whole former yard area was covered in, and improvements made to the foundry building. A fourth smaller furnace was built for casting small quantities of metal, and the area over the offices was substantially rebuilt with a fire-proof room and a large safe! A site plan of the works bore little similarity to the 1860 building, and the Taylor bellfoundry was now definitely the biggest in the world.

In 1897, Queen Victoria very conveniently celebrated her diamond jubilee, so more work flowed in, and the tonnage of bells cast was a record amount of ninety-five tons. This work, with the money that it generated, helped to offset the rebuilding costs. In 1900 his son John William II was forty-seven and had been fully involved in the business for some years. His other son, Edmund Denison, was thirty-six and another useful member of the family.

In the years after 'Great Paul', John William I and his sons started making visits to the continent and looking at bells cast in Holland and Belgium. He found how influential the Hemony brothers had been but had taken their tuning expertise to the grave. 'Tell you our secrets? No way. Find out for yourselves!' Taylor's started intense investigation to see if they could emulate this lost technique of tuning bells to a high standard. I will come to tuning later on, but tuning forks were being purchased from about 1860. In 1878, John William wrote 'the tuner can but give the bell the tone or keynote required, and must leave the harmonics produced by the peculiar form of the bell to themselves, having no power to control such.' Gradually, their understanding of how the notes within a bell could become more accurately tuned became less of a mystery.

Improvements in tuning were as a result of a basic tuning machine that took metal off the inside of the soundbow and lower down to some extent. A photograph of the works, probably about 1868, shows this machine, but this was all they could do or was the limit of their understanding. As the outside profile of Taylor bells had basically been fixed except for making small alterations now and then, altering the inside shape was the only recourse to try to improve the sound. I think they adapted their tuning machine to give a degree of machining further down the inside of the bell, at least for experimentation on test bells.

They became confident that they were on the verge of major improvements that were nothing less than rocket science. They built a new extension on the side of the foundry nearest to the offices and bellfoundry house, using part of their garden. In this 'tuning shop' they installed a vertical boring machine that John William I had sketched out and ordered in 1895. His specification was quite detailed and left no doubt as to what he wanted. He had asked for quotes from two manufacturers, but one of them was slow in replying. The other company promptly received the order! There was no time for messing around!

Right: *Ronnie Edwards in 1972 machining a bell about two tons in weight on the largest 15 ton tuning machine, custom designed by John William Taylor I in 1895. The medium size tuning machine is just visible behind.*
Photo by author

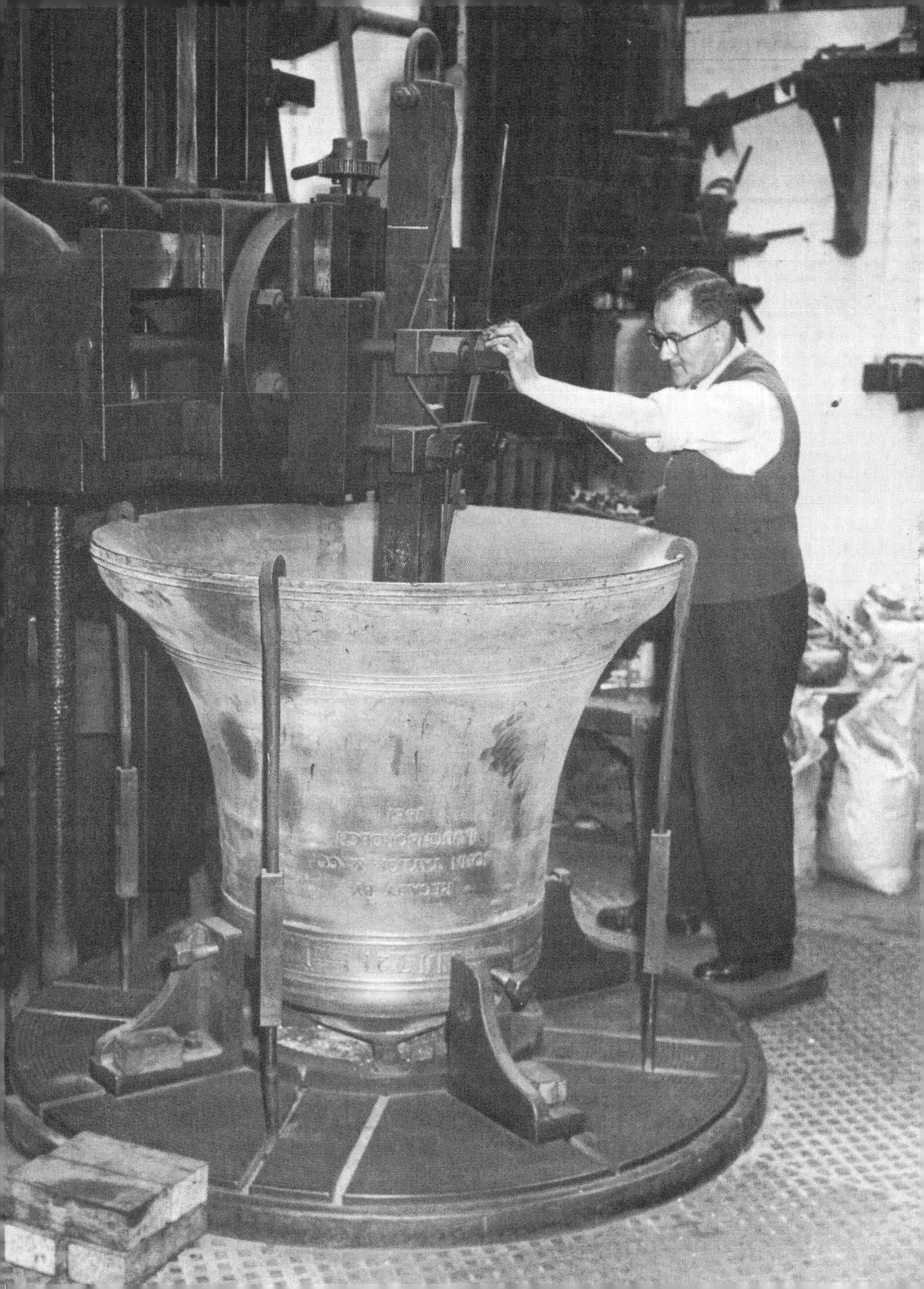

It had a turntable that was five feet six inches in diameter onto which the bell was clamped, mouth uppermost. The turntable revolved at different speeds, and a tool post with a cutting device could be dropped right down into the head of the bell. A set of gears slowly brought the tool post all the way back up to the lip, and the machinists brought the cutting tool in sideways, to follow the profile, by turning a wheel by hand. This beast weighed fifteen tons and must have been installed with the greatest of difficulty! Very encouraging results meant that a second smaller machine was purchased and quickly put in use. There was an instruction to the manufacturers that it needed to be speedily dispatched, so as to be used 'in connection with Queen Victoria's Diamond Jubilee.' When they needed any new equipment they were always in a hurry and continually chased up the manufacturers. By 1899 they had ordered a third machine for bells up to two feet in diameter.

In 1900 they invested in a huge version that had to be put in the building near the foundry proper, which had evolved from being a wood store to a girder store as well. This machine could take a bell up to ten feet in diameter and was put into use immediately to tune the five ton 'Great Bede' for Beverley Minster. The church was very impressed with 'Great Bede' to the extent that they ordered the seven ton 'Great John' in 1901. After just twelve months at Beverley Minster, 'Great Bede' was then transferred to Downside Abbey. With their total furnace capacity of a safe weight of twenty-five tons, Taylor's could now tune any bell they could cast. It is a tribute to the manufacturers, and the skilled men in the works of course, that with the required maintenance they are all still in use today!

Over the years, several smaller bell foundries had sprung up and were getting trade in the areas where they were based. John William I had kept a close eye on these but still obtained a lot of work from his reputation. He wrote to one of his patrons, 'some (other companies) are under the impression that they could establish a business without soiling their hands.' The Mears foundry in London had absorbed several minor bellfoundries, but between 1883 and 1903 John William I passed over several purchases he could have made. One of these was for the Mears foundry when their lease only had five years to run. Lord Grimthorpe (Edmund Beckett) was still well disposed to Taylor's, ensuring they received many orders, and John William sought his advice. He went to look over the premises and was allowed to see the accounts, but his conclusion (that Lord Grimthorpe agreed with) was to take no action. In later years, Denison Taylor was of the firm opinion that he should have bought Mears, liquidated any assets, and closed it down! Another couple of potential purchases were similarly rejected. He preferred investing money into purchasing copper and tin.

John William I retired and unexpectedly died in 1906. During his lifetime he had become a major landlord buying small cheap terraced houses, and the rent was very useful in lean years. Three small houses were demolished that split the foundry proper from the large

Right: *John William Taylor I inspecting 'Great Bede', the first bell put on the new enormous tuning machine installed in 1900. Initially cast for Beverley Minster, it was transferred to Downside Abbey a year later after a larger bell was ordered for Beverley Minster.*
Photo: Taylor archive

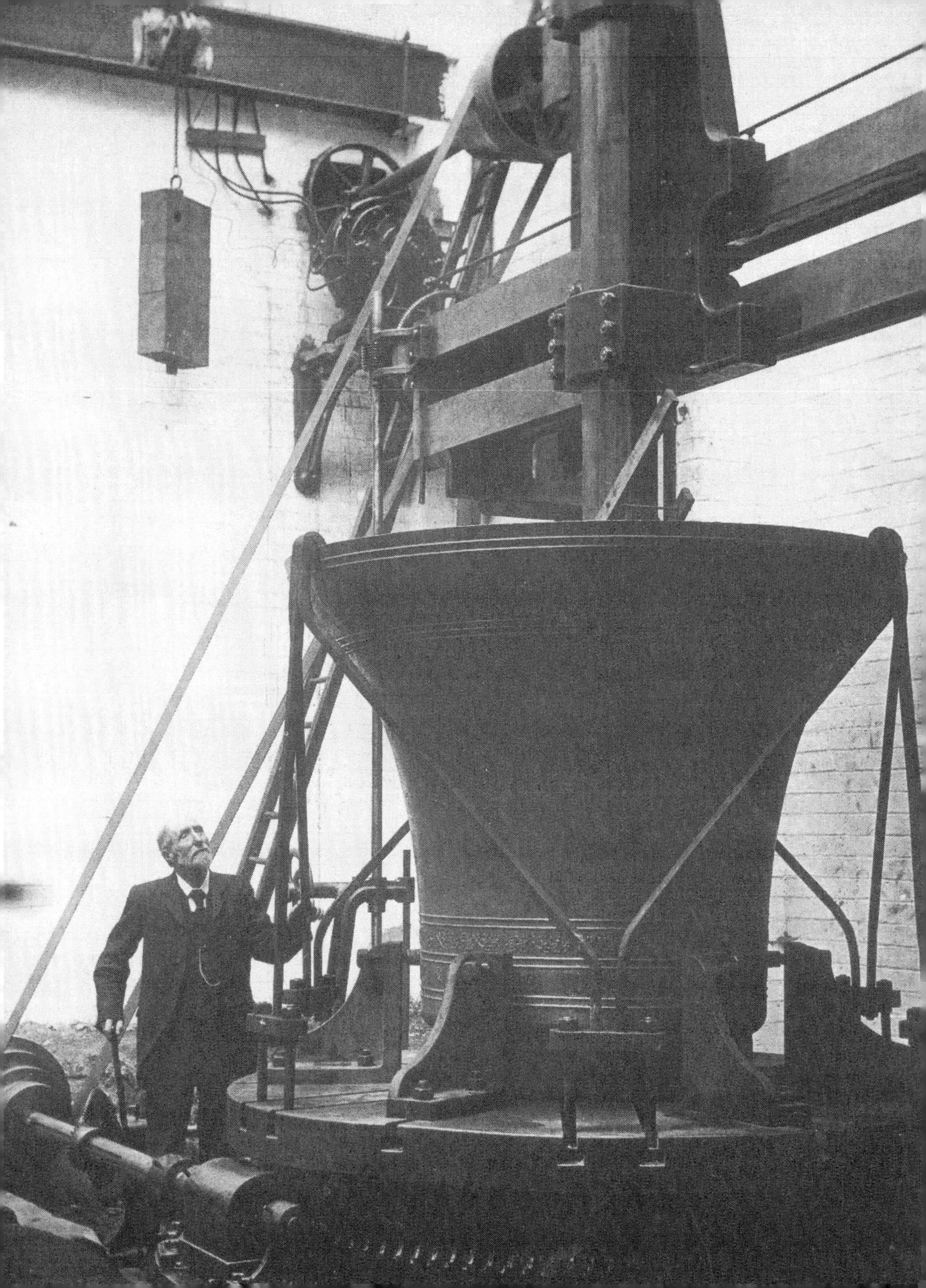

tuning machine and girder store building. This space was then turned into a yard where they built the brick-lined pits to mould enormous bells.

The bellfoundry was able to be taken onwards and upwards by his two sons, John William II and Edmund Denison. They were both very musical, and Edmund Denison developed a keen business sense.

A clock maker, Gillett & Brand from Croydon, were casting small bells needed for their clocks and eventually were to become a fierce rival to Taylor's in building carillons. A complaint to Lord Grimthorpe from Taylor's that they were implying they had cast the Manchester town hall bells merited a quick reply. 'Though Gillett & Brand are good clockmakers, I am sorry to say I consider their behaviour in matters of this kind so discreditable that I shall be less inclined to recommend them than I have been.' So that was a justified complaint with a very good result! Any company that was out of favour with Lord Grimthorpe was going to have problems! Apart from Lord Grimthorpe, the Taylor foundry was still looked on benevolently by John Stainer, the organist at St. Paul's, and Canon Cattley from Worcester Cathedral. William Wooding Starmer (1866-1927) was a prolific composer of religious music and a devotee of carillons and had heard Jef Denyn play many times. He was to become a real friend of the Taylor family and very influential in helping them to develop tip-top carillons. It's not just what you know; it's who you know as well!

In the first year that John William II and Denison were in charge, new bell work was slow to come in. The tide soon changed, and there was an enormous amount of work being done for Irish Roman Catholic churches. Work for Trinity House picked up as well, and this company looked after all the buoys at sea, a lot of which had bells. As the sea rocked the buoy, hammers hit the bell. From 1900-1909, the total tonnage of bells cast was 710 tons and in 1910, a record eighty-one tons. All these new bells were an enormous amount of work and the re-hanging of existing sets of bells continued as well.

In 1905, just before he died, John William I had come to an arrangement with a Dutch company. In return for any work which they steered in Taylor's direction, they were given 5% commission. This was a 'Gentlemen's agreement' with no legal documentation and fell by the wayside after John William died. In 1913, this contract was properly drawn up and was very productive until World War I broke out.

Work in the UK and the colonies continued to come in, and John William II spent a lot of Sundays going to do inspections, suggesting work, and clinching the deal. All work when war broke out was severely curtailed, with real difficulties in transport. The Midland railway, their main incoming and outgoing route for bells and fittings, could only transport items for war use. The Ministry of Munitions restricted normal trade from metallurgical suppliers, and even if Taylor's could find a supply of copper and tin, it was now 'money with order' only. No cheque in the post, no metal!

Taylor's were forced to apply for work along with other companies in Leicestershire whose work was controlled by the War Department, and they were given the job of machining two types of high explosive shell cases. 60% of the output from the foundry was now devoted to war work. At one stage, Taylor's were told that their production of shell cases was higher in number than they had been instructed to produce. Making too many shell casings? Surely that was a good thing? Obviously not! Many of the workforce, apart from moulders in the foundry proper, had been called up to fight, but moulders were considered to be carrying out essential war work. Taylor's were told to employ female labour to operate the machines in the main works with a night shift. Female machinists? Whatever next!

John William II had been married since 1884, and his first son (John William of course) was born in 1885. Another son followed in 1886, two daughters in 1888 and 1889, and a son, Pryce, in 1891. Together with a further son, Arnold Taylor born in 1894, Pryce became involved in the bellfoundry until war broke out, when all the sons enlisted. At the end of 1894, another daughter, Gwendoline, came into the world. All three daughters finished their education at a 'finishing academy' in Leipzig in Germany. Finishing schools for young ladies continued their academic learning, but the emphasis was on culture and the correct manner of becoming a member of society with social graces. Another subject taught was how to snare a good husband! Obviously a very useful thing! Young ladies spent one year learning how to be accepted into society and flutter their eyelids when considered appropriate.

After the first two daughters came back home, they were set on to work for the bellfoundry and sent off to trade fairs (often abroad) to promote Taylor bells. An ability to mingle with posh people who might order bells was considered very useful, and the daughters had language skills as well. Gwen, as she became known, was set to work in the tuning office attached to the area where the new machines cut metal off the inside of the bells. She learnt the vital skill of being able to say, 'Cut here' and tuned a great many bells including two complete carillons.

John William II lost his wife in 1904 after an illness that had stopped them travelling abroad as much. He married again in 1909 and had a daughter, Margaret, born in 1911, and a son, Paul, in 1914. John William had developed a real interest in the new-fangled 'auto mobiles' and volunteered himself and one of his cars to help the War Office. He drove senior army staff around the country during the war from January 1916. By the end of the war, he had clocked up 20,000 miles! Wars herald tragedy, and three of his sons who had enlisted were killed in the war in France. This was terrible for him, and it is said he never recovered. He was taken ill whilst inspecting some bells in March 1919 and died the following June at the relatively young age of sixty-six.

His youngest son, Pryce Taylor, was the only one of his sons who came back from the war, although he had been wounded in France and invalided home. He returned to the bellfoundry to become the manager at the beginning of 1919, so he and Denison both took over the reins. Until he died in 1919, John William II and Denison had managed to clock up 717 tons of new bells coming out of the foundry, despite the war curtailment.

13. Post 1919

'For bells are the voice of the church; They have tones that touch and search the hearts of young and old.'
The Bells of San Blas - Henry Wadsworth Longfellow

From 1919, when Denison was aged fifty-five, he found himself in sole charge of the foundry apart from his nephew Pryce who was aged twenty-eight and had survived World War I. His two nieces, Josephine and Phyllis, still went to exhibitions and trade fairs, and a bell was certainly taken to a Dublin exhibition. His other niece, Gwen, started tuning bells in 1920. Paul, his nephew from his father's second wife, was only five years old. Both Denison and Pryce were quite capable of tuning bells, but they were often away. Chris Pickford, an extremely respected archivist and bell historian, is jointly in charge of the Taylor archive company, as well as being a bellringer with a very good ear. He recounts that, one day in the 1960s, a ringer was in the works when the tenor bell from St. Thomas's church at Stourbridge, cast and tuned by Denison in 1935, had come back to Taylor's as part of a re-hanging project. Paul was very impressed with bells that Denison had tuned and hearing this bell in the works from his office he immediately remarked, 'Ah, Denny!' in admiration of the tuning.

Cyril Johnston, from the bell foundry Gillett & Johnston in Croydon, had not yet decided that he was going to compete with Taylor's in the carillon market, and in 1920 a tentative meeting between Denison, Cyril and Mears took place. It was agreed that they would standardise their prices and quotes, so forming a cartel. Denison and Mears soon decided that Cyril was under cutting them if it suited him! So after eighteen months it all fell apart. Gentlemen's agreements in 1920 were not of much use in a competitive market place. In 1920, John (Jack) Fidler came to work at the bellfoundry and soon became a very important employee. He carried out inspections of bells all over the country, so that quotes to carry out work could be drawn up. He is another person who stayed at Taylor's for yonks!

I have seen, or have, lists of carillon jobs, large single bells, and important rings of bells produced after the war. Some of them we have dealt with already, but when the lists are all amalgamated they are staggering! Try not to nod off; it took me ages. Denison had prepared publicity brochures that were widely distributed in the US, and between 1921 and 1929 there were eighteen carillons and chimes sent off. It was unusual if the largest bell was less than two tons. Large single bells were pouring out, such as 'Great George', the nine and a half ton slow swinging bell for Bristol University in 1925. Other large single bells went to Seoul in South Korea, Harvard University, a church at Ann Arbor in America, and a Catholic church in Ireland, that were all over two tons. Clock bells went to Shanghai with a six ton hour bell, and Brisbane town hall in Australia had a four ton hour bell. How did they get all these orders from all over the globe?

Church bells were a market that Denison and Pryce knew they could always rely on but never ignore. They split the country into areas and both went out getting work. New bells, re-hangs, and other work were their bread and butter, and what if carillons dried up? Their relatively new tuning achievements helped spread their fame, and some 'old style' rings were recast. St. Margaret's in Leicester was one of the large jobs that John William I had done before he settled in Loughborough, and a recast ring, augmented to twelve bells, was put in during 1921. Bradford and Rotherham had a new ring of ten, and in 1928 their flagship 1868 ring of twelve plus semi-tone bells at Worcester Cathedral was recast.

They had complied with Edmund Beckett Denison who insisted that the Worcester bells were to his contract terms, so very heavy and thick, but because Taylor's made them as he told them to they had put in the new ring of twelve at St. Paul's Cathedral. Well worth keeping him happy! By now, Taylor bells were of a better profile and were also very accurately tuned as well. So they boiled up the whole lot from 1868 except the four ton hour bell.

The major job in 1926 was the glorious ring at York Minster. The one bell still left was 'Great Peter', a slow-swinging bourdon bell cast by Charles and George Mears in 1845. We have commented on how the soundbow was three-quarters of an inch thicker on one side, but at over ten tons it was the largest bell ever cast in Great Britain up till then. It was supposed to be a slow-swinger, but twenty men couldn't get it horizontal, and neither could thirty men. Thirty men? Where did they get them all from? A big hammer was made to hit the bell that by now was going to be stationary. So not a shining example of English bellfounding! Denison was dying to recast this bell, and one of his very useful patrons was Canon Nolleth from Beverley Minster. He pushed for 'Great Peter' to be recast and undertook to cover the cost when money was slow in coming in. The order was placed with Taylor's who started making the moulds for this eight feet eight inch diameter bell in the big pit in the foundry yard as soon as the case and core plate arrived. The old bell was to be broken up for scrap of course, but the moulds were ready before it had been lowered down the tower. Denison had enough metal in stock so the cast went ahead.

When the six ton Sydney hour bell was cast a few years before, the moulds came apart and the bell was scrap. To the horror of everybody, the same thing happened again. Two useless moulds and metal everywhere in the pit. What a tragedy! Denison was ill at home at the time, so Johnny Oldham broke the news to Canon Nolleth. He was very upset, but decided he would give Denison three-hundred pounds 'to bear my part in the loss.'

Right: 'Great Peter', the ten and three quarter ton slow-swinging bourdon bell for York Minster, cast in 1927, fitted with 'balanced' headstock, wheel, and counterbalanced clapper that weighs just over one ton.
Photo: Taylor archive

"GREAT PETER"
THE BOURDON BELL OF YORK MINSTER
WEIGHT 10 TONS 16 CWTS 2 QRS 22 LBS.   NOTE E♭

What a nice man. Otherwise, the disaster was kept a big secret! Second time round, on April 22nd, 1927, it was a splendid bell and went onto the very large tuning machine before being sent off to York with a balanced horse-shoe headstock.

This was the first bell that tipped the scales over ten tons, apart from 'Great Paul', closely followed by the Lake Wales Bok Tower carillon bourdon of the same weight, and soon afterwards an identical Ann Arbor carillon bourdon. At York Minster, 'Great Peter' was handed over by Denison to Mr. Green, their Clerk of Works, for 'safe keeping'. They seem to have made a good job looking after it so far!

David Potter, in his booklet about the bells at York Minster, narrates that after the bell had been dedicated and swung in the cathedral, a local newspaper reported, 'It was a thrilling moment. The sound reverberated through the great cathedral and was heard all over the city and far beyond.' Instead of hordes of men needing to be rustled up, one man can ring it up to the horizontal. This magnificent bell weighs close to eleven tons at 216 hundredweight. The counterbalanced clapper came back to Taylor's in 1983 to be refurbished. It is absolutely enormous and weighs well over one ton! There was one fly in the ointment. The old Mears bell, that was stated to weigh just less than eleven tons, weighed three quarters of a ton (fifteen hundredweight) less than it was supposed to! Just some more metal to be paid for! If Mears took it somewhere to be weighed, like 'Big Ben II', the scales were duff, or it was a big fib. In 1987, a special dedication service was held as it was sixty years since the work on the ring of twelve, and 'Great Peter', was completed. A plaque made of bellmetal was put in the ringing chamber recording the vision of Canon Nolleth. When 'Great Peter', which has been accurately tuned, is rung with the ring of bells as a bourdon bell it really sounds sensational!

It is fairly easy to see where the 1,000 tons of bells went to from 1920-1929. In 1927, Taylor's advertised for a works manager to look after 'about 100' employees! The early 1930s saw a depression in trade throughout the country, but there was still work coming in, and Denison continued to invest in copper and tin whenever the price was right.

'Emmanuel', a slow-swinging bell just less than four tons, went to a Catholic church in Exeter in 1931. A ring of ten was installed in 1932 at Boston Stump in Lincolnshire where there had originally been a thirty-six bell carillon from a Belgian bellfoundry, installed in 1867. Amongst other rings of bells, 1936 was when a superb ring of twelve bells and two semitone bells were put in at Buckfast Abbey in Devon. This abbey is really interesting! It was resurrected in 1882 by French Benedictine monks who were apparently exiled from a monastery in France. Whatever had they done? Dr. James Gale owned the land from 1872, and when he wanted to sell it, he advertised it as 'a grand acquisition that could be restored to its original purpose'. He got that right! The monks bought the land and started building on the site of the first abbey, demolished in the 1500s. Handily, it was now partly a quarry.

Right: The Buckfast Abbey seven and a half ton slow-swinging bourdon bell 'Hosanna' in the works with the headstock fitted, in 1936. This was installed along with the ring of fourteen bells.
Photo: Taylor archive

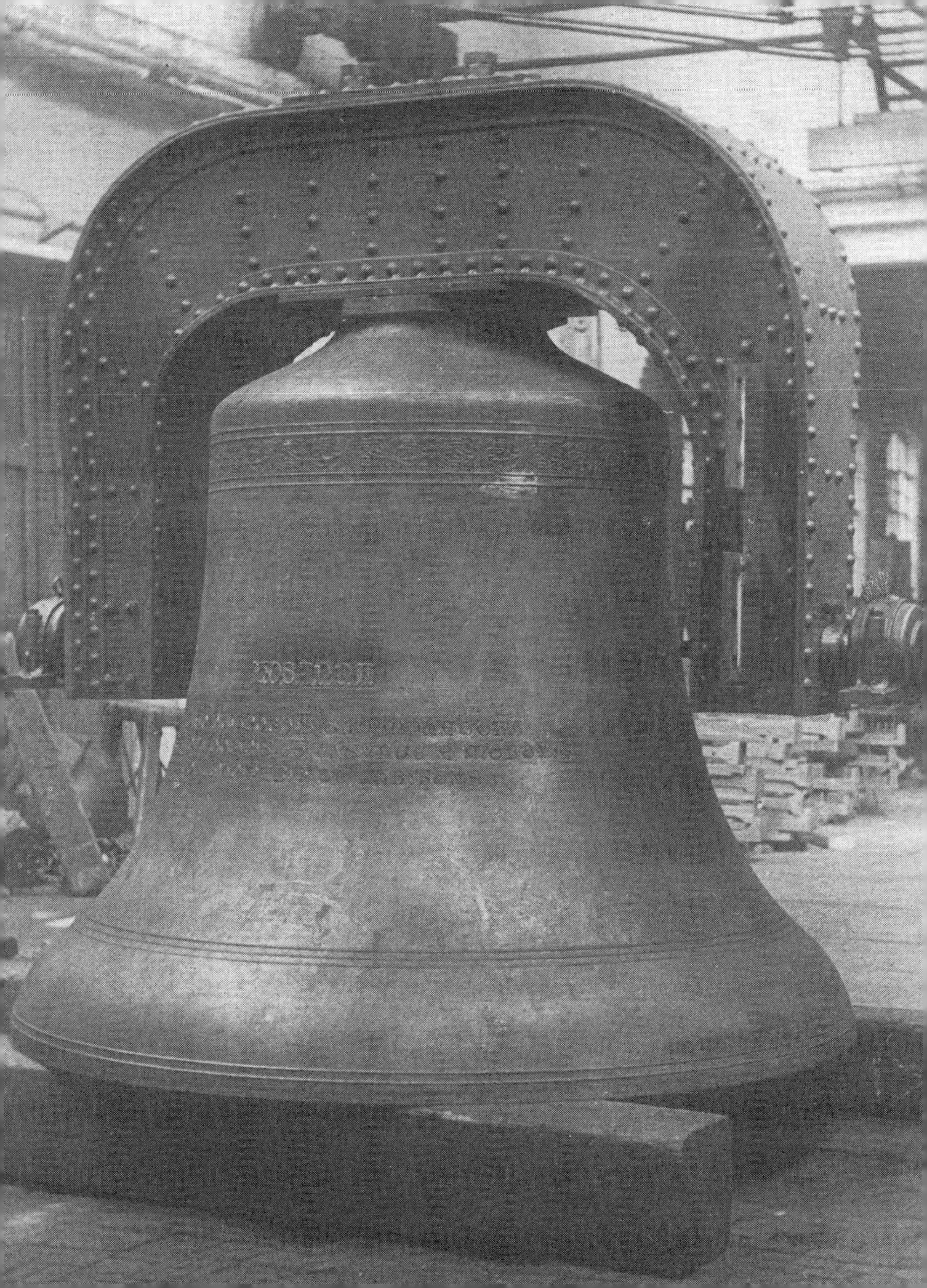

To get some money in, in the 1890s the monks started peddling 'Buckfast Tonic Wine' which was very potent and linked to antisocial behaviour, especially in Scotland! Oh dear. The abbey was re-consecrated in 1932 and fully completed by 1938. A previous 1910 ring of fourteen from Warner's had only been installed after the war in 1922 when the central tower was completed, but Taylor's boiled them all up to make the new ring. These wonderful bells from Taylor's were completed with a slow-swinging bourdon bell called 'Hosanna', which tipped the scales at over seven tons.

Walsall now had a new ring of twelve, and thirteen bells went to Leeds Minster with a two ton tenor, and ten bells went to Ripon Cathedral. Just after the Buckfast Abbey job, Wigan had a ring of ten, and Manchester Town Hall had a ring of thirteen with an additional ten bells to form a complete chime. In 1937, they cast a ring of thirteen for Winchester Cathedral, with a tenor over one and a half tons, and another early ring from Taylor's, at Leicester Cathedral, was boiled up to make a new ring of thirteen.

What amazes me is where did they put all this lot in the works? In the foundry proper, it must have been extremely hectic. They were splodging cast iron everywhere as well, for headstocks, frames for church bells, clappers and a lot of other bits and pieces for carillons. In the main works it was a tradition that all new bells with new frames were completely erected for testing, with the wheels and the whole shoot except for the ropes. So this takes up space, and they were erecting complete carillons as well, the whole lot.

Carillon frames were made from girders and might be twenty feet square and thirty to forty feet high, and all the bells, transmission, and the clavier were connected up. There was a brick-lined pit under the erection area where the clavier usually went. They often seem to have had two carillons on the go at the same time, so how did they manage that? I have absolutely no idea. If there were rings of bells where they were being re-hung in an existing frame in the church, they still had to give the bells and fittings house room. At least there was no frame!

In 1910 the plans for the Anglican Cathedral in Liverpool were approved. It was designed by Giles Gilbert Scott who was only twenty-nine years old, although his father and grandfather were famous architects. Apart from his age, it turned out he was a Roman Catholic! A Roman Catholic? Designing an Anglican cathedral? Was it legal? This wasn't just any old cathedral, it was only the third new Anglican cathedral in England since the Reformation (When the Protestants told the Catholics to get lost). It is the longest cathedral anywhere, from end to end, and the fifth largest in the world, with an enormous central tower rising up 300 feet. So this was serious stuff. It was built in bits, and the tower was eventually started, but in 1939 work almost stopped for the second time because of World Wars. The central tower was handed over in 1941, but it wasn't totally finished as Scott was still installing twiddly bits, and there were no bells yet. Thomas Bartlett had left a load of money for a ring of bells in 1912, but Giles Gilbert Scott, for some obscure reason, went to Whitechapel. Oh dear!

Apart from these thirteen ringing bells there was to be an enormous bourdon bell as well. Sounds better now! A circular reinforced concrete base was constructed, with reinforced concrete slabs sticking up in a circle, like spokes on a wheel, with one bell between every pair of spokes. Whitechapel suggested this design which was termed a 'radial frame', and the weight went down via steel trusses. Whitechapel had been fuming since 1878 when Taylor's supplied the wonderful ring of twelve at St. Paul's Cathedral, just up the road. To get back at them, Whitechapel installed the heaviest ring of bells in the world at Liverpool. Where St. Paul's tenor was just over three tons, they put in a ring of twelve with the tenor just over four tons. So ours is bigger than yours! The ringers really, really need a semitone bell to ring the eight 'lightest' ones. Apart from being the heaviest ring, they are about 230 feet up the tower, and a space between the ringing chamber and the bell chamber was to act as a sound-deadening area. It obviously works very well as ringers complain that the acoustics are terrible, and one comment describes them as 'abysmal.' Well, never mind. After Whitechapel cast these bells in 1939, the war and uncompleted work in the tower meant they weren't taken to Liverpool until 1951.

Taylor's were given the order for the enormous bourdon bell that was going to sit on some more concrete pillars sticking up above the centre of the frame. Giles Gilbert Scott must have had some doubts about his tower at this stage, or the radial frame, because he designed it so that the really big bell was hung dead. This bell was to be called 'Great George' in honour of King George V. The first letter of the biblical inscriptions on each bell had to spell out the fourteen letters of Thomas Bartlett's name, so this was done with the ring of thirteen bells, and the Taylor bell, 'Great George'. Thomas Bartlett's ashes are kept in the ringing chamber.

Taylor's thought they ought to get some more use out of the case and core plate for 'Great Paul', so they dusted them off for the event. As they were designed for a nine feet six inches diameter bell, why not make another one? The money had been donated in 1937 by a baronet and his wife and other family members, so when they had a few spare days they started on the core and case. They knew it wasn't going to be rushed up to Liverpool any day soon, but the war chiefs said they could cast it in 1940. Probably Taylor's thought the sooner they cast it, the sooner they would get paid, or perhaps the Liverpool baron put the finger screws on the war department. Perhaps he said, 'I want my bell. Let them cast it!' There was one condition. All the windows in the foundry had to be covered with black-out material, as work was done in the late evenings and sometimes through the night. I don't suppose they were curtains with valances and nice tassels; just plain sheets. The disaster with 'Great Peter' was still fresh in everybody's minds, so when the case and core were clamped together and lowered into the pit, twenty men worked in shifts for thirty-six hours to ram sand and soil down from the bottom up to the top. I would have thought there weren't twenty left at the bellfoundry, so perhaps they hired some local muscle. The inscription on the bell reads that Baron Vestey had provided the dosh in 1937.

In 1940, Denison was still having bouts of bad health, but Paul Taylor had been working at the foundry since he finished his university education, and had been made a junior partner in 1935 when he was twenty-one. He would definitely have been involved in closely watching the moulds being prepared, which were heavily reinforced with metal pegs. All four furnaces were loaded up with just over twenty three tons of metal, and getting the metal up to temperature in all the furnaces at the same time was going to be really tricky. If they had to slightly slow down melting the metal in one furnace or speed up another one, burning off metal may well have occurred. They started lighting them at 11a.m. on July 20th and cast the bell just after 8p.m.! Nine hours shovelling coal, but they had never used all the furnaces at once before! Some of the bods had to stay on to feed the head of the bell, which took another three hours! Everybody then called it a day, or a night, and they left the bell to cool for nine days. I bet they knelt down and said a few prayers (or a lot), before and after.

Trevor Jennings tells us that the bell was put on a low-loader lorry and driven straight round to where the big tuning machine was. I don't think this is right as bells need a hole drilling in the top before anything else! Bells can initially be lifted up with chains that have end bits that go under the lip, but they have to have a hole to go on a peg on the tuning machine. There are special lifting devices that fit into a hole whenever any other lifting is required. Really big bells had to be taken to Brush Engineering, about a mile away, where they obligingly drilled the centre and bolt holes. I think this would have been possible, even in the war. Trying to drill holes by hand (and they needed five) is not at all easy. The other thing that was always done was to weigh the bell 'as cast', and this meant a trip to the weighbridge. On the way to be drilled (assuming I'm right), it was weighed as being almost exactly the same weight as 'Great Paul', at sixteen and a half tons. It didn't mean that all the metal put in the furnace had disappeared because there would have been a lot left over. And why not!? Running out of metal? God forbid! Taylor's could have established the weight 'as cast' by weighing all the metal chippings as they were machined off and then the finished bell, but I think it went onto the weighbridge!

When 'Great George' came back, it was taken to the big tuning machine, and Paul Taylor would have been climbing all over it. To mark 'cut here', he would have been climbing down a ladder! The note required after tuning was one whole note, or two semitones, lower than 'Great Paul' to match in with the ring of twelve from Whitechapel. At least this time, the nine feet six inches diameter bell could be tuned, and in the process they machined off nearly two tons. What happened to the tank turrets they were supposed to be machining on the big tuning machine for the war office? Were the army told, 'Just postpone the invasion for a few weeks as Taylor's are tuning a big bell.'

It then went back to the weighbridge (and it had to be taken there then) for the finished weight which was fourteen and three quarter tons. 'Great George', destined for Liverpool, was then the second heaviest bell in Britain, the largest tuned bell, the bell with the deepest musical note, and the same diameter as 'Great Paul'. The bell was suspended off the ground in the open yard beside the foundry with a simple (well, very large) girder bolted on at the top. Lots of people came to see the bell and have their photographs taken, but there was no big hurry. It wasn't put onto another lorry for the journey to Liverpool until April 15th, 1951! Good job bells don't go rusty.

Right: *The fourteen and three quarter ton 'Great George' cast in 1940, with the substantial girder headstock.* Photo: Taylor Archive

MAKE A JOYFUL NOISE UNTO THE LORD ALL YE LANDS

TO THE GLORY OF GOD
IN THANKFULNESS FOR GREAT MERCIES
RECEIVED AND IN AFFECTIONATE REMEMBRANCE
OF THE CITY OF LIVERPOOL
WILLIAM BARON VESTEY OF KINGSWOOD
AND HIS WIFE EVELYN
WITH
SIR EDMUND HOYLE VESTEY BARONET
AND HIS WIFE ELLEN
GAVE ME IN THE YEAR
1937
AND IN MEMORY OF KING GEORGE V
NAMED ME
GREAT GEORGE

So let's stick with 'Great George' for the moment, after it set off in 1951. Pickford's turned up with a substantial lorry, so none of the problems with 'Great Paul' in 1882. It was ready to be taken off the lorry at Liverpool on May 7th, but to get it under the tower, where it was going to be hoisted up, was a big problem.

On April 25th, Frank Godfrey, Taylor's carillon designer, was in Kansas installing a carillon. He was interviewed by a local newspaper, *The Lawrence Daily Journal*, and 'Great George' was mentioned. Frank told the story that the cathedral aisle (the bit you walk down between the seats) was laid with marble tiles, but the floor was hollow in the middle. Giles Gilbert Scott had not thought about manoeuvring this very heavy bell. Frank told the reporter that it took him over two months to work out how to pull the bell down the aisle with the weight only at the sides! He also told the reporter that he only remembered two scrap bells in twenty-three years of working at Taylor's! Well, he was away a lot. No! I'm being facetious. I'm sure he was right, and he started work the year after the 'Great Peter' disaster.

When 'Great George' was finally under the tower, the company Machinery Installation Ltd. from Acton, with Ronald Harris in charge, were at the top with a specially built winch. The day before, they had whizzed the Whitechapel bells up, but the time it took to hoist 'Great George' sounds like the hours put in when it was cast! Twelve men were in three teams of four, and they hand operated the winch, with each team working for ten minutes, and then a twenty minute rest. They started at 9a.m., and got the job done nearly twelve hours later, with the winch continually turned 25,000 times.

It was quite a tight fit when it was 160 feet off the ground because of another round hole in the ceiling like at St. Paul's, but this time the stonemasons didn't have to make it bigger. When it got to the top, an Irishman, who was one of the labourers, hit it with a lump hammer to see if it sounded all right! He didn't crack it, but they tore strips off him. 'It's not supposed to be struck until the Queen is here.' So well done Paddy! It was officially dedicated on June 11th and officially rung with a rope fixed onto the counterbalanced clapper. Paul Taylor went there with Johnny Oldham, and he told me decades later, 'It sounded magnificent!' The men who told Paddy off had lied because the Queen didn't turn up until 1978, when she declared the whole shoot of this enormous cathedral finished and broke out the champagne. Or, as this was Liverpool, probably barrels of stout.

After the war, metal prices were controlled until 1949, so if it was available it was not too expensive. Casting bells and other work could be carried out again, with things slowly returning to normal. I think Denison virtually retired during 1945 as Paul was back from his war service, and Denison suffered from intermittent illness and gout. He died in 1947, a very clever man business-wise who readily adapted to new markets.

The fifty-five bell Niagara Falls carillon was completed in 1947, and two chimes for Malta. The largest bell for one of them was just over four tons, and the other just under this. Malta (they like bells there) was the destination for another two single bells of four tons and two tons. The Kansas University carillon helped keep the pot boiling, and also a ring of bells supplied to Adelaide in 1946. A ring of ten for Grantham were followed on in 1947 with a new ring of thirteen for Wakefield Cathedral, and ten bells went to Lichfield Cathedral. Blackburn had a ring of ten in 1949, and in 1951 a splendid ring of thirteen was put in the free-standing Evesham Bell Tower. This tower was built about 1530 for the bells at Evesham Abbey, and John Molder is credited with starting it off in 1524 by leaving some loot in his will.

In 1950, a three ton plus hour bell went off to Oporto in Portugal, the second largest city, famous for the fortified wine called port. If you don't know why port is a fortified wine, I don't either. A recast eleventh bell at Cirencester went off in 1952 to go with the remaining ring of twelve, mostly cast by Rudhall's, a Gloucester bellfoundry, between 1713 and 1786. Taylor's had recast one of the bells in 1895 and supplied a semitone bell. Tonnage of bells increased during the 1950s, and 300 bells were cast in 1959. Between pauses for breath, in 1961 the Southwell Minster ring of twelve were recast with a semitone bell added. I know where that is. Stamping ground of my early childhood! Tewksbury had their bells recast in 1962 into a ring of twelve, and St. Andrew's Cathedral at Sydney in Australia had a ring of ten in 1964, later made up to thirteen.

A chime went off to Nicosia in Cyprus in 1962, with the largest bell weighing in at over four tons, and Archbishop Makarios came to see them cast, which is where the photographs came from. He was the head man of the Greek Orthodox religion, and the first Prime Minister of Cyprus for two terms, starting from 1960. He probably came to Britain for some high flying meeting, and they ferried him up to Loughborough to have a gander at his bells. When he died in 1977 he was buried in a tomb he had specially designed, on a hilltop at a monastery, where he had first been an apprentice monk in 1932. Going to see his tomb in Kykkos is included in a list of the ten things you should go and see if you are dropping into Cyprus. I'll try and remember that, just in case.

14. 'A Thirsty Market'

'Music is God's gift to man, the only art of Heaven given to earth, the only art of earth we take to Heaven.'
Walter Savage Landor

From 1895, Taylor's were producing bells that were absolutely in tune within each bell and with all the other bells in a set. Their experiments and solutions were intended to make rings of church bells sound better, but they had found out how to duplicate the tuning of the Hemony bells. Taylor's could now produce modern carillons unrivalled by any other bellfounder. A chime for Iowa State College in the US was supplied in 1896, the first accurately tuned bells to be installed out of Europe. On one of their trips to Belgium, John William II met Jef Denyn, and he became a firm family friend.

It was obvious that Taylor bells and his skilled playing could be an absolutely winning combination. In 1904 they made an experimental carillon of forty small bells installed adjacent to the tuning shop with a clavier of their design. It was the first accurately tuned instrument in England, and Jef Denyn came to give a short series of recitals. Through their agent in Holland, Taylor's supplied two replacement bells for Utrecht cathedral. English bells in a Dutch cathedral to rival the best bells in Holland? Whatever was the world coming to? Gradually, it was accepted that trying to repair old linkage systems was a waste of time. Install a complete new system like Mechlin, keep any Hemony bells, and boil up the others. This was exactly what the Hemony brothers had been doing in their time! Carillonneurs could now play on tip-top instruments and try to be as good as Jef. Nobody was of course; he was streets in front!

William Wooding Starmer, the very knowledgeable organist, composer, and carillon enthusiast, continually gave advice to Taylor's on how to improve the clavier design to give the ability to play with greater expression and standardise the layout of the levers, called 'batons', and pedals. He also discussed how the placement of the smallest bells gave the best sound. Whilst in Belgium and Holland he had decided which carillons had a poor sound because the installation or bell location was cruddy.

Taylor's installed a modern tuned chime of twenty-two bells at the Bournville suburb of Birmingham, and a two octave set at Appingedam in Holland in 1911. In 1913 they replaced the Dutch carillon at Vlissingen (Flushing, in English) that had been destroyed by fire, and the next year supplied a light carillon at Eindhoven. The onset of World War I then put paid to any more carillons being dispatched from Loughborough, and several Belgian ones were destroyed by shelling. Jef Denyn gave his last recital at Mechlin in August 1914, and as his house had been bombed, he came to England with his family and lodged with William Starmer. The Germans wanted an inventory of Belgian carillons (to be melted down of course) but Cardinal Mercier, who had his palace at Mechlin, forcefully pointed out that bells and churches were protected under the Hague Convention of 1910. It didn't stop shells destroying towers of course, but it did stop the Germans collaring every single bell.

I have mentioned that Gillett & Brand in Croydon were clock makers dating back to 1844. Arthur Johnston purchased a partnership in 1877 changing the name to Gillett & Johnston, and they soon started casting clock bells. His son Cyril joined the company in 1902, and he installed a small tuning machine in 1905 and a bigger one in 1909. A set of five clock bells he made in 1906 were condemned as being badly out of tune after William Starmer had been called in to give his opinion. His advice was that the bells should be sent back to Gillett & Johnston and they should order new ones from Taylor's!

Cyril immediately realized that somehow he had to produce bells that were as well in tune as Taylor bells if he was to compete with them. George Elphick, an acknowledged expert on bells, published a book in 1988 entitled *The Craft of the Bellfounder*. In a chapter on tuning he writes, 'The firms of Gillett & Johnston and John Warner and Sons are said to have obtained secretly a Taylor-tuned bell and cut it in half to see what they could make of it. Only Gillett's solved the problem'. Definitely industrial espionage and not the only example by far! Cyril basically copied the Taylor profile but told people he had studied the literature that a clergyman called Canon Simpson had published when Taylor's were perfecting their tuning in the 1890s. Cyril proclaimed to all and sundry that he had worked it out for himself and called his 'discovery' Simpson tuning! In 1907, he recast the five condemned clock bells.

Cyril Johnston is a very important English bellfounder, and from this period in time he certainly became the most famous. In 1919 he managed to wangle the order to recast the Royal Exchange ring of bells when they wanted some of them retuned and others recast. Taylor's and Whitechapel were obvious contenders for this work, but Cyril managed to get the job, a very important feather in his cap. He told the committee that was collecting quotes that there were no accurately tuned bells in London (which was true), and he was the only bellfounder who could rectify this as he had found out for himself how to do this! After the war, he proclaimed his bells were as good as Taylor's (they weren't, at that stage), and he entered the carillon field in 1921. He became a major pain in the bum for Taylor's, so I need to explain something about him.

Born in 1884, Cyril was tall and imposing, and even men described him as being handsome. Women fell at his feet, and he scooped them up. He was a dandy, loved dancing, was witty, urbane, and very good company. Two of the regular words used to describe him were 'debonair' and 'dashing'. He was unashamedly a big social climber and cultivated every person he thought could be beneficial to him. Wining and dining people, not just women, was a favourite occupation, ideally in his bow tie and tails.

Until he was forty-six, he lived in the family home in Croydon together with his sister Nora who was two years younger. His mother, who had French origins, was a perfect hostess. Nora had started off with a career in the theatre, and she never married. The three of them held court, and important visitors were often asked to stay the night. Cyril assiduously courted publicity, and he turned his works into a show room. Anybody who was anybody was invited along, and he made sure that important newspapers, not just in England, knew what he was working on, had completed in his works, or when he was arriving somewhere to open a new carillon. He was always good for a story particularly if he had completed, or was installing, a big carillon. Journalists found him extremely approachable and a really interesting person, apart from being very photogenic.

Business wise, he was brash, overrode any doubts that he might not be able to do the work, agreed to delivery dates that were impossible, and shamelessly undercut other quotes. Having got a job he then 'talked the price up' citing extras and unforeseen work. He was often involved in disputes about money. On one big carillon job he asked for 80% when the carillon was delivered and 20% when it was in action. Along the way he asked for several advances for unforeseen work or price increases he claimed because of the price of bellmetal.

At Taylor's, he was nicknamed 'the great pirate' because he swarmed over Taylor jobs, copied any good ideas he came across, and continually boasted they were of his invention. He was perfectly happy to distort the truth or engage in outright lies and consistently stated that he had rediscovered the lost art of tuning bells, even when people knew it was a lie. He was a competent bellringer, and at one enormous bash for ringers at his works he organized coaches to take them to different towers, a lavish tea, and a jazz band in the evening. Quoting for one ring of bells, he stated he would make a gift to the church of 10% of the price if he was given the job! This didn't go down at all well and was considered below board and very shady dealing. On other jobs, he told the client he would cast one or several of the bells at cost! One description of him was 'a ruthless professional'.

The Whitechapel bellfoundry supplied an eleven bell chime in 1918 to Middletown in Connecticut, their first venture into the American market, but they didn't adopt the Taylor new tuning system until 1926-1927. In 1966 it was enlarged to sixteen bells, but I don't know if the 'old style' tuning of the existing bells was amended. Taylor's had to delay installing a chime for Cobh (Queenstown) in Ireland until the war was over (later extended to forty-two bells), but immediately after this, a thirty-nine bell carillon was ordered for Armagh. In 1921, two Dutch emigrants ordered a Taylor carillon for Rotterdam with four complete octaves and a bourdon bell weighing four tons. This was the heaviest Dutch carillon for over 100 years and set new standards for carillon design and tuning. 1921 was the best year ever for Taylor's although there was supposed to be a recession, and they made a ten bell chime for Yale University with a 6 ft 9 ins bass bell. This was increased to fifty-four bells in 1954, with a total weight of forty-three tons.

Taylor's supplied a thirty-seven bell War Memorial carillon for the Parkside Mostyn School in 1922, and made the first modern twenty-three bell chime to be introduced into America for the Portuguese Fishermen's church in Gloucester, Massachusetts. It was then enlarged to thirty-one bells in 1924. The same year, Gillett & Johnston put in a twenty-three bell chime at a church in Toronto with the bass bell just less than four tons, and Cyril gained an important foothold in Canada. From a photograph that purports to show this bell on the larger tuning machine he bought in 1909, this was almost the biggest bell he could tune. Before the Toronto bells were sent off, Cyril erected it at the Wembley Exhibition centre!

Carillons produced by Taylor's for America from 1922-1926 included Gloucester, Andover, Birmingham in Alabama, Morristown, New Jersey, and Germantown near Philadelphia. Thirty-two bells had been sent off to Cape Town City Hall in 1923 to match existing bells, and the Prince of Wales obligingly cut the ribbon.

Cyril put in carillons in America at Plainfield in 1923 and Cohasset in 1924. This one was cast when Cyril was still finding out how to produce satisfactory small bells, and Taylor's recast thirty-seven of these in 1990. In 1924 Cyril put in a twenty-three bell chime at a large department store in Old Bond Street in Mayfair in London; a very good location!

Over in New York, there were extremely important decisions being made regarding a church built by John D. Rockefeller, known as Rockefeller junior (1874-1960), who was looking after most of the family fortune. He paid $1.5 million to build the Parkside Avenue Baptist church affectionately called 'the millionaire's church', finished in 1922, and he wanted some bells. In America and Canada, the first accurately tuned carillons had not yet arrived, and there were hundreds of chimes. Quite often there were ten, twelve, or fourteen bells, played from devices a bit similar to the batons on carillon keyboards. They were exactly the same as rings of bells in England that went up the scale in the same way. If the bottom bell of the chime was note 'C' then all the other bells were the white notes going up from that one with no black notes, or sometimes just one. They were all hung dead of course.

Rockefeller asked some of his staff to find out who made the best chimes, and the answer was that a company called Meneely in New York was the best American bellfoundry. This firm had been started by a Scotsman, and they were doing some tuning in the late 1890s, but they didn't undertake modern tuning until 1927. The next company that was suggested was Taylor's. Rockefeller decided he needed a consultant and approached Frederick C. Mayer who was organist and choirmaster at the very prestigious West Point Military Academy fifty miles from New York. Finished in 1920, a tower held twelve Meneely chime bells with the largest one weighing one and a half tons, and there was an organ with 14,000 pipes and 750 stops. If you remember this from an earlier chapter, the 'stops' determine what sounds you can make, and having 14,000 pipes resulted in a very swish organ! Mayer was delighted to be given the job of adviser, and the two men formed a partnership that would last for decades. He had heard that Taylor's were supplying a very heavy chime for Yale University with the biggest bell just slightly under six UK tons.

Top right: *The 6 ft 9 ins diameter largest bell of the chime of ten for Yale University being transferred to the large tuning machine in 1921.*
Photo: Taylor archive

Bottom right: *Leaving the works to be taken to Liverpool Docks.*
Photo: Taylor archive

YALE
UNIVERSITY
U.S.A.
CHIME OF TEN BELLS
JOHN TAYLOR & Co.
TELEPHONE
BANK 4845
LIVERPOOL.

Mayer had wanted to obtain a quote from Taylor's or Whitechapel in 1917 for his chime, but the war put paid to this idea. He told Rockefeller he had to check out the Yale job, but prices that Denison had been asked to supply for a chime were about the same as those from Meneely. Mayer didn't know too much about bells, but he was a quick learner, and he was told about the new Gillett and Johnston twenty-three bell chime very recently installed in Toronto.

The Taylor twenty-three bell chime at Gloucester that had not yet arrived had a bourdon bell the same weight as the bass bell in Mayer's Meneely chime. He went to see the Toronto chime that the Canadian carillonneur Percival Price played until 1925 and was absolutely bowled over! Install a ten or twelve bell chime? Forget that! He could see the possibility of Rockefeller having a really super perfectly tuned carillon, as the few existing ones in America were not at all well-tuned. The only trouble was, the Park Avenue tower was not very big!

Rockefeller trusted Mayer completely, and he hadn't ripped him off by asking for a salary or a big retainer; he was happy to have his expenses paid. Mayer knew that Rockefeller had a bottomless pocket, but he wanted to spend this money wisely.

Denison was asked to quote for a thirty-five bell carillon, and he sent over his standard prices. Rockefeller contacted the donor in Toronto who said their dealings with Cyril had been fine, and a musician sent to Croydon before they ordered it had been very impressed with Cyril and his hospitality! Denison arrived in America when the Yale chime was being put in and went to see Mayer and his Meneely chime. Denison was fairly blunt and said it was terrible which upset Mayer a bit! He also told Mayer that only Taylor's made good carillons and Cyril didn't really know what he was doing. Both these comments were basically true, but it wasn't very tactful.

So the stage became set for a contest between Cyril and Denison, not just regarding their products and achievements, but their personalities as well. Compared to Cyril, Denison was as dull as ditch water! He wasn't witty, debonair, or a social climber. He was a serious British businessman full stop, but he did have a very good product that greatly helped him achieve sales. He was a bachelor to the day he died, and as he was something of a martinet, he apparently had difficulty keeping male or female staff at his home. His main interests, apart from making bells, were playing tennis and occasional fox hunting. He was also a gentleman farmer who owned large areas of land. Mayer was regularly reporting back to Rockefeller and told him Denison had been quite rude about Cyril. Despite this, Denison was asked to supply a firm quote for the Parkside Baptist church, along with Cyril. Mayer stressed to Denison that an important carillon in New York with Rockefeller's money might lead to all sorts of things, but he didn't think Denison really understood this and thought it was just another job!

When the quotes came in, Cyril (who did understand that a New York carillon was a plum job) undercut Denison by over 25%. Mayer decided that he needed to know a lot more about carillons, so Rockefeller told him to go to Europe and see what they had there. When Cyril found out about this he told Mayer he could use Croydon as his base with free lodgings! Mayer was equally impressed, not only with Cyril and his big claims but also their family hospitality. The biggest bell that Cyril had produced to date was the largest chime bell at Toronto that weighed less than four UK tons and only four and a half US tons! Mayer was impressed with Cyril because he was so brash, promised everything, was obviously a bit of a wild card in the pack, and was almost American in his dealings. Mayer told Rockefeller, '(Cyril) rivals the most radical American business precocity – and with a good sporting spirit'. 'Precocity' means being a really pushy upstart!

Arthur Townsend, one of Cyril's right hand men who worked at Gillett and Johnston for twenty-seven years, went to see Mayer after completing the Toronto installation. He told Mayer that Taylor's had indeed rediscovered the art of producing perfectly tuned bells, not Cyril, but that Cyril's bells were now really good. He told Mayer to go and hear the Taylor Gloucester carillon and decide for himself. It doesn't appear that Mayer did this, but he was impressed by what he had been told. A Belgian carillonneur, Luc Rombouts, has written a book entitled *Singing Bronze: A History of Carillon Music* and narrates that Rockefeller sailed his yacht to Gloucester to hear the twenty-three Taylor bells for himself and was very impressed. He donated $500 for two more large bells providing his donation was anonymous. Whatever Rockefeller was finding out for himself, Mayer was making the important recommendations.

In October 1922, Cyril signed a contract to install a carillon that was now going to be forty-two bells, with a bourdon bell of four and three quarter tons that was the largest bell he could tune, and with a delivery date of nine months! In July 1923, Rockefeller, his wife Abby and three sons came to London and went to Croydon. They were suitably impressed with Cyril and family, but Rockefeller and his wife were also having a trip up to Loughborough.

To try and give a boost to carillons in England, a War Memorial carillon had been installed at Queen's park in Loughborough near the town centre. The free standing 152 feet tower was designed in 1919 by Sir William Tapper, an architect friend of the bellfoundry, and who built it? William Moss of course! He did the right thing in getting the *Cherry Orchard* job in 1859. Local businessmen, individuals, and the town council gave bells, and Denison Taylor provided the five ton bourdon bell in memory of his three nephews killed in the war. The range of the bells was four octaves, with the twelve smallest bells duplicated to try and improve their carrying power. Jef Denyn came to give the opening recital.

When Rockefeller and his wife arrived in Loughborough they were given a lavish lunch and taken to the recently opened War Memorial carillon for a recital by Jef Denyn, whom Denison had specially asked to come over. Pryce Taylor and Denison expounded on the benefits of memorial carillons of course. Rockefeller must have (presumably) decided it was Mayer, not he, who was suggesting who was given the order, and it seems unlikely that he mentioned that Cyril had already been chosen! Perhaps he just wanted to meet Denison, who must have been told he was coming to England to have invited him up to Loughborough? As I have mentioned already, Rockefeller had gone to see the large Taylor chime at Gloucester and donated two large bells. It's very likely that Cyril was well behind schedule with the Parkside Avenue carillon. Was he now in breach of contract? Was Rockefeller toying with the idea of cancelling the order? It's all a bit strange to say the least!

I would have thought that Denison and Pryce might have heard on the grapevine that Cyril was trumpeting that he had this order, but perhaps they thought this may not have been true, and it was just another boast! Rockefeller wrote a very nice letter to Denison the very next day saying how much they had enjoyed their visit and wrote, 'Your bells are wonderful. They open up a whole new field to me… I have never heard anything approaching them…it is really a splendid achievement'. He was absolutely knocked out by hearing a real 'grand carillon' this big, with a range of four octaves and a five ton bourdon bell, and realized just what he was getting for New York. Writing to Mayer shortly afterwards, he told him, 'I am, and always have been, desirous of installing the largest and finest carillon which physical conditions will permit.' Mayer was happy to oblige, but the tower was very small!

By December 1923, there was still no carillon sent from Croydon to New York, but it seems Mayer was not too worried. Rockefeller must have told him about visiting Loughborough and being suitably impressed, but a new contract was signed with Cyril for a carillon with fifty-three bells! The new bourdon bell was going to be ten US tons, a very nice round number as it worked out at 20,000 lbs/nine and a quarter UK tons. To overcome the problems of space, the eight largest bells were going to be put in a steel framework on top of the church tower roof. It was the only solution! From the Rockefeller standpoint that New York merited the biggest of everything, this redesigned carillon had one more bell than the largest carillon at Gwent, and the bourdon bell was heavier than the heaviest one at that time at Mechlin, which weighed just less than nine tons.

Denison and Pryce made several trips to America, and their sales pitch and expertise resulted in various orders, even if they weren't as smarmy as Cyril. Denison investigated having a film made to highlight their work, but it proved to be too costly, so he continued to distribute an immense number of brochures instead. Cyril Johnston was doing the same thing and still telling everybody how he had personally reinvented the lost art of tuning perfect bells! He really was a pain! A chime Cyril made for Tilburg in Holland was erected and played at the Albert Hall in London before being sent off. He didn't miss a trick! In 1926, Taylor's supplied a replacement three octave carillon for Zutphen in Holland, the first order that Frans Hemony had obtained, but it had been destroyed in a fire. As well as this one, another forty-two bell carillon for Holland was completed and sent off.

A young Belgian carillonneur, Anton Brees, started giving recitals in North America and tried really hard to get Taylor's to appoint him as their technical adviser in return for putting work their way, but Denison was a bit wary. They should have said, 'Yes please', because he was a firm devotee of Taylor carillons. In 1923 he came to England and became the first carillonneur for a few months at the Loughborough War Memorial carillon. In 1926, he performed the opening recital at the Taylor carillon in Cape Town, and from 1928-1963, when he was mostly in America, he gave the opening recital on every major Taylor carillon!

Top right: *The mayor of Loughborough at Taylor's inspecting the Loughborough War Memorial carillon on display in the works in 1923. The photograph shows the 47 bells but not the 12 duplicate ones.*
Photo: Taylor archive

Bottom right: The *Queen's Park, Loughborough, carillon.*
Photo: Duncharris

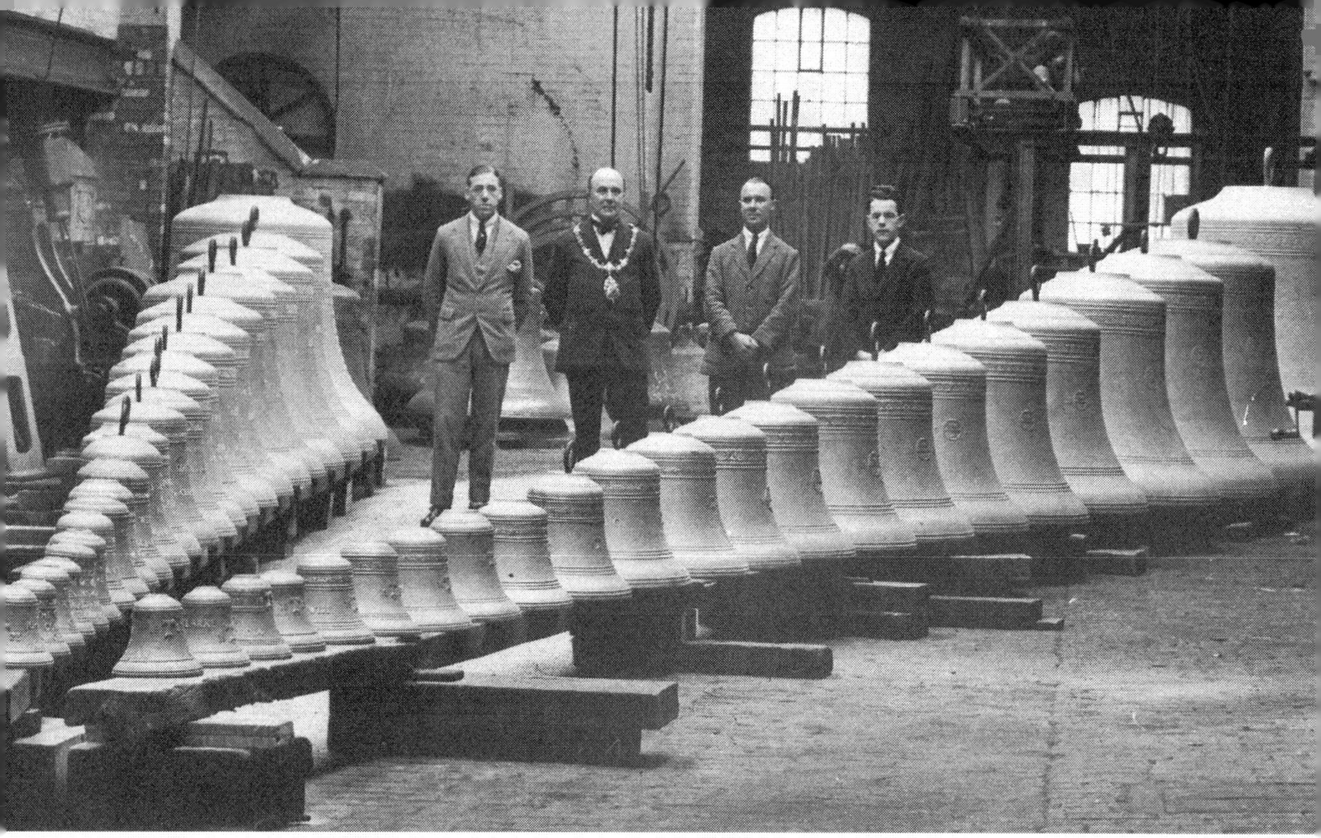

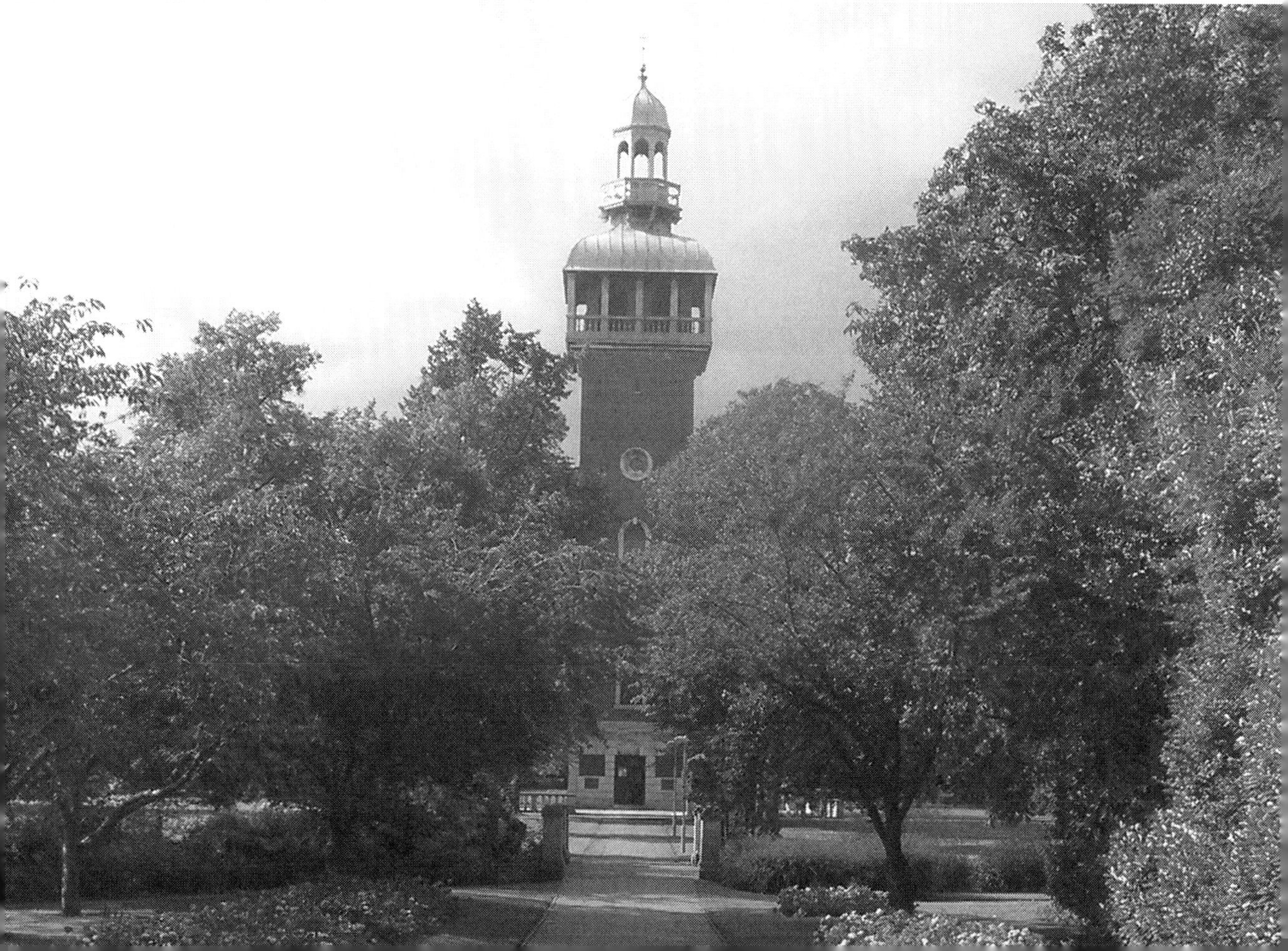

Meanwhile, in New York, Mayer had written to Rockefeller telling him, 'I believe everything rests on Mr. Johnston's courage', and this was absolutely true. Mayer was quite worried about his lack of experience in casting big bells and inadequate furnaces. Perhaps he was quietly wondering, *Should I have gone to Taylor's to start with?* Or was Rockefeller thinking the same thing? This massive project was now far removed from a ten or twelve bell chime! Cyril was very reassuring and told Mayer there was absolutely no problem, and he thought that the carillon would be finished by the end of 1924. It was a long way off from the nine month delivery date agreed in 1922! Cyril had a bit of luck when Warner's shut shop about 1924, and he bought their monster tuning machine, very similar to the one Taylor's had bought in 1900. He now possessed a tuning machine big enough for large bells.

By May 1925, along with all his other work, Cyril had cast all the bells and built the two frameworks that were needed, as one was for the roof of the tower. This was a really big job for him, so he pulled every string he could, including buttering up a minor member of the royal family whom he knew. He was able to tell Rockefeller that no less than King George V and Queen Mary were coming to see it and hear it played in his works! He invited Rockefeller over as well, but he declined the invitation. The consequent jamboree was spread over three days, and Cyril wore his morning suit, dickie bow and spats to greet the royal couple. A cast had been laid on, and fortunately the King and Queen were not spattered with molten metal!

Mayer had decided that they needed a tip-top carillonneur, and they managed to get Anton Brees to sign up in 1924! Mayer had assumed Denison was paying him a retainer to inaugurate every Taylor carillon and was very surprised this was not the case. Mayer knew all about Jef Denyn, but he was now aged sixty-one and Anton was only twenty-nine. As the carillon had not yet arrived, Anton was sent to Croydon to see it in the works, but Cyril was not at all impressed and didn't get on with him one bit! It was far removed from the Taylor carillons that Anton was so familiar with. Mayer was still worrying about squeezing the carillon into such a small tower, and Rockefeller started musing about building another much larger church!

Anton started playing the Parkside Avenue carillon after it was installed in October 1925, and gave the official opening recital in December when Cyril went there on his first trip to the US. Mayer hadn't fallen out with Denison, and he went out of his way to write to him apologising profusely that in the printed booklet distributed at the official opening Cyril was still stating that he had personally rediscovered the lost art of tuning perfect bells!

The carillon wasn't good news as there were much higher apartment blocks alongside where well-heeled New Yorkers lived, and they objected strongly! The sound of the big bells on the roof was extremely loud, but the smallest bells were difficult to hear. Anton was very upset and started to get really bolshie! He described the carillon as being, 'The most freaky installation imaginable'. Anton's complaints became really intense, and he didn't like where he was living either (paid for by Rockefeller), so they sacked him one month later! Anton went back to his beloved Taylor carillons and inaugurated the one in Cape Town in 1926. The Park Avenue carillon now became a 'project in transit', as Rockefeller was planning to build an enormous new church where, apart from everything else, the carillon was going to be reinstalled. Mayer now had a completely new canvas to paint on and started major new plans.

To give an idea of the weight of carillon bells, a four octave carillon with a ten ton bourdon bell would be a total of sixty-four tons, and with a six ton bourdon, forty tons. This is a lot of tons, but there is one way to reduce the weight and cost. The bottom octave of a carillon with a ten ton bourdon bell weighs fifty-six tons, but because we know that the next octave up reduces in weight eight times (remember this?), the next octave is only seven tons in total.

Frans Hemony had told his customers that two of the bells right at the bottom weren't really necessary. If we go back to Middle C, between this key and the white key E two keys up, there are two black keys. Frans expounded on this in 1678, and published a small booklet, *The uselessness of C sharp and D sharp* (the two black notes) *in the Bass of carillons*. He stated that in playing normal music these notes were rarely needed, and if music was being written specially for carillons he said, 'Don't use these notes!' If we ditch these two bells in a modern carillon with a ten ton bourdon it saves just over fourteen tons of bellmetal! Some carillons don't have these two heavy bells, so a four octave one then has forty-seven bells, not forty-nine. People like Rockefeller wanted all the bells they could have and didn't care how much it all cost, but other customers said, 'Really good idea'. So you can save weight and cost if you do this. Bellfounders have to offset the extra money they make if there are forty-nine bells against the saving in money for the customer with only forty-seven. Not having two of the big bells also makes it easier to fit a carillon in an existing tower. This is a consideration to be taken into account when a carillon is being designed.

It has to be remembered that in a carillon all the bells are hung dead. They do however require enormous girder frameworks custom designed for the tower, complicated 'transmissions' (the mechanical linkages), and loads of clappers (quite different to change-ringing ones). Somewhere for the clavier and carillonneur is needed, often in a special cabin, along with a practice clavier. Taylor's always built the whole shemozzle (except the cabin) in the works as a fully working instrument so that patrons, donors, or musicians such as William Starmer could come and see them in action. Carillonneurs such as Jef Denyn or Anton Brees could then come and give recitals.

Cyril did this as well of course, but one of his trademarks as we have seen, if the carillon was not needed straight away, was to erect it at another location in between times, and not only those in the UK. He could achieve maximum publicity, and although it was a lot of work, he balanced this against the interest that might be shown by other prospective donors. It also got it out of his works!

With the Park Avenue carillon installed, Cyril was working on a large fifty-three bell carillon for the Ottawa War Memorial Peace Tower. It was a very good order and next door to the new Houses of Parliament, considered to be of national significance. Both buildings were started after a major fire destroyed the parliament building in 1916. Within just a few months, the corner stone for the new building was laid by HRH, the Duke of Connaught, then Governor-General of Canada. Mayer had been involved in the initial plans, and the main tower was very similar to Big Ben but with enough height for a major carillon. As far as I can tell, I don't think Denison was asked to put in a quote. This was an order he never even smelt as a result of Cyril obtaining the Park Avenue order. It had a ten ton bourdon bell and a very large tower clock that Gillett and Johnston were able to supply as well. Cyril had managed to get the Canadian Prime Minister, Mackenzie King, to Croydon when he was casting some of the bells. The official dedication in 1927 was an enormous event.

The first Taylor carillon for a city council was installed at Albany City Hall in New York State in 1927, with four octaves and duplicate bells and a five ton bourdon. It was another very important carillon as it was a memorial to Americans killed in World War I. In the works at the same time there was a major forty-nine bell carillon for Sydney University, installed in 1928, and another big one for Cranbrook in Michigan. Pryce Taylor was in Canada in 1927 trying to halt the flow of carillons made by Cyril, and caught pneumonia, then peritonitis, and then died in hospital. A real body blow for Denison who was now on his own!

By now, Taylor's often cast bells before lunch, then loaded up the red hot furnace for a second cast in the late afternoon and sometimes even had a third one in the evening! From 1920-1929 they cast 1,099 tons of bells! In 1927, a really flagship carillon was installed at the Mountain Lake Sanctuary in Florida in the custom designed 'Bok' tower, situated in a lagoon at a large landscaped bird sanctuary. Edward Bok was an immigrant who had made his fortune in publishing, and he presented the tower, carillon, and gardens to the people of America. This was four octaves with duplicate smaller bells, and the bourdon bell was just over ten UK tons. It became a reference carillon, considered to have a tip-top state of the art design. Anton Brees gave the first recital, of course, before he became the permanent carillonneur for many years. He was invited back to perform a special forty-year anniversary recital in 1967, during which he collapsed and died at the clavier.

At the official inauguration in 1929, President Coolidge classified it as a 'National Historic Landmark'. Denison was involved in every aspect of the design and told the architect that the bell chamber should be open to the sky to help the smallest bells be fully audible. The climate in Florida is fairly benign, but maintenance was always necessary and very difficult. Anton Brees soon told Denison that duplicate bells were not a good idea, and these were disconnected. Taylor's replaced the smallest bells in 1969, and an acoustic reflector roof was put on. This noticeably increased the audibility of the smallest bells! The experiment of having no roof was never tried anywhere else. Good try Denison, pity it didn't work!

Denison wrote to William Starmer, 'I am capturing the thirsty market in North America, Australia and South Africa,' (apart from carillons in Holland and Belgium!) The Taylor achievements were absolutely super, and in general, carillonneurs thought their carillons were better than Cyril's. Taylor's pioneered the use of friction-free ball bearing races for the transmission bars which made playing a carillon need a lot less effort. They continually upgraded all the gizmos, but Cyril was still copying any new idea.

Right: *The very impressive 1927 'Bok Tower' carillon at Lake Wales, Florida, faced in pink marble.*
Photo: Averette

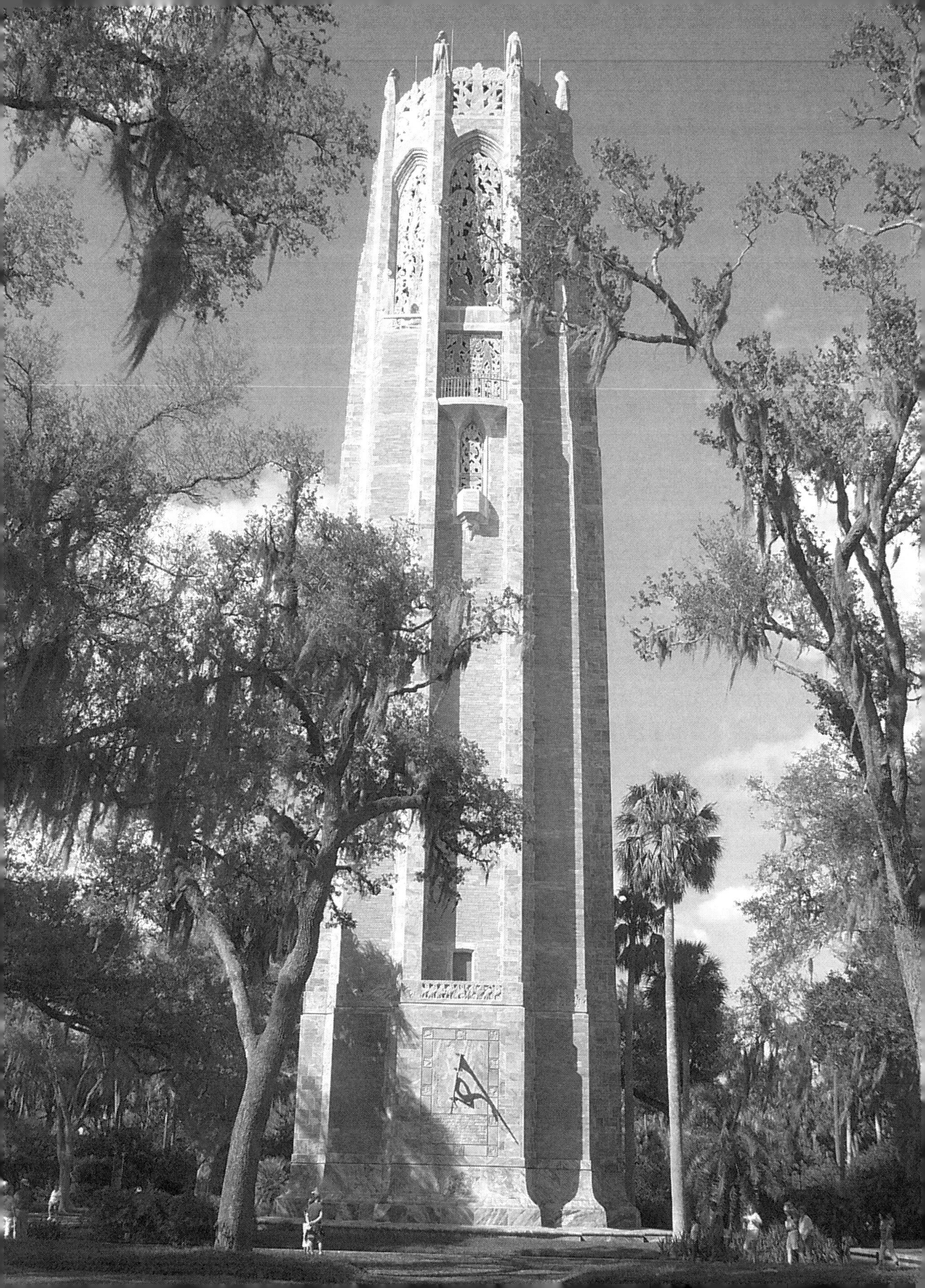

John Gouwens, a very experienced American carillonneur at Culver, wrote a book in 2013 about carillons (particularly in the US) and observes that often, an original good idea in one of Cyril's carillons was not carried on in the next one. He thinks this was a big mistake.

A big problem from 1928 was that in the US they introduced punitive tariffs on imported goods to protect American industries and manufacturers during the depression. This was known as the 'Smoot-Hawley Tariff Act', named after the two senators who came up with the idea, and it encompassed 2,000 categories. This applied to bells and was to give companies like the Meneely bellfoundry in New York a big advantage. The import duties levied on carillons with more than thirty-four bells was a whopping 40%. Why thirty-four bells was a deciding factor I have no idea! (Even stranger was the high tax on pianos that had more than sixty-four keys!) The only explanation that I can up come up with regarding the magic number of thirty-four bells is that a three octave carillon with the two lowest semitones omitted is thirty-five bells.

There were various appeals by people ordering large carillons, as they pointed out that no American company could produce them. They argued (successfully in some cases) that a carillon was an educational item when installed in places like universities as pupils could learn to play them, or that in churches they were for religious use. *The Brooklyn Daily Eagle* newspaper reported that Edward Bok at Lake Wales paid $35,000 in customs duty for his carillon from Taylor's, which was 40% of the $88,000 cost. It's a good job he was a millionaire!

The bells for one large carillon were loaded onto three railway box cars that were sealed by the US customs. They were trying to ensure that the bells weren't split up and put in different places, and as a result, claims made for a reduced amount of duty! A customs man at the destination checked that the seals were undamaged. The vast majority of customs tariffs were kept in place until World War II, but a Senator in Nebraska managed to get congress to pass an amendment in 1931 to junk the customs duties on carillons. With the money his church saved from the 40% tax being cancelled, they were able to increase their new carillon from thirty-five bells to forty-seven, with all the extra mechanisms. Well done that man! A big help, particularly for English bellfounders. The carillon at Lincoln in Nebraska came from Taylor's, and Anton Brees gave the opening recital in 1932. It was estimated that 25,000 people turned up, so Anton was extremely happy.

Back in New York, Mayer had been very busy. The new Rockefeller gothic-revival style church that was almost the same size as a cathedral, was designed to have a tower that was 392 feet high, with a belfry forty foot square and fifty foot tall. There was room for a lot more bells! Mayer wanted Rockefeller to have a carillon that would outdo every other one in the world by a long way. The Park Avenue carillon did have one more bell than at Gwent, and the bourdon was slightly heavier than the next heaviest at Mechlin, but Mayer, who now called himself a 'carillon architect', had set his sights on creating a monster carillon. He mounted his white charger, picked up his lance, and set off to find the Holy Grail!

Right: *The Riverside church tower from West 121st street.*
Photo: Petri Krohn

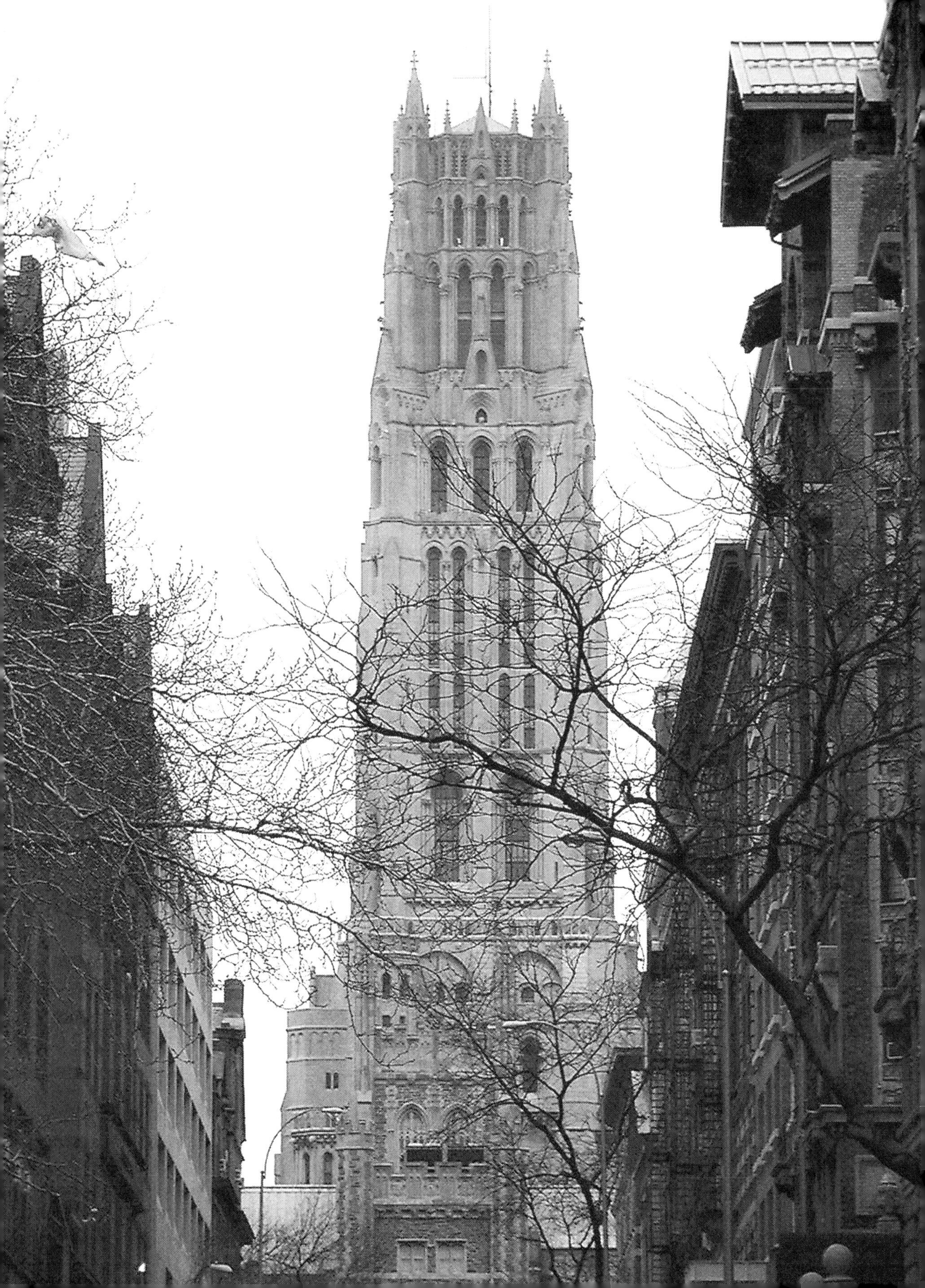

15. 'A Thirsty Market', Act Two

'I am assuming that there is no danger of getting the carillon too high?'
John D. Rockefeller Jr., 1926

The bourdon bell at the Park Avenue church had been designed by Mayer to be ten US tons/20,000 lbs, and Cyril had achieved this with the finished bell weighing 20,510 lbs. After he had tuned it however, the corresponding A bell (number 48 of 53) finished up at A=448Hz, not A=440Hz which Mayer had specified. I think Cyril was worried that if he tuned the bourdon bell down any more, the weight may have finished up less than 20,000 lbs. It was note E, so coming back to our piano it was two white notes up from C. Coming back down again including the black notes, there are two white notes and two black notes, so four notes in all. No carillon had ever been conceived that would have a very large bourdon bell that was note C, but Mayer thought that this was what Rockefeller needed for his new 'Riverside' church; so called because it was beside the Hudson River. Having decided they needed a low C bell, and as Mayer worked in nice round numbers, he wanted this monster bell to be twenty US tons, so 40,000 lbs! Another three monster bells would take him up to the existing bourdon bell that would now be the fifth largest of all the bells. He thought the new bourdon bell would probably need to be more than 10 ft in diameter.

Carillons often have four octaves, so forty-nine bells, although there were fifty-three in the existing carillon. Mayer decided he wanted six octaves, never even contemplated before, so he needed seventy-three bells. This was going to be the 'mine is bigger than yours' carillon of all time! Rockefeller was suitably impressed. He did ask one very pertinent question when he observed to Mayer, 'I am assuming that there is no danger of getting the carillon too high?' Mayer thought not, although there had been problems with the existing smallest bells, so he decided that twenty-eight of them needed replacing! The cornerstone of the Riverside church was laid with all due pomp and ceremony (and a lot of champagne) in November 1927.

People with carillons, despite having skilled carillonneurs, often still wanted some system of 'automatic' playing, although there could be no expression with loud and soft sounds. Denison approached the 'Aeolian Piano' company in London. They produced 'pianola' pianos that were magic. They looked just like ordinary pianos, and you could play them normally, but the wooden bit at the front under the keys hinged down to reveal several controls. Where the printed music went, on a ledge above the keys, there were two sliding doors. Open these, and stand back in amazement! There was a horizontal brass bar with a large number of square holes in it. A paper roll with the same size holes was driven over the brass bar by an electric motor. Another electric motor sucked air into the mechanism through the holes in the brass bit. As the roll of paper went over the bar, and a hole in the paper roll coincided with a corresponding hole in the bar, the piano played automatically, but there was no pianist! All the keys went down as if a ghost was playing it, and the Aeolian company marketed a large number of rolls with different tunes.

Denison and the manufacturer modified it so that the air being sucked in operated a valve which pulled down the normal carillon transmission wires connected to the clappers. They patented this as 'The Taylor-Aeolian Patent Electro-Pneumatic Automatic Player for Operating a Carillon of Bells.' So there you have it. A time clock could start it off, and the music available on these rolls was specifically punched to be suitable music for bells. The pianola did not have to be right under the transmission as electrical cables operated the valves.

Various carillons, particularly in North America, had these automatic gadgets fitted, but there was a multitude of small rubber pipes inside, and the valves sometimes stuck. Nevertheless, it was a really good way of replacing the mechanical drums linked to the clock. Over a period of years, if in damp conditions, they stopped working, and none of them lasted for ever. A competent mechanic could usually sort everything out with suitable spares, if they had a competent mechanic! They are now often to be found in a carillon museum, but were a good idea at the time, and really nifty gadgets. Denison hardly ever took out patents as he couldn't see the point, which is why he couldn't do anything about Cyril rushing off to inspect a new Taylor carillon to see what they had done and copying it. On this occasion, he thought it might stop Cyril in his tracks for a little while!

When Mayer told Cyril about his plans for Riverside, I have no idea what he thought! If he could pull it off it would be one of the carillon coups of the century, but this was extremely ambitious. He worked out that the four new bells would probably weigh about sixty UK tons, and apart from all the new cases needed to make the moulds, casting them at his works was impossible. Almost certainly, because the Croydon maximum furnace capacity was 'about' ten tons, the 15 ton US 'Wanamaker' clock bell, cast in 1926, had been made at the London bronze foundry J. Stone & Company at Deptford. Cyril had leased part of the works, and his workers moved into this foundry to make all the moulds. The 1950 'Freedom-Peace Bell' for Berlin, weighing about ten tons, is modelled on the US 'Liberty' Bell, and is stated to be the largest bell ever cast at Croydon. In 1974 it cracked and was welded in 2001.

Mayer then made quite a smart move and asked Denison to quote for the four monster bells! He wanted another price to make sure that Cyril was not charging him or Rockefeller an absolute fortune. There had been a lot of friction between Cyril and the Rockefeller bean-counters before and after the Park Avenue carillon had been installed. There were arguments, claims, and counterclaims over the final cost and requests for payment for 'extras'.

When Denison read the letter from Mayer asking for a quote, I am quite sure he screwed it up and threw it in the bin. Making bells to complete a Gillett and Johnston carillon! Whatever next! I bet he stomped into the works and gave a bollocking to the first person he saw who didn't seem to be fully occupied. Probably after lunch he smoothed the letter out and read it again. He had quite enough work as it was, and despite having the furnace capacity, the case and core plate used for 'Great Paul' would not be big enough for the bourdon bell. He would need a bigger case and core plate, and he would have to use all four furnaces at once. I think he probably thought he needed this job like he needed a hole in his head! He did work out a price, but I'm sure he thought getting the job was extremely unlikely. When Mayer compared the two quotes, Cyril's was more money, so he used Denison's quote as a stick to beat Cyril who reduced his price! After a bit more discussion, Cyril offered an increase in the total weight of metal for the same price, so Mayer was now happy. Recasting the top twenty-eight bells from Park Avenue meant that there were only twenty-five original bells left, so the number of the new and recast bells came to forty-eight.

Cyril seems to have told Mayer in mid-1927 that he was getting ready to cast the bourdon bell, but it wasn't actually cast until December. The casting was fine, and it went onto the big tuning machine. He now had an enormous bell, ready to be exhibited to all and sundry in his works, that weighed eighteen and a quarter UK tons. Then Mayer announced that he wanted five bells, including the bourdon, to be slow-swingers operated by electric motors. The plan was that they would all be swung for five minutes before the Sunday morning service and on other special occasions. Mayer came to see the Riverside bourdon bell, and everything seemed fine.

Cyril had ordered 2,000 post cards with a photograph of the bell (and himself, of course), but then in June 1928, Rockefeller sent a cable to Cyril saying that Mayer was not happy with this bell and wanted Cyril to have another go! They weren't accepting it, and for some reason Mayer wanted the second largest existing bell at Park Avenue recast as well. This bell was a mere six and a half tons! Who was paying for all of this? Was it Cyril? Mayer was not just relying on his own ears. He had asked Jef Denyn to go to Croydon when he was in England to listen to the bourdon bell and tell him what he thought. In very large or enormous bells there is often a 'rogue' note which is about a musical interval of a fourth; so note F coming up three notes from C. (I will come back to this in a chapter on tuning, but it is partly a problem because the human ear emphasises this note in very big bells.) He advised Mayer that this fourth was quite obtrusive. Cyril sent quite an emphatic letter to Rockefeller, without being too strong, telling him that only Mayer would have rejected the bourdon bell (he didn't know what Jef Denyn had said) and that first of all Mayer had said it was perfect! He pointed out that in the contract he had agreed that 'the fourth is to be subdued as much as possible', and he said it was. I bet he bitterly regretting agreeing to this! He went on to say that producing bells this big was in 'the category of highly experimental productions'. He finished up complaining that he had been forced to reduce his price 'to combat a rival bid'. He meant Denison's price of course!

It was gradually smoothed over with Mayer obtaining permission from Rockefeller to give Cyril a £5,000 interest free loan for twelve months to buy more metal, and Cyril agreed to stand the cost of recasting the other rejected bell. Percival Price, the Canadian graduate from the Belgian carillon school, criticised having very large bells over ten tons in a carillon as he thought this rogue fourth was far too strong and a big problem in these bells.

Adding insult to injury, Mayer asked Cyril to make a trip to other European countries to listen to very big bells and see which of them had the troublesome fourth and which didn't! Cyril was suitably outraged! His expertise as a bellfounder was being severely questioned.

Unfortunately, Cyril had another big problem that was nothing to do with bells. He had met an American woman, Olive Crowe, who was a nurse and seventeen years younger than he was, on a transatlantic liner in 1927, and she became one of his conquests. In October 1928, she told Cyril she was pregnant and refused not to have their child. Jill was born in England in May 1929, and this wasn't in Cyril's plans at all. Basically, he dumped her, and Olive went back to New York. Olive's cover story for her family and Jill, when she was old enough to understand, was that the father was Cyril Johnston, a famous English bellfounder who had died of pneumonia when Jill was a baby. Both mother and daughter adopted the name Johnston.

In 1950, when Cyril did die, Olive told Jill that she had lied because of the stigma of a divorce and showed her Cyril's obituary from *The Times*. I may be wrong, but I don't think that when Denison died in 1947, he merited a similar obituary in *The Times*. Cyril left Olive £500 in his will, but five years later Jill found out they had never been married. Jill became a famous authoress and a respected book and art critic, and she wrote a book in 2008, after years of research, entitled *England's Child*. The word 'child' refers to carillons, not herself. This book is a biography of Cyril and Gillett and Johnston, and Jill's autobiography. It is a very bitter-sweet account of events. She was the subject of one of Andy Warhol's films, 'Jill' in 1963. She died in 2010. Cyril had another iron in the fire when Olive went back to America, and he became engaged to Mollie O'Leary, and they married in November 1930. Despite her surname, and being a Roman Catholic, she had an impeccable English heritage and direct ancestral roots back to at least King Edward III. When they got married she was.... seventeen years younger.

St. Mary's Catholic church at St. Helens in Lancashire took delivery of a forty-seven bell Taylor carillon in 1929 with a bourdon just over four tons. During the 1930s they supplied carillons in America at Michigan University, Duke University, Rumson, Richmond War Memorial, Hartford College, Lincoln Nebraska, Ann Arbor, and Luray Caverns, home of some very famous caves. Frank Godfrey had started work at Taylor's in 1928 and eventually became their chief carillon designer, continually improving the mechanism.

Top right: *Frank Godfrey, the Taylor carillon engineer, checking the linkages from behind the clavier for the Washington National Cathedral carillon, in the works in 1963. The large bourdon bell, weighing nearly eleven tons, can be seen on the right.*
Photo: Taylor archive

Bottom right: *The first of a large number of lorries taking the fifty-three bells, framework, and fittings to be shipped to Canberra in 1970. The bell on the right is the six ton bourdon bell. Employees from left to right are Peter Cake (carillon engineer), Harold Freestone (works foreman), George Morley (accounts department), Charlie Philips (chief carillon builder) and Derek Powell (the frame builder).*

53 BELL CARILLON
FOR
CANBERRA A.C.T.
AUSTRALIA
CAST BY THE
JOHN TAYLOR BELL FOUNDRY
LOUGHBOROUGH ENGLAND

JOHN TAYLOR & Co.
BELL FOUNDERS

He made loads of visits to North America, and as he refused to fly even when he could, he always went there on passenger liners! In the 1951 American newspaper interview, he told the reporter that he had made thirty-one trips to America to twenty-five different states! Frank put in forty-two years until he retired in 1970, and everybody involved with Taylor carillons were very impressed with his expertise. He had some bad luck before World War I as his father had sent him to Germany to learn German and study engineering. His German must have been absolutely perfect when he came back home because he was interned there for four years!

Another extremely important Taylor employee was Johnny Oldham who had joined the company initially as works manager and progressed to general manager. After Pryce died, he started dealing with correspondence, orders, and shipping, and he went with Denison to America on various occasions becoming his right-hand man. He finally retired about 1969, having been a major force in the company.

Cyril cast the second 'Riverside II' bourdon bell in spring 1929, but both Cyril and Mayer agreed it was worse. 'Riverside III' was cast in January 1930, having a completely different profile, and was considerably heavier. It was the worst one of all three! In February, Mayer told Rockefeller he was accepting 'Riverside I' that was then sent to New York! There had been one change to the four biggest bells when Mayer decided that they didn't need the next heaviest bell up from the bourdon. This was the 'C sharp' bell which Frans Hemony had said was not necessary, so the number of bells was then seventy two. The three largest bells of the carillon weighed forty UK tons.

In the meantime, Mayer was given the job of consultant for a carillon at Louvain University in Belgium which was a memorial to the hundreds of American engineers killed in World War I. It had forty-three bells, a bourdon weighing seven tons, and Cyril was given the order. When it was erected in his works he invited the UK American and Belgian ambassadors, the mayor of Louvain and other important guests for a recital by Jef Denyn.

When the guests came along, Cyril had another important carillon in his works! It was a four-octave National War Memorial for Wellington in New Zealand, which was a sister carillon to the Ottawa one, but the tower was not ready. As it was completely clogging up his works, he erected it first of all at Newcastle upon Tyne for a 1929 exhibition and then moved it to Hyde Park! He made sure there were regular recitals, and when they dismantled it they shipped it straight off. Was there any way of stopping him? Taylor's were trying hard, but Denison always rightly considered that getting important people up to Loughborough was much more difficult than it was in Croydon and London. He complained, '(London) let in the Croydon people, so handy for influential visitors.'

All Taylor's could do was keep forging ahead, but they weren't short of work! A Taylor carillon with four octaves for a splendid cathedral tower in Indianapolis had been finished in 1929, and this was another one considered to be 'state of the art'. A three octave carillon for a War Memorial at Bathurst in Australia was in the works waiting for the tower again. Good publicity for visitors but 'please finish the tower, we hardly have room to move!'

Rockefeller sold his Park Avenue Baptist church to the Presbyterians for two thirds of the cost of building it, and the Riverside church and carillon were duly opened. Another Belgian carillonneur, Kamiel Lefévere, had been employed in 1927, and he took over from Percival Price, the Canadian carillonneur, who had replaced Anton. Percival's three year study course at the Jef Denyn carillon school at Mechlin had been subsidised by Rockefeller who thought a North American carillonneur was a good idea. Kamiel Lefévere subsequently stayed at Riverside until 1960.

Unfortunately, the smallest bells were almost inaudible at street level, even with light traffic, as the tower was 392 feet high. Compared to the 10 ft 2 ins diameter 40,900 lbs bourdon bell, the smallest bell was tiny at just over 5 ins in diameter, weighing 12 lbs. Rockefeller had been right with his question about the height of the bells. In 1931, Mayer suggested that thirty-seven of the smallest bells were re-tuned to try and get a louder and brighter sound! The bell that would have been the smallest if it had been a four octave carillon was 14 ins in diameter, weighing about 28 lbs, so this bell may have been audible - just!

There was a big spat again over Cyril's final bill which was quite substantial. Rockefeller's accountants said they had overpaid him the same amount he was now claiming he was entitled to! Eventually, for the sake of good relations, they paid him what he wanted on the understanding he sorted out the smallest bells, but he didn't. If you have to re-tune the smallest bells coming down to number thirty-seven, the only way is to junk bell number thirty-seven and re-tune bell number thirty-six to replace it. Then number thirty-five is re-tuned to become number thirty-six, and so on. All the bells would have had to be shipped back to Croydon and then shipped back out to New York, with no working carillon in the meantime. Mayer could see this was a bad idea so suggested thirty-seven new bells! If you spend a whole week re-tuning a five inch bell which only weighs twelve pounds, despite whatever you achieve, there can be no substantial increase in volume! This was the major problem.

By now there was another big Rockefeller project in the making. He wanted another carillon, to be called the Rockefeller Memorial Chapel Carillon in memory of his mother, at Chicago University. This was seventy two bells with a bourdon bell weighing sixteen and a half UK tons and having the C sharp note missing in Riverside. By not having another low note C bourdon bell at Chicago, Riverside was still the biggest carillon, with the heaviest bell! Cyril obliged, and it was finally opened in 1932 with the bells much lower down. I hope Cyril had a really watertight contract because Alan Buswell (who has compiled an extremely comprehensive data bank of Gillett & Johnston tuning records) kindly provided me with the Chicago information. 138 bells were cast to arrive at the seventy-two!

Some were quite large ones, starting with bell number sixty which weighed one and a half tons. I expect the rejected bells were put in another carillon or sold as clock bells as they were still making a large number of clocks. The bell that was number twenty-three was fourteen and a half inches in diameter and was cast seven times, as was as a slightly larger bell. Casting seven bells before you have one that is acceptable? It's back to the post-Hemony days! Gillett and Johnston cast all carillon bells less than twenty-four inches in diameter as 'sand castings' using patterns, so no loam cases and cores. When Cyril cut a Taylor bell in half to give him a crash course on how to tune bells, he finished up with two halves. Using a similar half bell pattern (probably cast out of aluminium) for bells that are not too big is fairly easy and does speed the process up significantly. It's a good job it's quicker!

Percival Price, like the Hemony brothers, thought that three octaves were ideal, and above this, with a four octave carillon, it became more difficult to play. The physical layout of the baton spacing on the clavier meant that even with lots of furniture polish on the seat, trying to reach the baton at the extreme left hand end, and the baton at the extreme right hand end, was very difficult, apart from the pedals. The distance between the two ends was five feet. With five or six octaves, this was completely impossible! You could play duets with two carillonneurs at the same time if you could rustle up another one! The other snag at the Riverside church and Chicago was that the carillonneur could not exert enough force to pull the clappers onto the enormous bells. The solution adopted for the eight largest bells was an electro-pneumatic system with air pistons. Percival Price thought this was a very bad idea, but obviously Rockefeller and Mayer were going for gold! Cyril thought these two carillons were excellent as he charged a fortune!

Percival Price became an extremely accomplished and famous carillonneur and wrote a comprehensive book in 1933, entitled *The Carillon,* dealing with the design, bells, musical range, architecture and ideal playing conditions. In this book he details all the working carillons in 1931 throughout the world and the ones destroyed in World War I. His list of Taylor carillons from 1904 until 1931 totals thirty-five, and he defined a carillon as having more than two octaves of bells. This number was exactly matched by Gillett & Johnston from 1921 to 1931. What an enormous number of carillons!

A Taylor carillon in 1937, with twenty-five bells, was for the Springfield Hillcrest cemetery in Massachusetts. For a cemetery? Was it just sad music or hymns they played? Must have been! In 1938 Cyril made a carillon of forty-four bells with a six ton, slow-swinging bourdon bell, for Grace Cathedral, San Francisco (where the reverberation time is seven seconds). A donor had given the money for a new tower and carillon but as the tower wasn't finished the carillon was erected on nearby Treasure Island at San Francisco Bay. It was the centrepiece of the 1939-1940 Golden Gate International Exhibition. Another stroke of genius by a very determined businessman and showman! This is not a traditional carillon as the bells are all rung electronically with a piano-type keyboard. It is one of just two Gillett & Johnston carillons of this type in America. In the 1930s, the work Cyril obtained in the US dropped off quite dramatically.

Cyril's unmarried sister Nora had been sent by Cyril in 1926 to study at the Belgian carillon school under Jef Denyn, so she became very proficient. During some recitals in 1933 at a new Gillett and Johnston carillon in Jerusalem (where the idea was that she also trained someone else) it became clear that she suffered from fairly severe alcohol related problems. These recitals were quickly stopped and immediate plans made to send her back home. Cyril had planned to have her play on his carillons in the US when they were officially opened, but he had to think again.

Nora responded to this end in her career as a carillonneur by having the equivalent of a practice clavier made, with bars and resonator tubes. She took it to America twice in 1938 where she gave recitals and often a lecture at the same time entitled *The Romance of Bells*. She played when some American TV documentaries were being filmed, once with an orchestra, and was received at the White House by Eleanor Roosevelt! It sounds as if she was a true sister of Cyril apart from her alcohol problems. A third American tour in 1939 was cancelled because of the impending war. After the war there was a period when she stayed at an alcohol rehabilitation clinic in England. She died in 1952, just two years after Cyril.

Frederick Mayer had asked for slightly amended tuning for the smallest bells at the Chicago carillon, officially opened in 1932, but this did not increase the volume. As the Riverside carillon was still a bit of a white elephant, and nothing had happened about re-tuning or re-casting any of the bells, he started again in 1936. His new proposal, which Cyril would be paid for, was to re-tune sixty-one of the seventy-two bells. Sixty-one? That only left eleven! Mayer was still organist and choirmaster at the Military Academy, and would remain there until 1964. He obviously had a good ear, and he now knew a great deal about bells, but why was he suggesting so many bells should be re-tuned? Did he think that by now Gillett and Johnston bells had improved dramatically? Or that they still needed to be improved?

The biggest bell he wanted to send back was five feet in diameter and weighed a smidgen over two tons. What was wrong with this bell? Eventually Cyril came up with a price, but by 1939 nothing had been done, and then World War II intervened. After the war, the idea was aired again, but Cyril's price had nearly doubled. It was still 'on the cards' in the mid-1940s when Cyril was losing control of the company, so that was the end of that as far as Gillett and Johnston were concerned. The last idea Mayer came up with was to have sixty-one new bells, make a forty-nine bell carillon from the biggest bells that were taken out, and give the remaining twelve smallest ones to the Rockefeller family as souvenirs!

World War II put a brake on all the extensive work Taylor's was churning out, and other work in the pipeline was put on hold. Denison told the Ministry of Supply that they could cast bronze up to twenty tons and cast iron up to two tons. The work they received was mostly miscellaneous items, aircraft parts, tank turrets, buoy bells and some ship bells. This assorted work still allowed them to carry out some normal production when the labour force had time, as they were only being required to work one shift, not two, like in World War I.

An estimated 175,000 bells were seized by the Nazis from 1941-1944 in all of the European countries they occupied. 6,700 were removed from Holland and 4,800 from Belgium out of a total of about 12,000. After the war, bells were found in Germany at Hamburg docks where there was an enormous dump of 14,000, and another 4,000 were at Ilsenburg. Other bells had not yet left the ports of Amsterdam and Antwerp where they were waiting to be shipped to Germany. Austria lost about 72% of their bells, and 22,500 bells were taken from Poland. They were all intended to be smelted down, tin being the prime requirement. It is thought that about 2,000 tons of tin were obtained in this way. Organ pipes were considered a good way of obtaining tin, but this was never instigated. Good news for organs!

As cultural items of major historic value were considered to have some status, bells were systematically categorized into groups A-D. Group A bells (1850-1940s) were considered to have least value historically, were relatively modern, and were melted down immediately. This applied to about 90,000 bells. Group B (1790-1850), that were more important historically, were to be melted down after all the group A ones had been, and then Group C bells (1740-1790) after that. Luckily, several thousand of the groups B and C were found in Germany after the war. Category D (pre 1740) were medieval bells, together with all early carillons providing they were capable of being played, and these were (thankfully) left in the towers. A sub category was bells dated before 1450 that were not to be removed under any circumstances. In theory! Burying these bells to protect them was allowed.

Modern carillons were in Group A, so in Holland the 1913 Taylor carillon at Vlissingen (Flushing), the 1914 Eindhoven carillon, the 1921 Taylor Raadhuis carillon at Rotterdam along with the 1925 Taylor carillon at Zutphen, were all requisitioned and smelted down. The 1925 Gillett & Johnston carillon at Tilburg was one that suffered the same fate, as well as a 1928 twenty-four bell chime, and the thirty-eight bell carillon at Amelo in Holland. How tragic, for some of the best carillons there. The 1911 Taylor carillon at Appingedam had the bells requisitioned right at the end of the war, but as they were in transit in Holland they were located and brought back! Phew! At Ath in Belgium the carillon had been destroyed in a fire in 1815, but the locals took as many church bells as they could to the carillon tower to hide them. A gramophone record of another carillon was played over loudspeakers when the Germans arrived, and they showed them details of recitals that were really from 1814! The Germans left the bells there without asking to see them. What a smart move! Even in Germany, to aid the war effort, bells from about 100,000 churches were removed.

After the war, commissions were set up to try and identify all the bells which was an extremely difficult task! Once this had been done, they were returned to the various countries and places of origin. In 1943, President Roosevelt had established the 'American Commission for the Protection and Salvage of Artistic and Historical Monuments in War Areas', and the British Occupation Forces undertook a lot of this work. The British Foreign Office files on investigations and repatriation of bells were finally closed in 1949.

There was a bit of a spat about 500 tons of broken bellmetal that was ready to be melted down and came from German churches. The refineries wanted payment in exchange, and one argument was that they had voluntarily been handed over, not actually requisitioned! Eventually, legal opinions were that the 1910 Hague Convention, which banned bells being taken away, was considered to apply to these as well. The metal was ordered to be apportioned between the churches for casting new bells.

Right: *The Zutphen carillon tower, and typical market place, where the Hemony brothers provided their first ever carillon in 1642. After being destroyed in WWI, Taylor's provided a new one in 1926 that was taken away and melted down by the Nazis in 1942 during WWII.*
Photo: Michielvertbeek

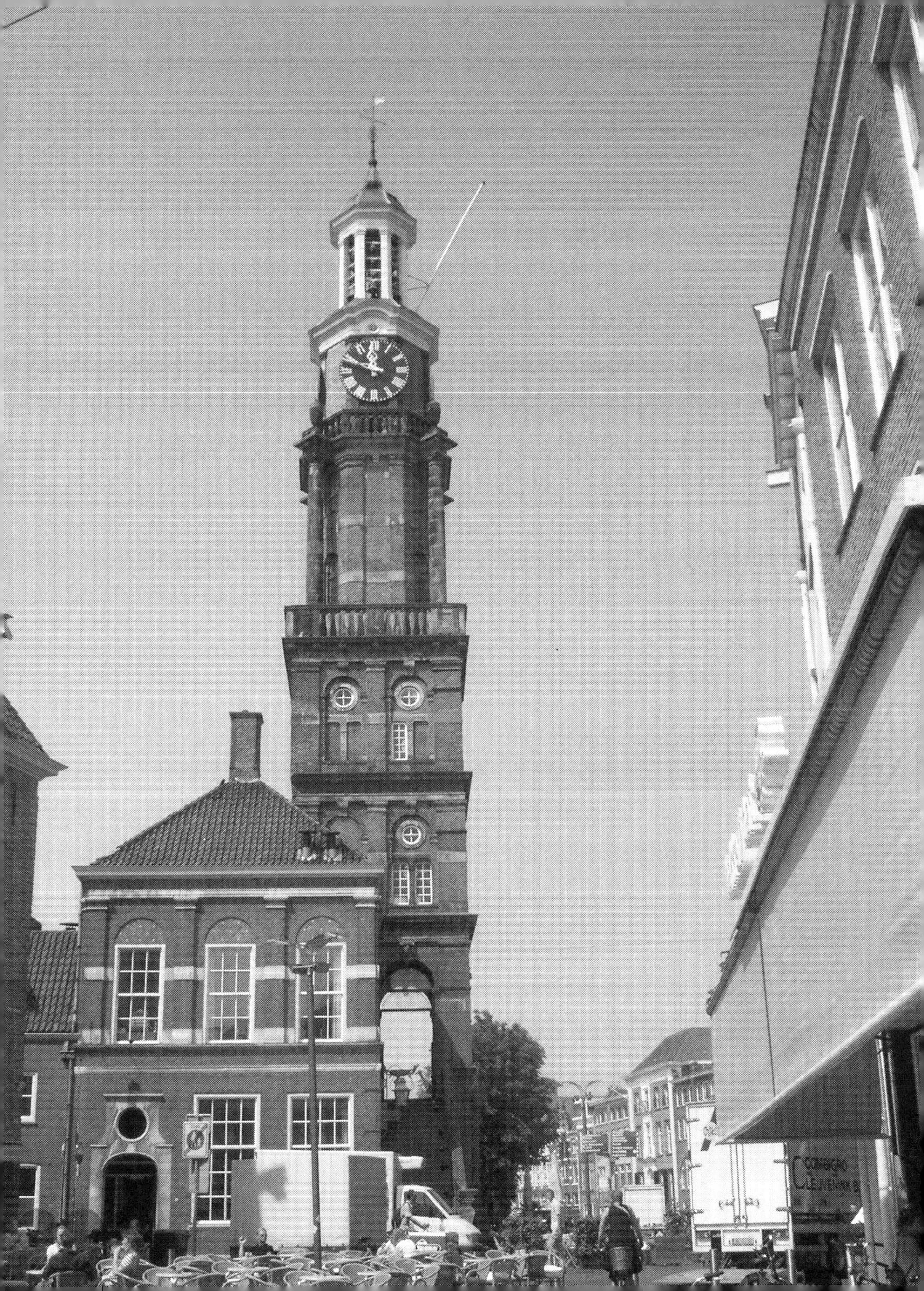

The Red Army collected nearly 10,000 Russian bells after the war from storage sites where they were waiting to be shipped off. They loaded them onto 700 railway wagons to use them as scrap metal themselves! They thought their metal shortage took priority! Throughout Europe, another estimated 150,000 bells were destroyed in bombing raids and fires. In some towers where incendiary bombs landed, where there were very strong up draughts of air, the bells not only melted but they completely vaporised as well, leaving only deposits of ash. Incredible! This happened to several bells when a carillon in Rotterdam was bombed by mistake, and at Rouen Cathedral in France. So once again, war was a very tough time for bells.

The heady days of the 1920s and 1930s never materialised again, and competent Dutch bellfounders appeared including the Royal Eijsbouts bellfoundry near Eindhoven, who started casting bells in 1947. They had previously just made clocks and mostly bought any bells they needed from Taylor's or Gillett & Johnston. They had already installed various carillons for different bellfounders. In 1949, they employed a nineteen year old young man called André Lehr to be a bell tuner. He went on to be one of the most famous bellfounders until he died in 2007. Initially, just like Cyril and Paccard in 1986, large bells were cast at a propeller factory. They soon became a major force in Holland and in 1952 opened a subsidiary foundry in Belgium that kept going until 1969. A much older Dutch bellfoundry, Petit & Fritsen at Aarle-Rixtel, started producing bells in the 1930s that were quite well tuned, and they re-opened in 1945. A young Dutch engineer, Engelbert 'Bert' Van Heuven, was asked to undertake a major study of the acoustical properties of Dutch bells that were at Hamburg docks, and the idea was that he might find another metal, apart from bronze, to make bells. He didn't, but I will come back to him later on.

With the wholesale destruction of Dutch and Belgian bells, many restoration projects were given to their bellfounders by the authorities in a controlled manner, without any possibility of bellfounders from other countries quoting for this work. There were also major financial considerations regarding claims made for grants of money for replacement work to be undertaken. So seems fair, even if a great pity!

The superb 1921 Taylor carillon at Rotterdam was replaced by Petit & Fritsen in 1948 with forty-nine bells, but as they weren't much good the top thirty-seven were recast in 1975. They were given the order to replace the Vlissingen (Flushing) carillon in 1949, but the city did not receive any compensation until 1956 and then not the full cost. The Dutch Van Bergen bellfoundry made a new carillon in 1949 to replace the Gillett & Johnston chime that was melted down, and one for Zutphen in 1950. The Royal Eijsbouts foundry replaced the Eindhoven carillon in 1969. In 1950, the Dutch government had decided to present the USA with a forty-nine bell carillon in gratitude for their help during the war. Unfortunately, Royal Eijsbouts, Petit & Fritsen and Van Bergen were all asked to make a third of the bells, in the Hemony style. It was first erected at West Potomac in 1954, but then moved in 1960 to the very important Arlington National Cemetery that had started up in 1864 and now has 400,000 graves or urns. It was not a good example of Dutch carillons at all, as perhaps might have been foreseen, coming from three different bellfounders. The vast majority of the bells were re-tuned in 1995. It did make it a bit better, but in 2010 the free standing open tower was closed to the public for safety reasons. A $2.7 million restoration was proposed in 2016.

Gillett & Johnston had been bombed during World War II but regrouped afterwards. At one stage Cyril had tried to merge with Whitechapel and set up a new joint foundry in Crawley, but this didn't happen. In 1948, Cyril resigned from Gillett and Johnston after a financial dispute. He died suddenly in 1950, and the casting of bells finally ceased in 1957. In the last couple of years, after their foundry foreman suddenly died, Taylor's cast about thirty bells for them using their crooks. These were tuned in Croydon. When they finally shut shop, Paul Taylor purchased all their tuning forks for £40, and documentation such as the tuning books. Their tuning forks went up in frequency further than the Taylor set, but these ones were found to be inaccurate as regards the actual and claimed frequencies. The Whitechapel foundry employed four of Cyril's workers, and Paul Taylor also offered some of them work.

The first Taylor carillon installed after the war, in 1947, was at Niagara Falls, with fifty-five bells and an eight ton bourdon. This was in Canada! At last! Well, it was in Canada, but about a five minute walk over the bridge into America. This carillon became famous when Marilyn Monroe climbed to the top and was murdered by her husband in a 1973 film, *Niagara*. It served her right as she and her lover were both trying to murder her husband!

Fifty-three bells with a seven ton bourdon were made by Taylor's for the University of Kansas carillon in 1951 where Frank Godfrey was interviewed by a local newspaper. This was a very important carillon as it was a memorial to Americans killed in World War II. In 1956, thirteen bells were added at Ames, Iowa, taking them up to forty-nine. Peter Cake joined Taylor's in 1962 and shortly afterwards took over as carillon designer, apart from later becoming the works manager and then a company director.

At Riverside, after Cyril left and Gillett & Johnston was in different hands, the Belgian carillonneur Kamiel Lefévere held talks with the Dutch bellfounder Van Bergen, and in 1955 a total of fifty-six bells starting with the smallest ones were recast! It doesn't appear that Mayer was involved very much for some reason, but the Rockefeller gang agreed to come up with the loot. Van Bergen added two new bells at the top to make seventy-four!

Milford Myre, the very skilled carillonneur from the Bok Singing Tower, said the result was no better than the Gillett & Johnston bells, and the small ones were still almost impossible to hear at street level. Apart from being inaudible to a large degree, as no carillonneur can play six octaves at the same time, the smallest Gillett & Johnston bells and their replacements were hardly ever used. There was a proposal (never carried out as it was an extremely bad idea) that the smallest bells were tripled in number to try and make them audible! An American carillon consultant, who always thought adding Dutch bells to an English carillon was never successful, commented decades later that the original Gillett and Johnston bells must have been 'perfect'. Mayer didn't think so! He wanted to junk sixty-one of them.

Taylor's never had bourdon bells or any others rejected by donors or consultants, but they stuck to the largest bourdon bells being only a tad over ten tons. In the 1960s onwards, when duplicate bells were being replaced, this was done to make the new bells louder, but nobody ever said, 'Take forty of the forty-eight bells back to Loughborough and see if you can make a better job!' Was the Taylor profile rightly considered to be superior or were the bells tuned better? It seems very likely that the tuning was more accurate. Gillett and Johnston bells do have a characteristic sound with some people saying they are very mellow.

In 1963, a prestigious fifty-three bell Taylor carillon with a ten ton bourdon was completed for Washington National Cathedral, and it became the third heaviest in existence. The donor, Bessie J. Kibbey, who died just before the carillon was installed, donated in memory of her grandparents. What a pity. She never heard the bells but had watched some being cast. Milford Myre, the famous carillonneur from the Bok tower, gave the opening recital and described it as 'the most responsive action of any carillon I have ever played.' It was almost identical to 'his' Bok tower carillon, but with a much improved design of the twiddly bits. In 2001 Taylor's replaced some of the clappers, re-ground others back to the original shape, and replaced the wire linkages. The frame was entirely repainted by hand. There was nothing wrong with any of the bells of course! The weight of the smallest bell is eighteen pounds, much heavier than the corresponding bell in earlier carillons, and one bell not two.

1963 also saw a twenty-five bell carillon put in at Newcastle upon Tyne Civic Centre, with a three and a half ton bourdon in a flash modern tower. In 1965, work started on adding forty-three bells at the Harkness tower at Yale University. With the original heavy chime supplied in 1921, this gave a total weight of forty-three tons. 1968 saw a forty-nine bell carillon installation at Spokane in Washington, with a two ton bourdon bell. They obviously had plenty of spare loot because in 1957 they had put in an organ with 4,000 pipes. Bet that sounds good! No doubt they were looking round to see what to buy next and probably heard about the Washington Cathedral carillon.

In 1969, another very important 'Grand Carillon' order given to Taylor's was for the National Carillon at Canberra. This has a six ton bourdon and fifty-three bells (with another two added in 2003), and the free standing tower beside a lake is extremely impressive, to rival the setting of the Bok tower. This carillon was a present from the British Government to celebrate the fiftieth anniversary of Canberra being the capital city. Nothing to do with convicts, I was wrong there! Queenie went and opened it in 1970.

In 1955, Whitechapel installed a carillon with thirty bells at Kilmarnock in Scotland. The West Hartford carillon in Connecticut is unique as it is the only American one with all of its bells from the Whitechapel bellfoundry. They started off with twenty-four in 1969, and under the watchful eye of one of the very influential carillon consultants, Timothy Hurd, another twenty-six were added in 1985, although the smallest bells are minute in size and weight. I have a full-scale profile of the smallest bell which is just over five and a half inches in diameter and only weighs ten pounds; so very diddy and almost identical to the smallest bell

Right: *The 1963 Washington National Cathedral carillon, with a bourdon bell of nearly eleven tons, fully assembled in the works with the bourdon bell on the right.*
Photo: Taylor archive

N3
N4

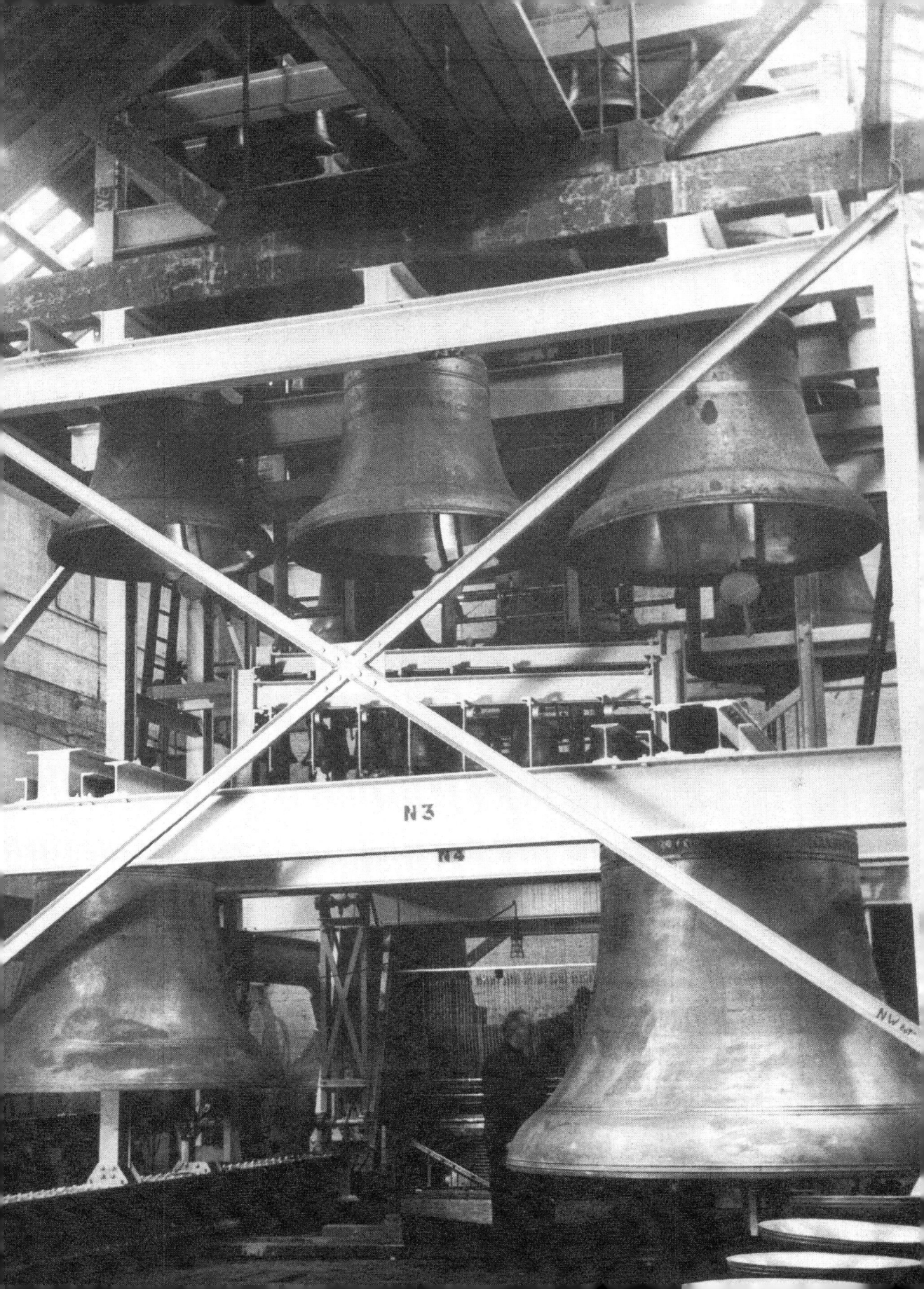

at Riverside. This carillon is tenth from the bottom in a list of 118 carillons with the largest bell weighing a maximum of 6 cwt/672 lbs/300 kg. These 'baby' carillons are popular where there are constraints of size and cost, and are a trademark of Petit & Fritsen.

In his book, Trevor Jennings gives a numerical list of carillons cast by Taylor's through the years, but this is poorly thought out. He credits Paul with making six carillons, and has two down to me. I wish! A 'grand carillon' with forty-nine bells and a ten ton bourdon bell? I would love to be able to lay claim to one of these. Trevor counted the carillons made up to 1947 when Denison died as being ones he was responsible for, but he had retired before then and Paul Taylor had been made a junior partner in 1935. From then up to 1978, with the Berkeley carillon in the US, there were eleven major carillons that Paul certainly had a hand in, or was totally responsible for. I was involved with the large extension to the Taylor chime from 1912 at Berkeley, making a carillon of forty-nine bells in all.

The early Taylor policy of duplicating the top one or two octaves of small carillon bells was never a success, as Anton Brees had pointed out. Designed to increase the sound level, making two identically tuned bells was not possible at that period in time and still very difficult now, although not impossible given enough time. Trying to get two very small bells to strike exactly the same time was also a real bind. Paul and I recast the twenty-four duplicate bells at Lake Wales in Florida just after I joined Taylor's, and increased the weight of the smallest bell from 11 lbs to 16 lbs. We did the same thing with eighteen bells at Richmond in Virginia in 1970 and a lot at Cranbrook in Michigan in 1978. I replaced thirty bells at Albany City Hall in 1986 (including duplicate bells) and recast and added more bells at the Gillett and Johnston carillon at Wellington New Zealand. Some of these recasts of up to two octaves or more, or extensions, are the 'carillons' that Trevor writes were made by me! I do wish he had asked around!

The Wellington War Memorial carillon by Gillett & Johnston in 1932 is a typical example of a lot of work by different bellfounders. In 1984, Timothy Hurd, the carillonneur there at the time, decided to increase the number of bells from the original forty-nine and have some recast. Originally there had been a plan that this would be another seventy-two bell carillon! He gave the job to Taylor's in 1986, so I recast twenty bells (as you would) to a Timothy Hurd/Gillett and Johnston profile and added another sixteen to make sixty-five bells. In 1998, which was the fiftieth anniversary of the ending of World War II, four larger bells were added at the bottom end. Timothy Hurd decided that Whitechapel were able to make the best 'clones' of the Gillett and Johnston profile although Taylor's had previously cast several bells to their profile. The new bourdon 'Peace bell' weighs just over twelve tons, and as Whitechapel couldn't cast any of these bells they sub contracted them to the Royal Eijsbouts bellfoundry in Holland! Definitely a precedent here! Taylor's could have cast all these bells with their existing furnaces as they had cast and tuned a ten ton bell for Malta in 1992. Timothy then donated five new top end bells that Eijsbouts cast, and this made the total number up to seventy-four. Oh dear! Not again! Mine is bigger than yours? The bourdon bell is the largest in the southern hemisphere, and the complete carillon is now the third heaviest in the world! Perhaps they found a friendly octopus and taught him how to reach seventy-four batons and pedals at the same time!

I think casting bells in Holland using Taylor's, Whitechapel, or Gillett and Johnston profiles is very suspect. I don't mean morally, which is my objection to the 2012 Whitechapel/Royal Eijsbouts' Olympic bell that is now just a sculpture; I mean from a technical stand point. Taylor's have never abandoned making moulds the traditional way using loam that is a consistent mix of materials, and I think this is absolutely right. They bury the moulds before pouring the metal, and the bell consequently cools slowly. Along with the current owners of Taylor's I am sure this is very important. The techniques used in Holland are totally different and so are the mould formers, and the bells are cast completely above ground. I am sure a Taylor profile bell cast in Holland would be different to one cast at Loughborough as regards the sound.

In 1990, Taylor's recast thirty-seven bells and added four more at Cohassett in the US, an early carillon of fifty-one bells put in by Gillett & Johnston from 1924-1928. The Taylor carillon at Fife was steadily augmented from the original fifteen bell chime installed in 1924 with additional bells in 1938 and 1962. In 1998, four more bells made this carillon up to twenty-seven bells. In 2000, three extra Taylor bells took the Lake Wales Bok tower carillon up to sixty bells. York Minster took delivery of twenty-four bells in 2008. (13 of them came from a mobile chime at York cast by Taylor's from 1999-2001.) They had been tuned to match in with eleven other Taylor chime bells cast in 1933 that the Minster had acquired from Nelson in Lancashire in 1989. This thirty-five bell carillon was (and still is) the first traditional carillon in an English Cathedral. It took a very long time for this to happen! In 2011, the top two octaves at Michigan University were replaced by Taylor's, and in 2014, after the Mostyn School was closed (where Paul Taylor had gone as a boarder), the carillon was transferred by Taylor's to Charterhouse Public School.

In 2015, twenty-five bells were installed at the Bournville carillon in Birmingham where Taylor's had put in a carillon with a total of forty-two bells between 1906 and 1925. Cyril had been absolutely delighted to be egged on by the then carillonneur to recast almost all of these bells in 1934, but the result was never satisfactory. This carillon is now returned to its former splendour with the new Taylor bells.

Remember the Riverside carillon? Timothy Hurd waved his magic wand here as well from 1999-2002. A total of fifty-eight bells including all the Dutch ones were replaced. Taylor's were undergoing a bit of a reorganization so Timothy went to Whitechapel. The profiles of the first half dozen largest bells were exact copies of the Gillett and Johnston profile. The next few bells were a fudge of Gillett and Johnston and Whitechapel profiles, and then they reverted to the Whitechapel shape. Major rebuilding of the carillon took place at the same time. I have hunted high and low to find any account that says this carillon is now fine again but there is only one I have found that states, 'The authentic sound of the Gillett and Johnston bells has been restored'. Really? I have been told that there was a great deal of problems (put politely) when the work was being done from the standpoint of the consultant and contractor relationship. It's quite possible that Whitechapel, who were thrown in at the deep end, wished they had never heard of Riverside!

There is a YouTube video of the five swinging bells in action dated August 2014, and the bourdon bell starts to swing first. But what happens then? There must be a big problem with one of the two motors that should drive it up in either direction as the bell only swings about half way up to the horizontal, if that. So does the clapper strike the bell? Unfortunately not!

If this whole shoot had been a big success, you might have thought that a similar renovation would have been carried out at the Rockefeller Chicago Memorial carillon when it was done up from 2006-2008. The Royal Eijsbouts foundry took the top forty-three bells back to Holland. They were found to be substantially flat in pitch and needed re-tuning. It appears that this is characteristic of many Gillett and Johnston carillons, and a Dutch carillonneur and carillon expert, Gideon Bodden, has made a tonal analysis of several of them. He reports that many of the top octaves with very small bells are not well in tune. This would appear to be because the highest frequency Gillett and Johnston tuning forks were not accurate, as Paul Taylor and I found out. In 1977 I was able to re-calibrate all these forks, so at least we knew the correct frequencies rather than those marked on the forks.

I managed to get to the Riverside carillon in 1986, but it was a whistle-stop visit on my way to Boston. The plan was that I would be there when it was struck twelve times at noon as it is also the hour bell. It would have worked if there hadn't been a major traffic jam with me stuck in a yellow taxi! Just before one o'clock, the security guard at the belfry said no-one was allowed in when the hour bell sounded. He wouldn't budge even when this pushy Brit told him he was a bellfounder, because I needed some chit from the office eighteen floors down! I managed to get back down to street level in the lift, but the traffic noise was a problem. With only the one bong as the bell struck the hour I couldn't hear it very well.

As can be seen, replacing top octaves or large numbers of carillon bells is commonplace. The Dutch bellfounders, Van Bergen, Petit & Fritsen, and Eijsbouts, have carried out a lot of this work, and so have Fonderie Paccard, Taylor's and in one or two cases, Whitechapel. The big Gillett and Johnston carillons at Riverside, Chicago, Wellington in New Zealand, and others such as Princeton, Cohasset, Mercersburg, East Lansing and Stamford have been substantially modified. Suggestions to replace some of the bells at Ottawa have been resisted so as to keep this carillon one of only two complete large Gillett and Johnston instruments in North America, along with Culver.

The list of Taylor carillons where there are still only Taylor bells includes Albany, Ames (Iowa), Ann Arbor, Armagh, Canberra, Charlotte, Charterhouse school (moved from Mostyn), Durham in North Carolina, Fife, Hartford, Kansas, Lake Wales, Loughborough, Luray, Newcastle upon Tyne, Richmond, Spokane, Springfield, St. Helen's (Lancashire), Washington, Yale, and the very first one in the US in 1922/4 at Gloucester. Any work carried out including replacing the duplicate bells that were never a success, has been done by Taylor's. I think this tells us a lot about the quality of Taylor bells and their musicality. I told you they're the best!

In conversations with Sheila, the widow of Peter Cake who had a long career designing Taylor carillons, she told me that he had outdone Frank Godfrey and had travelled to every US state except Alaska! He went to prepare quotes and meet up with architects and construction bosses, including the ones from the Canberra project several times. He also supervised the installation of all the important carillons. He was away a great deal, but it was quicker for him than Frank Godfrey as he hopped over on a jumbo jet! Peter was one of those people described as 'what you see is what you get', and he became firm friends with a host of people he met through work when he was abroad. Following on from Frank Godfrey, he made a very important contribution to perfecting the art of carillon building so that carillonneurs had the best carillons available, giving them the best sound from the highly responsive action. Peter was seventy-eight when he died, and he had met Sheila when they were both seventeen, so a long marriage.

16. A Really Interesting Job

'Dear Bells! how sweet the sound of village bells When on the undulating air they swim.'
Ode to Rae Wilson, Esq. - Thomas Hood

On the day that I joined Taylor's bellfoundry, I was shown round the works properly, as when I had been offered the job it was a whistle stop tour. In the main works there were bells everywhere! Some dark grey ones had come from the foundry and were waiting to have a hole drilled in the top or to be dispatched. The ones that were an assorted shade of green were old ones that were being re-hung or were in storage waiting for some action. I was shown some that were waiting to be returned to the respective churches, with nicely painted red things bolted on called 'headstocks'. There were also a lot of wooden wheels, particularly in the joinery shop.

Across the road was another large building. This was the foundry where men were putting wooden patterns into boxes on the floor that were for making cast iron frames. At the far end there were moulds being made in things that looked like bells but were made of iron, and they all looked very weathered and rust coloured. There was a large door in the wall that had been raised up revealing the drying stove. Other iron cases were in there on their sides with shiny-grey linings, and there were also bell-shaped things that I was told were 'cores'.

The sensational thing in the works was an enormous framework of girders with lots of bells strung from then. I was told, 'This is for Canberra. It's a carillon.' There were lots of bars with levers and wires that went up to the bells, connecting to what I was told were clappers. Below the frame was a big hole with brick walls and a wooden set of steps. In this pit was a large wooden contraption with horizontal pegs sticking out. These seemed to be the same as keys on a piano, in two sets, one above the other, but all made out of polished wood. The wires coming down from all the levers came into the top of this gadget. 'This is a clavier.' Fine! It looked quite strange, and it had pedals as well, like an organ. I was told the enormous bell (except there were several) weighed six tons. I didn't really have any idea what six tons looked like but it was a very big bell! The bells that you could see from underneath were all a shiny gold colour as these had been tuned. So this was what tuned bells looked like! Grey on the outside and a gold colour on the inside.

The part of the works where I was going to be based was called 'the Tuning Shop.' It had large doors into the main works but otherwise was a self-contained building. Here all the bells were mouth up, and there were three special machines. The biggest of these was enormous.

These 'tuning machines' had wide leather belts coming down from pulleys that then went round other pulleys. There were lots of gears and cogs mostly covered in grease. Bells on these machines had some strange clamps that went down from the edge of the bells into slots in a turntable. They were going round reasonably fast, and metal was being cut off by men who were peering in and turning a device like a star fish. These star fish things brought a cutting tool into the side of the bell, and bits of metal fell into the bottom. 'Chippings', I was told. 'They go into paper sacks.' Several bags were being put on a large wooden trolley that came into the tuning shop on a railway track that was sunk into the ground, pushed in and out by hand. 'Chippings are weighed and then go to the foundry.'

The man who was explaining all this was called Harold. He had wiry grey hair, a sports jacket, a bow tie, and he smoked a pipe like Paul Taylor. It turned out this was his habitual dress style; it wasn't just for me on my first day. There was a room at the end of the tuning shop that was called the office but was not much like other offices I had worked in. There was an old desk and a lot of different shaped books with one open on the desk. At the side of this room there were loads and loads of tuning forks mounted on wooden boxes, with a number on the front of the box. I knew what tuning forks looked like, and they are shaped like a letter 'U' with two very tall sides and hardly any space between them.

At this stage, the man operating the big machine did something that made it slow down, and the funny clamps were undone with a spanner so they came away from the lip whilst the bell was still revolving! It ground to a halt, and a second man on a slightly smaller machine seemed to take this as a sign to stop his machine as well, but he didn't undo the clamps. The third man, called Stan, had pushed the wooden trolley into the works with the paper sacks. The man on the big machine, who was called Ron, then picked up a wooden mallet from several on a row suspended on cup-hooks, and Harold looked in his book. Ron hit the outside of the bell with his mallet, and Harold went over to the tuning forks and hit several ones close to each other with a thing like a soft drum stick. After hitting several of these tuning forks he came back to his book and wrote something down, and Ron was now hitting the bell on the outside, a bit lower down. Harold switched to a different set of tuning forks, and he seemed to know where he had to go along the line. Another entry was put in his book, the bell was hit again, and more forks were selected. Harold seemed satisfied, and then Ron hung his mallet back up and selected a piece of what looked like iron with a ball at the end. This time the sound was quite different, and Harold scurried to another section of the tuning forks. Ron waited patiently whilst Harold looked in his book, sucked his pipe, and then came to a decision. He went over to the bell and put two chalk lines in a particular place joined up with an 'X' between them. He did this in two different places, and Ron started the machine up again along with Sid.

Top right: *The first tuning machine installed about 1868 that allowed metal to be machined from the inside of the bell. Unlike later tuning machines, the bell is fixed and the cutting mechanism rotates.*

Bottom right: *The specially built tuning shop with the three tuning machines installed 1896-1897.*
Photos: Taylor archive

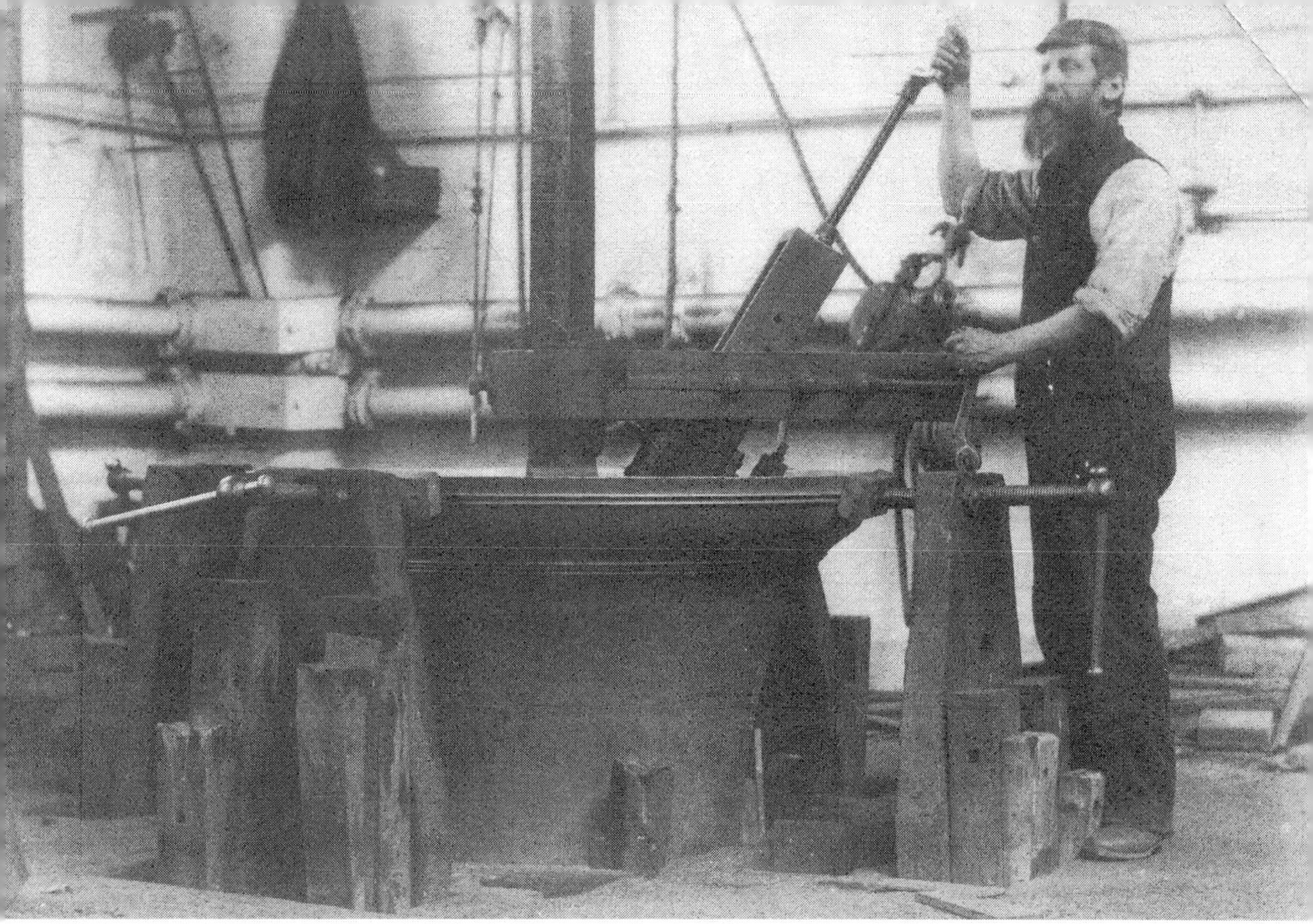

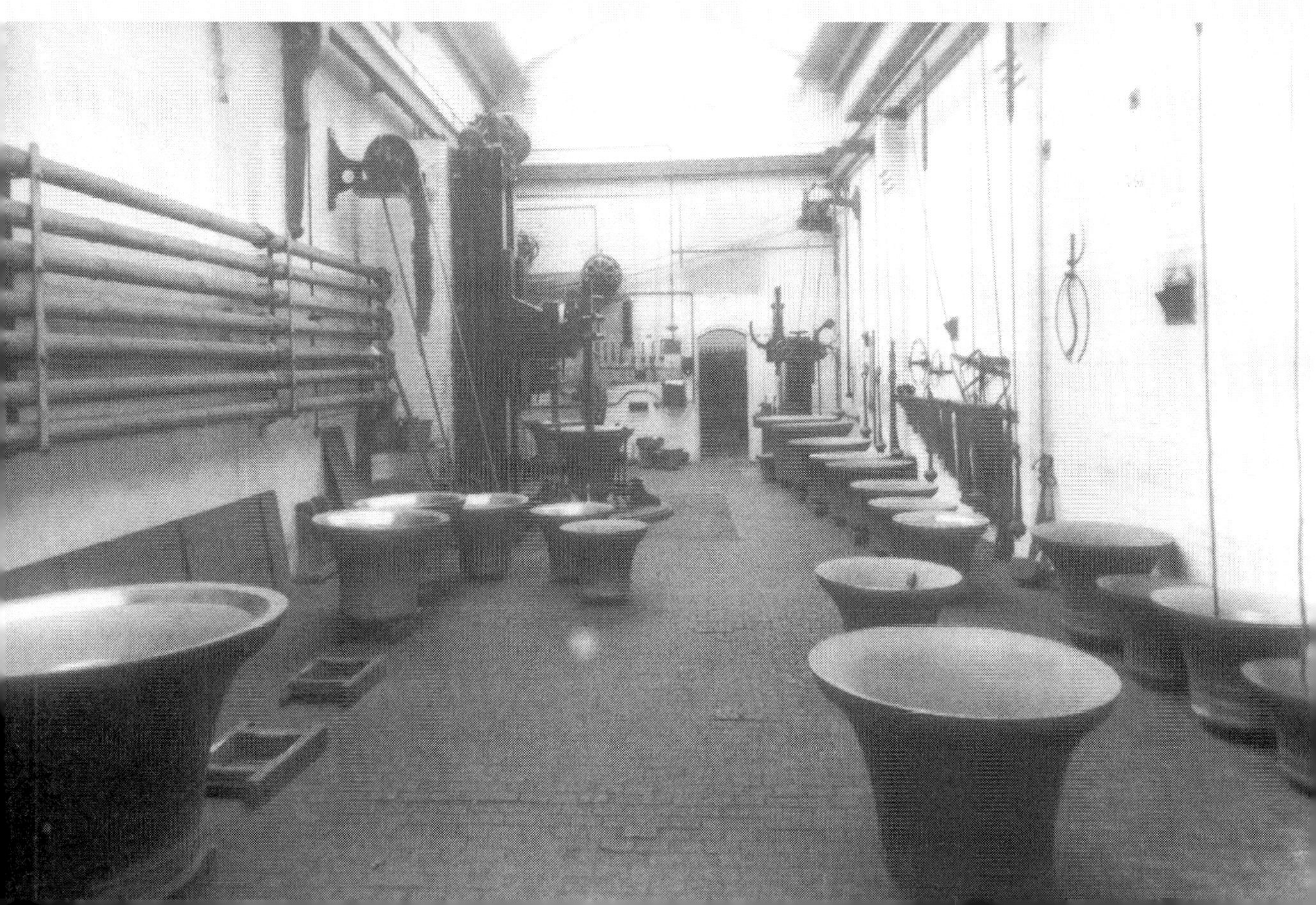

What was all this about? How did Harold know where to put the chalk marks? Was it black magic? Harold explained that he was keeping track of five different notes in each bell, and the numbers on the forks were frequencies. Right! So the one that had 440 written on the end of the box was 440Hz. Remember this? 440Hz is the note A above middle C. So the next fork along that said 444 was 444Hz, and the one that said 436 was 436Hz. Some light dawned! So between 440Hz and 220Hz, an octave down, there were fifty-five tuning forks 4Hz apart. Harold was comparing the note he could hear coming from the bells with the forks. I was beginning to get there, and after about a week I was able to match some bells to the forks. I'm going to explain exactly how this is done later, so contain your curiosity a bit longer.

Harold Marcon, a kindly man, was a ringer from Lincoln when he joined Taylor's in 1949 but was now about to retire. He told me one day that when he came for his interview he brought his wife (like you do), and Johnny Oldham, the general manager, drove them to see three houses. Taylor's must have owned these, and Harold's take home pay depended on which house they selected to rent! Good scheme! Eventually they owned it because he wasn't moving house when he retired. So Harold had worked at Taylor's for a long time.

After a couple of days Paul Taylor appeared. He had been off somewhere when I turned up so I was officially made welcome. He invariably wore a suit, cuff links, nice ties, and a handkerchief in his front pocket. He had a silver 440Hz tuning fork in the same pocket, but not one of the ones that needed a resonator box which would be silly. He was obviously extremely clever, and some years later in different circumstances, I decided he was a genius! Being clever was only half the story.

It turned out that the office that was called the tuning office was actually the nerve centre of anything to do with bells. If the foundry bods were being told that they had to make some bells, they were given a chit of paper with the sizes and the appropriate crooks. This came from our office, and this was the first they knew about it. This was one of Stan's jobs, and he was first given another bit of paper with the crook or strickle number that went with a particular size bell. In a big ledger there were details of all bells ordered and cast for a very long time, listed with their diameter and the crook number.

Plates on the crook that would determine the core size could be changed, and the tuning office decided which set of plates were required and wrote this in the ledger. Stan then went up some rickety wooden stairs to the crook room where the crooks were stored with their sets of three plates. One was for the soundbow, another for the waist, and a third one for the shoulder. The ledger had a record of the set of plates put on the crook the last time it had been used, the weight of the bell from the foundry, the notes within each bell 'as cast', and the finished weights after tuning.

Stan went to see if the plates on the crook were going to be the same as last time or needed changing. If they did, he brought the crook and the different plates to the tuning shop. He changed the plates, got them signed off as correct, and took them to the foundry. He had to bring all the crooks to the tuning shop even if the plates were the same. We had to check they were right and agree everything was tickety-boo. Any inscriptions were written on another sheet and then taken over as well. Each bell had the job number, and this number and the crook number were put into the case mould just above the shoulder. This was a good plan. When bells were brought to the main works, pushed over from the foundry, the blokes just dumped them there and went back for any others. We went to have a look and could identify each bell by the job number and the diameter or crook number. It usually worked! Otherwise they were just grey bells of all different sizes. Having decided where they figured in the scheme of things, they were weighed on the scales. Bells without a hole in the top are pretty useless. You can't tune them as the hole goes over a peg in the tuning machine, and the lifters we have talked about for moving the bells round the works needed a hole. Ultimately, a hole was really useful for stuffing the clapper in. So Charlie on the drill was the next person you needed. If some client had ordered a single two foot diameter bell, it was made to our standard crook setting, giving a weight of three hundredweight, note E.

If it was a complete new ring of bells, Paul was heavily involved. He decided the diameters, and when they were ready to be tuned he worked out the frequencies and put them in the tuning book. We tuned the bells to correspond to these figures.

If we were re-tuning old bells, or recasting a cracked bell, to start with we needed the notes of the bells in the tower. Jack Fiddler, who was usually carrying out inspections, had to lug round a very heavy reel-to-reel tape recorder, get it up the tower, and plug an electric cable in somewhere. He had a particular tuning fork, and he started the tape recorder going, hit the tuning fork and then all the bells in order. He used the tuning fork more than once during the recording, and if he did a good job we could play back the tape and determine the notes. Quite often we told him he had not hit the bell enough times, but it wasn't easy! He was grovelling round the bell chamber in all the dirt and pigeon guano, balancing the tape recorder where he could, with a microphone and a clapper to hit the bells. This was after he had found the nearest power point!

When he was back at base we listened to the tape and wrote the notes down. The tuning fork on the tape was compared with an identical one of ours to ensure that they both matched in frequency. There was a knob on the tape recorder that adjusted the speed slightly altering the frequency of the recorded fork if necessary to ensure the two tuning forks were spot on. We then decided which bells we could tune to make them better, or which ones might be scrap, and Paul did this normally. We had lists of bells by other bellfounders from present day to well back in time, and when an old bell came through our hands we made a record of the notes and weight. So the report on the state of the old bells, and how we could improve them, or how we hoped we could, went into a general report. This was winged down to the lot at the church, and hopefully we got the job. When these bells did come in we checked them for cracks. Remember the iron crown-staple cast into the head of the bell? Always good for cracks! We used dye or an electronic gadget to look for cracks, and if we found any, new plan, extra quote, new bell needed.

Harold Marcon obviously had a keen ear. He must have tuned thousands of bells of all sizes, but he hadn't been hired because of his knowledge of the physics of music or mathematical ability. Paul wrote calculations on bits of envelopes that the two secretaries supplied him with after the post was opened. 'Waste not, want not'. These scraps of calculations usually went into the bin in our office before he went off to do something else more important. Harold would often smooth out these crumpled bits of envelopes, light his pipe and study them, usually without too much understanding. It was a struggle for me as well. My maths was all right, I always knew if I had been short changed at the pub, and I did know something about the maths relating to acoustics and musical scales, but what Paul was calculating was quite often gibberish to both of us. Well, he was the bellfounder, and we were minions!

Eventually, it was just me who was the minion because Harold retired. I didn't find the tuning too difficult, and knowing where to machine metal off was just something you acquired with practice. Paul was always in the background, and quite often in the forefront, and the tuning office was where he headed off to the most. Sometimes the phone on my desk summoned me to his office which had portraits of previous Taylor family members hanging on the walls. Peter Cake was often called in as well, as Paul was preparing some quote and we were involved.

Another way of making bells ring was to fit electro-magnetic clappers. You get a thing like a cotton reel (but not so fat) and a lot of fine copper wire is wound round it. The hole in the middle of this cotton reel (called a bobbin) goes over an iron pin. When you plug the two ends of the wires into the wall socket, electro-magnetic force is created, and this snaps down a plate on top. The plate flips a lever which propels a cast iron clapper into the bell. These came from a company in Germany after we told them the basic size. An electrical control unit could be ordered as well, with a time clock if needed. I got the job of testing everything and repairing old ones when the coil on the bobbin had burnt out, or the clapper was going rusty and needed cleaning.. Before I worked there they sent for a friendly electrician, but it was decided I knew enough to test everything without burning down the works, and the same with motors that swung the bells. This was why they sent me to oversee 'Great Paul'. It was usually all right, and I didn't get too many shocks or swear unduly.

When there was a carillon being made, there was usually a practice clavier. This was identical to the normal one, with batons and pedals but not connected to the bells. When the batons were pushed down, a little hammer hit an aluminium bar, with one for each note. Basically, these are like the xylophones they sometimes have in orchestras, or the little ones your children play when you are trying to have a quiet nap. The longer the bar, the deeper the note, like pan pipes. There has been a stupid advert on the goggle box recently. A dog is sitting beside a park bench and appears to be playing some pan pipes. The producer of this advert does manage to get the dog to appear to blow from the smallest pipe to the biggest. But guess what? The music has the smallest pipes playing the deepest notes! Pan pipes just don't work like that. Surely somebody should have known that the longest pan pipe makes the lowest note and the smallest one the highest! It's not very complicated.

Right: *The practice clavier for the Canberra carillon showing the seat, foot pedals, batons and music rest. The aluminium bars and resonator tubes are hidden from view in the top section.*
Photo: Taylor archive

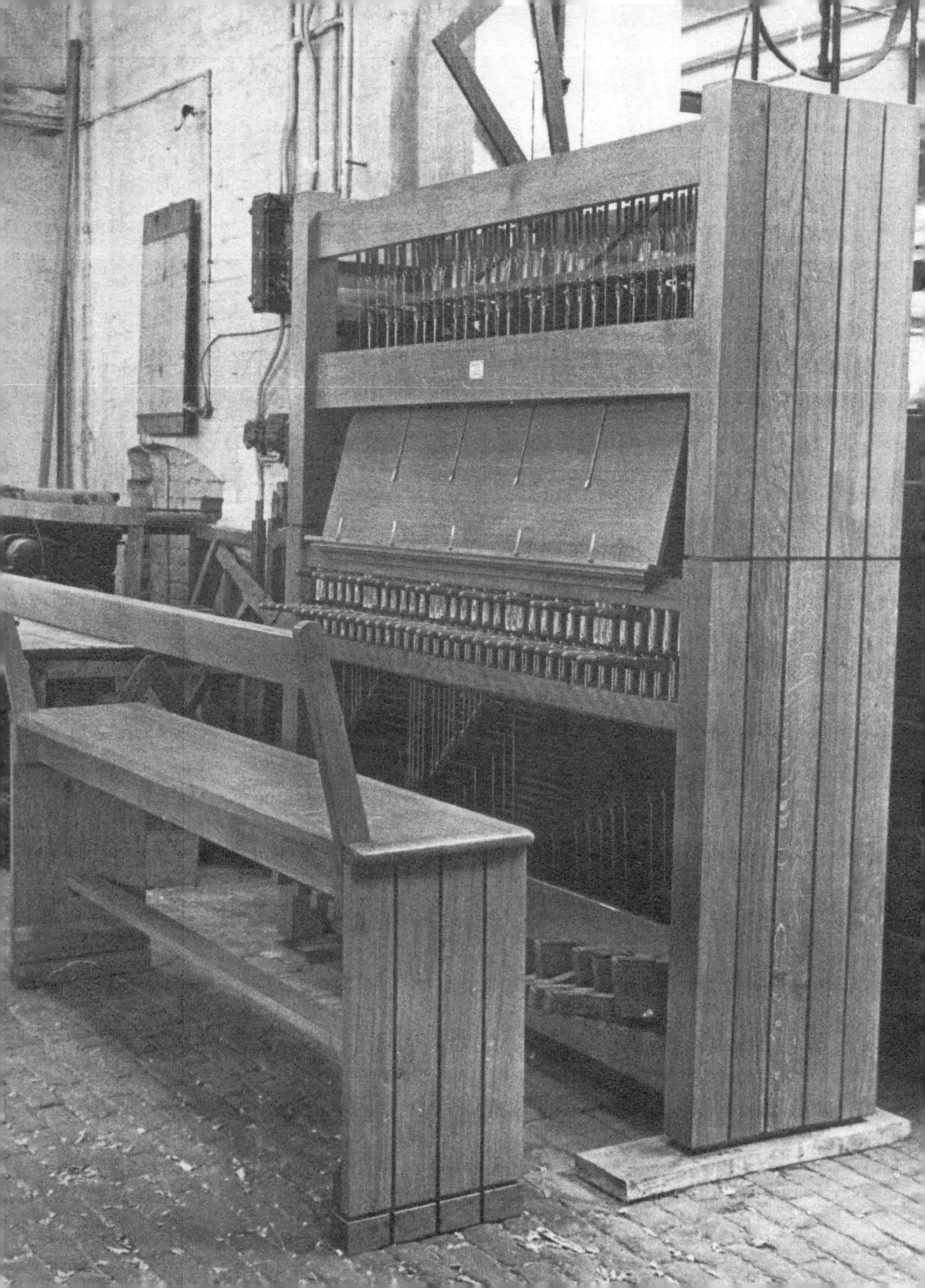

The aluminium bars were cut to different lengths but with as many bars as there were bells. To tune them we had to carve them underneath with a big file, continually checking with tuning forks until we had achieved the right note. It took ages! Forty-nine bells, forty-nine bars. When we had done this, we cut lengths of aluminium pipe. Forty-nine bells......yes......unfortunately, one tube for each bar. The tubes were suspended above the bars to improve the sound, and the smallest were only a few inches long. The longest ones were cut in two, and then brazed back together at an angle. A lot of work! The bars and tubes then went off to be plated, so they looked all shiny. Stan did this (not the plating; he filed the bars), but if he was busy I did it sometimes. He didn't cut the tubes to length as that needed applied maths, so I did this while he just beavered away shaping the bars. The carillonneur could practice his recital without the surrounding neighbourhood complaining. Listening to mistakes when someone is playing a piano in the next room is bad enough! Listening to a badly played carillon is excruciating, and the sound travels a long way.

One night before they dismantled the Canberra carillon to send it off, everybody in the works had gone home, but I was finishing something off, and there were only a few light bulbs on here and there. Paul Taylor decided to play this gigantic collection of bells sitting at the main clavier with some sheet music in front of him. It was one of those, 'This is what it is all about moments.' A bellfounder making heavenly music on a whole set of carillon bells he can put his name to. Excellent; I loved it.

The only thing was, the pay was lousy! Peter Cake had previously worked for a very large crane company in Loughborough as a draughtsman, like my father had first started out doing. When he came to Taylor's, he made it a condition that they paid him the union rate. He was still a member of the union, so when there was a general pay rise he got it. Clever boy! By now I had married the high-flying secretary who now had a plum job at Loughborough University, and she was being paid much more money than I was. The thing was, Denison had created a trust in his will. The bellfoundry was supposed to produce loot for people he named, and then their children. Trustees (usually a solicitor and an accountant, or the odd bank manager thrown in) administered the trust. If a lot of money was going out on things like wages, there was less (or none) to pay out. Denison obviously thought he was doing the right thing in 1947 – unfortunately.

I was a bit silly at this time in my life, and I thought I should be bringing home more bacon than I was. I should have clapped my wife on the back and said, 'Good for you! Well done!' It didn't seem likely I would be getting a pay rise any day soon, or perhaps not for ages. Peter cunningly enrolled me in his union that was for draughtsmen and technicians, but our accounts bloke said it didn't count. Fair, I suppose. So after three years, I got another job and left. Sad, but I thought I was doing the right thing, although a bit unnecessarily macho on my part. The next job was well paid, and then I was working for Leicestershire County Council doing an interesting job with good pay and prospects. I had kept in touch with Peter Cake socially, so he knew where I was and what I was doing. In 1977, he came to see me and had a proposal. Paul wanted me back at the bellfoundry, and there had been a dramatic re-arrangement of the company. Phase two?

17. Back in the Fold

'Revenons à nos moutons.' (Let us get back to the subject.)
Anon.

Well, I've given the game away now! The fundamental proposal was that in 1979 Paul was going to be sixty-five. He wanted to ease himself into retirement gradually, coming in just two to three days a week initially, but would always be involved. No doubt about that! When I joined Taylor's originally, Johnny Oldham had just retired from being a forceful General Manager. Frank Godfrey was retiring as well but with Peter Cake compensating for this. A foundry manager who had been there for ever had also just gone. So all the manpower had been sorted out, and everybody knew what they were doing, but the trust Denison had set up had not been working well for several years. Paul had decided how this could be solved and came up with a proposal. John Taylor & Co. (Bellfounders) Ltd. came into being, with directors, the same as any limited company. This company rented the premises from the trustees, so they now had some guaranteed loot every year. They in turn gave us all the equipment, so it could be upgraded if it needed to be, or scrapped. This sounded sensible and looked like good thinking and killed several birds at once.

Where I came in was that Paul wanted me to be his sorcerer's apprentice and to try to teach me loads of the things I needed to know. Well! That was going to be a big job! One day probably in the dim and distant future I would be fully in charge of the bells side. Riveting! When Peter first made this proposal, my first reaction was to ask, 'Well, how are you going to pay me? Where is the money going to come from?' He assured me that they might well pay me what I wanted and enrol me in a pension scheme. He didn't go too white about the gills when I told him what I was being paid currently, so talks became serious with Paul involved. Eventually I asked, 'Where do I sign?' Everybody in the works seemed pleased to see me back so a good start. I expect there might have been a couple who thought, *what's he doing back here?* but nothing serious, so I became a sorcerer's apprentice.

The new format of the company was that Paul was a director, and the boss of a company in Derby that had made big clocks for aeons (we often supplied them with bells) became head honcho as managing director. Douglas Hughes, one of the owners of Whitechapel, came in as another director. Well, all right, he knew a lot about running a bellfoundry even if his bells were second rate to ours, and his nephew Alan was in the shadows as well. Paul was always interested in some form of loose business association which Denison had tried in 1920. And there was a new general manager sent to manage us in general. Nobody was exactly sure how he fitted in. Well, I wasn't, and Peter was in the same boat.

So Peter continued his valuable work as works manager and carillon boffin. When Paul semi-retired I was given the title 'Bellmaster.' Seemed very premature to me, but when the letters weren't going to be signed 'Paul Taylor O.B.E.' it might look impressive if I was firing off letters. I haven't told you this. When the Canberra carillon was installed and opened by Queenie, Paul was awarded an O.B.E. Quite right! Well deserved!

I had been amazed to find in the tuning office two large scientific gizmos made by a world famous Danish company, Brüel & Kjaer, that made tip-top acoustical measuring equipment. This was the bees-knees and normally found only in acoustical laboratories. Where had these come from? I had come across this equipment when I went down to a manufacturer in Kent who made state of the art drive units for loudspeakers. Whilst I was waiting for some to be boxed up they gave me a guided tour, and they were using equipment from the same manufacturer in their research and development laboratory. These were really sophisticated bits of kit.

Paul explained that a boffin at Loughborough University of Technology was doing serious research into the way bells vibrated as they were just about unique. So this equipment appeared to be on permanent loan! They rang Paul up if they wanted to come and play with them, and as we had so many bells lying around continually it was the ideal place to come. It may have influenced their project to start with! Where can we find some bells? How about Taylor's? Let's see what they say? We had never used any electronic equipment ever, as we always thought that ear lugs and tuning forks were the perfect choice. It had worked well for over one hundred years.

The two large acoustical devices had the dust covers over them. As they looked so technical, Paul took the covers off when we had important visitors who might be impressed! They weren't plugged in of course! Why would we do that, just wasting electricity! They were on a new desk in full view from outside the office door, but it wasn't actually a new desk; I just hadn't seen it before. I think the accounts department slung it out after it had its hundredth birthday. It had a sloping desk top, ideal for writing in big ledgers with a quill pen, and the shelf at the top was for dusty tomes. In due course, the equipment and the boffins were very useful to us and visa-versa.

Top Right: *A collection of various tuning forks with assorted soft felt strikers. The one on the left is a 440Hz reference fork with resonator box. The two hammers are for testing and ascertaining partials in small bells.*
Photo: By author

Bottom left: *A 'Revox' professional reel to reel tape recorder, of the type used for recording bells in the works and dubbing recordings onto a second machine.*
Photo: By author

Bottom Right: *A Brüel & Kjaer acoustical laboratory beat frequency oscillator.*
Photo: Brüel & Kjaer, Copenhagen

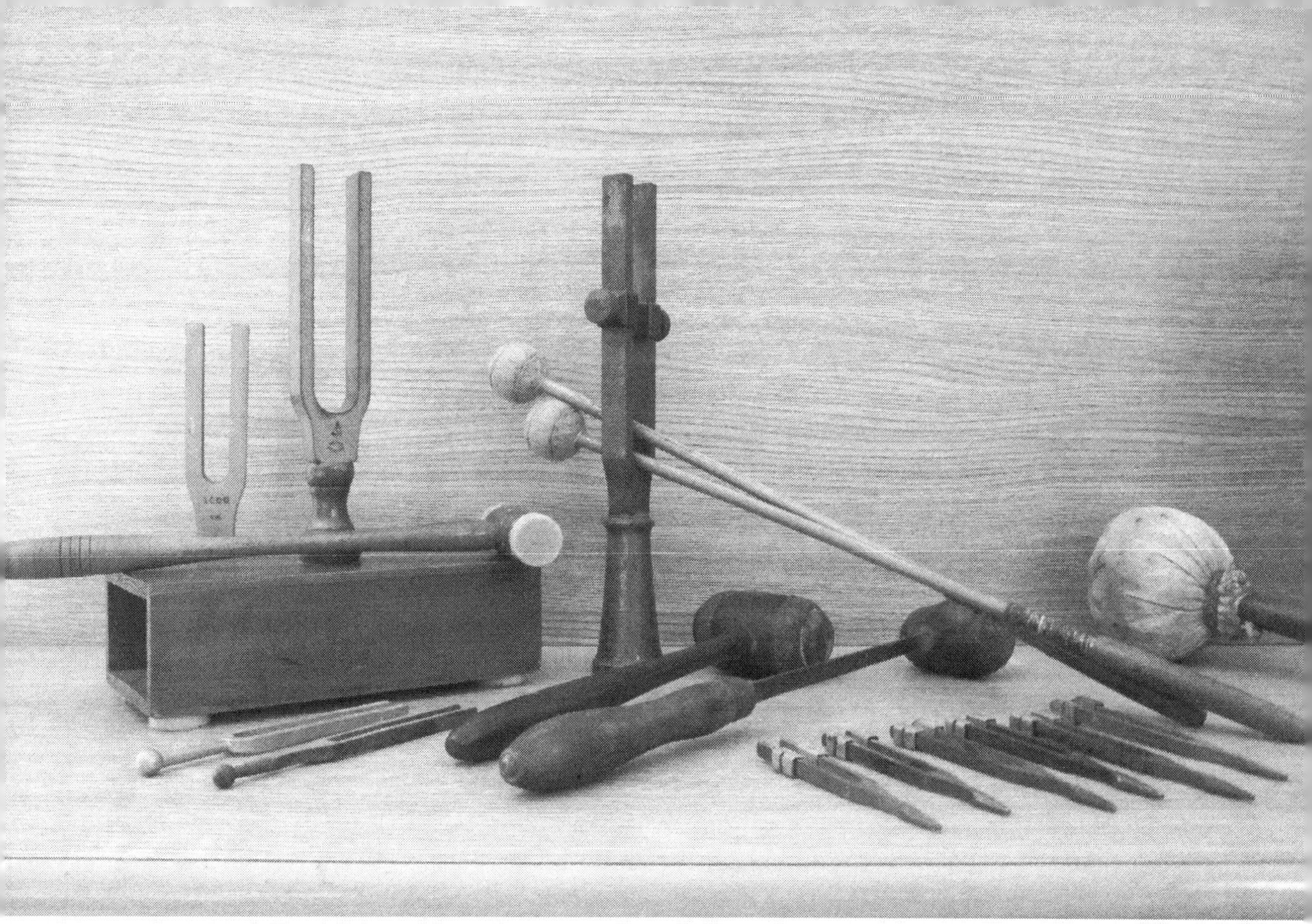

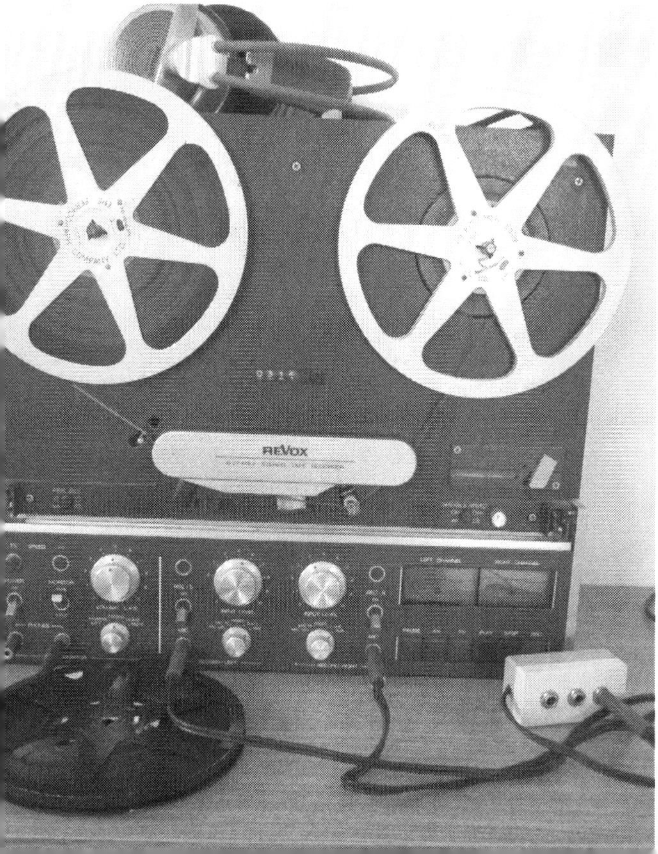
REVOX

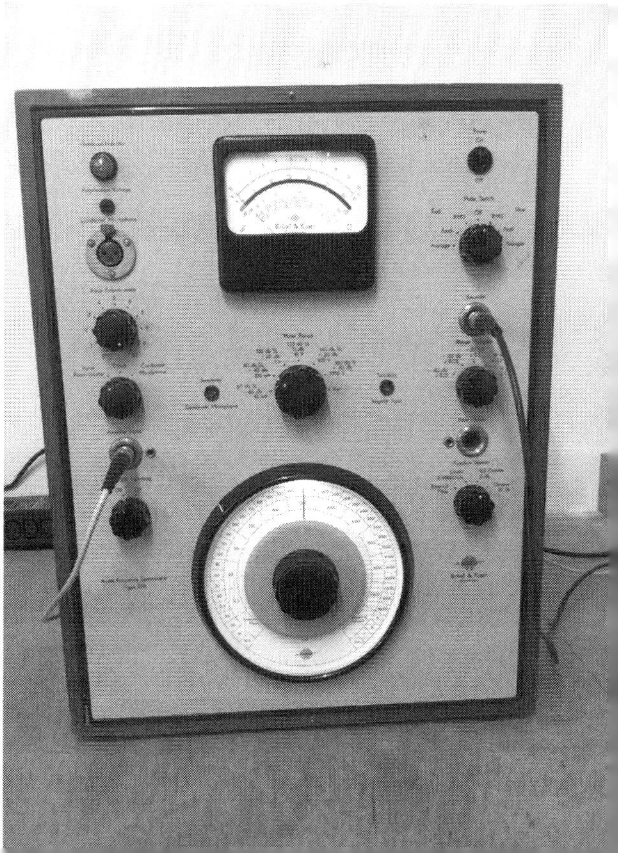

One of the magic things that Paul used every day was called 'A Fowler's "Magnum" long scale calculator'. On the front of the instruction book it proclaimed, 'The World's Best'. It had cost forty shillings but another shilling for the instruction book. Hardly fair, was it? You bought this thing like a very large pocket watch with another knob to twiddle apart from the one normally found on a watch. You didn't wind it up, but you rotated a disk with an amazing amount of scientific and maths scales. It was an all singing all dancing, circular slide rule type gadget. But the instruction book cost another shilling! Dear me. It dated back to about the 1930s when Paul had bought it.

Slide rules are gadgets that have lots of mathematical symbols on them, and they are extremely clever if you know how to work them. I consequently bought the normal sort and a book, *Slide Rules for Dummies*. Peter Cake used one, and my father had done as well. After about three weeks of reading the book I could see that I wasn't going to be able to compete, so I bought a scientific calculator instead. Much better! You hit various keys, and the result came up in numbers at the top. I am now the proud owner of Paul's magic circular calculator in the very nice leather case, and I will explain how I came to have it later.

If you are really clever and are trying to explain something to a lesser mortal, you may get a bit frustrated if they are not following you. Paul was very patient with me about 90% of the time! When I could carry out the same steps as him in some long calculation on my humble calculator, just now and then I could correct his finished numbers! You can 'round-up' a long calculation on slide rules by making the number 99 up to 100, or 49 up to 50, or some other slight change to make it quicker. Just once or twice I could tell him, 'You're not exactly right!' Only sometimes! His calculations on the backs of envelopes began to make sense. There is a lot of maths in music, and we have seen how octaves are a doubling up or a halving of a frequency, and diameters and weights of bells are linked through maths. Working out the numbers or frequencies of every note from (for example) the A below middle C up to the A above in twelve semitone steps is just maths.

One thing that always needed close attention was when new bells were being put into a ring of old bells, often cast by different founders over a span of centuries, and we had them in the works. We kept records of every bell that came through our hands, but the thing was, we were trying to get the swing of all these assorted bells right. If we could do this, the ringers had more of a sporting chance. This was back to the centre of gravity which we knew in relation to new Taylor bells, but old ones didn't obligingly match in.

In the tuning office, because we were supposed to know more about old bells than anyone else, we worked out the measurement known as 'bell hangs'. This was the distance from the lip of the bell to the centre of the axles on the headstock. The technical term for the axle is a 'gudgeon' but nothing to do with fish! Every bell with new fittings went on a 'ringing up stand' that had two substantial pillars, one of which could be moved. The bell, headstock, clapper and wheel were assembled and bolted to these pillars. It was then 'rung up'

Right: *The Taylor employee Girdar Vadukar checking the clapper swing and position on the recast two ton slow swinging bell for Harvard University Chapel, in the works in 2014.*
Photo: John Taylor & Company

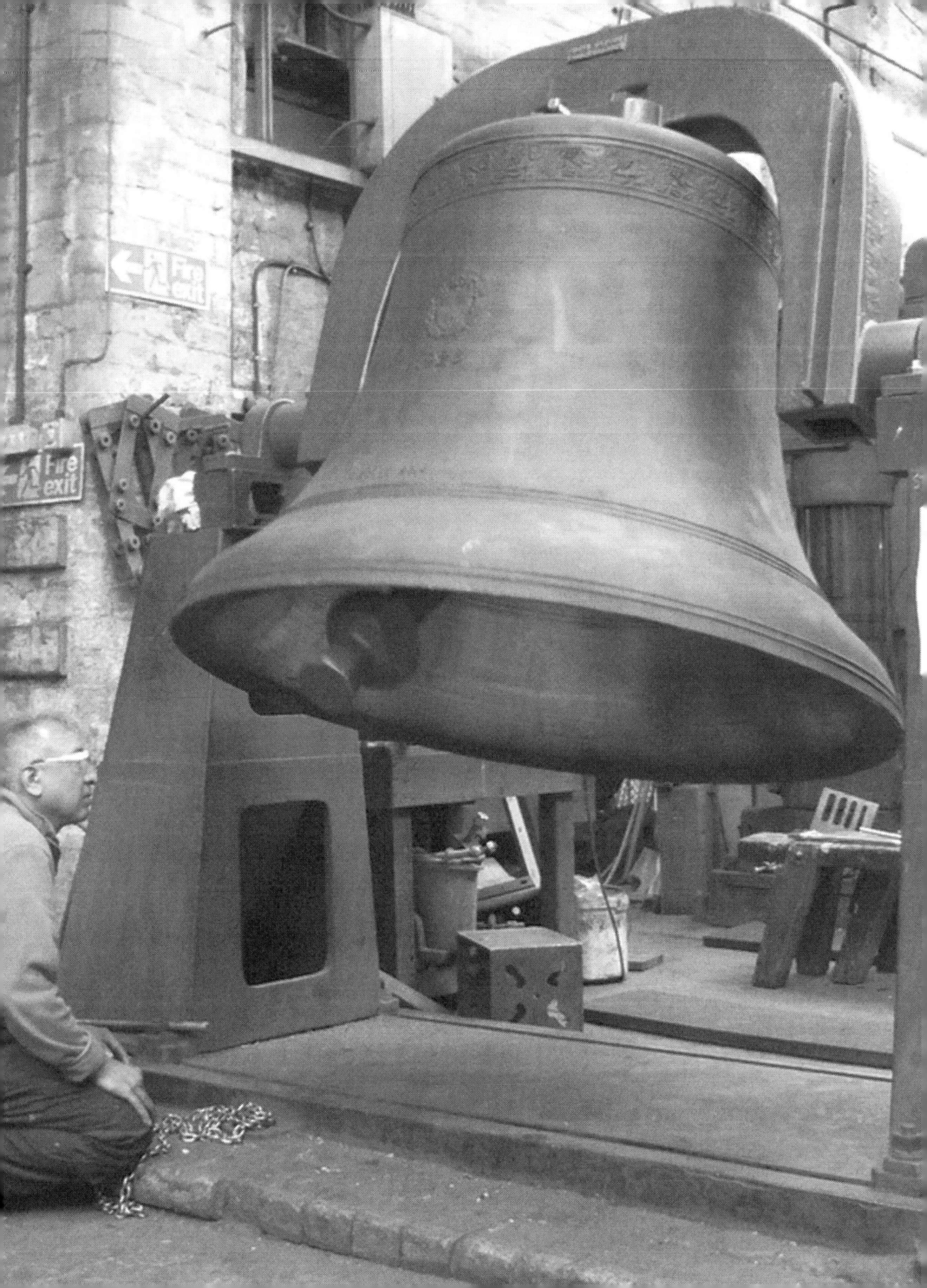
Fire exit
Fire exit

by hand. You could hear this was being done throughout the works and the offices and often way up the street outside, and this was a signal for someone to come out with a stop watch. The bell was released to swing down like a normal ringing bell, and the time it took for five swings of the bell and clapper was noted and written down. If there was any adjustment needed to the clapper it was done at this point in time. The minions in the drawing office came and did this or Peter Cake, or, as a last resort, me!

We juggled with these 'bell hang' measurements a lot. Paul often went back to previous rings with bells from the same founders where we had the period of swing times written down. One evening, probably after having a bell casting session that day, I was in the bath washing off the grime, and there was a very decent tide mark! When I got out to dry myself off, another tide mark appeared a bit lower down. So this gave me my personal eureka moment! The next day I said to Paul, 'Suppose we had a big tank of water with a glass tube at the side that joins the tank at the bottom, so the water comes up the tube as well. If we dunk a bell completely up to its top, the water will go up the tank and tube to a higher level. So we mark that and then start slowly lifting the bell back out. When the level of the water in the tank and tube is halfway down from what it was, then we have found the centre of gravity.' Paul was very impressed, but we decided it was not feasible as where would the tank go? Good idea though!

Our managing director from Derby was tall and imposing and a magistrate to boot. He sat on the 'bench' and handed down fines and prison terms for relatively minor offences. He was soon very useful when we sacked the newish foundry manager! There were a host of good reasons including that his 'people-management' on a scale of one to ten was minus fifty. Because the foundry was completely separate from the main works he had decided it was his own empire. Not cricket, not team work. He was given the right amount of warnings, and then we waved good bye! We didn't really wave, we cheered instead. The young man who was promoted was Roger Johns who was very capable and skilled, and he still works there now. The only thing was, his workload suddenly went up dramatically.

It was decided that I would be much more involved in supervising which bells we needed when, and juggling case sizes if we had orders for three bells all at the same time with the same diameter. It's called Sod's law. The amount of metal we were going to put in the furnace when we were having a cast also needed careful calculations. I worked all this out after Roger and I agreed when we were going to have a cast, and of which bells.

At some stage the small coal-fired furnace had been equipped with an oil blower instead. We squirted diesel oil in with a big air blower to make a spray. You had to get the air and oil mix exactly right otherwise the metal might oxidize, and keep increasing or decreasing the strength of the jet of flame as the metal became molten. To make sure that this was done correctly I took over lighting the furnace and adjusting the flame. If there were visitors to see a cast, we needed to get the metal up to temperature whilst they were being shown round the works and then send a runner to say, 'Come over to the foundry. Now!'

We were now short of one person when we poured the metal, so I took over tipping the ladle and molten metal into the runner boxes, and Roger was the one who let it down into the moulds. The other important person was the man on the crane. He had to nudge the controls gently to move the ladle from one mould to the next. I also bought more safety gear bearing in mind that 'familiarity breeds contempt'. Just because you haven't been splattered with molten metal for a long time doesn't mean it won't happen one day! Remember Matthew Bagley? I also arranged to obtain two large propane gas heaters, the sort you wheel about, that made the lives of the workers a bit more tolerable in winter. So everything was under control; well nearly.

When the furnace needed re-lining we did it ourselves. It had been done scores of times over the years by a local builder, but I decided we could do it ourselves. When it was out of action we couldn't cast bells, so some of the foundry lads were a bit spare. There was a company we dealt with regularly who supplied free standing furnaces and crucibles used for melting cast iron. I decided we didn't need an arched roof which was a throwback to when the coal-fired flame was being reflected back onto the metal. With the oil and air blower we blasted the flame over the metal, and as the fire brick company sold big interlocking slabs we could have a flat roof. Peter was a bit doubtful about this as every other time the furnace had been re-lined it had been done with an arch, including after we converted it to oil. The fire brick man agreed with me, so we took the lid off, replaced all the bricks, and used flat slabs for the roof. We also dropped the floor down slightly to give us a bigger capacity. When we had finished it and tried it, everything was fine. A good job as it was all my idea!

I checked the inscriptions with a mirror after Roger had carefully tapped the letters into the moulds. We also checked them in the tuning shop, but it was a bit late then! One day, a churchwarden's name had a letter missing. He had a complicated surname, like Braithwaite-Llewellyn-Smythe, or something like that, and there was a letter missing that was impossible to correct! So we tuned the bell for Mr. Braithwaite-Llewellyn-Smythe, now re-christened something slightly different, and sent it off! We never heard so much as a murmur. If he did see it perhaps he thought someone had spelt it wrong at their end? I had signed it off in the foundry as being correct of course!

So everything seemed to be proceeding to plan until the directors announced we were very short of work. It happens sometimes. It's like buses that all come along together when you have been waiting for half an hour! So the chiefs had a pow-wow. I think that after Paul, who was still the big boss of course, it ought to have been politely mentioned to Peter, and probably Jed Flatters and myself. Jed had by now taken over from Jack Fidler and was doing all the inspections. (He had started as a bellhanger, balancing on girders in the sky, pulling bells around in mid-air, and had now progressed to inspecting bells. He was often in the same boiler suit in the tower and still up to his neck in dirt and guano but a much more important job.) I think there were some 'smoke and mirrors' I never understood at the time, and still don't, but the crisis was averted. To give them their due, Whitechapel did divert to us some work they could have done involving Taylor bells. So a big thanks for this. Still not crystal clear though, and a hidden agenda somewhere! Peter clinched some carillon jobs, and Jed and I rang round the bods on church councils responsible for orders that we thought were going to be coming our way. This bore fruit as well and we were able to continue.

In 1979 Paul officially retired but came in at least two days a week, and I bought him a matching scientific calculator as a present. Small carillon bells were still an area we were constantly trying to improve. Duplicate bells had not been the answer, and one bellfounder even put them upside down! That didn't work either! Putting them on the outside of the frame in the tower openings was all right if you were listening on that side of the tower! So Paul and I did a lot of work together making little bells much heavier. By now, jobs for the States often came with a 'carillon consultant' who was usually a carillonneur from somewhere. They dreamed up specifications and came to sign off the finished bells. There were a few of these, so we dealt with that in our stride! Being a carillonneur didn't necessarily guarantee that the person had a really good ear. We had, but why did they think they had? One day, one of them was checking our new shiny bells and he queried the exact frequency of one of the bells with an electronic gadget he was using. Paul and I wandered down to have a look, and he was making out one of the notes was not exactly right by a smidgen. When we looked at his gadget he had set it to the wrong octave! He was booked into a hotel, so we told him that by the next morning it would be all tickety-boo. We didn't touch the bell, and the next morning we made sure his gadget was measuring the right note; which was, of course, perfect. Paul was suitably scornful and complained that if he couldn't tell by ear what he was listening to, why was he in the works at all? The simple answer was that he was being paid to be a consultant, along with all the expenses he put through. Other consultants were fine and we had fruitful discussions with them when major work was being done.

Because they were getting a bit nit-picking, I wanted to know the exact temperature that 440Hz related to. I rang the head tuner at the Steinway piano company in London and asked him. He told me that they factory tuned their pianos to 440Hz international pitch, but if they took a piano to the Royal Albert Hall or the Festival Hall they fine-tuned it there. He did agree there must be a standard temperature somewhere, and the answer came back that at a laboratory in Paris there was a 440Hz reference fork, that was kept at exactly twenty degrees centigrade. He was quite interested in how we tuned bells which turned out to be the same way they did, by ear, listening to beats! We told the consultants that 440Hz applied to an ambient temperature of twenty degrees and nothing else! So there were various discussions with these consultants before they went back home and left us alone to get on with it.

The university profs were still churning out scientific papers in publications such as *The American Journal of Acoustics*. I started using their equipment as it was silly just having the dust covers on them, and they provided another string to our bow. The main prof was Tom Charnley, and Bob Perrin was one who came to Loughborough from Auckland to get involved in the research during a year off. He was very good and stayed much longer than had initially been planned. As far as I know he never went back! Another American prof, Tom Rossing, also dropped in now and then. It was very valuable research with extremely technical, cutting-edge, acoustical investigations. Sometimes it was a bit above my head, but they were very useful people to chat with. It didn't take them long to cotton on that Paul knew a great deal about bellfounding! They thought the Taylor profile was just about perfect and continually asked to see the master drawing with the geometric construction. We hadn't got it to show them because we didn't know where it was! I discovered it much later on.

They decided that the University would award Paul an honorary Doctor of Science (D.Sc) degree. Degrees like this are ones they hand out to people who have become very eminent in their field and usually have important links to the university. Paul already had a normal degree in engineering of course, from when he was at Sheffield University. When it was the summer degree ceremony, Paul was awarded his honorary degree. Quite right! A truly eminent person who rightly deserved this recognition. At award ceremonies like this, the recipients of honorary degrees give a little speech. Paul's speech was not at all like anything they were used to hearing! I'll tell you what he said in a bit.

18. Some Special Jobs

'Find a job you enjoy doing, and you will never have to work a day in your life.'
Mark Twain

In April 1980 a phone call was put through to me that was one of these 'how much is a big bell?' enquiries. Our secretary told me it was somebody from Birmingham, and it turned out to be a company, Light & Sound Design, with an enquiry regarding the rock band *AC/DC*. This time cost didn't seem to be an issue, and the question was simply, 'Can you supply a big bell?' After I said, 'Yes, this is what we do,' the *AC/DC* manager, Ian Jeffery, then rang me and told me they needed a big bell, note C, with the *AC/DC* logo in very large letters that would show up from the back of a US auditorium. This meant a sixty-inch bell weighing two tons. I began to think, *this is a really serious enquiry.* The problem was, they wanted it in six weeks, so I then thought, *probably the last we will hear of this then!* I explained about moulds and casting a bell that then had to be tuned, and the next question was, 'Well, how big a bell can we have?' I suggested a forty-eight inch bell weighing one ton, note E, and they could drop the note of the bell down to C in their recording studio for the album. This was agreed to be quite feasible, and they thought that a bell that weighed one ton was probably the heaviest weight they could suspend over the stage for their live concerts.

I went home thinking, *they really do want a big bell, but who are AC/DC?* I was a fan of *Dire Straits* but wasn't really up to date with *AC/DC!* The order was placed the next day, and the bell had to have the *AC/DC* logo in very large letters polished up to reflect the stage lighting and spotlights, but they didn't really want the bell to be a grey colour. I promptly suggested we would paint it gold! Good plan. If there were any slight imperfections from rushing the moulds we could remove them before we painted it.

I told Peter about this and all he asked was, 'Will we get paid?' I told him I thought we would. With the written order that I had insisted on, I had been given a contact name and address for the London office of Prager & Fenton, an extremely large firm of accountants in New York.

I found out later that their Scottish born singer Bon Scott had choked to death in a car in London on Feb. 14th, 1980. *AC/DC* thought of disbanding but eventually decided not to as they thought he would have wanted them to keep going, so Bon Scott was replaced by Brian 'Jonna' Johnson. It was a good career move for him as he had been working at a car factory putting in windscreens! The *Back in Black* Scott memorial album was being recorded over six weeks in April-May at Compass Point Studios, Nassau, which gave them some reduction in taxes. Malcolm Young later commented that whilst they were there, 'I was just taking a piss and I just thought, *hang on, why don't we get a big f.....g bell.*' The weather in the Bahamas was unusually foul with constant tropical storms, and Brian Johnson recalled, 'It wasn't a tropical paradise. It wasn't all white beaches. It was pissing it down, there was flooding, and often all the electricity went out!' The *Hell's Bell* track lyric reflect this: 'I'm a rolling thunder, pouring rain. I'm coming down like a hurricane..... I got my bell, I'm gonna take you to Hell'.

Jake Berry, their very important general factotum and road manager, was now really on my back to know when the bell had been tuned as the album was being mixed in New York, so a recording was needed forthwith. As soon as it was finished being tuned, Tony Platt, their recording engineer, came to the bellfoundry with a mobile recording studio. I opened up the works in the evening so it would be quiet. I was chosen to toll the bell as it had to be struck exactly on one of four places round the circumference. The very large raised *AC/DC* logo made the bell out of balance on this side, producing a slow pulsing sound. Carillon bells often had this problem, which we could deal with (we called it a 'wobble'), but I had never experienced it on a big bell.

In an interview in November 2014 in *SOS Magazine*, Tony Platt stated that, because the recording was so urgently needed, he used sixteen microphones of two types, recording the sound on tape over twenty-four channels so he could edit it later. The finished tape was then flown immediately to New York. It did take a long time setting everything up at the foundry. I have bragged over the years to family and friends (or anybody who would listen) that it is my 'performance' on the *Hell's Bell* track as it's me hitting the bell! Tony Platt comments, 'The guy who made the bell was the guy who hit the bell on the record, and there was a specific spot painted red where he had to hit it'. I should have asked for a fee or a share of record sales and 1% would be nice, but I didn't think of that! When the album was released it zoomed into the charts at number one in the US & UK. To date (well, the last time I looked), total album sales are given as over fifty million, the second highest number of sales ever, except for Michael Jackson's *Thriller*. The note of the bell was dropped down for the album recording so it sounds really good, and at six minutes it is the longest track.

As we were being pushed so hard to finish the bell quickly, there was a proposal within Taylor's that the bell that had the same note at Loughborough's World War I Memorial Carillon was recorded instead. I discounted this as it was difficult to get a mobile recording studio near enough, and traffic noise and cooing pigeons on the outside of the high tower were a problem we couldn't solve. We could have shot all the pigeons, but stopping the traffic was unlikely. Tony Platt agreed with this, but the recording of this carillon bell has been erroneously put in an *AC/DC* magazine article as being 'fact'.

Right: *Initial sound checks for microphone placement to record the 'AC/DC' one ton bell in the works. The author is on the left, and their recording engineer, Tony Platt, is on the right.*
Photo: David Humphrey

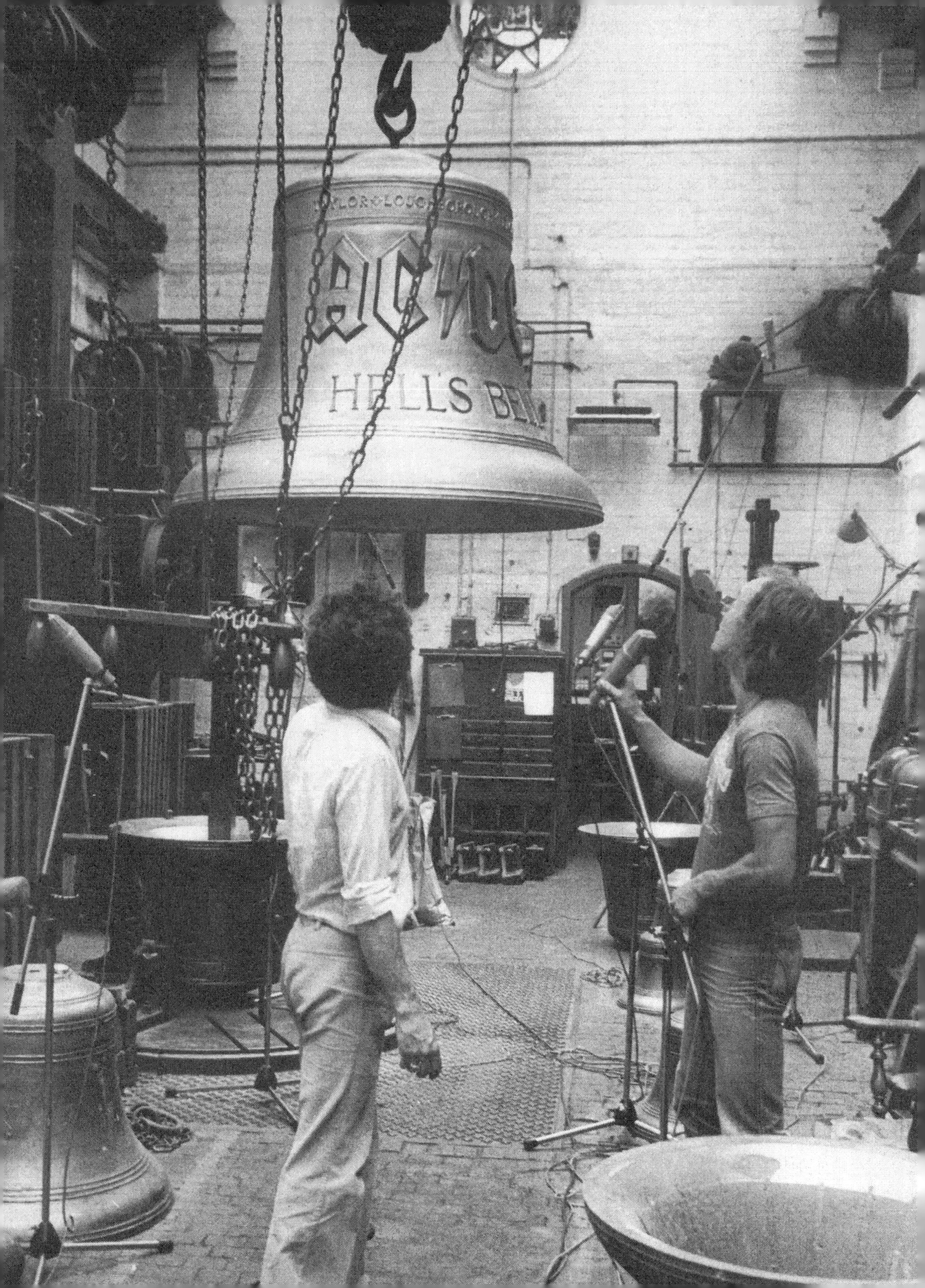
AC/DC
HELLS

I didn't tell Paul that it was going to have *Hell's Bell* on it as well as their logo! He came to inspect it on his next day in the works, and apart from raised eyebrows he took it very well! The lads in the works were very excited, but neither Paul nor I thought it was a big deal. We had no idea the bell would become so famous.

I was sure that the bell would soon crack if they were smacking it with a hammer on stage, so because of this I reduced the tin content slightly to make it a smidgen less brittle. We initially supplied six hammers, but they were continually needing more! They did break one or two, but frequently they didn't know where they had put the last ones! Making multiple sets of hammers was quite profitable, and Jake always needed them air-freighted to different parts of the globe yesterday, but Prager & Fenton kept signing the cheques. One day when he was panicking, I said to him, 'So you are in dire straits!' He replied, 'Very good, Mike', and then something really rude to do with how soon we could send the hammers off!

Our normal work progressed, and Paul and I recast the smallest bells for the Cranbrook carillon in the US that we had produced in 1928. A big job was the recasting of the bells for Christchurch Cathedral in New Zealand, and making them up to thirteen. These were considered a flagship ring of ten back in 1881, but 'old style' of course. In February 2011 the cathedral was badly damaged in a major earthquake, and aftershocks in the following December caused more damage. What bad luck! More problems with tremors in 2016 haven't helped, and a drone was sent in during June 2016 to assess the damage. Engineers say that it is not safe for anyone to be inside, and no part of the cathedral is considered structurally sound! There is a big argument as to whether they reinstate the ruined cathedral or demolish it and build a new one, with no firm decision as yet. All the bells fell down, but amazingly only one cracked. They all came back to Taylor's to be checked and the cracked one recast. A semitone bell was ordered to make a light ring of eight. So far they are far from being back in use. The ringers are proposing a temporary tower made from six shipping containers. Well why not? You can do all sorts of things with shipping containers.

In 1981, Wellington Cathedral in New Zealand had a new tenor and a treble bell, recast from the flagship ring of ten supplied in 1884. Two trebles were added to make a ring of twelve along with two semitone bells, and the remaining bells came back to be re-tuned. I was involved in frequent phone calls to the Dean who was the boss man, but Wellington is thirteen hours ahead of the UK, so we had to schedule the calls to suit us both. In the end we both swapped home phone numbers as well as the work ones! When I was talking to him it was quite often the next day there as well. In the end I used a spare digital clock and set it to be local time there. Really weird!

Top right: *The mobile recording studio from 'Manor Recording Studios', Shipton-on-Cherwell, owned by Richard Branson & Virgin Records, in the works.*
Photo: author

Bottom right: *Setting up final microphone placement with a CCTV link to the recording engineers.*
Photo: author

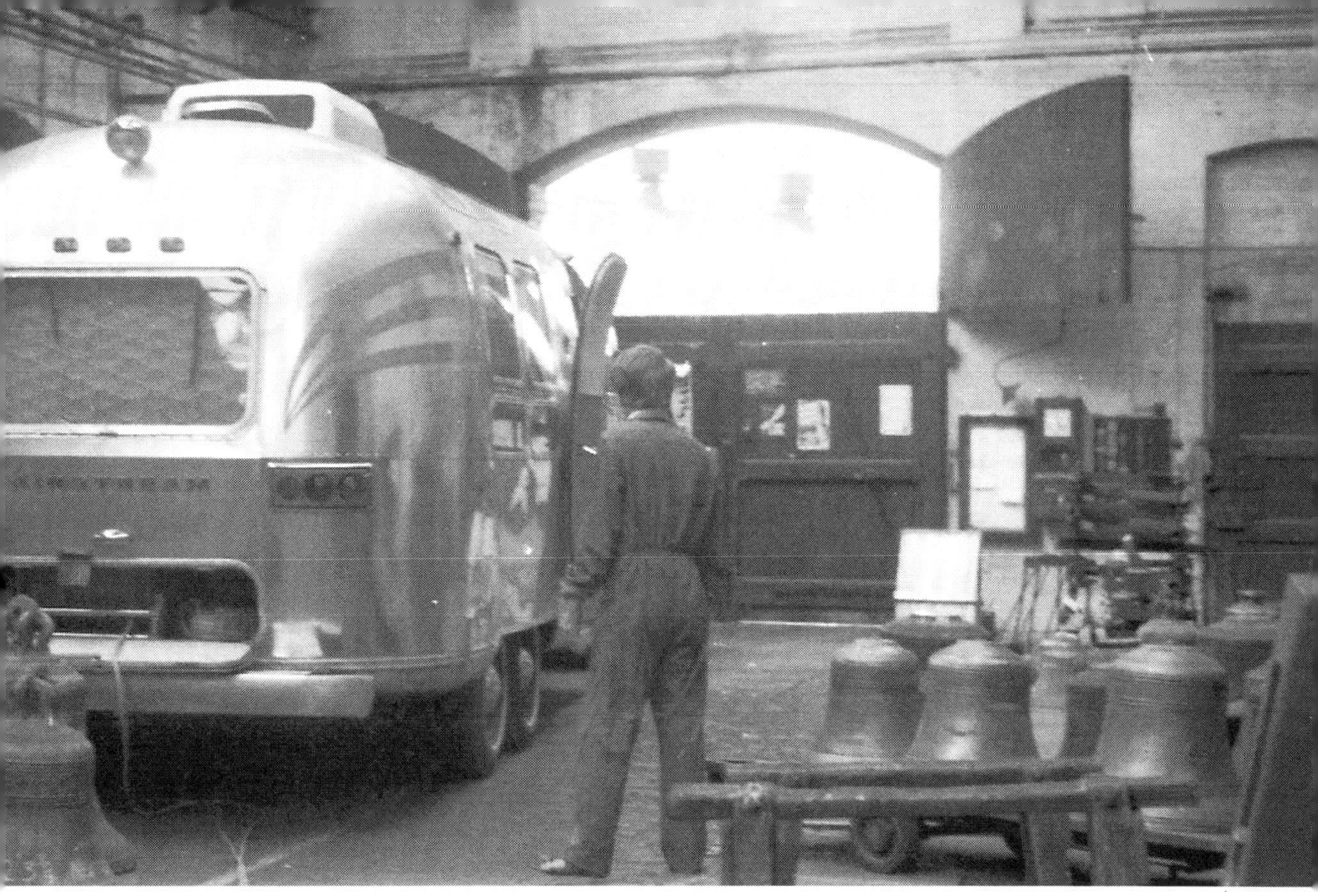

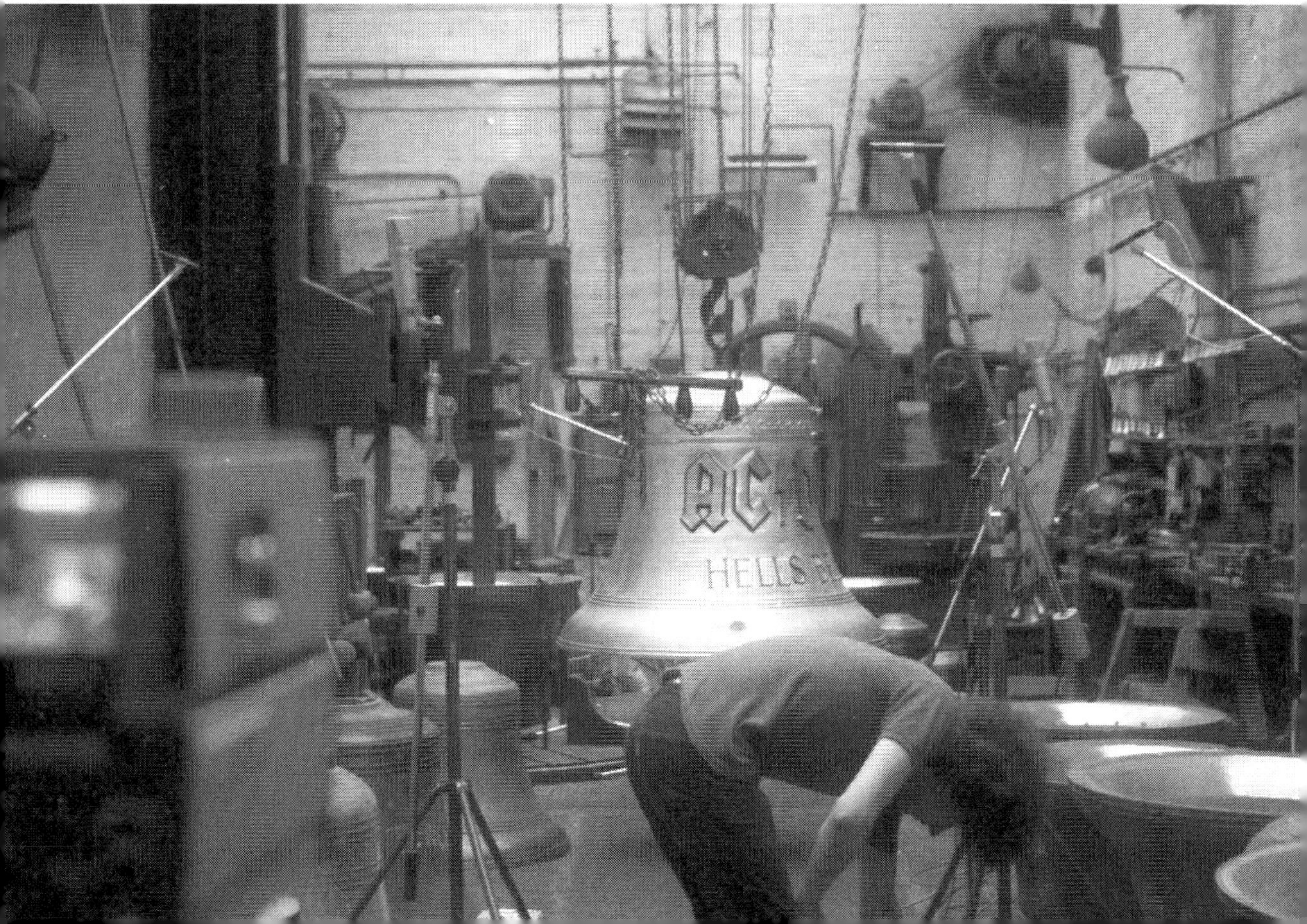
HELLS

Everything appeared to be going swimmingly until Paul died in October 1981. Just like that, no warning, in the blink of an eye. He was only sixty-seven, for God's sake! Twelve hours after I had had a conversation with him on a Saturday night that had now become the last one. He had said that he had something really interesting to tell me! This hadn't been in the forward plan. Horrendous. Suddenly I was left without his advice, his fount of knowledge, and not least importantly, his friendship. I like to think he had explained 90% of the things I needed to know and that he wanted me to understand. But was it 90% or only 80% or less? And what would the other 10% or 20% or more have been? Impossible answers. Peter and I took stock of the situation, and we agreed that small carillon bells still needed more research. What I could achieve on my own remained to be seen. The Loughborough University gang were still in frequent contact, and we had cast one or two small bells of different profiles for them to play with, so I could bounce ideas off them if I needed advice.

By now, a friend of mine called Marc, who was a wizard electronics designer, had set up his own business. He had worked at the factory in Leicester when I was peddling their audio equipment. We were still equipping bells with motors and chain drives to turn them into slow-swinging ones, and we had always been buying these motors from our German supplier. This was silly as there were thousands of motors available in the UK from a variety of suppliers. Marc told me that you could now buy motors that reversed direction, and although they were more money, were far more useful. A motor that could be reversed was going to be a lot easier to set up. The exact period the motor was actually driving the bell was always very tricky to get right. When the bell was swinging gaily up to the horizontal, you had to be really careful it didn't keep creeping up a lot further. It took us about two days when 'Great Paul' was being motorized with two motors! With these new-fangled motors we put two sensors in, so a piece of metal on the wheel went past each sensor when the bell was about horizontal. This switched the motor off, so the motor only drove the bell until the exact time it was told not to! We had to play around to start with, sticking the bits of metal on with 'blu-tack', but we got there eventually.

Marc started making us swish control units to go with the electro-magnetic clappers. Roman Catholic churches want bells that ring at a particular time when a mass is being held, or in the evening, so we made a good few of these. Convents and monasteries liked these as well. We were still buying these clappers from Germany which was unnecessary. Two more of Marc's friends, who owned a metal bashing company, made them to our improved design. Bigger coils meant more oomph, so another contact supplied these. We even sold them to the clock company in Derby where our managing director came from. At a good price of course! The only fly in the ointment was that Marc was getting lots of other work. His particular skill was making gadgets with the least number of bits, and it was paying off. He did one job for a very large national company. Well, lots of jobs actually (can't tell you who it was). When they saw one of his first quotes, they politely said that as his price was so much less than anyone else, they might have difficulty with their bosses. They might think Marc didn't know what he was doing! So he adjusted his price up at their request and was given the contract! He worked best under pressure, when his mind became completely focused on a particular technical problem, but it wasn't always good for delivery dates.

People with chimes of bells still wanted some sort of automatic play equipment as well as playing tunes manually. In 1985 a lot of work needed doing somewhere near Edinburgh where there was a two octave chime. They wanted automatic play as well as manual, and it was decided to put solenoid clappers in all the bells. This made it easy when you wanted to play tunes yourself with a keyboard. But how was it going to be operated automatically? Marc decided we could install a small keyboard, just like electronic organs had, in a nice wooden case (joiners' shop very useful again) with a built-in cassette recorder. The human being who wanted automatic play hit the record button and recorded his tune. He could play it back to see if it was okay, and if he had played a duff note, he did it again. Then he pressed the switch that energized the clappers, and his cassette tape played the tune on the bells. Simple! The only thing was, it wasn't simple at all. A big chunk of digital software was needed for this. Bear in mind we are talking about the early 1980s when digital software was very complicated. Marc farmed this bit out to another boffin.

I think he probably started putting the whole caboodle together the morning of the day we needed to send it off as this concentrated his mind. I went over about 6p.m. to collect it and send it 'red star' on a train. It worked fine putting a tune on the cassette tape, but the bit that sent electricity up to the bell clappers didn't work at all! I went off and bought some sandwiches from a corner shop, and Marc told his wife to put his dinner on hold, but I missed the train and then the deadline for an overnight lorry. About 1a.m., after I had gone out for two lots of fish and chips, it worked fine with a few more components soldered onto the printed circuit board. Phew! 'Servisair' at East Midlands airport said they needed it by 6a.m. to go on an Air Ecosse flight, so I took it there, had a quick kip, and went into work. Peter asked, 'Keyboard go off all right?' and I just said, 'Yes.' Well, it did! I kept quiet about the last minute flight, and Marc disguised the airfreight cost on his bill and paid me back later! I told our bellhanger it wasn't at the station and to go to the airport! The next one we put in was easy, and it worked first time.

The other changes we made were regarding the claviers for carillons. Our head joiner was occupied for a long time with the wooden frame and batons and pedals. Peter found a whizz carpenter who made them for us in our works. It was better than his own workshop, and this took the pressure off our carpentry bods. I was still getting Stan to carve out aluminium bars for practice claviers, or I was doing it. If you can find someone else to do an awkward job, go for it. In Leicester there was a company called 'Premier Drum'. Apart from drums, they made professional xylophones and marimbas. So I went to see them and asked, 'How about we buy musical bars off you, and resonator tubes?' So we did, and a really tedious job became a thing of the past. When the first set was delivered, I checked them with the tuning forks and note A was not 440Hz international pitch, it was 444Hz. So I rang them and asked, 'What's going on here then?' They told me they always tuned their bars slightly sharp as it made them stand out a bit more in an orchestra. Well, how about that? It tied in with a technique that Paul had been using on new rings of bells.

A lot of reps from different companies came to see us, and as most of them had no idea at all what skills and materials bellfounders needed, they came to have a gander. One made better cutting tools for our tuning machines, so he got an order. Another one from Ciba-

Geigy sold resins and adhesives. The resins were a two part mix, so you got one tin of gunge and mixed it with another one, and it very quickly hardened. If you weren't quick it went off in the bucket!

The joiners' shop hand crafted circular oak pads for the top of the old bells where we had lopped the canons off. They chiselled them for hours so they fitted flush and gave us a level surface on top. They often did this in the tuning shop, making a real mess with bits of wood everywhere. So we made circular rings out of a sheet of celluloid, and sat them on the top of the bell. We stuffed plasticine all round the outside at the bottom and then filled them with resin. It now took about fifteen minutes for each bell, and we machined the top of the resin pad on the tuning machines to make it level. Job done! We tried it first on several old bells that were going to be broken up, and it worked fine. There was no way you could get the pad off unless you took a large hammer and chisel to it. They still do this today, and it saves no end of time.

In May 1982, Pope John Paul II came to England to see everybody and say mass in Coventry at an enormous open site where 300,000 people turned up. I persuaded the bosses that we should make a special bell, take it there and bonk it at the right moment. I said we would be bound to sell it afterwards. And look at the publicity! We suggested this to the high ups in the Catholic Church, and when we said we were doing it for free they quickly agreed! It was a carbon copy of the *AC/DC* bell but without their logo, and definitely without the *Hell's Bell* bit. We painted the bell gold again and put an inscription on it about his holiness coming to Coventry. We made a framework with a nice yellow awning at the top, and a bellhanger bolted the frame into a cement base. I went over to press the start button that fired up the solenoid clapper. There were photographs of the bell in all the local and national press, and loads of TV companies turned up. They focused on the bell when there was a lull in the proceedings, and I was interviewed by a very dishy reporter.

Where about 1,000 Catholic priests, nuns, bishops, and cardinals were seated on a large platform, a carpet company had laid acres of grey Criterion cord carpet. When I was dismantling our control unit, there were various blokes rolling it up. I asked the one who looked like a foreman what they were doing with it, and he replied, 'No idea! May be scrap, do you want a roll?' Luckily, I was in one of Taylor's trucks as it helped me get past security, so I carpeted nearly my whole house including the stairs, courtesy of the Pope!

It wasn't quite as easy as I had thought to sell the bell afterwards, but eventually a church in Dollis Hill in London bought it. I didn't know then that various bells exhibited at special exhibitions in the past were difficult to sell. Really good publicity on the day though. A day away for me in Coventry, loads of grey carpet, and another sale.

By now I had purchased three semi-professional Marantz cassette recorders. Jed had one, and there was one if somebody else was inspecting bells. Mine had a variable speed control for matching up the forks. I didn't need it much for this, but the variable speed was really useful for other applications. These portable cassette recorders were much easier as they worked off batteries as well as a wall socket, and were one hundred times easier to take up a tower. Tape recorders are good toys, and a bellringer from Hull that was a firm believer that

Taylor bells were best (well, of course they were) asked me if I wanted to buy two professional reel-to-reel tape recorders that had come from Radio Hull at some stage. One was stereo and the other one was mono, but both of them had been matched up by BBC engineers. So if you played a tape on one of them that had been recorded on the other one the sound level and frequency response were identical. I bought these off him along with oodles of cables, two microphones, and stands. I paid for them myself, so they were my toys. The stereo one weighed a ton and had a carrying handle that was in two parts so if a weakling was trying to carry it he could get someone to help. The second one was slightly lighter.

In those days there were no digital gadgets that enabled you to do all sorts of clever things with sound, so magnetic tape was still used a lot. Professional machines whizzed the tape along at fifteen inches per second which compensated for any slight defects in the magnetic tape, and they always had a second speed of seven and a half inches per second. Domestic tape recorders were usually just three and three quarter inches per second, and cassettes chugged along at one and seven/eighths inches per second. I'm telling you this for a reason! All these different speeds are 50% of the next one up. So seven and a half inches is half of fifteen. Okay? If you record a 440Hz note A tuning fork at fifteen inches per second and then play it back at seven and half inches per second the frequency of this fork is now 50% less. So it becomes a 220Hz note A, coming back to our octaves. Copy this onto the first machine at the higher speed and play it back again at the lower one, and it becomes 110Hz. So, really clever! This is how I made the cassette recording for Stephen Roman in Toronto. I kept dropping the speed of a big bell I had recorded.

Tape was very good for another reason. You can chop bits out and splice the tape back together to edit it. I often recorded big bells in the works, and once we were dropping the clapper slightly so it hit the soundbow a fraction further down to give a better sound. Making a recording 'before and after' showed the improvement straight away. 'Endless loop' cassettes had a piece of tape already spliced internally, and they went round once for fifteen, thirty, and sixty seconds (well these were the ones I bought) before the first bit came round again. If you made a recording for any of these time periods and then pressed go, the tape loop just went round for ever and kept playing back the same chunk. These were very clever, but the only thing was, you definitely had to put the tape in on the side it told you to. If you put it in upside down you wrecked it! With my variable speed cassette recorder I could alter the musical note and make it one or two notes lower down or higher up. Given time, I could produce tapes of bells with the notes of any bells we could make, using all the tape recorders! If I was bothered enough to do this, and it didn't become a real bind.

In 1980, an Irish television film-maker from R.T.É. (Raidió Teillifis Éireann, so you can tell it was Irish) came to make a film about the Dublin Cathedral bells at Taylor's. Cameramen and sound recordists came in their Volvo estates with all their kit, and everybody stayed at a local hotel. The film-maker, Norris Davidson, was very famous for his old-style filming techniques and wanted to film the new tenor bell being cast. There was a lot of opposition to this idea from one of our bosses. What if we had a disaster? We never had one normally, but what if? I became a studio manager! At last! I mediated between the crew and the person who had come to manage us generally, who was very opposed to the idea. Eventually this was solved with a firm promise (I think it was in triplicate) that if anything went wrong with the cast they wouldn't show this in the film. So they did film it and everything was tickety-boo. How could they all have gone home and not filmed the Dublin tenor being cast?

Norris Davidson completed the filming at Cork and at our carillon at Cobh. The film, entitled *Let Steeple Bells be Swungen*, was scheduled for a New Year's Eve and midnight transmission in 1980/1. He wrote me a nice letter when there was a cock-up with the scheduling meaning it didn't go out! He told me he would let me see the film when it had been broadcast the next year, but I never did see it, and I can't remember how I was going to get a copy. Recently, I contacted the archive department at R.T. É., and they agreed they had the original film. For a fee of €61 I obtained a DVD copy. As I live in Euro land as well, it was an easy transaction, and it is a very interesting film. When a TV company come to somewhere like Taylor's, they pay a certain amount of money called a 'facilities fee'. This is for the lecky they use and any inconvenience. Norris came to me and said it had been agreed that I would be given this fee, not the company, for smoothing everything over. There had been one or two other problems that I had had to overcome on their behalf.

Two people came to the bellfoundry in 1982 that became firm friends of mine. They were husband and wife Diane (Di) Shelley and John Merchant, who lived in Bristol. Di was a freelance radio producer who the BBC had declined to employ when she first applied to join as a reporter in her youth. Silly mistake! She has always been a talented writer and so started off as a journalist before becoming freelance and working in radio stations. Later on, the BBC realized what an excellent producer she was and decided to employ her. Her husband John was a wizard organist. He played a pipe organ in church, and electronic ones, and taught budding organists. They both knew a great deal about broadcasting.

We were re-doing the bells at Winscombe in Somerset, just up the road from Bristol, so Di decided there might be material for a programme. There was, and with the BBC man who had the hair shirt and was responsible for outside broadcast religious programmes, Di put together a production for BBC Radio 4. It went out live from Winscombe church on New Year's Eve in 1982, from 11.30p.m. to 12.15a.m. I know the exact times because I have the piece of thin card shaped exactly like a bell (Taylor profile of course) with all the times on it that was given to all the people in the congregation. There was a rehearsal at 9.45p.m. followed by soup and sandwiches, and the programme was entitled *With Iron Tongues*. Clappers. Get it? I went down there for the broadcast and they put me up, and over the years we saw a lot of each other. Di edits books and manuscripts, writes stories, and has an M.A. in Creative Writing, apart from all her production work for programmes she dreams up. A very talented lady.

Right: A new use for a bell. Diane (Di) Shelley working on her schedule for the Radio 4 'With Iron Tongues' documentary broadcast on New Year's Eve, 1982, at Winscombe Parish Church, Bristol.
Photographer: Michael Martin

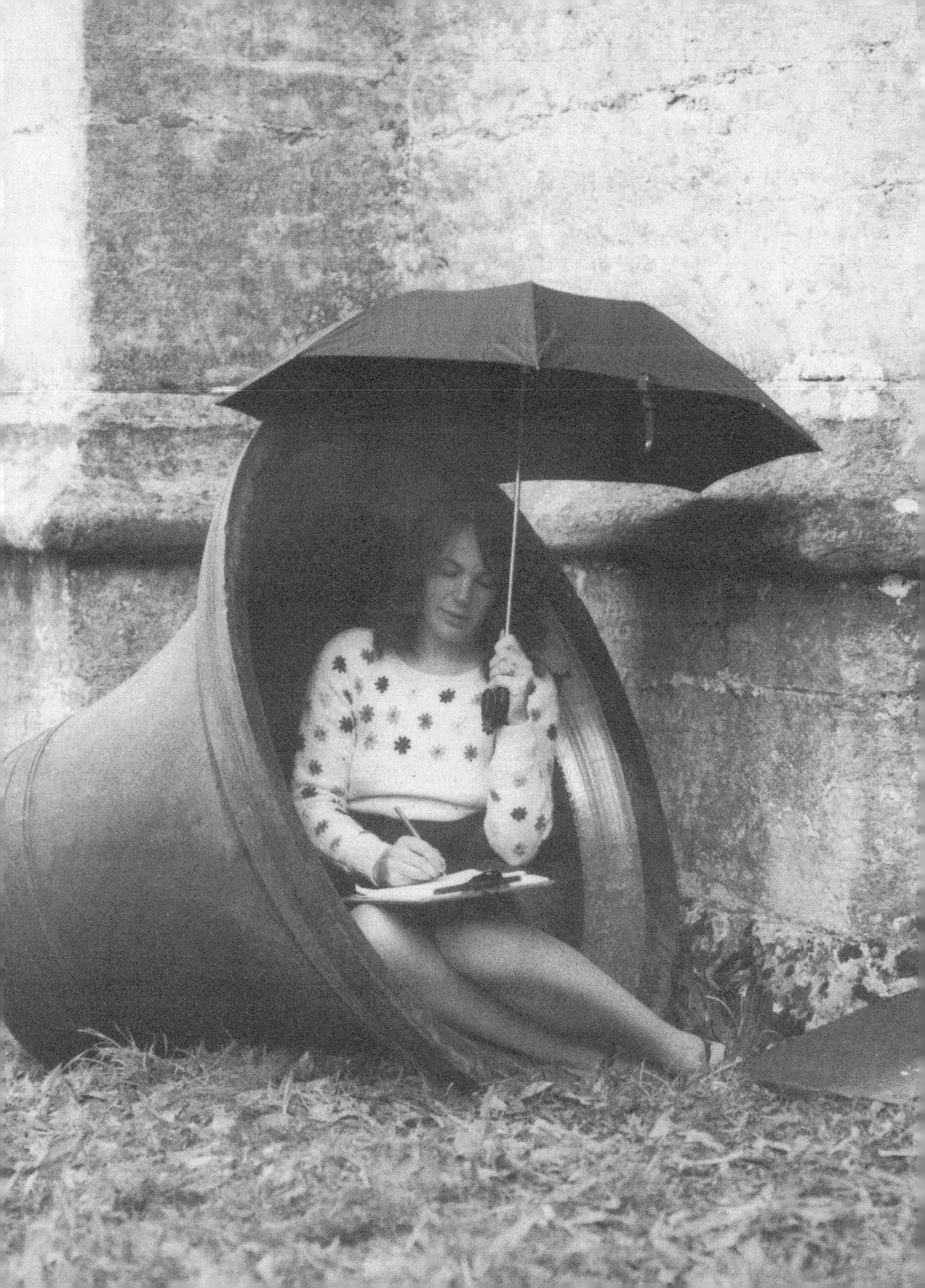

John broadcast a Sunday evening organ programme from Bristol, and people requested different pieces of organ music. Di did the continuity and announcements, and I was there for a couple of them.

One time when they came up to Loughborough to stay with me, I had arranged for John to be given permission to play the electronic organ at a local theatre on a private estate. He didn't know it existed, neither the theatre nor the organ. He was very impressed, and it was a complete surprise as he had no idea where I was taking him. The organ rose up in front of the stage when you pressed the appropriate button. I had told Di beforehand of course!

So then Jake Berry got in touch again! Angus Young wanted the bell to swing over their heads on stage. 'Could we do that?' 'Yes.' So it would need a horse-shoe headstock, a custom designed frame above it, a wheel, motor, and chain drive. There was a catch of course. It had to sound in time with the *Hell's Bell* track performance that was ninety-six beats per minute. Thinking cap on again, as there was no way the swing of the bell and the time between the clapper hitting the bell could be made to be the same speed.

After a lot of thought I solved it! We put an enormous electro-magnetic clapper inside the bell, specially made for the event. Taylor's had an associated rope-making company that made bell ropes in a part of our works, so we wove a cable into a rope with the fluffy sallie right at the end, and it hung down from the frame, not the wheel. At the end there was a hidden bell push. Angus could press this in time with the music, irrespective of where the bell was in its own swing. Marc made a control unit that could cope with different voltages all over the world, and on the front panel we put another push button, behind a little cover, the sort of push button that fires off a nuclear missile. This was a fall-back solution if the one stopped working at the end of the rope. Not being stupid, we put a cable in with two spare wires just in case.

They had an American stress engineer called Tim on their crew, and he worked out what weight of speakers and lights, as well as the bell, that they could hang from the gantries on stage so they didn't keel over. He rang me to ask what the dead weight of the whole caboodle would be, and the swinging forces. When I told him, he said, 'You're joking aren't you!' I replied, 'No. Sorry about this but the bell has to swing, according to Jake.' Tim said something very rude about Angus and his big ideas.

We had told them that the chain had to be checked before and during each tour to make sure it was tensioned properly, and that this was very important. At Hamburg one evening when they hadn't done this, the chain snapped! Luckily, it just missed Malcolm Young, but

Top Right: *A general view of the main works in 1977 with a freshly cast bell being taken to the scales to be weighed. The frame building area is in front of the joiners' shop.*
Photo: Taylor archive

Bottom right: *A large case with the core plate clamped to it, lifted out of the pit after the bell has been cast and cooled.*
Photo: John Taylor & Co.

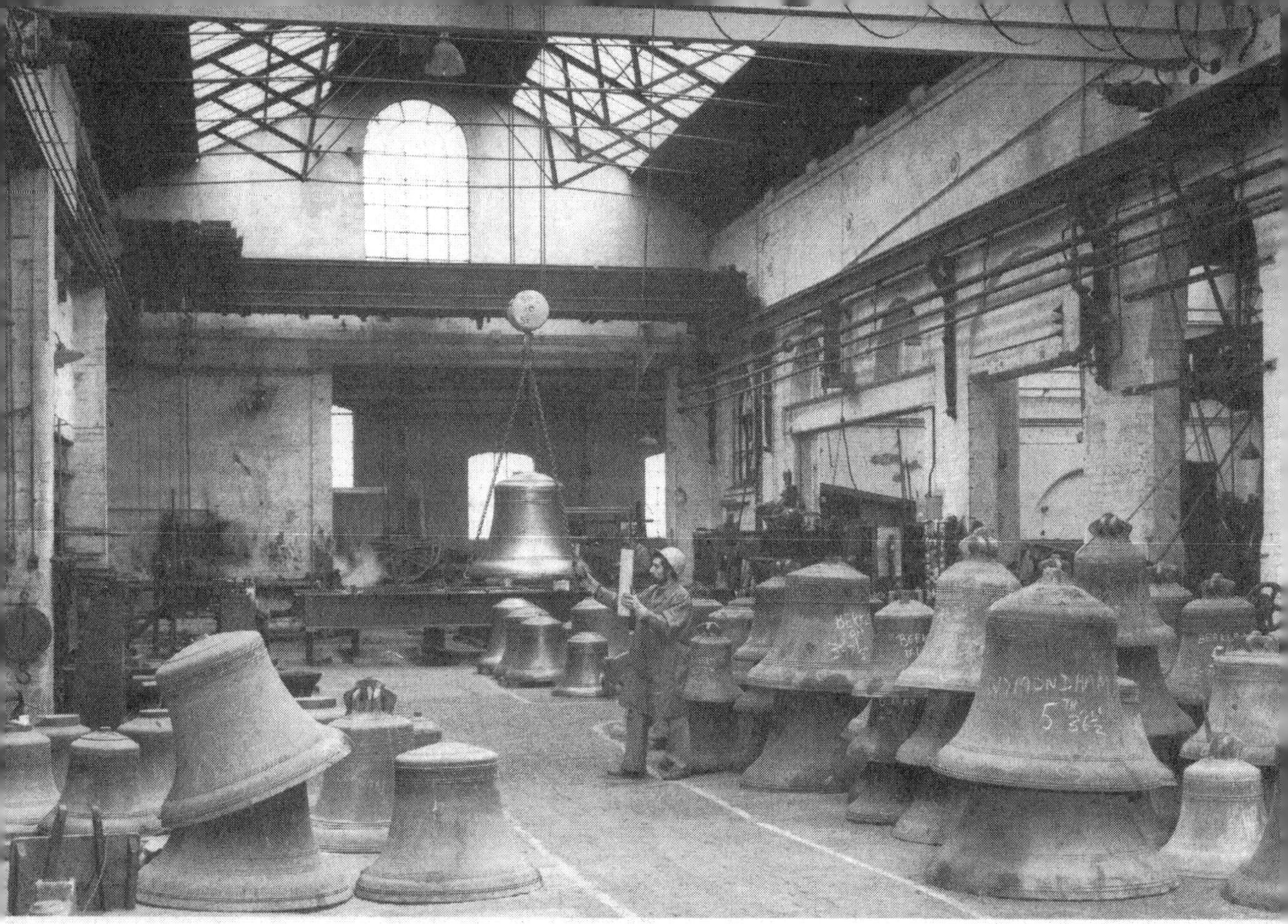

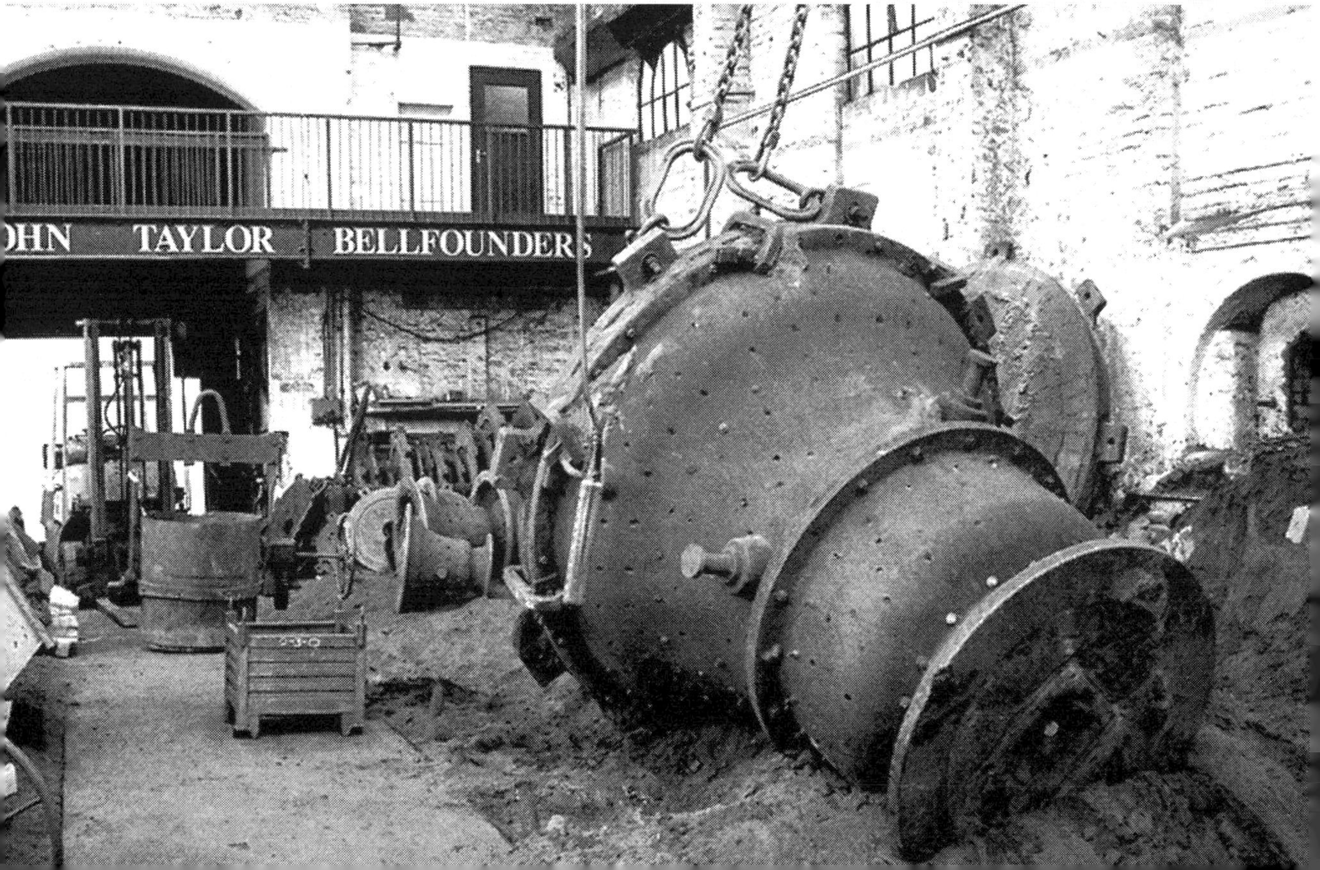
OHN TAYLOR BELLFOUNDERS

they should have flown me round the world to check the chain. Because of this, they stopped using the bell with the swinging mechanism which was a bit risky! At one stage, they had no idea where the bell was as they had lost it! Eventually they discovered it in a large warehouse where they stored their big bits of kit.

Several years later, a half size identical bell was ordered from Taylor's to go at the top of an ornate staircase at a house that Malcolm Young had in Hertfordshire. I have no idea if it actually rang or was just a big ornament as it was after my time. Over the years, *AC/DC* paid Taylor's quite a lot of money, and once, the bell was air-freighted back from somewhere to be repainted. Jake Berry told me one day, 'It doesn't really matter how much all the kit costs to motorize the bell, Mike. The sort of money you are talking about is petty cash to them!' Perhaps we should have doubled the price, or tripled it?

19. A Sweet and Pleasant Sound

'The temple bell stops but I still hear the sound coming out of the flowers.'
Matsuo Basho, 1644-1694

So how do you tune bells? It's not at all easy-peasy. To start with I need to explain why sounds from a bell are different from other musical instruments. Many instruments make their sound by plucking or sawing on a string with a bow, like violins. A guitarist sounds his strings with his fingers, and the female (well, it's usually a lady) hidden behind a harp plucks her harp strings, and pianos have strings. Then you have instruments where air is blown through them including organ pipes and orchestral instruments such as flutes. This is the same with school recorders that parents are supposed to buy their little darlings. All these sounds are produced by blowing.

A monk known as Marin Mersenne (1588-1648), or Père Mersenne because he was a French monk, did loads of research. Père is pronounced 'pair' or 'pear', you takes your pick. It's funny how in the English language there are two words spelt differently but spoken the same. If I was with a male friend of mine and an attractive woman went by he might say, 'What a lovely pair.' I would know from the circumstances that he was commenting on her ankles. If I was offered some fruit from a big plate I might say, 'A pear please.' I wouldn't expect to be given two pieces of fruit. Strange, isn't it?

So Père Mersenne was an extremely important mathematician and theorist regarding music. I told you the two go together, and he was called the 'father of acoustics'. Because he was so clever I expect they let him off working in the monastery garden and washing up. One day he was doing some research in what must have been a very long straight cloister. This is a covered-in passage where monks walk along reading their bibles. Quite often there are four cloisters on each side of a square with a garden in the middle, or a fountain. Whichever the monks or nuns think is a good idea. He closed it off and stretched a ninety-four foot rope from one end to the other as tight as he could get it. He tied a piece of ribbon or something else in the middle, and if he had been short of ribbon he could have used his sock. He stood there and pulled the rope up as much as he could like the string of a bow. When he let go, the rope went down to below where it had been before he pulled it up. It kept moving up and down, above and below. In doing this it pushed air aside which more air replaced. It did this for as long as the rope kept moving up and down. This is how sound is generated. We hear the air being compressed and then replaced with more air which is called a 'vibration', and if it's within the range of human hearing we hear a note. In this case, it would have made a note about 12Hz because this is the note you get if you have a ninety-four foot guitar string or piano string. It's straight physics, it just happens this way, so don't worry about it. He was using a rope because ninety-four foot guitar strings are difficult to come by. 12Hz is the posh name for 12 c.p.s. (cycles per second). It became known as Hertz (Hz for short) after another famous acoustical scientist, Herman von Helmholtz. He wrote a reference book on acoustics entitled *Sensations of Tone* that was translated into English in 1885. Père couldn't hear this note as it is below the level of human hearing, but he may have felt a vibration through his sandals. If he had an extremely large clock with a second hand he could have counted these twelve vibrations a second.

The reason Père Mersenne had used a rope this long was because he wanted to see the rope going up and down twelve times a second. He was also watching to see something else he knew was going to happen. The rope started going up and down each side of his ribbon as well, at the same time. This produced a note an octave up, so 24Hz. This is called a 'second harmonic' because the 12Hz note is the 'first harmonic'. If he hadn't got wax in his ears he probably heard this 24Hz note which is just above the lowest sound a human can hear.

The rope also goes up and down in three equal sections giving a 'third harmonic'. Then in four sections giving a 'fourth harmonic', and five sections that is a 'fifth harmonic', etcetera. So the second harmonic gave the note 24Hz (an octave up), the third harmonic 3 x 12 so 36Hz, then 4 x 12 so 48Hz (two octaves up), and then 5 x 12 so 60Hz, and so on. If you pluck any string it gives out these harmonics. This is called 'the harmonic series' and you can't say, 'I'll only have the second and fifth harmonic', you get all the lot free with no extra money involved. This particularly applies to strings and open organ pipes without a stopper at the top end. Mersenne probably used a ninety-four foot rope because the cloister turned a corner after that, but he could see and hear the vibrations and harmonics. We can say this harmonic series is in the ratios (the relationship between them) of 1 : 2 : 3 : 4 : 5 : 6 : and so on, from whatever frequency we start from.

So now you understand this, I need to tell you that bells are entirely different. Typical! A bell is a percussion instrument like a cymbal, gong, or xylophone bar. You clout all these to get the sound, and the correct name for this family of instruments is 'idiophones'. A bell doesn't have natural harmonics or the harmonic series, so when you hit it you don't get the related notes automatically. The profile of a European bell gives more than one note because of the shape, and these notes are called 'overtones'. The posh word is 'partials', but they are not harmonics. The shape of a bell was known for centuries to give several overtones or partials ideally related to octaves and other intervals.

There are lots of these, but let's talk about the first five. The bottom and lowest note/partial when you clout a bell is called the 'Hum'. The next note/partial up is about an octave, give or take. Above this there are two more notes/partials, then the fifth partial is another octave, ideally four times the hum but rarely exact. The first approximate octave is called the 'Fundamental' or sometimes the 'Prime'. The next partial is called the 'Tierce' (Latin for 'third'), and the next one up is the 'Quint' (Latin for 'fifth'). The fifth partial, approximately four times the hum or twice the fundamental (if you are lucky) is called the 'Nominal'. This is because this note was often said to be the 'name' note of the bell ('name' is 'nomen' in Latin). So if you thought this was note A, you said, 'This bell is note A and ignore all the other funny notes.'

So let's go back to our piano keyboard and 'middle C'. We called this 'C4' as well. Go down two C's to C2 and then jump up an octave to C3. The white note two up from this C is E. Go back to this C and go up four white notes to G. Then go up to the next C which is C4, so back to middle C. Have a fag or a tea break while you think about this. What we have is two C's an octave apart, then an E two notes up (a third), then a G four notes up (a fifth) and then another octave C. This is the simple ratios of 1 : 2 : 2.5 : 3 : 4.

If you know the song *Row, Row, Row Your Boat,* you have gone up two notes when you get to 'boat' so a musical interval of a third. If you were playing this on a piano starting on C you will be on the white note E when you get to 'boat', known as a 'major third'. This is the same if you are singing or playing the children's song *Frère Jacque* when you get to the 'Jacq' note.

Now think about 'The Sound of Music'. When the kids are going away they sing *So Long, Farewell*. If they started on a note C with 'so', the note they sing for 'long' and the 'well' of 'farewell' is not the white note E. It is the black note to the left of E. If you want another example it's the first two note interval in Black Sabbath's *Iron Man*. Just sing this to yourself for a moment seeing the difference between *Row, Row, Row Your Boat* and *So Long, Farewell*. You may think that the interval in *So Long, Farewell* sounds a bit sad. The kids were sad, not Julie Andrews. This interval is a 'minor third' in music. Bells have this minor third so therefore the ideal tierce frequency is 2.4 times not 2.5 times the bottom hum note. So in bells these ratios are 1 : 2 : 2.4 : 3 : 4. If the hum note is 100Hz, the tierce minor third interval should be 240Hz, not 250Hz. So bells often sound a trifle sad as well. (Not very sad, just a touch). Another example of a song with minor thirds, in a minor key, is the carol *God Rest Ye Merry Gentlemen*.

In the old days, after you had hauled your bell out of the pit, you gave it a clout. If it was a single bell and it sounded all right then you got paid and went away. If it was to be part of a set or a ring, somebody who knew about notes and music might say, 'This is not the right note'. So now you have a problem. This miserable person who says your bell is not right is probably talking about the nominal partial, the one people often say is the note name of the bell. If he says it is 'sharp', so too close in note to the next bell up, you get your chipping hammer out. It's a bit like a baby pickaxe, and you start at the soundbow inside the bell and chip metal off in lines going down. Above and below the soundbow mainly, and you do it in grooves so as not to weaken the whole of the soundbow. The more metal you chip off, the better the bell sounds to your critical man (hopefully)!

You are lowering the nominal note so that it gets further away from the next bell up and lower down, nearer to the bell below it. You can hear the difference yourself, but you have to satisfy other people. If you chip-tune from the soundbow down into the waist of the bell this affects other partials as well. The whole basis of tuning a bell is that you can lower the notes but not sharpen them. There is one slight exception regarding the nominal, and if you chip away at the lip effectively making the bell a slightly smaller diameter, you can sharpen the nominal a fraction and the tierce as well, but not quite so much. This is termed 'skirting', and some old bells have the lip chopped away a lot, but there is a point where no further improvement takes place. H. B. Walters in *The Church Bells of England* states that the tenor of the ring at Redenhall in Norfolk, cast about 1514 at the Bury St. Edmunds foundry, had the diameter reduced by three-quarters of an inch (the bell is just over four feet in diameter).

So if the bell you have proudly cast in the pit is hopelessly the wrong note, and it doesn't match up at all with the others already there you may not get paid at all. Just like the carillons we have mentioned where a whole set of bells were rejected. Really tough luck! Legend has it that Thomas Bilbie, one of a family of bellfounders from Cullompton in Devon, committed suicide about 1800 when he was unable to get his bells in tune. It's only a legend, but don't go as far as this if you have a bit of bad luck! If you have a bellfoundry and old bells are coming in to be rehung and retuned if possible, then before you have invested in any sort of tuning machine you will more than likely chip-tune some of them.

We have mentioned the Hemony brothers who made chimes and carillons in Holland. They became very skilled in altering the strickle board or crook to affect the thickness of the bell. After a lot of experimentation, they were casting bells where the five principle partials were very close to the ratios 1 : 2 : 2.4 : 3 : 4.

One account about Frans Hemony going to Amsterdam in 1654 states that he took his chipping hammers with him and a 'set of very small bells' tuned to the different notes of the musical scale. He wasn't just tuning the nominal, he was attempting to lower the notes of all the partials, so he was streets in front of the other bellfounders of the time. Another account states that he put some bells on a horizontal lathe, so he must have fixed the canons to some sort of plate. Men who had eaten lots of porridge for breakfast probably turned this plate with a treadle (like the foot treadles early sewing machines had), and they were removing metal with some sort of tool that went inside the bell. The two brothers were very religious, and they built a small private chapel on the bellfoundry site. Perhaps they just prayed hard that the bells the next day would turn out fine.

André Lehr from the Royal Eijsbouts foundry in Holland, who was one of the world experts, thought that they had a collection of iron rods of different lengths which they held against the bell to see which one vibrated the most. Frans obviously had a very good ear and so did Pieter his brother. Frans and Pieter weren't satisfied with just the first five notes or partials. In 1653, the Hemony brothers said there should be partials in tune that were three octaves apart, a minor third, a major third, and two fifths. The one up from the nominal is a major third, so the *Row, Row* interval not the *So Long* one. The next partial up is an octave of the quint partial, and then one that is an octave above the nominal. The ratios of this lot are

Right: *The Hemony carillon in the Zuiderkerk tower, Amsterdam.*
Photo: Yair Halkai

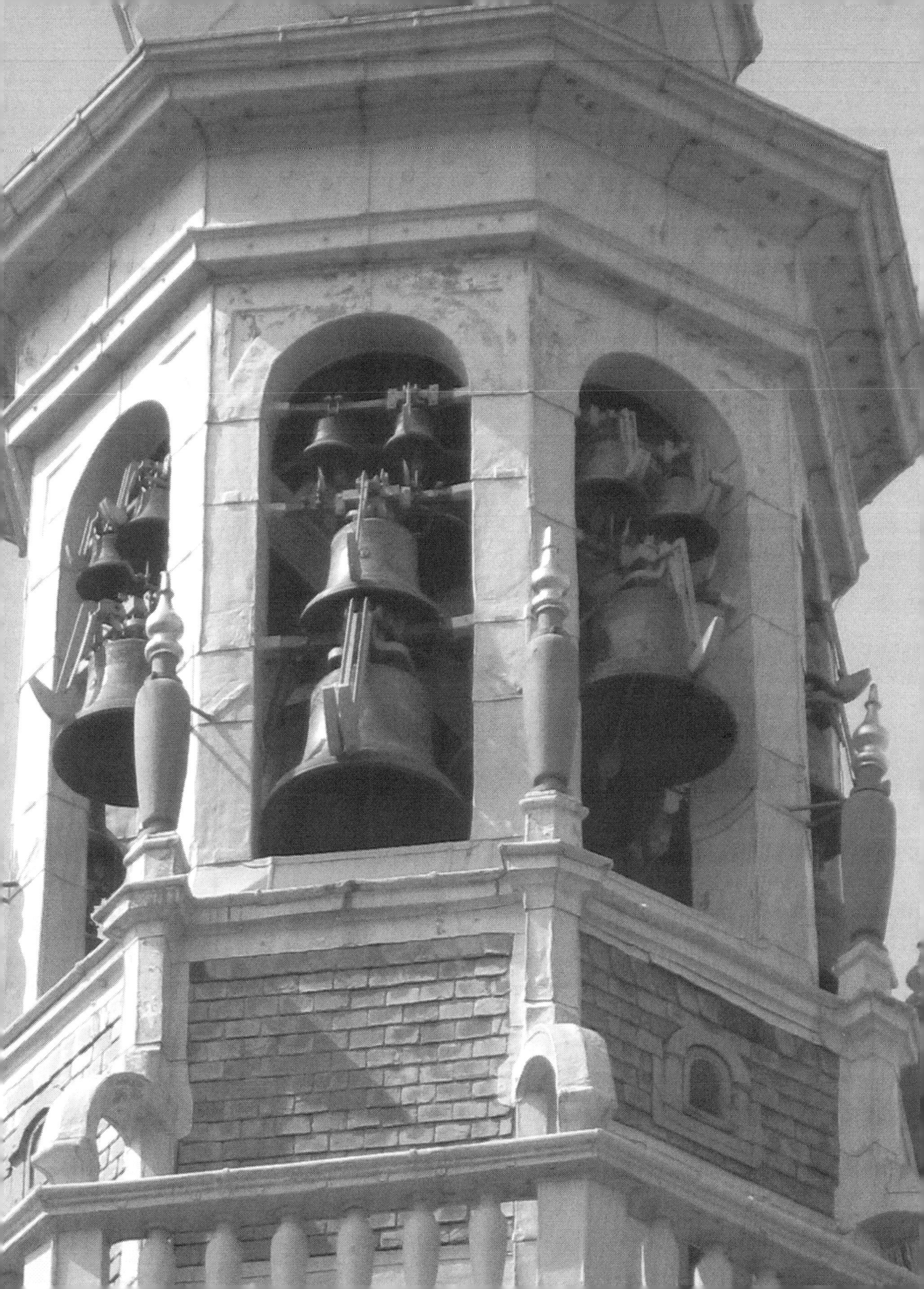

1 : 2 : 2.4 : 3 : 4 : 5 : 6 : 8. They were motoring along if they could do this, but along with other bellfounders they produced some bells that were less than perfect. We know that they built up stock chimes or carillons, and I think it is possible that if they had a bell that was a smidgen too flat, they put it on one side to go with any others that suffered the same fate. These were very useful for a stock chime if slightly re-tuned again. Another account is that they kept recasting any bell they were not satisfied with, and if they were charging enough money, or raking it in from cannon work, they could do this. I have commented how the Belgian bellfounder Van Aerschodt said that he cast twelve small bells for each note and picked the best one!

Bellfounders are a secretive lot when they have developed a unique technique. I expect it was the same with the artists who were mixing colours with all sorts of different powders and chemicals. We know some of them bought items from their friendly chemist (to make paint with not for other uses). They wouldn't have been at all keen to tell any other painter how they had made up a particular colour, and they may have carried this to their grave. De Haze, the apprentice of the Hemony brothers, who said he knew how to tune like they did, had to admit he didn't know 'exactly' how they did it! If the brothers had sons that were taking over they would have trained them up, but it looks like they didn't, so their secret tuning techniques were lost when they died.

At Taylor's, before they started buying posh tuning machines, I have mentioned that they had a basic one from about 1868 that machined metal off the soundbow and a bit further down, and there is a photograph of it. A drawing of the tuning area at Whitechapel about the same time shows a pit where the bell was put about half way down with lots of chunks of wood stuffed in around the sides to hold the bell rigid. A device that rotated from a wheel with cogs above the bell was lowered into the bell, and there was a handle that pulled a simple tool into the inside of the bell. This is very similar to the Taylor one that was much more sophisticated, but Whitechapel bought their basic machine when another bellfounder hung up his clogs and sacked the donkey that drove it, so it wasn't exactly new!

I wanted to know how Taylor's arrived at their new tuning skills about 1895, where they got their tuning forks from, and where the tuning machines came from. It wasn't too difficult to find this as there were lots of letter books. If someone wrote to Taylor's in their best joined up writing they obviously got a reply. Paul's father or Denison wanted a copy of the letter they were sending out. So how could they do this? They had a cunning technique. The letter, which they had written in special ink, was covered in a thin piece of tissue paper with a sheet of damp blotting paper on top. Then there was a piece of oiled paper that wasn't permeable, then another letter, tissue and blotting paper, and another oiled sheet. They put this lot in a hand press and wound a big handle down to squeeze them all together. The blotting paper sucked up some of the ink from their replies into the thin sheet. So magically they had a copy.

Eventually, with all the letters they had received and their copy replies they had enough to be bound into a book called.......a copy letter book. So they accumulated these for years, and kept them in a large cupboard in their fireproof room.

In the period that I was interested in there were a lot of letter books. Paul let me take various ones home so I could go through them when it was a quiet night with nothing on the goggle box. It was just a slow job carefully turning each page over. I haven't mentioned that I was no longer married when I went back to Taylor's. It was entirely my fault, and there is a nice Latin phrase that is 'Mea culpa, mea culpa, mea maxima culpa.' This roughly translates to 'I cocked it up properly; all my fault.'

If European bellfounders knew about partials in a bell from reading books by acoustical scientists, they could only suck their pencil thoughtfully. Père Mersenne, our French monk, was interested in notes from bells because he was so interested in acoustics and music, and he even drew out some bell profiles. He published *Harmonicorum libri* in 1636 that ran to eight volumes, with volume four being entitled *Campanas* (Bells). Bellfounders in general only had very hazy ideas about tuning bells, and Père's book was in Latin which probably didn't help too much either. Sir Gore Ouseley translated Père's book into English in the late 19th century.

Taylor's were trying hard to get the nominal in tune because they thought this was the most important partial. When a bell is clouted hard the hum is quite strong and decays (the time it takes for a sound to die away) the slowest of all the others. The fundamental starts off about the same but decays sooner than the hum. The tierce is stronger at the moment of impact and lasts a bit longer than the fundamental, and this is the partial that makes a bell sound a bit sad, because it's the minor third. The quint partial is much weaker and is not easy to hear unless you really know what you are listening for. The nominal is extremely loud and twice as loud as the hum or fundamental, but it quickly decays.

The vast majority of work carried out at Taylor's was, and still is, connected to rings of bells tugged upside down and back again by bellringers. We have seen that however many bells there are, the strike-rate is about five bells every second. So as soon as one bell has been hit by its clapper, another one is on its way up to strike 200 milliseconds later. The nominal partial sings out and is still going when the next bell sounds. So the nominal was rightly judged to be a very important partial, and if they could get all the nominals pretty well in tune the bells sounded in tune, and the other partials were less important.

If you have a decent size single bell, or particularly a slow-swinging bell, the sound splays out and the other partials are audible to a greater extent, including the hum, fundamental, and the tierce. From reading books on acoustics where bells were being discussed by European acoustics experts, John William and Pryce found that the fundamental was considered very important and was called the 'Prime'. When a musician or bellfounder in Europe was being asked what note the bell was, they usually said it was the same note as the fundamental or prime, not the nominal, so a different approach.

In the 1890s, John William I, Pryce and other family members were going to the continent to see what the European bell founders were doing. They wanted to be able to produce Taylor bells where the hum and fundamental were in tune with the nominal for rings of bells. They hadn't got as far as considering that they could produce carillons, but they came across them of course, and looked at the mechanism as well. John William I wanted his bells to be considered good by musicians, and he was very musical himself. They had bought a collection of small tuning forks that fitted in leather strips with a pocket for each fork. They rolled the strips up, and they were easy to take around.

In a bell that is perfectly in tune, the hum, fundamental and nominal frequencies are the same note one and two octaves apart. So if the hum is 100Hz, the fundamental should be 200Hz and the nominal 400Hz. In most European bells, including the ones Taylor's had been producing prior to 1896, this was not true at all. A very good example is 'Great Paul'. This bell could not be tuned, so they needed the nominal as cast to be a musical interval related to the nominal of the tenor bell of the ring. This is why they were really hot and bothered, even after casting a half size bell that they would have been able to tune to some extent on their fairly basic tuning machine. They told the St. Paul's lot that there was no guarantee it would be the correct note, 'so don't expect this to happen.'

The nominal of 'Great Paul' needed to be 308Hz to be exactly in the right relationship with the nominal of the tenor bell of the twelve. It is 317Hz so wunderbar, and not too far different, and not quite in the gap between this and the next note up on a piano. The fundamental needed to be 154Hz to be in tune with the correct nominal of 308 Hz, and it is 151Hz. Amazing! Stand back in admiration. John Stainer, the organist from St. Paul's, tested 'Great Paul' in the works and said it was 'exactly' in tune, so he may have been listening to the fundamental, not the nominal. I don't know what he brought with him to establish this. The bell the octave up from the bourdon bell, that is number nine in the ring of twelve, has a nominal of 636Hz. So to be half of this and an octave lower, the nominal of 'Great Paul' should be 318Hz and it is 317Hz as cast! So phenomenal, take your hat off, however you look at the relationship of the notes.

When you have found the notes of a bell, directly or from a tape recording, there is a quick way to see how the hum, fundamental, and nominal are in tune with each other. You multiply the hum frequency by four, and the fundamental by two. How much are they out? 'Great Paul' (I've done a 'Paul Taylor' and forgotten about decimal places) has a hum note of 84Hz. The fundamental is 151Hz and the nominal 317Hz. If you multiply these up, it works out as being 334Hz, 302 Hz, and 317Hz. So compared to the nominal, the fundamental is flat (a lower frequency) and the hum is quite sharp (a higher frequency).

This is absolutely typical of bells at this period in time, not just in England. If they could have tuned 'Great Paul' they could have lowered the nominal to 308Hz, the correct frequency in relation to the tenor of the ring, and also improved the hum a smidgen. If they had done this, the fundamental would have gone a bit further down, so it would still have been flat.

The rogue note is the fundamental because it is flat in relationship to the others to start with. If I am right about John Stainer observing that the fundamental was almost exactly in tune, this is how a continental bellfounder would have done it as well. They would have said,

Right: *The large tuning machine installed in 1900, capable of tuning a bell the same size as 'Great Paul'. Arthur 'Gunner' Underwood (on the left) and Jack Saddington (right) are levelling 'Great Peter' in 1927 to machine the head.* Photo: Taylor Archives

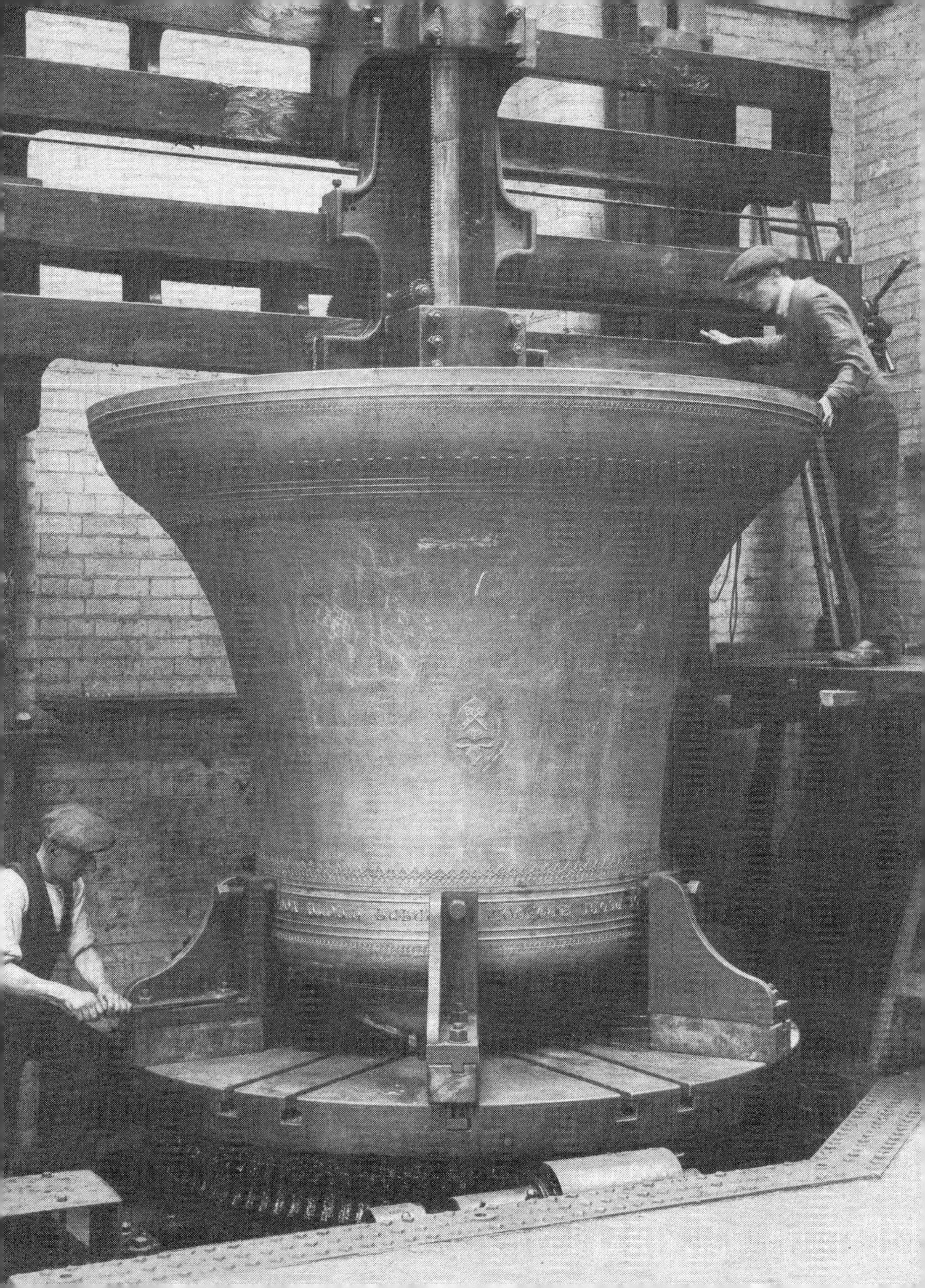

'The prime (fundamental) is exactly right, the hum is too sharp, and so is the nominal.' Anyway, everybody said 'Great Paul' was amazingly in tune for a maiden bell, and it certainly was. The Taylor family, when they were testing their own bells and charting the nominal in relation to the other partials, soon found out that a flat fundamental was common in all their bells. How were they going to bring it up in frequency? This was the big question. They played around with the settings on the crook to see what happened. A clergyman, Canon Simpson, rector of a small church at Fittleworth in Sussex, wrote to the Taylor family in 1894. He claimed he had tested the three and a half ton Taylor hour bell at Chichester Cathedral cast in 1877 (he was a Canon and Prebendary at the cathedral) and was criticising the tuning. Criticising the tuning! Who was this bloke? They invited him to come and see them which he did, and he said that English bellfounders were concentrating on the nominals, and the other partials were not well in tune! It transpired he had tried to get the Mears and Warner foundries interested in his observations, but they told him to stick to writing sermons.

Canon Simpson had examined some bells cast by De Haze and told Taylor's they were better in tune. He astounded them by saying European bellfounders were far more interested in the fundamental. He told Taylor's that when the 'Gloriosa' bell had been cast in 1873 for Cologne Cathedral, musicians could not agree what note it was. He said this was because the nominal and the fundamental were not in tune, and some were listening to the nominal, and others the fundamental. He said that Taylor's should try and get the hum, fundamental, and nominal in tune. This was amazing when they were already casting experimental bells to try and do this! A 'fine set of forks' had been ordered, and Taylor's told him this would greatly help in their research.

There was further correspondence between Canon Simpson and John William I, and they visited a few churches together and told him where new bells were being installed. The problem was, they didn't want to tell him exactly what they were doing and were on the verge of achieving. By December 1894, they had found out how to get the fundamental up in pitch by increasing the thickness right at the top of the shoulder and in the head. They told Canon Simpson that an experimental bell they had cast was very nearly in tune, and they had proved that the thickness of the shoulder did not affect the hum note. Canon Simpson suggested that bells should be taller and asked what they thought. A quick reply stated that they had already done this on various rings of bells including the 1887 Imperial Institute job!

They thought that if they kept saying they were interested in his theories he wouldn't go back to Mears or Warner's! They now had a new set of fifty-one forks that went from 340Hz up to 540Hz every 4Hz, (they cost £8 each in today's money!) but they soon extended the range even further. They sent various ones back of course! They told the Sheffield manufacturer Valentine & Carr that they were not accurate enough as they could test them against a small set bought from a famous acoustic expert, Rudolf Koenig (1832-1901). During 1895 they recorded the results of experimenting with the profile and carefully charted the five main partials. In October 1895, Canon Simpson wrote an article for *The Pall Mall Magazine* with all his theories, and he sent them a copy. They congratulated him on his very 'interesting' article but privately they were not at all impressed!

At Christmas in 1895, John William sent a small donation to the organ fund at Fittleworth and told him that a tuning machine that would allow them to machine right down to the shoulder of the bell had been ordered and would be put in a new extension to the works where it would be quieter. They were sure this would enable them to control all the five partials and had ordered even more tuning forks to extend the range again up to 1,400Hz.

The fifteen ton tuning machine was delivered in February 1896, and they soon let him know. By September 1896 they were able to tell him that all bells could now have the three octaves in tune, but Canon Simpson had published another article in *The Pall Mall Magazine* the same month, entitled *Why Bells Sound Out of Tune and How to Cure Them*. He wrote in his introduction, 'In particular I should mention Messrs. Taylor, of Loughborough, who were the first to appreciate the importance of the ideas which I have advocated, and who have faced the task of carrying them out to a practical issue with an energy and intelligence deserving of all praise.'

He also advocated that his knowledge should be available to all bellfounders 'to let bell-founders take it or leave it as they may think best'. Taylor's were horrified. He had a profile of a bell with claims where to cut it to get it in tune, with a whole series of guidelines. Fortunately some of this was inspired guesswork! He went on to say that he had tested 'Great Paul' and 'the fundamental and nominal are in perfect tune and true octaves.' Well, they aren't perfectly in tune! He criticised the frequency of the tierce as being far too sharp, and it was sharp but not as much as he said. He finished up his five page article by writing, 'I can promise to founders a most valuable help in their difficult work'. So the warm way that Taylor's had received him now went extremely frosty. They wrote to him one day that they were 'too busy on our own part' to conduct any more experiments for him. So there!

I think it is completely fair to say that Canon Simpson gave them some very good pointers regarding the ideal tuning of the partials at a time when they were discovering a lot of information themselves. This didn't include any technical information regarding the tuning that helped with their research as he couldn't accurately say, 'Cut here'. We have seen how he claimed to have analysed 'Great Paul' and determined the relationship of the partials which was far from being correct. John William wrote to another clergyman, 'Mr. Simpson (not Canon Simpson!) cannot claim to be the author of so called improvements. Mr. Haweis in England and many people on the continent maintain that a perfect bell must be so tuned.' Reverend Haweis was the person who had travelled a lot in Belgium and said church bells were dire and St. Paul's Cathedral should have a carillon instead of a ring of bells!

The Taylor family had been in correspondence with a German monk, Franz Klein, who was a carillonneur at an abbey in the large Dutch city of Middleburg. William Gorham Rice, in his 1914 book with a 'top ten' list of carillons in various countries, considered this carillon, with forty-three bells cast by Noordon de Grave in 1714, one of the best ones in Holland. They made several visits there as Franz Klein, who they described as a 'fine musician', was considered very knowledgeable regarding bells and their ideal tuning. In 1897 Taylor's added a seven ton bourdon bell and three smallest bells at the top end of the Middleburg carillon, so perhaps the abbey got a discount for Franz helping them somewhat! The carillonneur there in 1913 strongly recommended that Taylor's be given the order for a new carillon for the city of

Vlissingen (Flushing), and they got the job. The entire abbey carillon was destroyed in 1940 by a stray bomb, and the Vlissingen carillon was one of the ones nicked by the Germans in 1943 to use the metal. So that was that!

When Canon Simpson died in 1900, no-one from Taylor's went to his funeral. I expect they were too busy. Taylor's christened their technique 'Five Tone Harmonic Tuning'. They knew partials were not harmonics, but it was as good a name as any. Sometimes their invention was called 'Simpson Tuning', and I am sure that upset them. By whatever method they had employed, their achievement was hailed by themselves and others as being 'the rediscovery of the lost art of tuning'. Which it was, so well done boys. The first 'harmonic-tuned' ring of eight bells was sent off to Norton in Derbyshire in 1896.

So the big question is, how were they able to use tuning forks to test the partials in a bell? If you have a tuning fork that is 440Hz and the next one up is 444Hz, when you gently hit them both together there is a 'beat', a pulsing sound. Hz is the name for cycles per second remember, and when these two forks are hit together there is a pulsing sound that is the difference in frequency, so 4Hz or four cycles per second, or four pulses or beats per second. If you are comparing the forks with the frequency of a partial in a bell, and find there are four beats per second from first a 436Hz and then a 444Hz fork, the frequency of this partial in your bell is 440Hz. If there are two beats or pulses per second from first a 436Hz and then a 440Hz fork the frequency of the partial in your bell is 438Hz. It's just the same whatever frequency you are trying to ascertain. If you hit two forks at the same time that are 100Hz and 104Hz you still get a beat of 4Hz, and the same if they are 1,000Hz and 1,004Hz. The Taylor tuning forks right at the bottom end were 2Hz apart, not 4Hz.

Very slow beats can be timed with a stopwatch if you are trying to find the absolutely exact frequencies in a big bell. If you are listening to a partial in a bell that is a smidgen up from 100Hz, you use your stopwatch. If there is a beat of 5Hz every ten seconds, this is 0.5Hz every second, so the partial in your bell is 100.5Hz. If there is a beat of 3Hz every ten seconds the partial is 100.3Hz. When Paul Taylor was using a stopwatch in 1940 for the lowest partials in the nine feet six inches 'Great George', a comparison with the theoretical frequencies and 'as tuned' in brackets is: Hum: 69.1Hz (69.25); Fundamental: 138.2Hz (138.25); Tierce: 164.4Hz (164); Quint: 207.1Hz (208); Nominal: 276.5Hz (277.5); 'Continental 4th': 369Hz (371); Quint octave: 414.2 Hz (416); 'Super nominal' double octave: 552.9Hz (564). (The super nominal is invariably a bit sharp in most bells by most bellfounders and is very difficult to control). The 'continental 4th' octave that should have been 738 Hz was 750Hz, and other higher partials are very close to the theoretical frequencies with a total of eleven partials charted. From a photograph of when the first fifteen ton tuning machine was being installed, there isn't a door into the tuning office so it wasn't there! They must have kept the forks in the main offices or bellfoundry house and taken them to the tuning shop as needed. When this became three bells needing testing at the same time this would have been a

Right: *Harold Marcon, bell tuner from 1949-1969, checking a bell in the tuning shop.*
Photo: John Jackson

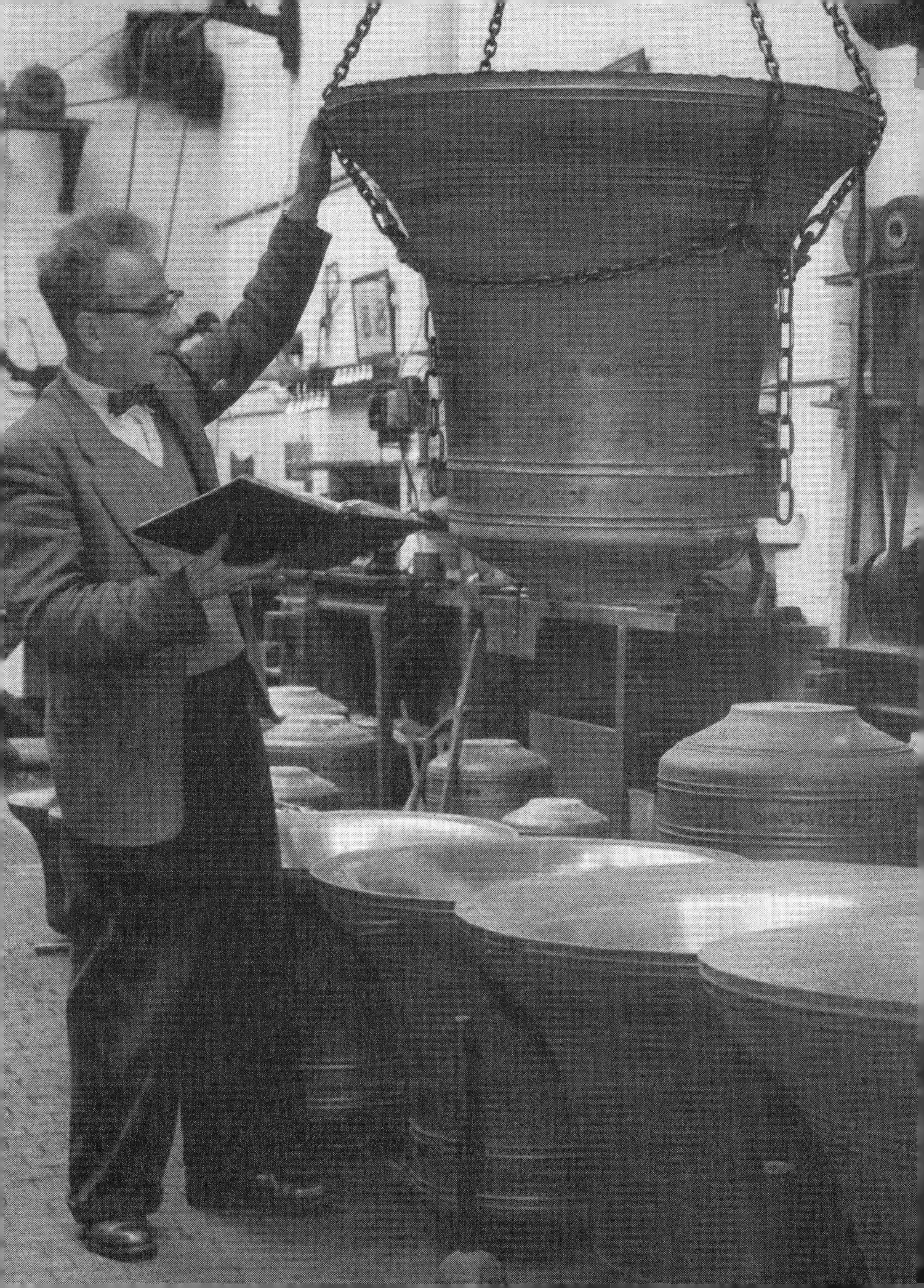

real fag. The solution? Knock a hole in the wall at the end of the tuning shop, throw up a lean-to brick office, and put all the tuning forks there.

The Taylor tuning technique was extremely hush hush. If I had told you about it in the late 1890s I would have had to kill you afterwards, unless you were a member of the Taylor family. When a bell was ready to be tested, the other two machines were shut off and all three men had to leave the tuning shop! The bell was then sounded and marked 'cut here' in chalk and the men allowed back in. Next bell to be tested - the same thing! Although these men were skilled minions doing the machining, there was hardly going to be any understanding on their part as to how the tuning process worked. Despite this, 'Wait outside and no listening at the key-hole.' (There wasn't a key-hole. The doors into the works are very hefty with big bolts, but you get the idea). Not very much metal was machined off at any of these stages. The men working the machines had no idea when they would be told that their bell was fine and to start on another one.

When Paul Taylor started tuning he would have been taught by Denison, and hearing beats is not difficult if you have an acute ear. Where to cut was the secret arrived at with much study and deliberation! Using electronics or computer programs to monitor the tuning is common nowadays, but a trained ear is still necessary to listen to the final result. At Taylor's, Andrew Higson, who took over after I left, eventually introduced a combined system that used a computer program as well as the forks. By the time I was marking up the bells, the men had been allowed to stay in the tuning shop for a long time whilst the notes were being established. You didn't have to go into the main works to see where they were. They still weren't told whether the next marked cut was the final one, and I decided this was silly! I started putting a number at the top of the bell when cuts were being chalked up. The number '50' meant there was a fair amount to come off. '25' meant getting close, and '10' meant just a light cut. If it was a big bell and I was trying to influence one particular high partial I might even put the numbers '2' or '3'. This gave Ron, Sid, or Stan an idea of what they were doing. If a hefty cut was required I had time to go over to the foundry and see how they were getting on.

During 1925-1926, Pryce and Denison decided that all the crooks had to be replaced as they were falling to bits! They took the opportunity to alter some of them slightly where there were discrepancies in the height or other small changes were needed. The old crooks were put in a cellar, and years later when they were finally scrapped accurate drawings were made of all the original profiles. If anyone needs to see how the pre-1925 profile compares to the present shape this enables it to be done. Andrew Higson has remarked that new crooks were badly needed before he left Taylor's. Re-cutting damaged threads on the bolts that tightened the plates was getting very difficult. At present there is an investigation going on at Taylor's to accurately establish the extent of all the changes in the various crook profiles, with possible modifications to the current ones.

20. The Nitty Gritty

'Let's skip the chitchat and get down to the nitty-gritty.'
Americanism of uncertain origin.

We have talked about learned experts deciding in 1940 that 'international A' was 440Hz. Before then, 'church bell pitch' A was 435Hz, but it wasn't crucial. In 1877, St. Paul's Cathedral organ was tuned to A 447Hz, and a note A tuning fork used by George Frideric Handel was A 423Hz. The Berlin Philharmonic orchestra A in 1858 was 452Hz - so not any general agreement anywhere! In the early days at Taylor's, if there was a new ring being tuned, the tenor was tuned first. When it was in tune with itself, not necessarily to A 435Hz, it was left at that. It wouldn't be miles out because the crook plates were now finely adjusted to the notes you expected the bell to have when it came from the foundry. If it was in tune with itself, leave it alone! There were always lots of bells in the queue. Other bells in the ring were then tuned to be in the right relationship to the tenor.

Old bells require special consideration, particularly if they are part of a ring cast by different bellfounders. Put bluntly, you are often trying to make the best of a bad job! Notes taken from a tape recording are useful for giving an approximate idea of what improvements can be carried out and put in a report. When the bells come in, you think again. Can you find any cracks? If you can, it's a really good thing for a bellfounder but bad news for the church. 'Dear Vicar, unfortunately your bell is cracked, and a new one will cost this amount of dosh.' There might be a plaque in the ringing chamber showing the founders, diameters, and the weights, but sometimes bellfounders were telling porkies. It might well be that when a bell was weighed in our works and the note compared to a standard bell of ours, it was amazing that this bell had not cracked. It might be extremely light, so a letter needed. 'Dear Vicar, we don't know why this bell hasn't cracked. The weight is all wrong, and we suggest you let us boil it up and make you a decent one.' Or like the bell from Dublin that I condemned, 'Dear Archbishop, the weight on the plaque in your tower is not true. Lead put in the head of the bell when it came out as a bad casting is also a big problem. We suggest you have a new bell.'

Any tuning of existing bells is not normally intended to lower the notes of bells that are the flattest. If you can tune other bells down to match the flattest ones they will sound better. There is no attempt to tune old bells so that an A bell is in tune with A 435Hz or A 440Hz. The only consideration is that the progression sounds reasonable. Nobody is going to complain, 'These bells have not been tuned to international pitch.' It doesn't matter at all unless one of the ringers has 'absolute pitch'. This is really interesting. Absolute pitch known as 'A.P.' or 'perfect pitch' is very rare. These people can stand with their backs to a piano and immediately tell you what note you have played. This applies to any sound such as a foghorn, the note that a circular saw makes when cutting wood, or the hum from a generator on a building site. Acoustical research suggests that these people store pitch in the memory part of the brain with some sort of exact coding taking place. Another theory from Daniel Levitin's book *This Is Your Brain On Music* was that these people had something called 'muscle memory' from the position of their vocal cords if they sang the note, but his experiments showed this wasn't true. So how do they do it? As yet no-one knows for sure. A really intriguing ability!

The other consideration when tuning bells is whether they have to sound the same notes that you get on a piano. Centuries ago, when not many instruments played together, the interval between notes was a simple mathematical relationship. There were various ways the musical scale was formed, and without getting complicated we will call these 'unequal temperament.' This is nothing to do with 'artistic temperament' from a performer or artist, often described as 90% temper and 10% mental. When different instruments were playing pieces of music starting on various musical notes or 'keys', mathematicians such as Père Mersenne decided that the octave should be divided into twelve equal steps. Every semitone is an identical 'distance' in relation to a semitone below or above. This tuning of the twelve steps of the octave is called 'equal temperament' and it makes the overall sound of various instruments much better. Let's suppose you are back at Aunt Mabel's piano. With a bit of experimentation you should soon be able to pick out *Happy Birthday to You* with one finger starting on C. If you then start on the black note just above C you can do this as well, using black and white notes if you persevere. If you go up another semitone to the next white note and start again, *Happy Birthday to You* still sounds fine. But really it's a big fiddle! The only good reason is that by using equal temperament, assorted instruments can all play together in any key, starting on any of the twelve semitones (black and white notes) in the octave.

Starting (for instance) from C, each semitone up in equal temperament is about 6% more in frequency than the one before, as you go up in the twelve semitones to the next C. This progression is 'logarithmic' so in the old days you used mathematical tables that gave logarithmic progressions known as 'log tables'. This is really complicated so don't worry about this at all. It's much easier with a calculator, and you can use a special number. Apart from having my mother's Co-op divvy number engraved on my memory for ever, there is another number that, as long as my brain is not completely addled, I shall always be able to recite. Wake me up at 5a.m. in the morning (but please don't do this) and ask me, 'What is the 12th root of 2?' I will reply, '1.0594631'. This is the magic multiplication number that each semitone goes up by. With a calculator you put in 1.0594631 and then press the multiplication sign twice. This converts the magic number into a 'constant'. When you put in 440 and press the equals key twelve times you get to 880. Exactly! Each time you press the equals key you are forming the progression from 440 to 880 in twelve steps. So if we are talking about A 440Hz, you are going up to the octave above which is 880Hz in these twelve logarithmic steps.

You can put in any frequency you like. 216Hz, 305Hz, 476Hz, 816Hz etcetera, etcetera, and you can read off the frequencies as being an equal tempered scale from this frequency up to the next octave, or the one above that. With carillons, where you are playing different pieces of music that have been written down, and start on different notes, you need the equal tempered progression. The Taylor carillon with the four ton bourdon bell sent to Rotterdam in 1921 was the very first carillon in Europe tuned to equal tempered pitch.

For old rings of bells you can use the more exact 'unequal' mathematical intervals if it works out easier. When I was in the crack cathedral choir and singing unaccompanied without the organ, or if a skilled violinist is having a bit of a solo in the middle of an orchestral piece, the intervals between the sung or violin notes will be unequal, not equal. It sounds better to the trained ear of the person singing or sawing on a violin. A boffin recorded a crack violinist when she was playing a solo bit on her own, in the middle of a violin concerto with an orchestra, and he analysed the notes she was playing. It might have been Anne-Sophie Mutter who is a wizard violinist. He found that when she was playing on her own she was using unequal intervals. Violins are not like guitars and there are no frets where you put your fingers; you put your fingers wherever you want to. When the orchestra came back in and she was playing with them again, she switched to equal tempered intervals. The difference is very slight, but it exists. Her musical ear told her to do this, along with her brain of course. If you see a CD with an attractive violinist on the front with a mane of hair it's almost certainly her. If it is the CD where she is playing the Tchaikovsky and Korngold violin concertos, buy it! It's magic. (It's a Deutsche Grammophon recording). The mathematical relationships between different notes are nice round numbers in unequal temperament, so I have used these previously for simplicity. In equal temperament they are far messier.

So before we leave this magic number, suppose we put it in the calculator as a constant and then put in 24 (24 inches). Every time we press the equals key it gives you the next size down in the diameter of bells. So 24 x 1.0594631 = 25.43 inches for the next semitone down, and so on. Now multiply the magic number by itself twice which is called 'cubing' a number. If you did it right you get 1.1892071. If you have a standard Taylor 24 inch bell that weighs 3 cwt, and you use this new number as a constant, it will tell you that the weight of the 25.43 inch bell is 3.57 cwt. A really good magic number! With rings of bells, there are some variations in the weight (particularly the treble bells) to make the bells easier to ring.

Coming back to rings of bells that have bells cast by assorted founders (bet you thought I had lost the thread), you can choose whether you try to tune them into an unequal scale or an equal one. You are trying to get old bells to sound better than before. Plotting the weight and frequency on a graph is a good way of showing which bells are 'out' the most. Rings of bells all cast by the same founder often came in to be tuned, and if they were the 'heavy' profile and weights there was a good chance of getting them all much better in tune. This applied to Taylor bells as well, cast before 1895. After Taylor's started the 'five tone harmonic tuning', Gillett & Johnston started copying this in 1907 after Cyril cut a Taylor bell in half. Warner's started the new tuning to some extent in 1908, but they stopped casting bells in 1924. Mears held out much longer until 1926-1927. Some ringers thought they liked the old style tuning, and Mears were not in the carillon market, but it was thirty years after Taylor's. It's a long time. Old rings of theirs before 1926-1927 were still out of tune and often had a heavy profile as well.

One of the posh Brüel & Kjaer gadgets that the university boffins had provided us with was a frequency oscillator. By twiddling knobs it gave me any frequency I wanted, the same as tuning forks and every frequency in between. With a loudspeaker I could use the oscillator as a variable tuning fork. Instead of running up and down the racks of forks I could make the oscillator give me the same frequency as the one I was testing in a bell (by ear of course, listening to the beats). I needed to know exactly what frequency I was dialling, so we bought a frequency counter. This gave me the frequency as 440.12Hz, 456.32Hz, 732.65Hz, or whatever I had dialled. This was a really good jape for rough tuning, and I only had to switch to the forks when I was very close to the frequencies I wanted the bell to have.

When there were important visitors we always told them how the Taylor profile of a bell was based on ellipses, not arcs of a circle. We rightly told them that this was why Taylor bells were best. The other thing we told them was that we tuned bells listening to tuning forks by ear, and not using electronic gadgets like Whitechapel and Eijsbouts did, and we made a point of telling them this! We told them that this was because bells change note with temperature and so did our forks. We said that if we tuned a new bell in winter when it was cold in the tuning shop, and then tuned another new one on a hot summer day when we were sweating, they would both be in tune with each other when they were at the same temperature. Dashed clever! Actually, it was a little bit of a white lie and was being slightly 'economical with the truth', a really good phrase. We were right with major changes in temperature such as days when the thermometer had plummeted right down in winter, compared to a day when there was a substantial heat wave.

Before I deal with the very complicated problems of tuning small carillon bells, which every good bellfounder from the Hemony brothers onwards agreed was very difficult (to put it mildly), I want to go back to partials in normal bells. After World War II, the Dutch engineer Engelbert 'Bert' van Heuven, (as part of his investigations paid for by the Dutch government), started charting as many bell partials as he could and also carrying out research into tuning. He produced diagrams he called 'tuning graphs' showing where the best place on the bell was to tune each partial. This was a genuine scientific investigation rather than Canon Simpson's ideas. His results were adopted by various Dutch bellfounders, and in 1949 he published his findings in a paper entitled *Acoustical Measurements on Church-bells and Carillons*. He was then awarded a degree by the Delft Institute of Technology. The Loughborough University profs eventually asked us if we would lend them a bell for a long time for protracted testing. We did this, and supplied them with a Taylor bell weighing just over four cwt that had been kicking around in our works for years and years.

Right: *A recent photograph of the tuning shop with a collection of tuned bells. The smallest tuning machine is just visible behind the present tuner, Girdar Vadukar.*
Photo: John Taylor & Co.

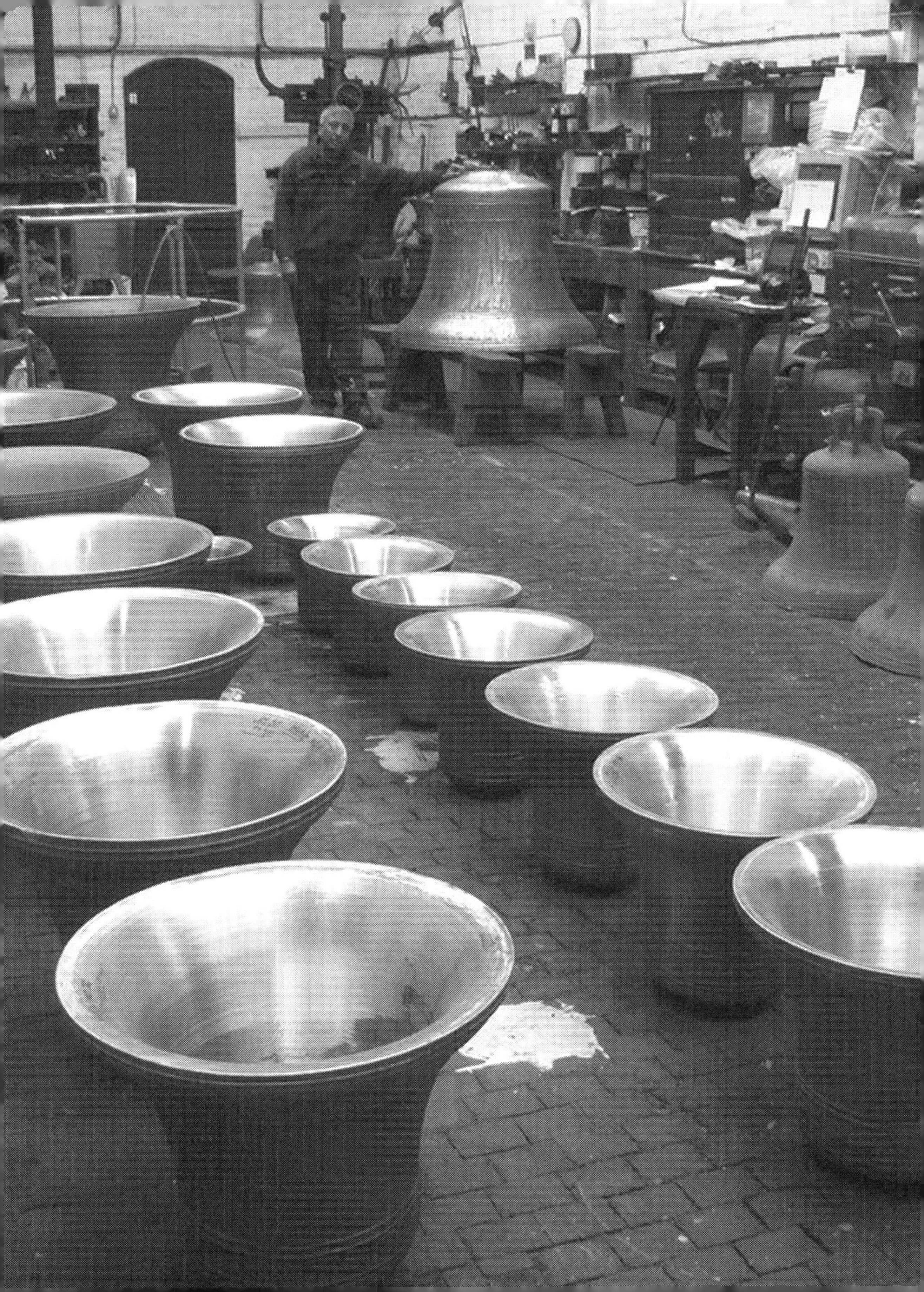

We had carried out 'normal' tuning of the first five partials, but they identified 134 modes of vibration with different partials, and a major scientific paper was published as a result in 1983. I was given an honourable mention in the list of people who had in some way contributed to this research project. At the university, they drove the bell into vibration via a variable oscillator, like the one they had supplied us with. This gave them as long as they wanted to see where the bell was vibrating, and I did this with small carillon bells using a loudspeaker, where the tuning forks at the top of the range only gave a short ping. They started with the hum note in the bell we had lent them which was 293Hz. They went up 1Hz at a time until they gave up at 9,286Hz! This shows real dedication and an enormous amount of time over months and months! They used a computer program to predict and confirm where these 134 modes of vibration should be, and their relation to families of different vibration modes. In one or two cases this indicated a partial where they hadn't found one, so they went back to the bell to find it. Over several years of study, various other boffins dropped in, and there were loads of learned papers published in scientific journals. The bell became very famous and it has subsequently been put in the Taylor bellfoundry museum.

Simplifying their results totally, they found that within the bell there were partials that they described as being 'ring driven' from the soundbow being clouted. These started off as being the hum, tierce, and nominal. Above these were the quint octave, the nominal octave, an octave of a 4th above the nominal (that Taylor's called the 'continental 4th'), an octave of an interval that is a 6th above the nominal, and then a 4th double octave. These simple ratios are 1 : 2.4 : 4 : 6 : 8 : 10.66 : 13.33 : 21.33, and then there are some more. I'm ignoring loads of others that are in some cases 'shell driven' so originate from striking the bell some way down the waist, and the quint partial is a good example. The major third, *Row, Row, Row Your Boat* partial, immediately above the nominal with the ratio 1: 5 is one of these 'shell driven' modes, but is just audible. One note up from this is the interval Taylor's called a 'continental 4th', ratio 1: 5.33 and the octave below (three notes up from the fundamental) is the note often described as being a 'metallic 4th'. I have explained that Percival Price stated he didn't like this interval and complained that in bells above ten tons in weight this note was too obtrusive. He thought a ten ton bell was the heaviest bell a carillon should have. Part of the perception of this 4th takes us into the realms of 'psycho-acoustics', that I will explain in more detail in a moment.

What impressed the university boffins and got them all excited was that in this bog standard Taylor bell a lot of these high partials were in the right ratios. They commented on this in their first scientific paper and said that in our profile of a bell these came out 'in the wash'; a nice description. They decided the Taylor profile was extremely good, and German bellfounders in particular, who were actively trying to tune the higher partials, were probably working with a bell profile that was not as good! This is why they tore down to the bellfoundry and wanted to see the Taylor profile geometric construction details using the elliptical shape. As I hadn't yet discovered it we couldn't oblige at the time. At one stage, when they were deciding from their own research that German and French bell profiles were based on arcs of a circle, they asked Whitechapel for their construction details, but they wouldn't play ball! As they had already decided they were probably based on arcs of circles from looking at their bells in our works, it didn't matter too much.

I had acquired the work sheet of the tuning process for the one and a half ton tenor bell at Westminster Abbey, cast at Whitechapel in 1971. Their tuner at the time wanted this bell to be as perfect as possible and charted a total of twelve partials. He was very successful in controlling the important ones, although nearly six cwt was removed in the tuning which is ever such a lot. When Gillett & Johnson packed up, I have mentioned how Paul Taylor bought all the tuning books and forks, so it is easy to see what they were achieving.

The Whitechapel bell finished up very close to a slightly larger bell that I had carefully tuned in 1980 when I tuned or followed down twenty partials as an experiment. A typical large Gillett & Johnson bell was not quite so accurate because they had the strange idea of tuning the notes within a bell to unequal temperament, which is really weird. I obtained the finished tuning figures for a four foot diameter bell cast and tuned by André Lehr from the Royal Eijsbouts foundry, but it appears to be not quite as good regarding the high partials. He was the expert Dutch bellfounder, and although this was not a recently cast bell, I suspect he may have been using a slightly different theoretical tuning system.

I need to explain something else that is vital, and hopefully you will find it really interesting. Let's pretend an upturned bell is like a tulip with four petals, and we super-glue the edges of the petals all the way down. Imagine that we puffed a large amount of air into the tulip and the centre of each petal moved outwards, but the edges stayed in place. If we could see the hum note 'pattern' when a bell is struck there would similarly be four places where it opened and closed, from the lip down to the head. Let's be more destructive to our tulip and glue a bit of wire all the way round, about a quarter of the way down. In this case, apart from the four petals expanding at the top, the petals also expand below the piece of wire. This is how the fundamental partial works, if we could see it.

In a bell, we call these places from the lip downwards, where the glued petal edges stay in place, 'nodal lines'. The circular places going round the bell, as you go down from the lip, where there is no movement, are called 'nodal rings'. There may well be more than one. So when the hum frequency is excited in a bell, there are four places round the rim where there is virtually no vibration, and in the case of the fundamental, a circle lower down as well. Where the bell is happy to vibrate between the nodal lines we call these 'anti-nodes', and they are generated from the place where the clapper hits the soundbow. The tierce is the same as a tulip with six petals super-glued at the edges, and the wire glued half way down. So we have six nodes and one ring, and the quint partial is the same. The nominal has eight nodes and one ring, along with the major 3rd two notes up, and the octave of the quint has ten nodes and one ring, as does an interval that is a 7th above the nominal. The octave of the nominal has twelve nodes and one ring, along with the major 3rd octave, and the 'continental 4th' octave has fourteen nodes and one ring, along with another one that is not related to a musical interval. Keeping going, the octave of the 6th has sixteen nodes and one ring, as does the nominal double octave. All these nodal lines come in pairs of even numbers, as you may have spotted. So let's stop there!

With scientific acoustical measuring equipment we can see this if we excite the bell at all the various frequencies. In the old days, someone found that a stethoscope was good for this, and we had one at Taylor's that I used once out of interest. Other notes or partials within a bell (that are basically related musical intervals) often have a nodal ring at the sound bow, and there may be another one lower down as well, making two nodal rings, or there might be three or more. Because one nodal ring is at the soundbow, when you hit the bell there the corresponding vibration is extremely weak with hardly any sound, or none at all. Some people interested in the acoustics of bells say that there is no point trying to tune partials that are not excited when you hit the soundbow. I don't think it is as simple as this, but let's forget it.

I can hear various people furiously sharpening their pencils to tell me that many of the upper partials I have detailed as having just one nodal ring have a second nodal ring, and in some cases they do. Quite often these are right up at the top of the shoulder and not very pronounced, so can be ignored. When it was being decided how the university bods were going to set up the test bell, they wanted it to be resting on nothing; so sky hooks! The alternative system chosen was to make a circular plate with four diesel engine valve springs that had minimal contact with the bell. Measurements of partials were taken right up the outside of the bell and over the crown. This produced various partials with nodal rings that would not be present when a bell was bolted up to a headstock or girder. So when we were all interpreting the results these were discounted as not being there in practice. The title of the major scientific paper was *Normal Modes of the Modern English Church Bell*, but in reality it should have been entitled *Normal and Abnormal Modes....*!

For various reasons that may be due to a bell not being uniform in thickness, or a slightly different metallurgical content because the cooling was not at the same rate, you can get a thing we called a 'wobble'. This is a 'beat' in the bell just the same as hitting two tuning forks at the same time. Other people call this a 'warble' because if it is fast it sounds like birdsong. The proper name is a 'doublet' or 'split partial'. This is a real pain, and small carillon bells often suffered from this problem. The original 'Great Peter' bell at York Minster, cast by Mears, that was three quarters of an inch thicker on one side than the other must have had a really good wobble. The Mears 'Big Ben II' has a wobble of two frequencies, 4Hz apart, which causes the pulsing sound because it is cracked. The only time I ever experienced this on a big bell was the *AC/DC* bell. The enormous logo put the bell out of balance, and there was a wobble on the hum note. If you remember, I put four circles of red paint on the soundbow as 'hit here' positions, but I don't expect they did this every time when they were cavorting round on stage!

I know you are dying to ask me how I knew where to put the blobs. Mother Nature does help us a bit. Suppose the hum note is 400Hz, which is correct, and there is a wobble of 4Hz because there is another note at 404Hz that you don't want to be audible. If you tap round

Right: *The AC/DC bell about to be dispatched. The two circles (out of four) on the soundbow denote where the bell has a clear note when struck. These places are where the 'anti-nodes' of the desired frequency are to be found. The very large logo had put the bell out of balance, generating a 'wobble' or split partial.*
Photo by author

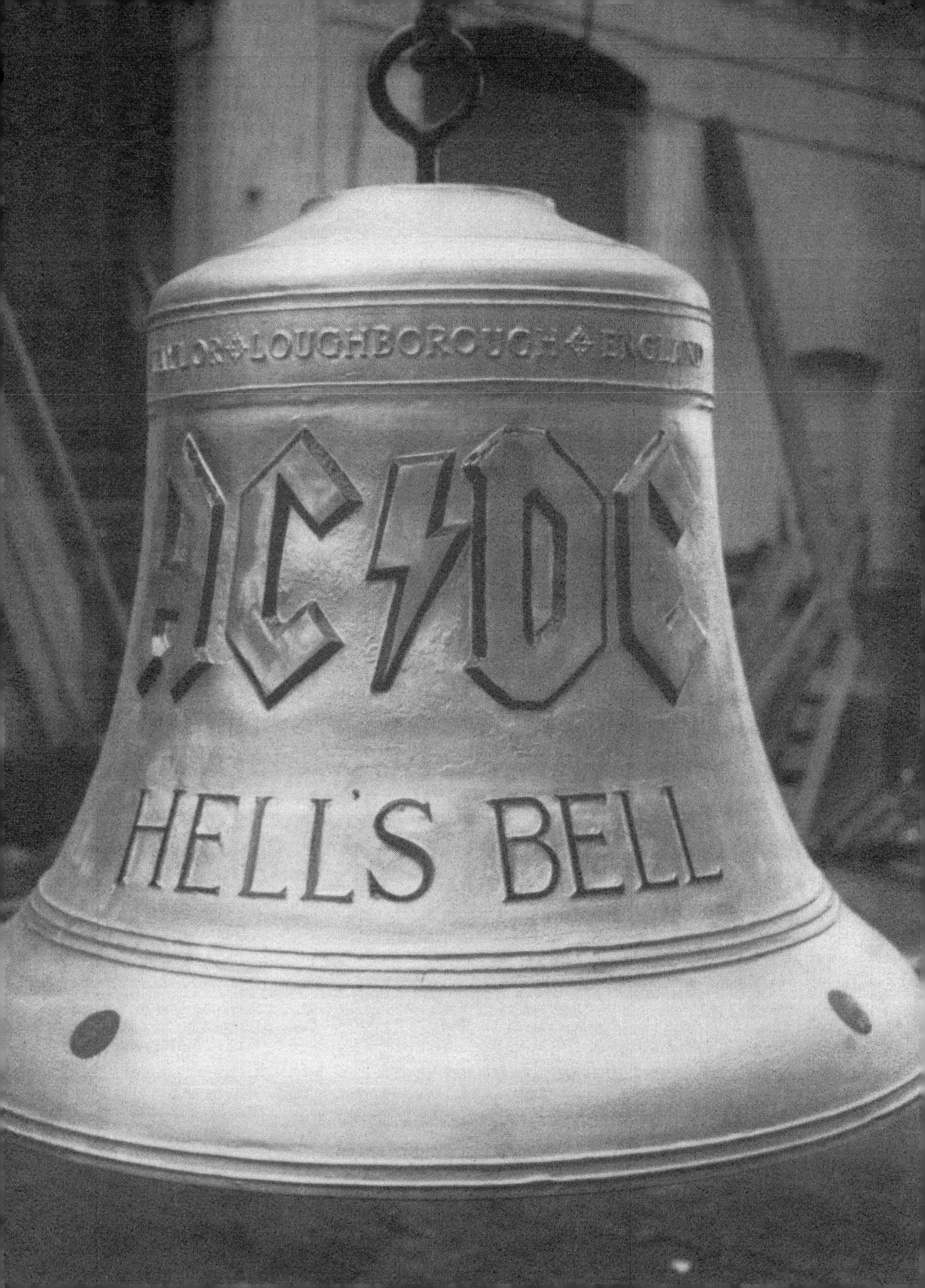
LOUGHBOROUGH
AC/DC
HELL'S BELL

the soundbow with a little hammer you can find the four nodes and anti-nodes of each frequency. Luckily for bellfounders, the node of one frequency of a wobble is the anti-node of the other one. Okay? Really handy! When you find the anti-node of the 400Hz hum note that you want, it is the node of the 404Hz note so it isn't audible. This is where you would put your four blobs of paint. If there is a wobble with the nominal, there are sixteen places with eight nodes and antinodes for the note you want, and eight pairs for the one you don't. Marking a 'hit here' place on a bell only works if you can absolutely guarantee that this is where the clapper will hit, which is often very difficult to achieve in practice.

When Paul Taylor and I were experimenting with small carillon bells we were progressively increasing the weight of the smallest ones. A simple concept: more weight more oomph, and a bigger clapper could be used to hit the bell without cracking it. If there was a bad wobble the bell might be scrap. One evening when I had stayed on to fight a small bell I determined where the nodes and anti-nodes were for a wobble on the nominal. In a moment of inspiration I cut a thin slot with a hacksaw on the inside of the soundbow on one of the anti-nodes of the highest frequency that I didn't want to be audible. This made it come down by a small amount and after several deeper cuts it was the same frequency as the lower one that I did want. I had managed to kill the beat wherever the bell was hit. Magic! Paul was extremely impressed and so were the university crew after I had managed to duplicate this on other bells. They had never even remotely considered this, so back to their computer to make a mathematical model, but I asked them not to write it up for a scientific journal! We wanted it to be another of the Taylor secrets. The slots didn't look very good to the casual observer so we filled them in with black wax so there was then just a thin black line.

On one of my 'watching the tide marks in the bath' times, I realized that the smallest bells were being sand cast in square boxes that we used for cast iron bits and pieces. Was the bell cooling differently because it was a round bell in a square box? It did make a difference when we stopped doing this. Another good idea! My university friends agreed that uneven cooling was liable to give wobbles.

After Paul Taylor died, the university bods were meeting up with another professor from America and going to Holland. A Dutchman who was on a year off from another American university was studying the perception of sound, including bells, at Eindhoven University. The perception of sound is a whole different subject, and as I have mentioned, comes under the general heading of 'psycho-acoustics'. To give an example, we have seen how the normal harmonic series (not overtones or partials) is 1 : 2 : 3 : 4 : 5 : 6 etcetera. If you have several oscillators that give the harmonic series, but not the bottom first harmonic, the brain decides that this is really a harmonic series with the bottom one missing, so it puts this one in! Isn't that clever! The brain 'concludes' that it has to supply the missing first harmonic.

Right: *A view of the 1963 Washington carillon assembled in the works showing the internal clappers and their return springs which bring the clappers off the smallest bells cleanly and reduce the 'dwell time'. The large clapper top left is designed to give a minimum contact area and dwell time, to improve the sound.*
Photo: Taylor archive

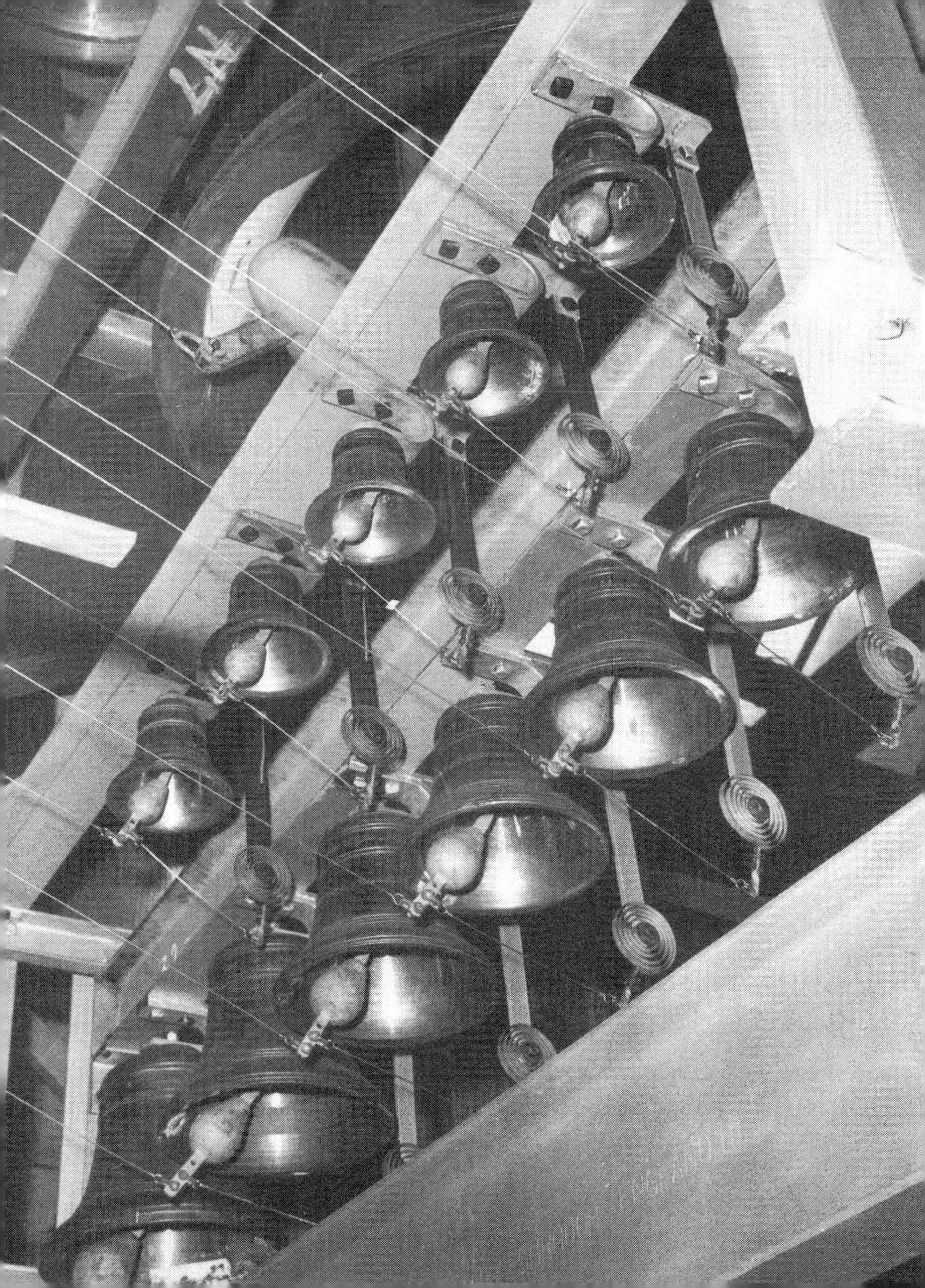

In very large bells, the perceived 'metallic 4th', three notes up from the fundamental, can be a big problem. Cyril Johnston was made very aware of this when Frederick Mayer made him cast the enormous Riverside bourdon bell three times! Very aware! Cyril cast three bourdon bells with different profiles, so they were different weights when tuned, and the second and third ones were worse than the first one! I imagine the metal composition was identical. When Pierre Paccard was casting the largest bell of the three for Stephen Roman at Toronto, he had a disaster with the first bell as the moulds split. He rejected the second bell because of the perceived 4th, so it was third time lucky with him as well! It is not absolutely clear why this note is so unpleasant in big bells, and the German bellfounder Peter Schilling thought it might be affected by the combined composition of the metal and bell weight, but I am sure the profile has a big effect as well. John Gouwens is the expert organist and carillonneur at the Gillett & Johnston carillon at Culver and has probably played on just about every single carillon in the US several times. He thinks that the 'dwell time' (the period of time when the clapper is in contact with the bell) has an effect on this rogue note making it audible to a greater or a lesser extent in large bells. Lots of theories!

Another reason is that the sound perception of the human ear is not linear. If you play a whole series of notes from low ones to high ones, and a microphone tells you they are all the same sound level, the human ear doesn't think so. It's called the 'threshold of hearing', and high partials in big bells come into a lower band of hearing than medium to small bells. The ear is most sensitive to frequencies between 1,000Hz and 2,000Hz so between C6 and C7 on a piano, and these frequencies are heard as being 'loudest'. Going up from C7 to C8 on our piano the 'perceived' loudness level starts to fall off quite rapidly. Relating this to actual frequencies, the nominal of the eighteen ton bourdon bell that is note C at the Riverside carillon should be 261Hz (middle C4), so the higher partials are lower down the frequency range. The smallest Whitechapel bell at the West Hartford carillon should have a nominal of 15,800Hz! This note or frequency, that isn't there on Aunt Mabel's piano, would be another twenty-three white keys further up from the last white key on her piano which is C8. This is one key/note below C10! Above the age of about thirty-five to forty, most people (particularly men) won't hear this note however loud it is. When I was selling expensive high quality loudspeakers with the high frequencies perfectly audible to young people, we joked that people who could afford them had probably lost their hearing at the top end!

One learned expert who has carried out an amazing amount of research on bells states that in a bell there are related partials that are musical notes or frequencies that form the simple harmonic ratios 2 : 3 : 4 : 5 : 6. He considers that the ear wants to hear the 'missing first harmonic' which is the same frequency as the unwanted metallic 4th. This assumes first of all that the very high partials are well enough 'in tune' within the bell that the brain can decide they are part of a harmonic series. Accurately tuning very high partials is impossible; the best that can be achieved is that the tuner keeps his eye on these. Tuning lower partials has some influence on the high ones but that's all. The second assumption is that the high partials that may make up a harmonic series are sufficiently audible. If you can't hear them the brain can't decide anything! I am not at all convinced that the ear has enough sensitivity to hear all of these partials loud enough to form a harmonic series. To 'perceive' this metallic 4th as being a first harmonic, the ear would have to hear the second harmonic (the 'continental 4th'), the third harmonic (the nominal double octave), and the fourth harmonic (the octave of the 'continental 4th, or the double octave of the metallic 4th). If we can't hear these three 'harmonics' (as a minimum), there can be no 'perceived' metallic 4th.

When tuning 'Great George', a very big bell, Paul Taylor charted and wrote down a whole series of partials, including the nominal double octave that he described as 'weak'. He didn't write down any frequency that would have related to the metallic 4th double octave. If he had heard it, even if being extremely weak, he would have written the frequency down. He was only twenty-six years old at the time, with acute hearing. If he didn't hear this note/frequency in 'Great George' his ear was not able to decide that it was part of a harmonic series with the first harmonic missing.

Another thing that the brain does is to perceive a 'difference note' generated by two other notes. The nominal (ratio 4) and the 6th (ratio 6.66) are both audible when you clout the soundbow as they are ring driven, so the 'difference' note is the ratio 6.66 minus 4 which is 2.66. This is the ratio of the unpleasant 4th, and I personally think this is the reason the brain decides this note exists as a very predominant one. Paul found both partials in 'Great George' that could well have produced a difference note. So this is my explanation!

Another difference note (Americans call these notes 'resultants') exists when various organ pipes are sounding at the same time which gives a 'perceived note' an octave lower. If you blast air through a thirty-two foot open ended organ pipe of note C, and a second one a fourth higher (so G in the scale of C) along with some smaller pipes, the ear puts in a note C an octave lower. This is equivalent to having a sixty-four foot C pipe. This is a feature of pipe organs which means these extremely long pipes are not needed. This is really handy for organ builders as they don't have to make a hole in the church roof to get them in, and these pipes are also very expensive to make. This is a really good wheeze that is normally used with the lowest notes in a decent size pipe organ, and organ builders call the perceived note of the pipes that aren't there, 'sub-harmonics'. (The equivalent sixteen foot pipes give the perceived note of a thirty-two foot pipe).

In listening carefully to recordings of large Taylor bells such as 'Great Peter' (that weighs nearly eleven tons), I don't think the 'nasty 4th' is an exceptionally strong note or frequency. No Taylor carillon ever made has a bourdon bell heavier than just over ten tons, which Percival Price thought should be the maximum weight of the bourdon bell. The very skilled carillonneurs, Anton Brees and then Milford Myre, were both official carillonneurs at the Lake Wales Bok tower for many years. They never complained vigorously about their ten ton bourdon bell. Coming back to John Gouwens, he can hear this fourth in the Lake Wales bourdon bell, but less in the same size Washington bourdon bell, but he doesn't think they are objectionable. Like Frederick Mayer, John Gouwens is a very skilled organist and former choirmaster, so he has excellent hearing. When Paul Taylor told me that when he heard 'Great George' at Liverpool Cathedral and 'it sounded magnificent' he didn't say, 'Apart from the metallic 4th', so it wasn't a big problem in this bell either. Let's stop here, because if I give any more explanations it will get even more complicated and probably really boring!

When I was invited to go to Holland there were some very interesting discussions. They all knew I was the one who was producing carillon bells to replace others that were duff or supplying new ones. What I was doing was extremely important, and I had to get it right as my reputation and Taylor's were on the line.

Fast forwarding in time again, I was experimenting with profiles for the little bells that were far removed from anything we had ever done before, except we always used a higher tin content of up to 25% that helped to give more zing. The bells were thicker still and very different in the internal profile, and I had also modified the external shape making the bells quite dumpy in height. I found on two occasions that a frequency I was charting and tuning suddenly disappeared! It was obvious it was related to the thickness but not a 'normal' partial. The university profs suggested that I identified different frequencies or partials by determining how many nodes and rings they had. I knew all about nodal lines and rings from killing wobbles of course, but it had never been relevant before to identify particular partials. I drove the bell into vibration with a loudspeaker again, and used a little gadget called a transducer that I could slide round the soundbow or lower down, and up and down the inside. Hooked up to an oscilloscope, this showed me the number of nodal lines and rings. (Oscilloscopes are clever devices that have baby TV screens). This identified the number of nodes and rings. Was it one I wanted to tune, or some odd one that I could ignore?

This was now getting extremely complicated! More felt tip pens and counting the lines and rings of almost every note I could hear. The American prof was going back to Holland to see his friend at Eindhoven University again, so I went as well. Whilst I was there I went to see André Lehr from the Royal Eijsbouts bellfoundry just up the road from Eindhoven, who gave me the benefit of his advice. We both agreed that small carillon bells were pigs!

On one of my trips to Canada I had been delighted to see the squat profile of the smallest bells at a carillon in Toronto cast by the Royal Eijsbouts foundry. The small carillon at Rostok in Germany, cast by Peter Schilling in 1986, is another typical example. Obviously a case of 'great minds think alike'! We were definitely all singing out of the same hymn book, even if in three different languages! In 2016 the Paccard foundry renovated the carillon at Rouen Cathedral and the additional smallest bells have a considerably reduced height.

Whatever the gadgets were telling me, I still had to listen to the bells very carefully. It wasn't just what we called the 'internal' tuning so the bell was in tune with itself, the 'external' tuning was very important. Did hitting two bells an octave apart (so with some identical

Right: *John Gouwens, carillonneur at the Culver Academies carillon in Indiana in the US. This 1950 Gillett & Johnston carillon is one of the only two in North America that still have all the original Gillett & Johnston bells.* Photographer: Gary Mills

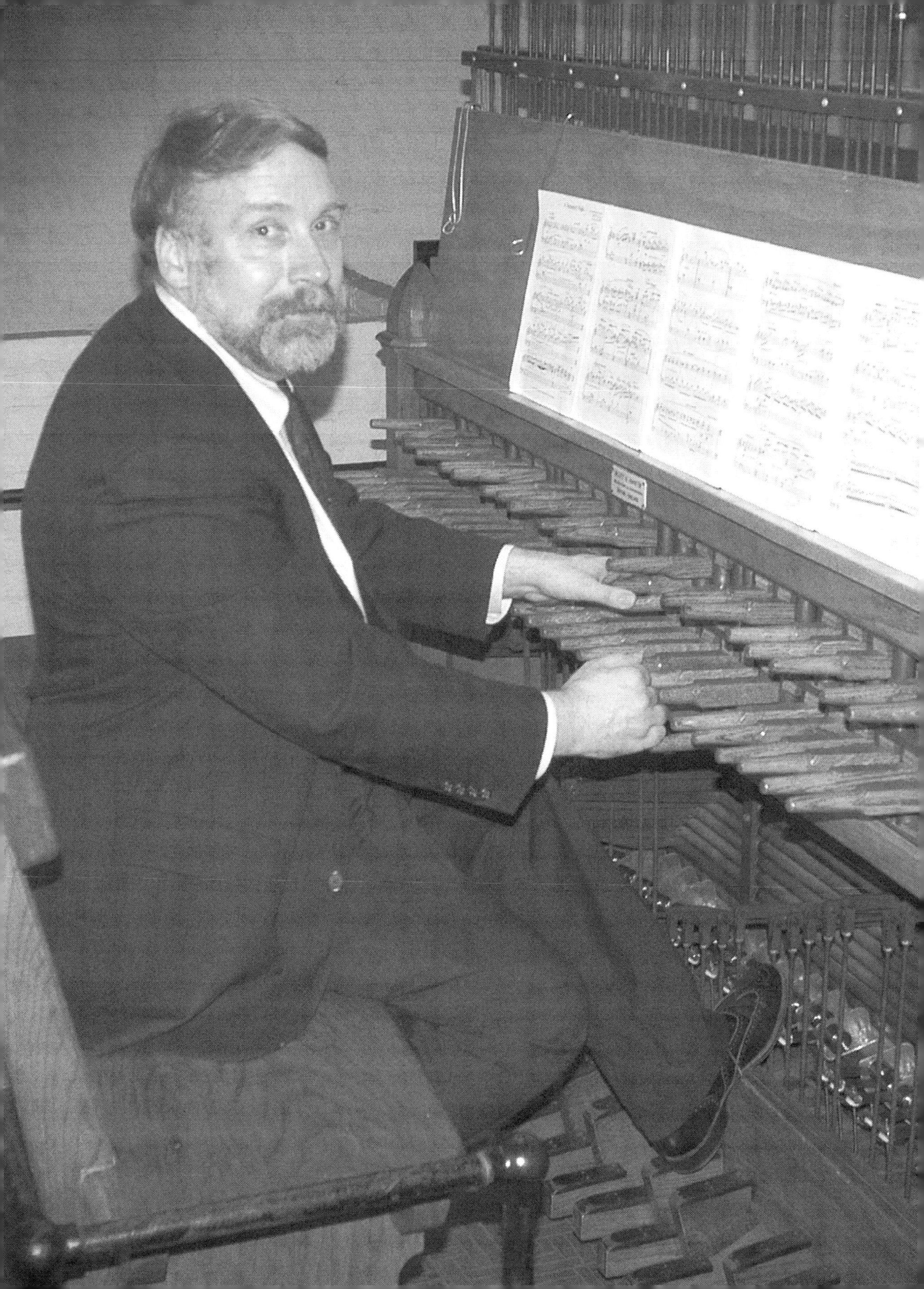

frequencies as regards the partials) produce a beat? If so, which frequency was not exactly right in which bell? At one stage the university bods suggested that if I wrote everything up it would go a long way to me obtaining a B.Sc. degree specializing in acoustic science! I thanked them profusely, but I couldn't see it would make me a better bellfounder.

I recently found some advice from Tom Charnley and Bob Perrin in 1995 gently suggesting to another acoustic bod (who had published a paper on bells in *New Scientist*) that he was wrong. They told him via the editor who had approved the paper to go back to his computer finite-element program. 'We suggest that Shippen re-runs his finite-element program using the values of 103 gigapascals for Young's modulus and 8.85×10^3 kg m-3 for density. The results should be insensitive to Poisson's ratio, which is about 0.38.' Well, I knew he should have taken this into account! Meanwhile, I was still producing carillon bells that the American consultants were coming to test in some cases. It was all getting a bit hairy!

On another matter entirely, Paul Taylor told me that when he decided to introduce a revolutionary new concept in the tuning of change ringing bells that was extremely successful he felt like 'a lonely pioneer'. I understood exactly. In 1986, at the 1927 Taylor carillon at Albany city in New York State, I replaced the duplicate bells and also some other bells just lower down from these. The smallest bell that I produced weighed just over twenty pounds, a large increase in weight compared to the original ones. I went out when they were being installed, and they sounded fine to me. Ronald Barnes, who was an extremely famous carillonneur, came to give the opening recital, and he thought they were excellent. Good job! A lot better than saying, 'These are dire!' I cadged a hard-hat off the bosses of the company putting steel girders in, which had their company name on it in big letters: 'Goode Erections'. Some Yanks have no sense of humour, and they were a bit puzzled why I wanted one!

By this time the smallest carillon bells were being cast with a cylindrical stump coming up from the crown, and this was carefully machined first. The bells were then put on a horizontal lathe and machined externally and internally to ensure that there was no irregularity in the thickness. After tuning, the stump was machined off and a hole drilled in the head. The finished bells then went to an amiable man called Charlie Phillips, who was the chief carillon

Top right: *The renovated carillon at Rouen Cathedral completed in 2016 by Fonderie Paccard. The very pronounced alteration in the profile and thickness of the smallest bells can be clearly seen.*
Photo: Jean-François Claire - 2016

Bottom left: *An 8 inch bell at the 50 bell Royal Eijsbouts Exhibition Place carillon in Toronto. The squat height and thick profile is typical of attempts to make the smallest carillon bells more audible.*
Photo by author

Bottom right: *Two small carillon bells being tested at Taylor's when the recasting of the duplicate bells at the Albany City hall carillon was carried out in 1986. There is a much reduced height and a large increase in weight.*
Photo by author

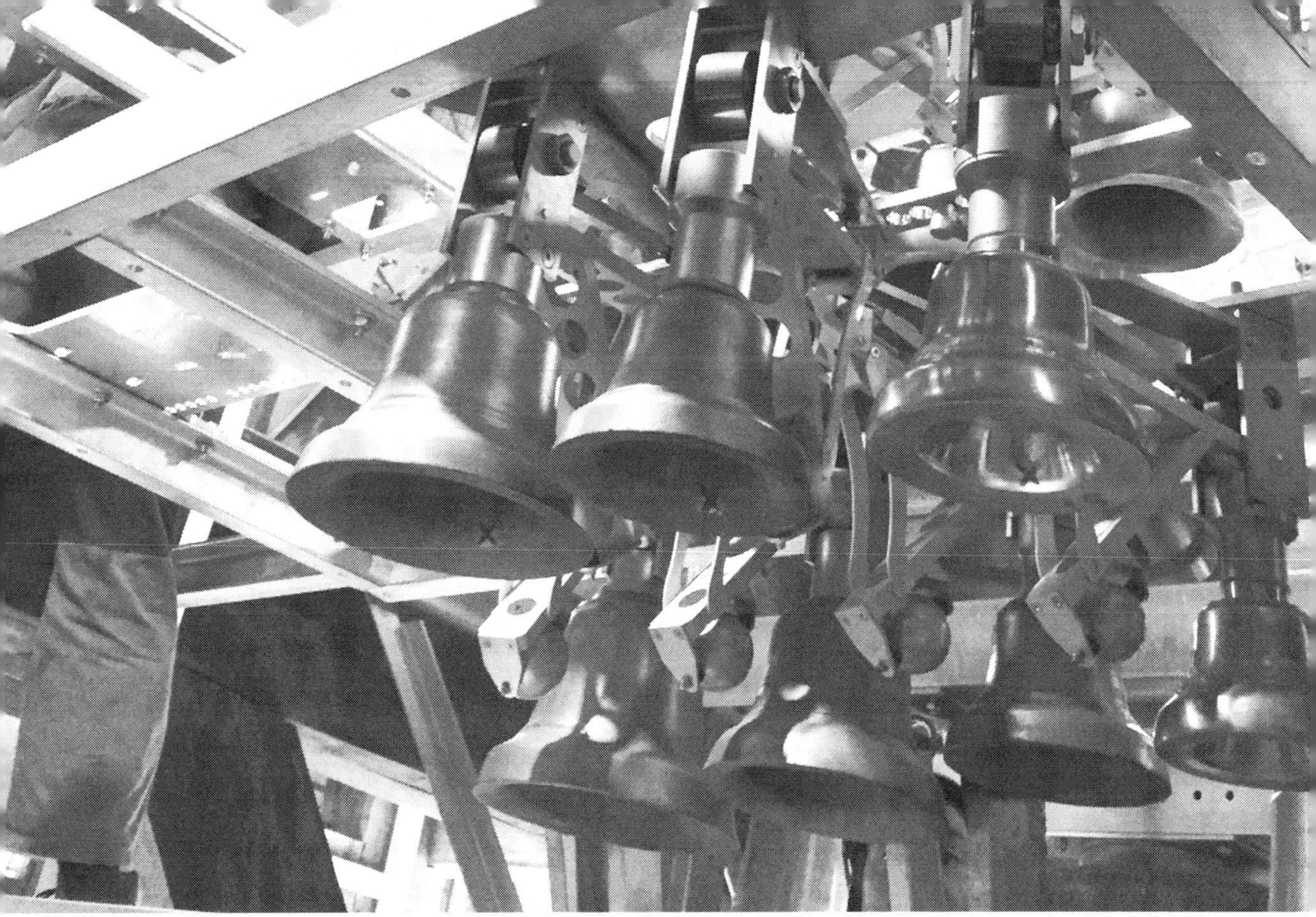
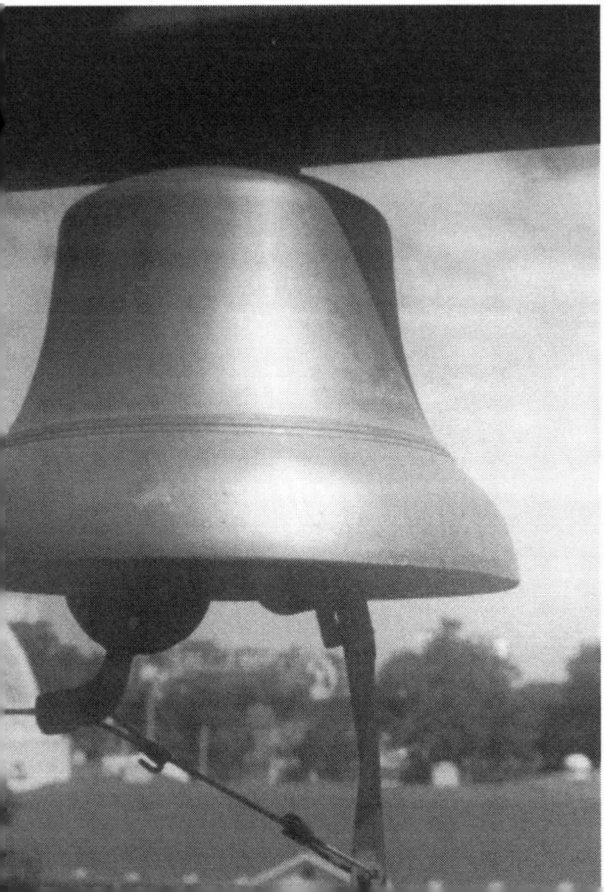
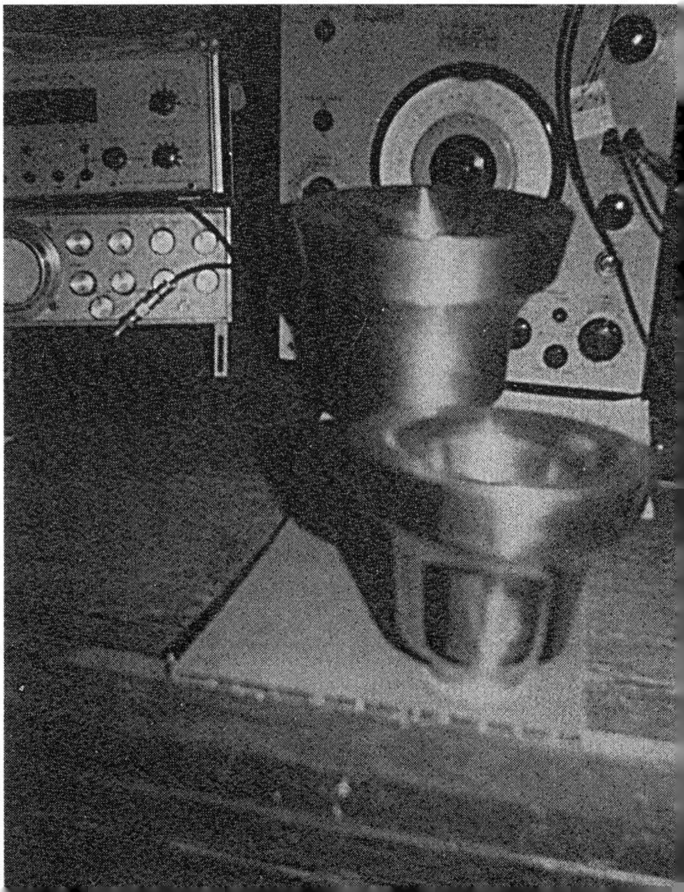

builder, and he used a series of punches, 0-9, along with a big hammer, to stamp the number of the bell in the carillon on the crown of the bell. Peter Cake and I joked that if the bell survived this process there was no problem. Once or twice the bells cracked! New bell needed!

Towards the middle of 1987, I was beginning to think that my stint of just over ten years at the bellfoundry was probably enough! The 'quit while you are ahead' principle seemed very valid! To have helpful discussions with another bellfounder regarding small carillon bells and their problems I had to go to Holland. Perhaps I could have gone to the Paccard foundry if I spoke French, but they had stopped making complete carillons in 1981. I thought a new set of ears might well be a good idea. I privately told Peter Cake well in advance what I was thinking, and I trained a young man called Andrew Higson over a period of a few months to take my place. He had the right credentials and a good ear, and he already worked at the foundry doing another job. At the end of March 1988 I bowed out, but I should have waited until 1992 when the ten ton bell for Malta was cast! As it was a complete success I was absolutely correct in thinking I was not indispensable.

Andrew Higson took over my job for twenty years and has narrated a hilarious story about this bell. Two furnaces were used, and the biggest one needed to be converted to use oil as the fuel, like the other one. It had twin burners that blasted the flame over the metal, and when they used it flames came out of the top of the chimney. A neighbour, Mr. Patel, rang 999 and several bulky firemen turned up, axes in hand. They asked, 'Do you know your chimney is on fire?' 'No', replies Bill, 'But if you hum me a couple of bars I think I'll pick it up!' By the time they had come back after the next three 999 calls everybody was on first name terms, and the firemen were given cups of tea! The only fly in the ointment was because the biggest furnace was just about under the museum. Trevor Jennings was extremely upset as the museum slowly filled up with smoke, and he complained bitterly. What is it they say? (Actually it was John Lydgate). 'You can please some of the people all of the time, you can please all of the people some of the time, but you can't please all of the people all of the time'.

21. Paul Taylor: Last of the Line

'He hath a heart as sound as a bell, and his tongue is the clapper; for what his heart thinks his tongue speaks.'
Much Ado About Nothing - William Shakespeare

Paul Lea Taylor, named after 'Great Paul', was born on January 25th, 1914, just a few months before war broke. This just about qualifies him as being a 'war baby' like I was but in different World Wars. He had one sister, Margaret Lea, who had just turned three when Paul was born. Lea was the family surname of their mother who came from Whalley Range in Manchester. She was thirty-three years old when she married Paul's father, John William II, in 1909. He was then aged fifty-six, so a great difference in ages, and it was his second marriage. Three of his four sons from his first marriage were killed on active service during the war, and apparently he never recovered from this tragedy. He died in June 1919, aged sixty-six, when Paul was five and his sister was eight.

One of Paul's four half-brothers had worked at the bellfoundry with Pryce before he was killed. Pryce was injured in the war but otherwise returned unscathed in 1919 to become the bellfoundry manager. Edmund Denison was fifty-five years of age when the war finished, and he became the driving force until he died, aged eighty-three, in 1947. He and Pryce devoted a lot of time to obtaining carillon orders in the US. When Pryce contracted peritonitis whilst on a sales trip to Canada in 1927, and died, Paul was only thirteen.

Paul's three half-sisters were aged between twenty and twenty six when he was born, and Gwen, who was the youngest, worked in the tuning shop tuning bells. In 1921, when the very heavy chime of ten bells for Yale University was made (later made up to a full carillon with an additional forty-four bells in 1966), she tuned all these with a bit of help from Pryce on the largest bell, which was six feet nine inches. She tuned the first Taylor carillon to be sent to America, for Gloucester, in 1922, and then the large 1923 War Memorial Carillon in Loughborough. She stopped tuning soon afterwards when she became married, and Denison and Pryce took over again.

Paul was sent off to boarding school when he was eight to the Mostyn House Public School at Parkgate in Cheshire. Denison and Pryce had installed a thirty-six bell War Memorial carillon so Paul must have felt proud that a substantial Taylor carillon was there. Going to boarding school was nothing new for the family. In the 1901 census, when Pryce was ten, he and his brothers John and Gerald were boarders at a school in Dorset where their uncle, Pryce Thomas Taylor, was the headmaster. There was probably a large discount in the boarding fees! From Mostyn, Paul went to another extremely famous public school at Oundle in Peterborough. They took children from the age of eleven until school leaving age. It seems that Paul's mother was not in good health, and there is an indication that she may have moved back to Manchester. She died in 1929 when she was fifty-three, and Paul and his sister became orphans in their teens.

General education in those days finished at the age of sixteen. In common with many of the Taylor family, including Denison, Paul was sent off to serve an apprenticeship. In 1931 when he was seventeen he started work at 'Metropolitan Vickers' in Manchester. This large company made heavy electrical engineering goods so perhaps Denison chose Manchester because Paul's maternal family were there? As well as serving his apprenticeship, Paul then obtained a degree in engineering from Sheffield University. In 1935, when he was twenty-one, he was hands on at the bellfoundry and was made a junior partner.

I assume Paul and Margaret were still living in bellfoundry house, possibly with their half-sister Josephine. She had married a local Leicestershire man in Nairobi on May 23rd, 1920, but for unknown reasons she came back alone on July 30th the same year. There is no record that she ever went back! In 1939, she was living with her sister Gwen and her husband in Welwyn Garden City in Hertfordshire. Pryce had been married in 1925 and left a widow, Kathleen. Whether she lived in bellfoundry house before or after she became a widow, I have no idea.

I have commented that Paul's father was very musical, and in bellfoundry house there was a collection of string instruments and a piano. He had asked William Wooding Starmer what make he should buy. Paul took up playing the viola (it's the next size up from a violin) and became a very accomplished player. Denison eventually moved to a posh house in one of Loughborough's best addresses near the boys' Grammar School and girls' High School. He never married and had difficulty keeping staff as apparently he was a bit of a martinet.

Paul told me how his pride and joy was the acquisition of a Bentley Sports saloon car that was first unveiled in 1934. It was a hefty 3.5 litre with twin carburettors and was being manufactured at the Rolls Royce works in Derby as they had taken over Bentley cars in 1931. It was a four-seater with a bit of a squeeze in the back and an enormously long bonnet. Denison was very keen on cars so perhaps this was a 21st birthday present. In 1922, Denison had purchased a brand new "Hudson Super Six" car made in Detroit, and then a car made by the Scottish company Galloway. Paul was an active bellringer, and he told me that if he was going to some tower with Johnny Oldham, he complained that Paul drove far too fast! If you had a 3.5 litre Bentley you could certainly drive fast.

Right: *Denison Taylor, Paul's "Uncle Denny", beside the ten ton "Little John" hour bell for Nottingham city; the hour bell with the deepest note in England.*
Photo: Taylor archives

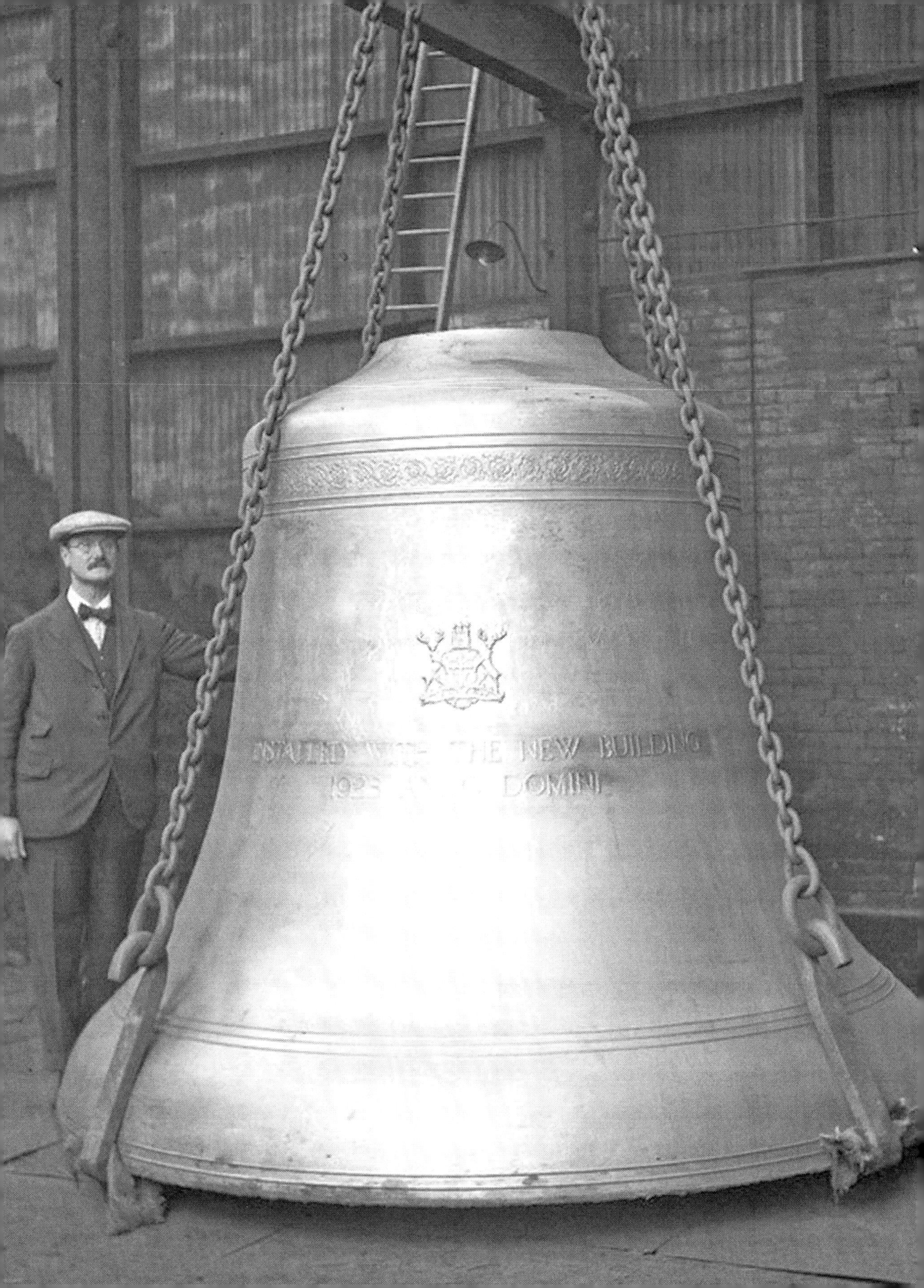
NEW BUILDING
DOMINI

Paul had a really good story about going to Buckfast Abbey in 1935 with Johnny Oldham to discuss the large ring of bells and the slow-swinger 'Hosanna' bell installed in 1936. Perhaps they bombed down in Paul's new car as he probably acquired it on his birthday that January. They stayed the night, and the monks found them two spare cells. When Paul turned in he found there was a glass of their famous and potent 'Buckfast Tonic Wine' on his bedside table. He told Johnny Oldham about this the next day at breakfast, and he just replied, 'They left me the bottle!' I wonder how many bottles the monks drank themselves every week? I suppose if you know you are going to be stuck in a monastery for the rest of your life you need something to take your mind off it.

We have seen how some work on bells was being carried out at the foundry during World War II, and how 'Great George' was cast in 1940 when Paul tuned this extremely large bell. In 1941, he joined the RAF as a Flight Engineer and was a Flight Lieutenant in 1945 when he was demobbed. He had met his future wife Merle (she was really Muriel) at some stage, and they were married on April 8th, 1944, when he must have been on leave. Merle had a large collection of family photographs and showed me the ones from their wedding. Paul was dashing and she was a beauty. Paul must have been thrown straight back into the deep end when he came back from the war as Denison appears to have already retired.

Paul told me that 'Uncle Denny' came down to the foundry on various occasions although he was often ill and was very crotchety! If Paul asked him a question the annoyed reply was often, 'Surely you know that!' When Denison died in 1947, Paul was thirty-three, and he told me there were lots of things he had wanted to ask him. When Paul was indoctrinating me into the art of bellfounding he was very aware that even if he was a little short with me sometimes because I was a bit slow on the uptake, he had to make sure I completely understood what he was telling me. One of his favourite expressions if he thought I was being dim was, 'Bloody hell, man!' Then he explained it again!

Apart from not obtaining all the information he wanted from uncle Denny, Paul told me that as small children, he and his sister played in the works. It was obviously an exciting place with wood shavings and sawdust in the joinery shop, and metal turnings from lathes, and I'm sure they hit the assorted bells. According to Paul, Denny wasn't keen on any equipment when he couldn't see how it worked. I don't know how he reconciled this with buying cars, but the scales in the works for weighing bells were the sort market traders used to have, called pan-scales. The thing to be weighed is put on one pan and weights on the other one until they balance. There were oodles of one hundredweight weights in the works. How they balanced the weight of a bell that weighed several tons I have not the slightest idea, but Paul and his sister played on these scales. They are like the ones on the statue at The Old Bailey Criminal Courts in London where you put a criminal on one side and the prison term on the other until they balance. They don't work nowadays because judges are too soft.

When he became a full member of the foundry management, Paul needed to know various things from the workers. One of these was how the position of the 'garter hole' was worked out on the rim of a bell wheel where the rope went through. He consequently asked the elderly joinery foreman who replied, 'That's the trick, lad.' Hardly fair was it, just because he had played in the works as a child! He told me that one evening when the works was shut he went to the joinery shop and worked it out for himself!

Paul was 'a man of the moment', and everything had to be done at the speed of light if not sooner! Any correspondence normally merited a reply by return post, the same as with my mother. If it was a carillon quote there may have been a delay of two or three days but not longer. Peter Cake and I often thought we had the morning planned until both our internal phones went, and we became closeted with Paul. His secretary was under strict instruction to slit open all the incoming envelopes so he had a ready supply of bits of paper to use for calculations.

He regularly delved into a directory that he replaced every time a new one was published that is called *Crockford's Clerical Directory*. This is a comprehensive guide to all the clergy in the Church of England, like a religious *Who's Who*. It was first published in 1858, and you can look up anyone you fancy and see where they obtained a degree (if they did), if they come from good stock, and all the places they have worked. It's now online of course, with 27,000 entries. If a clergyman had been struck off for some reason I bet it tells you this as well. Paul's knowledge of the clergy was consequently encyclopaedic! He could decide in two minutes whether a letter was from some vicar of any importance. He had a lovely phrase for some rural parish that was in the sticks, calling it 'Slocum-in-the-Mud'. He knew a great deal about Roman Catholic clergy as well, but I don't think there is a similar bible to consult.

Paul was only very infrequently unable to think of a quick retort in conversation. One day after he had retired, a clergyman was coming to the bellfoundry to meet Paul and myself. He was mostly friendly to Taylor's and was a diocesan adviser. This meant that he gave advice in his diocese as to which rings of bells should have work done to them, and whether very old bells could be melted down or must be preserved. He was due into Loughborough on a London train that I was meeting mid-afternoon. To my great surprise, he rang me from the station just before lunchtime to tell me he was there. When I queried which train he had come on he told me that he had caught an earlier one, but whilst at Leicester station he heard an announcement that the next stop was Nottingham, not Loughborough. As the train pulled out he went and found the guard and told him he was conducting an important funeral service at Loughborough and needed to get off the train. The guard went to see the train driver who got through to the station master at Loughborough, and the train made the unscheduled stop! I rang Paul at home straightaway to tell him the story, and after a long pause he said, 'Tell the bugger he has to wait until I have finished my lunch!' Being diplomatic, I collected the clergyman and took him for a pub lunch. Fancy that! And he was a man of God, to boot!

Paul was an accomplished bell ringer becoming a member of the Ancient Society of College Youths in 1949, and was a leading light of the Leicester Diocesan Guild of Church Bell Ringers, along with being influential in the Central Council of Church Bell Ringers. In 1950, when Paul was entirely on his own as regards the design and tuning of bells, he decided to embark on an ambitious change relating to the tuning of new rings of bells. Apart from his tuning skills Paul had an extremely developed musical ear from his viola playing. If he hadn't been a bellfounder he could probably have become a professional viola player. He decided that as the bells were rung down the musical scale (as in rounds), he wanted them to go down slightly further in frequency. This could be achieved by flattening the tuning progressively so that the tenor bell was flatter than normal.

He didn't want to do this, so turned his attention to sharpening all the bells progressively with the tenor bell having the normal note/frequencies of a bell of its size and weight. He decided the amount he wanted to sharpen every bell upwards from the tenor, and he tried this on several old rings of six or eight bells for 'Slocum-in-the-Mud' parishes. When he listened to these rings of eight bells sounded for him in the works, he decided that the new tuning was all right but was on the limit of what was acceptable, and his 'stretching' technique might be audible to other people. He couldn't therefore sharpen additional bells going upwards in a new ring of ten or twelve by the same amount as this would stand out too much. He refined his sharpening of a complete new ring so this was now carried out with a reduced progression, and this became the standard tuning for new rings from 1951. (There is a popular misconception amongst UK bellringers that the 1950 Evesham ring of twelve bells was tuned to the new method, but it wasn't!) This perception of the descending scale takes us right back to psycho-acoustics. As we have seen, a musical scale using equal temperament is built up in a logarithmic formula where each bell is approximately 6% higher in frequency than the preceding bell. By altering the logarithmic progression he increased the pitch of every bell apart from the tenor in a seamless progression.

This tuning technique was considered a success for nearly all new rings of bells and took the Taylor reputation to new levels, but it was a complete secret of course, and the tuning figures put in the tuning book were personally calculated and written down by Paul. I am sure that I was the first person whom he had fully indoctrinated into this technique, and he had to make sure that I understood it (and be really patient when explaining it to me!) so that I could carry on calculating it the same way. Without a scientific calculator it was extremely complicated! Paul told me that he had 'no-one to hold his hand', and he felt 'like a lonely pioneer.' This is now less of a secret as more and more people interested in church bells have electronic gadgets that tell them the frequencies of the notes within a bell, and the external tuning within the ring. I think some ringers have become 'wise after the event' and decided this technique is not a complete success, but in many cases only after they found that the frequencies 'according to their gadgets' seemed to be wrong! Some ringers with acute hearing think that on rings of ten or twelve it stands out and is too noticeable. It was consequently discontinued after I left, and another tuning formula for new rings put in place instead by Andrew Higson. Some of a ring of ten bells I cast in 1983 for Amersham had the 'sharp' tuning modified in 1993 when they were augmenting to twelve, and this wasn't the only time it happened. Nevertheless, a very great number of the new Taylor rings of bells after 1951 are

Right: *Paul Taylor in the tuning shop with the bells for Wellington Cathedral, New Zealand, shortly before he died in 1981. The varnished mallet was kept for special occasions like this one!*
Photo: Nicholas Sargeant

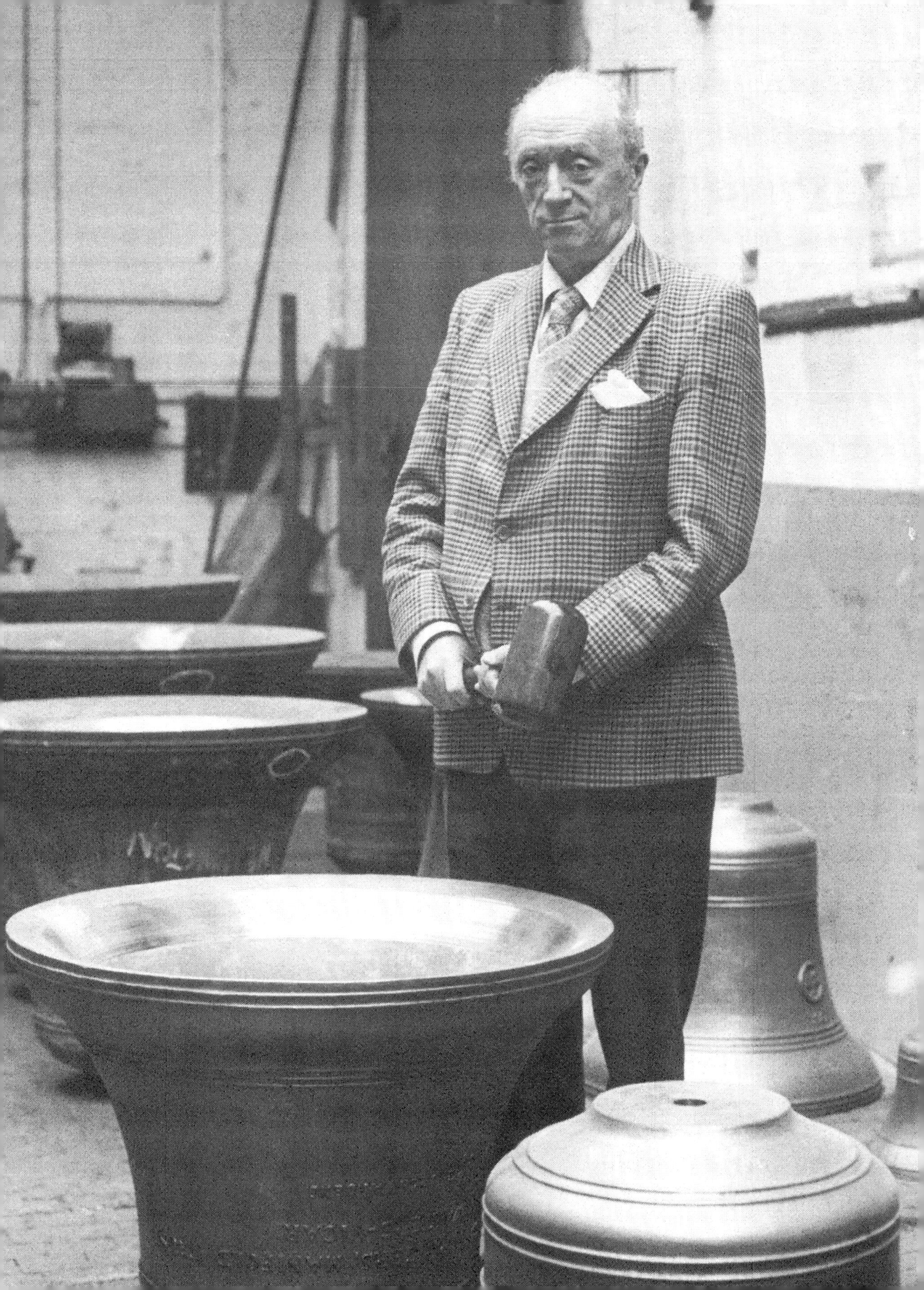

generally considered to be superb! The proof of the pie is under the crust!

The technique he had adopted was very well known as regards pianos being tuned and is called 'Stretch-tuning'. On pianos it is necessary because of the way the strings are made and the resultant harmonics (particularly from the steel strings) that are generated when the string is struck. Because of this, the tuning of the top octaves of a piano are sharpened, and the bottom ones are flattened. Pianists in the UK seem to consider that in the US the degree of stretch tuning is too much! The human ear also comes into this equation again as the perception of high sounds is that they are apparently flat in pitch. Really complicated! Stretch-tuning is never carried out on traditional pipe organs, but Frederick-Mayer persuaded Cyril to try it on the smallest bells at the Chicago Rockefeller carillon. This didn't work because of the defects in the marked versus actual frequencies of the Gillett & Johnston highest pitch tuning forks. They are all flatter than the frequencies stamped on the forks. It's a manufacturing defect present from day one, not something that happened over time. Paul was stretch-tunings rings of new bells, but not carillons of course, and neither was I when I was producing replacement carillon bells. Stretch tuning of carillon bells is guaranteed to produce beats.

In October 1982 I wrote a letter to *The Ringing World* and in a section of this letter I commented on Paul's aural acuity. I recollected, 'Paul Taylor possessed extreme aural perception - and could "process" the partials of a bell being rung up or sounded in the works whilst carrying on a telephone conversation from his office! I well remember helping him chart the progress of a pile-driver, a few streets away, by taking the frequencies of the impact of the machine - which came down as the pile progressed! He knew the note his car boot made when closed, and was most scornful of any person who could not recall the road number of the Ashby/Loughborough motorway turn-off on the M1. As it was the A-512 he readily identified it as being note "C": 512Hz in old church bell pitch. When our young machinist asked me one day why a small scoop that he used for collecting chippings from the tuning machine had 684 stamped on it, I was unhesitatingly able to inform him that it would be the frequency in Hz which it made when struck!'

Part of the reason that Paul was attempting to pass on his knowledge was the result of a very tragic event. Paul and Merle had two daughters born in 1946 and 1948. In 1954, Merle gave birth to a son, and there was only one name to be considered. He was christened John William; what else? He was not a child in good health, and many doctors and consultants gave their opinions and diagnoses. He was found to be afflicted with childhood leukaemia that was then incurable, and over a period of eighteen months before he was seven years old he was frequently in hospital. To the horror and desperation of everybody, John William died on December 27th, 1961. Coincidentally, this was on the same date that Paul's mother had died. Can you imagine the anguish? My sister had a son after two other children, and he died from a complicated heart defect when surgeons were operating on him when he was just five years old. Losing a young child is completely devastating and for Paul and Merle it was obviously intended, God willing, that he would be a son and heir in the bellfoundry. It was not to be.

In 1962/3, Taylor's had received the order for the 'Grand carillon' for Washington Cathedral, with a ten ton bourdon bell. It was a copy of the flagship carillons installed in bygone years at the Bok tower and Ann Arbor. A large difference was a major improvement of the transmission linkages from the clavier to the bells. Frank Godfrey had continually upgraded the system, and polished steel transmission bars rotated in friction free bearings. Levers transferred the downward motion when the batons were depressed to a linkage further along near the bell, which pulled the clapper in. Return springs quickly restored the linkage to the original position, and stainless steel wires were everywhere. Peter Cake continued with similar important improvements when he became the carillon designer. This is why Milford Myre thought the Washington carillon was the pinnacle of carillon building, as playing loud or soft sections of music was much easier, and repeat notes on the same bell were able to be played considerably quicker. When we replaced the duplicate top bells at a carillon we had to make sure there were no audible 'joins' between the last of the traditional shape bells and the new ones. With duplicate bells there was always this join where they started.

When the Washington carillon was inaugurated and dedicated at the cathedral, Paul was there with Merle. There was a lot of media interest and interviews. One of the regular TV shows invited a guest along who had an interesting job description. A panel asked questions to see if they could decide what this person did for a living. Paul was invited to appear and nobody guessed what he did which was hardly a surprise! At the end of the programme the chosen guest revealed what they did if the panel were still in the dark. Paul explained that he was a bellfounder who had produced the Washington carillon, and his family involvement in bellfounding went back to about 1780. The host then said, 'So you are a Johnny come lately!' This American phrase refers to a person who had suddenly sprung up from nowhere or is a late starter! The last major carillon project that Taylor's and Paul carried out was the carillon for Canberra, and I have mentioned how the custom built tower and setting is very impressive. Paul and Merle were there when Queenie opened it and a meal for the bigwigs followed. Paul was subsequently awarded an O.B.E. in 1971 for his achievements over the years and services for export. The whole family went down to Buck house for the day.

Paul had become a member of the Institute of Mechanical Engineers, so he was entitled to put 'M.I.Mech.E' after his name. His next major award was in 1979 when the Loughborough University awarded him an 'honorary' degree that made him a D.Sc., Doctor of Science. If a person has a normal degree in science or engineering from a university, as Paul had from his time at Sheffield, their degree is a B.Sc. which stands for Bachelor of Science. People can study for a higher degree, or other persons can be awarded one by a university for their outstanding achievements in their field, and this is termed an honorary degree. The boffins in the acoustic labs put his name forward, and on the due day he went to receive it at the end of the summer term degree ceremony, and I tagged along. Recipients of an honorary degree usually give a brief speech about their technical achievements and links with projects at the university. Paul had carefully prepared a true story that he told the assembled academics and guests. He mentioned a country parish church at Slocum-in-the-Mud (of course) where Pryce had inspected the bells at the end of World War I. The request had come because they wanted to ring a victory peal. He told them the bells were all right but pigeon guano had to be dealt with forthwith. His uncle inspected the bells for the coronation in 1937 and stressed that it was still possible to ring them but the guano level was now getting critical. After the finish of World War II, Paul was asked to go, and he told them that the bells were in a very serious state, only just capable of having a victory quarter peal rung, if new ropes were purchased, as the guano was getting very deep! In 1953 when it was coronation year, again he was asked to go back and told the vicar it was not safe to ring the bells, and if nothing was done immediately the bells might come adrift. The wooden frame was now in a perilous state, and the guano was now all the way up. A couple of years later he received a letter. It stated simply, 'Mr. Taylor, you were right. The bellframe has collapsed, and the bells have fallen down. Can you send some men?' Everybody was in stitches when he got to the punch line! This wasn't at all how honorary degree acceptance speeches were normally given. Brilliant! He had everybody in hoots. The University Chancellor was still laughing when he presented Paul with his scroll. I bet they talked about his story for months!

Paul suffered from angina which is a heart condition when not enough blood is being pumped by the heart. It can be controlled by tablets that are nitro-glycerine called 'TNT' tablets as they contain the same ingredients as dynamite! Extra tablets have to be taken if needed, and the dosage is critical. In 1981, when everything seemed to be progressing smoothly, and I was still absorbing vital facts, he went to London to attend a European bellfounders meeting. Obviously Whitechapel were there and I assume it was to consider some sort of standardised pricing that Denison and Pryce had tried to enter into with Whitechapel and Gillett and Johnston. The meetings started on a Friday morning in a posh hotel and went on until Saturday afternoon. I duly drove Paul to the railway station to catch the early London train on October 9th. On the Saturday evening I collected him and took him home, and he seemed quite tired and a bit subdued, but he told me, 'I have lots to tell you!' The angels were looking after me, and at home that night I unusually left various doors wide open so I could hear the downstairs phone if it rang. I must have had some premonition.

It did ring about 8a.m. in the morning, and Merle told me Paul had had a slight heart attack during the night at 2a.m. and she had called an ambulance that took him to Leicester Royal Infirmary. Immediately before ringing me, the hospital told her that he had experienced another heart attack, and she was to come immediately. They lived about ten minutes away from me and I zoomed over. My friend Marc had sold me a Rover SD1 car and Leicester was normally about a half hour drive away. I told Merle to shut her eyes, and I broke the land speed record. I knew Leicester quite well, and at one stage there was a drive round part of the ring road on the way to the hospital. A one-way street was a much quicker route, but I was going down it the wrong way! Fortunately, at that time on Sunday morning there was only one cyclist who quickly got out of the way. I screeched to a halt in the area that was completely reserved for ambulances, and Merle rushed in to find the ward. After I had parked properly I followed her in, but when I got to the ward she was coming out in floods of tears. She silently showed me Paul's wedding ring and his watch that were clutched in her palm. Paul had died on our journey to the hospital. Having a heart attack on a Sunday morning was far from being a good time then and apparently not much better now. Paul would have been seen by a consultant in the normal course of events on Monday morning.

The journey back to her house was much more sedate, and I started ringing round all the people that needed to know. Neither of her daughters could get there until late afternoon. Peter Cake, like everybody else, was astounded to hear the news, and he offered to come over if I needed him. By late afternoon I was able to leave her in the hands of her daughters and their husbands. What a blow. Advice for people suffering from angina is to take it steady (no chance of that in Paul's case) and avoid rich food. I am sure this was not an option whilst he was in London, and he probably had more than he should of his favourite alcoholic drink which was a pink gin. At the time of his funeral, 'Great George' at Liverpool Cathedral was tolled at my request which I thought was suitably appropriate.

Faced with the sudden loss of such a fount of knowledge, I went to London to see Michael Howard who had joined Gillett & Johnston in 1935 as part of a financial rescue package from his father. He designed the last two Gillett and Johnston carillons for Culver in the US, and Aberdeen in Scotland, after Cyril had left. He tuned the ten ton 'Freedom bell', a gift from the American nation to the people of Berlin, cast in 1950. Cyril had obviously taught him about good publicity as well as the American Ambassador came when it was cast! In 1957, the bell side of the company went into liquidation.

When I started back at Taylor's in 1977 I was soon using the Loughborough University equipment that was tip-top accurate. Paul and I already knew that the Gillett and Johnston tuning forks that had the highest frequencies, and were part of all the ones we bought in 1957, were wrongly engraved regarding the frequencies. They weighed about two pounds each and were very substantial chunks of metal! If you hit them with a small metal hammer they just went 'ping' for about two seconds! I was able to calibrate all the forks and write down what the real frequencies were. Michael Howard claimed he never knew they were wrong and neither did Cyril! He was quite adamant about this, and they never used any electronics for tuning, just the forks. This meant that frequencies for finished bells written in their tuning books where these forks were being used were incorrect! He agreed this must be the case. Extremely interesting, but they had no way of calibrating them against other forks or electronics. I have already mentioned that a Dutch carillonneur, Gideon Bodden, has done a comprehensive tonal analysis of many of Cyril's carillons and all the smallest bells are flat, with consistent errors from one to the next. In 2008, Eijsbouts took 43 of the Chicago bells back to Holland for remedial tuning, and the carillonneur wrote a report that states, 'Eijsbouts has possession of what appear to be the tuning specifications that Cyril Johnston was aiming for when he cast the instrument. From several sets of measurements that were taken, by Eijsbouts and others, it was clear that a number of the highest bells had gone seriously flat'. They hadn't 'gone flat', they were always flat since they were cast and tuned! Eijsbouts edged (skirted) the lips of all the smallest bells to get the nominals up in frequency.

I wanted to meet Michael Howard because there were various questions to which Paul and I had no answers. He lived in Kensington, and after a pub lunch he patiently explained some of the procedures he had adopted. He said it was a very long while since anyone had discussed bells with him, and Paul would have been very interested in what he told me. One of the puzzles related to the internal and external tuning of carillon bells, and as we have seen, all the desired tuning figures should be in equal temperament. In the tuning books Paul had bought, it was obvious Michael Howard was trying to get the tierce in every bell tuned to unequal pitch (so the 2.4 ratio) when the equal ratio is 2.378. In a particular size bell of note A, where the unequal tierce frequency would be C 1056Hz, the equal tempered frequency is 1046Hz, and this note/frequency would have been present in the correctly tuned nominal of another bell. All the bells were tuned the same way. In the above case it would have given a fast beat of 10Hz per second. Michael Howard said this was a deliberate policy for some years, and he quite liked the result! Some carillonneurs complain that these beats between bells are too obtrusive, and it doesn't work. They think he should have left the tierces in tune with all the other bells! Luc Rombouts, the gifted Belgian carillonneur, is quite dogmatic that this technique is 'to the detriment of the harmony created by the different bells together'.

Michael Howard also told me that when he was designing new bells for the Aberdeen carillon owned by Aberdeen City Council, at the Kirk of St. Nicholas church, (the last one they made), he asked for the smallest bells to be doubled in weight to give them 'breath'. This is very revealing. The eleven smallest bells were added in 1954 to the existing thirty-seven cast in 1952, with a bourdon bell weighing four and a half tons. "Breath" is the word he uses for volume and audibility, and doubling the weight is quite a drastic step. It is clear from his explanation that he considered the smallest bells they were producing prior to this date still had a problem, to the extent that he needed to double the weight. Gerda Peters, a Dutch organist and carillonneur, played on this carillon during a visit in 2014. She commented that the bells had a "full sonorous sound". She also stated that a "technical revision" carried out since she was last there in 2005 was a big improvement. It appears that Michael Howard's doubling of the weight was successful!

He also marked the smallest bells with a 'hit here' line to reduce wobble. All bells below two feet in diameter were machined on both the outside and the inside, but Taylor's never remotely considered this on such large bells. When he was trying to control high partials in a decent size bell he often cut small circular grooves in them. He told me that he tapped down the inside of the bell with a small hammer to find 'where the note was loudest' (so the anti-node), and the groove was machined there. As a result, these bells were no longer completely smooth on the inside. From examining some of their bells, Paul had guessed this was what he was trying to do. Another example of a bell profile not being quite as good as the Taylor one?

When the dust had died down Merle started inviting me over for evening meals, and I was delighted to accept. There were usually a few minor jobs that she wanted doing beforehand, such as hanging pictures, dealing with blown light bulbs, and all the things that

Right: *Paul Taylor playing on the clavier keyboard of the 1963 Washington National Cathedral carillon, completely assembled in the works.*
Photo: Taylor archive

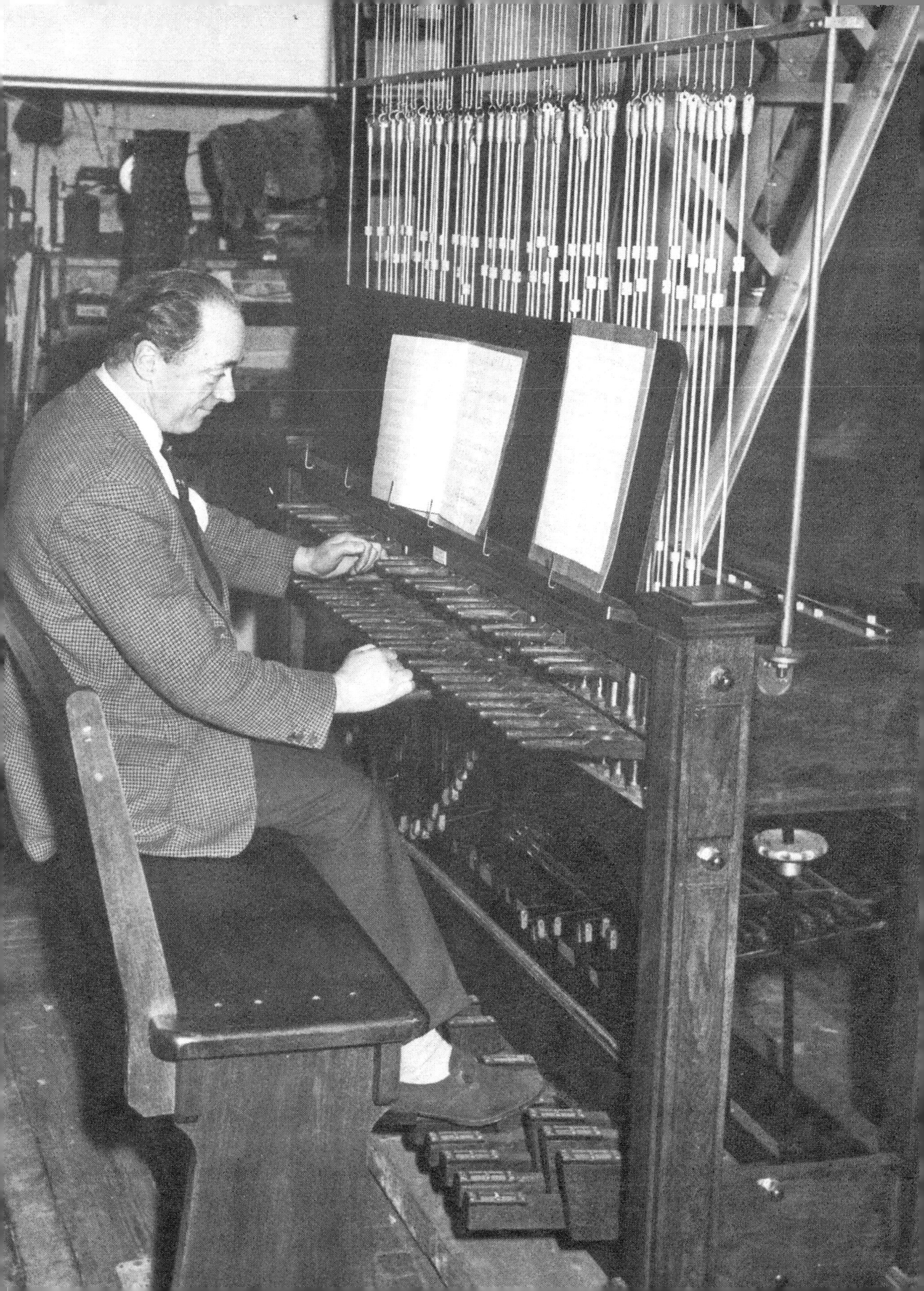

Paul would have done. Every time I went I took an assortment of tools, but I gave up trying to fix her dishwasher which was an excellent make but very old. I took her to buy a new one instead! Merle had never been able to drive as she suffered from petit mal syndrome which is a slight form of epilepsy also known as 'absence seizures'. When she had these she would stop talking in mid-sentence and go rigid for about twenty seconds. She had a fixed gaze and then returned to normal and carried on talking where she had left off! People with epilepsy thrash around and can hurt themselves but not with petit mal. I was very scared the first time this happened and after the second time I rang one of her daughters. She told me it was nothing to worry about and Merle had these attacks every now and then.

It turned out that Merle usually only had these seizures at meal times, and Peter knew all about them. I once mentioned this to a highly qualified nurse I knew, and she immediately said, 'They quite often only happen at meal times as it can be brought on by a saliva release!' I asked Merle once if it was worse or better after Paul died, and she told me she had fewer attacks as Paul was always 'in such a rush'. That was very true! The first time I ate there I polished off my food quickly, and Merle burst out laughing. She said, 'You eat just like Paul. You both went to boarding school!' Boarders might occasionally get 'seconds' or if not, there were much more interesting things to do.

It was fascinating talking to her, and she liked to have news of the bellfoundry, apart from directors' meetings and lunches as she had been made a director after Paul died. She often showed me various photographs and gave me the social side of all the places she had been to with Paul. Who was there, and what was said. From Paul, I had been given all the technical details but not this side of events. As she couldn't drive, I took her out sometimes to visit local beauty spots and have afternoon tea. Eventually she moved house and had a 'companion' who moved in and helped out. Years later she went to a residential home near one of her daughters and died at the very good age of ninety-two. After Paul died, she asked me what I would like to have that belonged to Paul as a memento, and I chose his circular calculator. It rarely left his side, and he had worked out millions of important calculations with it, so it then became mine. After a lot of heart-searching I gave it to the Taylor museum on permanent loan in 2016 to become a prized exhibit.

I have a last story to tell you, and some of you will doubtless say 'piffle' and 'rubbish'. Even in these days of most things having a logical explanation there are many things that we have no answer to. How can identical twins of the same sex and separated at birth get married on the same day to a person of the same name, have a dog with the same name, and have identical jobs? And then get divorced on the same day. How does this work? And then there are mediums or clairvoyants. They can't all be faking messages 'from the other side'. Oodles of years after Paul died and I was living in Spain, a friend of my wife and I died very suddenly. Slightly hesitantly I went to see a person who was reputedly a talented medium. She hardly knew me and nothing of my life history. After she had settled me down she explained that she had no control over who might 'come through'. She immediately told me that right before I rang her front door bell a man had come through who said he didn't know me as a child. I promptly suggested it might be my father who was always kept in the background, and I had gone off to boarding school. She replied it wasn't my father and this person was now becoming very impatient. When I gave her a blank look she asked, 'Is the name Taylor/Tailor of any significance to you?' Well, knock me down with a feather! I was astounded. If you think mediums are total rubbish fair enough. If you do believe they are sometimes right this is a good example. There was no message from the person called Taylor, and no doubt, assuming it was Paul, he had rushed off to do something else! So there we have it. I was extremely thoughtful on the way home. My wife and I decided to go to a general meeting this woman was holding one evening. We were planning a business venture but nobody at all knew this, only us. The woman embarrassed us by picking us out and telling us we should go ahead with something we were planning. As this venture is now in its twelfth year it appears she was right!

If I have piqued your interest with regard to bells, you have to go and hear them as bells are only made to be heard, or at least see them in a new light. If bellringers ring at your local church you will have a better understanding of what they are doing. You could change your life by becoming a bellringer yourself! If you go to Nottingham you can listen to 'Little John' which weighs ten tons and is the largest intact hour bell in the UK, unless it has been substituted for 'Big Ben' temporarily. Or, in York Minster, the ten-ton-plus bell 'Great Peter' that is a slow-swinger and rung manually every day. This bell is absolutely superb and makes the hairs on the back of your neck stand to attention, and so does 'Great George' but this is only rung on special occasions.

At Valletta in Malta there is the 1992 'Siege' bell that is a slow-swinger of ten tons and is rung every day by a motor at midday. Remember that notices in various lingos tell spectators that the bell is very loud! At the large Queens Park carillon at Loughborough, recitals are given every Thursday at 1p.m. and also on Sundays at 1p.m. from Easter till September. If you are in exotic locations such as Florida, Washington or Australia, go and hear the Taylor carillons at the Lake Wales Bok tower, Washington Cathedral or Canberra. Hopefully before too long 'Great Paul' will boom out from St. Paul's cathedral in London once more. You could combine one of these trips with going to hear a crack cathedral choir at somewhere like York Minster and listen to a large pipe organ as well. If one of the small boy choristers with an angelic voice looks as if he might be a bit mischievous, his nickname might just possibly be 'Milly'!

With the death of Paul Taylor, the amazing endeavours of the Taylor family personally involved in bell founding for over 200 years came to an end. In 1960 Paul published a booklet about the Taylor heritage to mark the 200th anniversary of the birth of Robert Taylor, and a meal was organized with various members of the Taylor family attending. Paul was a modest man, but I am convinced that he would have been fully entitled to describe himself as 'Master of My Art'. His implementation of the special tuning for new rings of bells was extremely progressive and inspired, and he and then I continued to do this for a total of thirty-seven years. There was also continuous experimentation regarding the improvement of small carillon bells that resulted in considerably more volume. Paul and I did a lot of this work together, and I carried on after he died. The ties with Loughborough University of Technology that Paul was happy to foster were very beneficial to both Taylor's and their own research. It didn't take them long to realise that Paul could easily hold his own when discussing cutting edge technology.

In my opinion, as regards innovation and continual improvements in the art of bellfounding, Paul Taylor was equally as important as any other member of the Taylor family, and from 1947-1981 he was 'on his own' from the age of thirty-three. His achievements were substantial, even at this age.

Postscript: The Present Situation

'Rising like a phoenix from the ashes'
A metaphor from Greek mythology

The changes in the running of Taylor's bellfoundry in 1977 were designed to safeguard the company and cater for the future. Despite this, many further changes took place over the years, and in 2009 the company trading as 'Taylor's, Eayre & Smith Ltd.' went into liquidation with substantial debts. A group of experienced businessmen, mostly accomplished bellringers, applied their expertise to the problem and bought the previous company from the administrators. The traditional name of John Taylor & Company was resurrected and John Taylor Ltd. was formed.

Subsequently, all the land, buildings, property, equipment, intellectual property and records were gifted to a newly formed charity – The Loughborough Bellfoundry Trust. As had happened in 1977, John Taylor Ltd. rent all the assets from the trust, and the income is available to pay for the upkeep of the buildings and other expenses. This new format entirely protects the assets which are now totally separated from the trading company.

The premises on the original 'Cherry orchard' site are exactly as designed in 1860, along with the additional casting areas from 1875 and the tuning shop built in 1896. No extensions have ever been built, and only a few non-essential areas have been dispensed with. Bellfoundry house was eventually demolished which I personally think was a great shame. This land and adjoining land was sold to build council flats so this generated funds. Even with the major carillon work that developed from the 1900s, the works were able to absorb this. The substantial and comprehensive industrial premises are a testament to the vision of John Taylor I and, of course, William Moss the builder.

Any buildings dating back to this time eventually need repairs, and the conservation company 'Heritage England', along with the Heritage Lottery Fund, stepped in after surveys revealed emergency repair work was needed, particularly to the roofs and the sixty-seven foot chimney, put up when the steam engine was installed. £860,000 has been spent so far, and the bellfoundry trust has provided 20% of the money. A far more ambitious plan for further restoration and the opening of a comprehensive visitor centre is being discussed, and a project team and architects are working with Heritage England. The budget price to carry out all the work is estimated to be in the region of £10 million, with a five year plan. On-going talks between the bellfoundry trust and the grant making bodies are in an advanced state with very positive signs that the whole project will duly take place.

It is not intended at all that Taylor's will finish up as nothing more than an industrial museum. The whole concept is that it continues as a working bellfoundry with the potential to cast twenty-five tons of bellmetal. In 2016, total turnover was just less than £2 million, and the order book continues to entail work for at least an eighteen month period. Many bell installations that date back in time need refurbishment and conservation, and the nature of bellringing is that ringers are continually campaigning and raising money for work they want carried out. This work will never dry up, and a complete restoration in 2016 of the bells of the Cathedral Church of St. Saviour, Southwark (known as Southwark Cathedral), is a good example. The opportunity of recasting the tenor bell of the ring of twelve was carried out with the new bell weighing 49 cwt. Other work completed in 2016 included a new ring of twelve with a 27 cwt tenor and three semitone bells for St. Mary Magdalene church at Taunton in Somerset, a new ring of twelve bells and a semitone bell for Cheltenham Minster, and a ring of eight bells for Godalming in Surrey. New rings have been installed at Liddington in Wiltshire and Horringer near Bury St. Edmunds, and a recast ring of eight has been installed at Richmond in West Yorkshire. A chime of twelve bells was completed in 2016, with six new bells to match the Gillett & Johnston profile of the other six bells, and sent to the Maritime Museum at Valletta in Malta. The chime is in memory of all seafarers who died defending the island.

A very interesting project during 2017 was a new ring of eight for St. George's Memorial Church at the Menin Gate in the Belgian city of Ypres in West Flanders. This church is a World War I Memorial to British and Commonwealth forces that were killed, and was erected as a tranquil place where relatives of the dead could come to look at the memorial plaques and find a focal point for reflection. The installation of the bells marks the centenary of the end of the war. The church comes under the jurisdiction of the Church of England Diocese in Europe, although it is interdenominational. This set of change ringing bells is the first new ring of church bells in Europe for a very long time. The only other lightweight ring of eight was supplied in 1882 by Warner's for the very large Royal Basilica of San Francisco el Grande in the centre of Madrid and is completely unringable and derelict. At a special ceremony in Loughborough, the Ypres bells were loaded onto two World War I lorries prior to transport.

Work on civic installations, such as places where existing clock bells are to be found or where new clocks with new bells are required, will always need to be carried out. Carillon work is another area where continual work will be done, with new projects including bells, restoration work or the modernization of old transmissions and claviers. The 1904 Taylor carillon at the bellfoundry, which was the very first carillon tuned to equal temperament, is being reinstated with the original number of forty bells made up to forty-nine. Some restoration of the small campanile needs to be completed first, but twenty-seven bells have already been cast.

Another major job is for the Cathedral of St. Francis Javier at Geraldton in Australia where they are having an automatic carillon of twenty seven bells. This is made up of the previous ring of eight bells from Godalming in Surrey, where a new ring of eight has been cast by Taylor's, and a further nineteen new bells. The Godalming bells will be retuned, and the new bells will be cast between the end of 2017 and the early part of 2018. The bells will be sounded by electro-magnetic clappers from a programmable control unit.

In January 2018, the twelve bells from St. Paul's Cathedral in London will be taken down and transported to Loughborough. The bells will be cleaned, and an entire set of new fittings will be manufactured. At the cathedral, the original wooden frame, now 140 years old, will be strengthened and renovated. 'Great Paul', the largest bell in England, is being restored as part of this major project, and new motors will be fitted so that it will once again "Preach the Gospel". Taylor's are steadily increasing their work force to cope with an increase in demand for their products.

'Sic Transit Gloria Mundi' – Worldly things are fleeting. Since May 2017, Taylor's is now the only bellfoundry in England. In a shock announcement in December 2016 the Whitechapel bellfoundry issued a short press release, 'The Whitechapel Bell Foundry Ltd. announces, with regret, that by May 2017 it will cease its activities at the Whitechapel Road site that it has occupied since its move there in 1738. The company intends to complete work on all projects presently in hand during the coming months. It will not be entering into new contracts for the time being, whilst discussions with the company's staff and other interested parties regarding the future direction, ownership, and location of the company, are on-going.'

Alan & Kathryn Hughes expanded on this decision and reminded people that the Hughes family involvement began in 1904 on the site in use for 250 years. Alan Hughes concluded, 'So it is probably about time it moved once again. We hope that this will provide an opportunity for the business to move forward in a new direction.' Various bodies and individuals asked that the Mayor of London should step in and raise the historic Grade 2 listed building to Grade 1, and petitions to keep the bellfoundry on the same location were launched. These pleas and suggestions did not prosper, as the premises, now in an area much more desirable than previously, had already been sold.

An established company, 'White's of Appleton' in Oxfordshire, who have carried out bellhanging work as a family business since 1824, have purchased all the Whitechapel headstock patterns. They have also acquired one of the tuning machines together with the electronic tuning equipment. A very large foundry, J. T. Price at Stoke-on-Trent belonging to the Westley Group of foundries, has added bells to their list of non-ferrous products. Any new bells required by White's will be cast there. Nigel Taylor, a key member of the former Whitechapel team, is carrying out the tuning and will train somebody else. He is also overseeing the moulding and casting techniques.

The John Taylor bellfoundry museum is normally open on Tuesday, Wednesday, and Thursday from 10a.m. till 12 noon and 2p.m. till 4p.m. with a modest entry fee. Full tours of both the museum and works are available for groups of ten or more people by prior arrangement. It is advisable to telephone the main works on *01509 212241* before travelling to the museum to confirm opening times for individual visitors. The museum is closed to the general public when tours are taking place, or periods when work on the building is being undertaken.

The Taylor Family History, 1780-1981

Dates given as 'circa' are calculated to be the start of 'hands on' involvement.

Robert Taylor: Apprentice, 1780, and in his own right, 1784-1830 (death)

Robert Taylor's sons
    John Taylor: circa 1807-1858 (death)
    William Taylor: circa 1805-1854 (death)

John Taylor's sons
    John William I: circa 1837-1906 (death)
    Pryce Taylor: circa 1845-1862 (death)
    Robert Taylor: circa 1840-1856 (death)

John William I's sons
    Edmund Denison Taylor: circa 1882-1945 (retired) 1947 (death)
    John William II: circa 1870-1919 (death)

John William II's sons & daughters
By first marriage:
    Arnold Taylor: circa 1912-1919 (death)
    Pryce Taylor: circa 1903-1927 (death)
    Gwendoline Taylor: 1921-1925 (bell tuner)
    Josephine Taylor: circa 1918 - date not clear (involved in exhibitions / sales liaison)
    Phyllis Taylor: circa 1909 - date not clear (involved in exhibitions / sales liaison)
By second marriage:
    Paul Taylor: circa 1934-1981 (death)

General Bibliography

Chapter 1: The Origin of Bells
China and The Chinese (1902) & *Religions of China* (1905), Herbert Allen Giles. Reprinted by Scholar's Choice, 2015. ISBN: 1-29-718884-5

Bells & Man Percival Price. Published by Oxford University Press, New York, 1983. ISBN: 0-19-318103-7

Nature Display'd: Spectacle de la Nature or Nature Display'd. Being Discourses On such Particulars of Natural History As were thought most proper to Excite the Curiosity and Form the Minds of Youth. Containing What belongs to Man confider'd in Society. Volume VII, Dialogue XXI. Originally in French, written by Noël Antoine Puche with English translation by Mr. Humphreys, 1740. Second edition published by R. Francklin, London, 1749.

Francesco Cancellieri. Exact title and date unknown.

A History of Bells and Description of Their Manufacture as Practised at the Bell Foundry Whitechapel. Anonymous author circa 1866, reprinted from "Cassels Magazine of Art". Published by Cassell, Petter & Galpin, London.

The Bell: Its Origin, History and Uses Rev. Alfred Gatty. Printed by J. C. Platt, Sheffield, 1848.

The Church Bells of England H.B. Walters, Oxford University Press, 1912.

Unknown Title Patrick Lafcadio Hearn a.k.a. Koizumi Yakumo

John Donne (1571-1631) Poem: *To Sir Henry Wotton, At His Going Ambassador to Venice*

Tomas Gray (1716-1771) Poem: *Elegy in a Country Churchyard*

Chapter 2: Making Moulds
Nature Display'd: (see chapter 1)
John Taylor & Co. Archives.

Chapter 3: Finishing the Moulds, Pouring the Metal
Nature Display'd: (see chapter 1)

The Doctor Robert Southy. Anonymous publication, 1843. Published under his name, 1847.

The Bells of England Dr. J. J. Raven, Methuen and Co, 1906.

Das Lied von der Glocke (Song of the bell) Friedrich von Schiller (1759-1805). Published 1800. Translated by Sir Theodore Martin, 1889.

Parish Records of Deaths St. Giles, Cripplegate. May 22nd & May 26th, 1716. Matthew Bagley & Matthew Bagley Junior killed.

The London Illustrated News 'Big Ben II', April 1858.

A History of Bells and Description of (see chapter 1)

John Taylor & Co. Archives.

Chapter 4: My Early Years
Personal Experiences.
Southwell Minster Village Cathedral. A Commentary for the Visitor H. C. L. Heywood Provost, 1957 (Third Edition)
The Minster Grammar School Southwell Headmaster B. J. Rushby Smith. General regulations for boarders. Undated.
Gandarva Beaver & Krause, 1971 LP, Warner Bros - K 46130/ WS 1909. CD 2006 Collectors Choice - ASIN: B000E112RU

Chapter 5: Setting Down Roots
A List of Bells Cast by John Taylor & Co, 1870. Printed by J. Bell, Nottingham. John Taylor & Co. Archives.
Master of My Art: The Taylor Bellfoundries 1784-1987 Trevor Jennings, 1987. ISBN 0-9511-988-1-5. Copyright John Taylor and Co. (Bellfounders) Ltd.
John Taylor & Co. Archives.

Chapter 6: The Cherry Orchard
A List of Bells Cast by John Taylor & Co, 1870. Printed by J. Bell, Nottingham. John Taylor & Co. Archives.
Master of My Art: (see chapter5)
The Illustrated London News August 23rd, 1856.
Clocks Watches and Bells (Sir) Edmund Beckett Denison. 8th edition, 1903.
The Engineer January 6th, 1860. Report on Big Ben Court Case Findings.
Hansard House of Commons record. June 4th, 1860.
Music & Morals Rev. H. R. Haweis, published 1875.
John Taylor & Co. Archives.

Chapter 7: The Ringing Isle
The Bell: Its Origin, History and Uses Reverend Alfred Gatty. Printed by J. C. Platt, Sheffield, 1848.
The Bells of St. Paul's William T. Cook, 1981.
A Book about Bells Rev. George S. Tyak. Published by Willaim Andrews & Co, 1898.
Loughborough Parish Church Peal Record Booklet. John Taylor & Co, 1909.
Central Council of Church Bell Ringers www.cccbr.org.uk
The Bells and Bellringers of York Minster David Potter, Ringing Master of York Minster Society of Change Ringers, 1987.
The Bells of York Minster David Potter M.B.E., President of York Minster Society of Change Ringers, 2015.
The Rings of Twelve W. A.Thow. Circa 1986.
Guardian newspaper. December 11th, 1893
The Ringing World October 2015 (South Petherton record peal).

Chapter 8: 'Great Paul'
The Times December 7th, 1881. Letter from John Stainer.
The Illustrated London News January 1st & 14th, 1882
The Illustrated London News May 4th & June 3rd, 1882
The Graphic May 20th & 27th, 1882
Master of My Art: (see chapter 5)
John Taylor & Co. Archives.

Chapter 9: Mine Is Bigger Than Yours
A History of Bells and Description of (see chapter 1)
Bells & Man Percival Price. Published by Oxford University Press, New York, 1983. IBN 0-1931-8103-7
Glockenkunde (in German) Dr. D. Heinrich Otte, 1884. List of large bells worldwide.
Sleeve notes: LP *Rostov Chimes* (Russian LP record), 1985. MOHO M90 46547 002
Russia Illustrated an Historical & Descriptive Account Linney Gilbert / Alfred George Vickers, London, 1844
Fonderie Paccard, Annecy, France   www.paccard.com
Royal Eijsbouts Foundry, Asten, Holland   www.eijsbouts.com
John Taylor & Co. Archives / website   www.taylorbells.co.uk

Chapter 10: Carillons & Singing Towers
The Present State of Music in Germany, the Netherlands, and United Provinces 1773 Charles Burnley. Published in London by T. Becket & Co.
Carillons of Belgium and Holland: Tower Music in the Low Countries 1914 William Gorham Rice. Published in UK by John Lane, The Bodley Head, London, 1914
Carillon Music and Singing Towers of the Old World and the New William Gorham Rice. Published by Dodd, Mead and Company, New York, 1915. Published in London by John Lane, The Bodley Head Ltd., 1926
The Carillon Frank Percival Price, 1933. Published by Oxford University Press, London, & Humphrey Milford
Bells & Man Percival Price (see chapter 9)

Chapter 11: Paradise Lost
Personal Experiences.
1st BBC televised broadcast of *Carols from King's*. King's College, Cambridge. December 23rd, 1954 www.youtube.com.
This Is Your Brain On Music: The Science Of A Musical Obsession Daniel J. Levitin, 2006. Penguin Group. ISBN: 0-5259-4969-0

Chapter 12: After 'Great Paul'
John Taylor & Co. 1882 & 1894 Catalogue and lists of bells. Taylor archive.
Master of My Art: (see chapter 5)

Chapter 13: Post 1919
Master of My Art (see chapter 5)
The Bells and Bellringers of York Minster (see chapter 7)
The Bells Of York Minster (see chapter 7)
John Taylor & Co. Archives.

Chapter 14: 'A Thirsty Market'
The Carillon Frank Percival Price, 1933. Published by Oxford University Press, London, & Humphrey Milford.
The Development of The Art of The Carillon in North America. Milford Myre. A paper delivered in July 1972 at the 50th anniversary of the inauguration of the Jef Denyn carillon school in Belgium. Restricted circulation.
The Uselessness of C sharp and D sharp in the Bass of Carillons Frans Hemony, 1636
The Craft Of The Bellfounder George Elphick, 1988, page 103. Phillimore & Co. Ltd. ISBN: 0 - 8503-3648-1
Singing Bronze: A History of Carillon Music Luc Rombouts. English language version, 2014, Leuven University Press. ISBN: 978- 90 5867 9567
Campanology. A Study of Bells, with an Emphasis on the Carillon John Gouwens, 2013. North American Carillon School. ISBN: 1-4840 3766-9

Chapter 15: 'A Thirsty Market.' Act Two
Europe 1945-47: A Report on the Condition of Carillons on the Continent of Europe as a Result of the Recent War. Percival Price for the US Army Special Services and the American Committee for the Protection of Cultural Treasures in War Areas University of Michigan, Rackham Foundation, 1948
England's Child. The Carillon and the Casting of Big Bells Jill Johnston, 2008. Cadmus Editions, San Francisco. ISBN 10: 0-9322-7471-4/: ISBN 13: 978-09 3227 4717
Campanology, A Study of Bells, with an Emphasis on the Carillon John Gouwens, 2013. ISBN: 1-4840-3766-9
Master of My Art (see chapter 5)
John Taylor & Co. Archives.
Tuning data for the Chicago Rockefeller carillon. A.A.J. Buswell.

Chapter 16: A Really Interesting Job
Personal observations.

Chapter 17: Back in the Fold
Personal observations.
Normal Modes Of The Modern Church Bell T. Charnley, R. Perrin, J de Pont. Journal of Sound & Vibration, Volume 90, Issue 1, pp. 29-49. September 1983. (Personal proof copy).
Tuning of bells Milsom, M. J. (1982). The Ringing World, September 3rd, p.733.

Chapter 18: Some Special Jobs
Personal observations.

AC/DC Personal conversations with Jake Berry & Tony Platt.
Tony Platt interview, SOS Magazine November 2014
Let Steeple Bells be Swungen Norris Davidon, R.T.É. (Raidió Teillifis Éireann) TV film shown December 31st, 1981. Copy from R.T.É archives.
With Iron Tongues Producer, Diane (Di) Shelley for BBC Radio 4, December 31st, 1982 (Personal copy).

Chapter 19: A Sweet & Pleasant Sound
On Bells Lord Raleigh. 'Philosophical Magazine', January 1890
Sensations of Tone (Herman L.F. Helmholtz, 4th edition, 1877) Translated from German by Alexander J. Ellis, 1885. Longmans, Green, and Co., London
The Church Bells of England H. B. Walters. Oxford University Press, 1912
Why Bells Sound Out of Tune and How To Cure Them Canon Simpson. Booklet, 1897.
Harmonicorvum libri Volume IV *Campanas* (Bells). Père Mersenne, 1636. Translated by Sir Gore Ouseley.
Tuning of Bells Milsom, M. J., The Ringing World (1982). September 3rd, p.733
British Standard Musical Pitch LL. S Lloyd. Musical Review, May 1950.
Normal Modes of the Modern Church Bell Charnley, Perrin, J. De Pont. Journal of Sound & Vibration. Volume 90, Issue 1, pages 29-49. September 1983.
A Comparative Study of the Normal Modes of Various Modern Bells, R. Perrin, T Charnley Journal of Sound and Vibration: Volume 117, Issue 3, pages 411-420, 1987
Group Theory and the Bell R. Perrin & T. Charnley. Journal of Sound & Vibration. Issue 31, pages 411-418, 1973
Science of Percussion Instruments Tom Rossing. Published by World Science, 1999.
The Physics of Musical Instruments Tom Rossing with N. H. Fletcher. Published by Springer, New York, 1998.
Acoustics of Eastern & Western Bells Tom Rossing. Published by CCRMA, Centre for Computer Research into Music & Acoustics. Stanford University, 2016

Chapter 20: The Nitty Gritty
Personal Experience.
This Is Your Brain On Music (see chapter 11)
Sensations of Tone Herman L.F. Helmholtz, 4th edition, 1877. Translated from German by Alexander J. Ellis, 1885. Longmans, Green, and Co., London
Temperament (An Elementary Treatise on Musical Intervals and Temperament) R. H. M. Bosanquet, 1876. Macmillan and Co., London
Acoustical Measurements on Church-bells and Carillons E.W. Van Hueven, 1949. Published by Van Cleef.
The Carillon Frank Percival Price. Published 1933, Oxford University Press London.
Component Tones from a Bell Arthur Taber Jones, 1933
Bell Tuning - Modern Enigma or Medieval Mystery R. M. Ayres. The Ringing World. September 23rd, 1983
Campanology, A Study of Bells (see chapter 14)

Tuning of Bells Milsom, M. J., Letter in The Ringing World (1982), September 3rd, page.733
John Taylor & Co. Archives.
Personal conversations with André Lehr, Bellfounder, Royal Eijsbouts Foundry, Asten, Holland.

Chapter 21: Paul Taylor : Last of the Line
Personal experience and conversations.
The Taylor Family History. Anonymous author – Commissioned by Denison Taylor. 1933.
Master of My Art (see chapter 5)
John Taylor & Co. Archives.
More on Tuning Milsom, M.J., Letter in The Ringing World (1982). October, page 812

Various Chapters
Personal conversations between Paul Taylor and author, or author only, with carillonneurs: Ronald Barnes, Robert Donnell, John Gouwens, Margo Halstead, Timothy Hurd, Andrea McCrady, Milford Myre, Gordon Slater & Richard Strauss. Email correspondence with John Gouwens and Carl Zimmerman. Email correspondence with David Potter, George Dawson, Chris Pickford & Andrew Higson.

Permission to use copyright material

Text Sources
Any references to John Taylor archives are with the kind permission of Bell Foundry Collections Ltd.
Any references to John Taylor & Co are with the kind permission of the company.
Any references to Trevor Jennings' book *Master of My Art: The Taylor Bellfoundries 1784-1987* is with the kind permission of John Taylor & Co.
David Potter MBE has kindly given me permission to quote from *The Bells & Bellringers of York Minster* 1987, and *The Bells of York Minster* 2015.
Mr R. J. Cook has kindly given me permission to quote from his brother W. T. Cook, *The Bells of St. Paul's Cathedral*, 1981
David Purnell has kindly given me permission to quote from his article in *The Ringing World* relating to the 2015 longest peal at South Petherton.
AC/DC quotes from Tony Platt, with kind permission of *SOS Magazine,* November 2014.
Bells & Man Percival Price. Despite being given contact details for the estate of Percival Price by Oxford University Press, I have been unable to contact this person.

Sources of illustrations

Any references to John Taylor archives are with the kind permission of Bell Foundry Collections Ltd.
Any references to John Taylor & Co are with the kind permission of the company and David Potter, webmaster: www.taylorbells.co.uk

Front Cover
'Great Peter' at York Minster. Photo from David Potter's collection.

Preface
Page xvi. John William Taylor I (Senior), 1827-1906. Photo: Taylor archive.
Page xix. An engraving of the bellfoundry between 1881 & 1891. Photo: Taylor archive.

Introduction
Page 7. The Cathedral of the Transfiguration. Photographer: George Socka. Creative Commons Attribution -Share Alike 2.0 Generic licence. Image cropped & converted to b & w.

Chapter 1
Page 11. 'The Great Temple Bell' in Beijing. Photographer: Sanshichiro Yamamoto: Pre 1906. Photo in public domain.
Page 15. A Chinese bronze crotal. Photos by author.
Russian 'Zvon' ringing. Photographer Matthias Kabel. Creative Commons Attribution-Share Alike 3.0 Unported licence. Image converted to b & w.

Chapter 2
Page 23. Forming a core for Notre Dame Cathedral. Photographer: Vincent M. 2012, with permission from the French Cornille-Havard bellfoundry, Villedieu-les-Poêles, France
Page 27. 'Johannesglocke' (John bell), cast by F. Schilling & Son in Apolda, Germany, in 1928. Photo origin unknown: in public domain.

Chapter 3
Page 31. Two foundry workers at Taylor's standing beside the case and core moulds. Photo: Taylor archive.
Page 35. Casting bells at Taylor's. Photo: David Humphrey.
Page 43. Anthony Stone using metal letters to indent an inscription. Photo: John Taylor & Co.
Bottom right: A conical case former at a foundry in Holland. Photo: Royal Eijsbouts foundry.

Chapter 4
Page 49. Southwell Minster Cathedral. Photo from Frith's Series-Reigate
Page 55. Southwell Minster choirboys. The Diocese of Southwell & Nottingham. Southwell.anglican.org. Image converted to b & w.
Southwell Minster choir area. Photo: Mattana. Put in public domain. Image converted to b & w.

Chapter 5
Page 61. Roger Johns, foundry manager, lettering a cope mould. Photo: David Humphrey.
Page 63. Making the outer cope inside the cast iron case for the bourdon bell 'Great Peter' at York Minster. Photo: Taylor archive.
Page 65. A diagram of an 88 note piano keyboard. Diagram own work.

Chapter 6
Page 69. A sketch of the bellfoundry that is post 1867. Sketch: Taylor archive.
Page 75. 'Big Ben I' cast by John Warner & Son in 1856. Origin unknown: in public domain.
Page 79. The West front of St. Paul's Cathedral, London, circa 1890-1900. Photo: Photochrom: in public domain.

Chapter 7
Page 83. A ringing bell assembled for testing. Photo: David Humphrey.
Page 87. The bellmetal plaque in the ringing room at Taylor's bellfoundry. Photo: Taylor archive.
Bellringers at Bury St. Edmunds. With permission of photographer John Hughes. www.johnhughesphotography.co.uk . Image converted to b & w.
Page 91. The Taylor 1936 ring of fourteen bells and the 7.5 ton 'Hosanna' bourdon bell at Buckfast Abbey, Devon. Photo: Taylor archive
The ring of eight bells after restoration with four new bells, at St. Mary's North Creake in Norfolk. Photo: John Taylor & Company. Image converted to b & w.

Chapter 8
Page 99. 'Great Paul' assembled for testing in the foundry. Photo: Taylor archive.
Page 101. 'Great Paul' securely fixed to the truck. Photo: Taylor archive.
The 14 ton case used for 'Gt.Paul'. Photo: John Taylor & Company. Image converted to b & w.
Page 105. The French engineer Pierre and Paul Taylor. Photo unknown, London press agency.

Chapter 9
Page 109. Russian Kolokov bell. Photographer: N.A.Naidenov: in public domain.
Page 115. Three bells at Paccard foundry. Photo: Fonderie Paccard. Image converted to b & w.
The Joan of Arc bell. Photographer unknown: in public domain.
Page 119. 'Great George' cast in 1940. Photo Taylor archive

Page 121. Cyril Johnston and the 18 ton 'Riverside' bourdon bell. Photographer unknown: in public domain.
Page 123. The John Murphy bellfoundry in Dublin. Artist and date unknown: in public domain.

Chapter 10
Page 127. St. Rombold's cathedral. Photographer: Donar Reiskofler. Creative Commons Attribution-Share Alike 3.0 Unported licence. Image converted to b & w.
Page 133. Set of jacks at Gloucester. Photographer: Jongleur100 in public Domain. Image converted to b & w.
The 1855 mechanical drum Gwent. Photographer: simonly. Creative Commons Attribution 2.0 Generic licence. Image converted to b & w.
Page 137. The Jef Denyn commemorative bell. Photographer unknown: in public domain.

Chapter 11
Page 145. Llandaff organ. Photos with permission of the Dean & Chapter of Llandaff Cathedral. Images converted to b & w.

Chapter 12
Page 155. Ronnie Edwards in 1972. Photo by author.
Page 157. John William Taylor I inspecting 'Great Bede'. Photo: Taylor archive.

Chapter 13
Page 163. 'Great Peter'. Photo: Taylor archive.
Page 165. The seven and a half ton slow swinging bourdon bell 'Hosanna' at Buckfast Abbey. Photo: Taylor archive.
Page 169. The fourteen and three quarter ton 'Great George'. Photo: Taylor archive.

Chapter 14
Page 177. The 6 ft 9 ins diameter, largest bell of the chime of ten for Yale University. Photo: Taylor archive.
Leaving the works. Photo: Taylor archive.
Page 181. The 1923 Taylor Loughborough War Memorial carillon. Photo: Taylor archive.
Loughborough War Memorial Carillon Tower. Photographer: Duncharris. Creative Commons Attribution-Share Alike 3.0 Unported licence. Image converted to b & w.
Page 185. Bok Tower carillon at Lake Wales Florida. Photographer: Averette. Creative Commons Attribution-Share Alike 3.0 Unported licence. Image converted to b & w.
Page 187. The Riverside church tower from West 121st street. Photographer: Petri Krohn. Creative Commons Attribution-Share Alike 3.0 Unported licence. Image converted to b & w.

Chapter 15
Page 193. Frank Godfrey, the Taylor carillon engineer. Photo: Taylor archive.
Canberra carillon bells on lorry leaving work. Photo: Taylor archives.

Page 199. The Zutphen carillon tower. Photographer: Michielvertbeek. Creative Commons Attribution-Share Alike 3.0 Unported licence. Image converted to b & w.
Page 203. The Washington National carillon at Taylor's. Photo: Taylor archive.

Chapter 16
Page 211. The first Taylor tuning machine installed about 1868. Photo: Taylor archive.
The specially built tuning shop and tuning machines, 1896-1897. Photo: Taylor archive.
Page 215. The practice clavier for the Canberra carillon. Photo: Taylor archive.

Chapter 17
Page 219. A collection of various tuning forks. Photo by author.
A Revox professional reel to reel tape recorder. Photo by author.
A professional Brüel & Kjaer oscillator. Photo: Brüel & Kjaer.
Page 221. Checking the two ton bell for Harvard University. Photo: John Taylor & Co. Image converted to b & w.

Chapter 18
Page 229. Initial sound checks, 'AC/DC' bell. Photo: David Humphrey.
Page 231. The mobile recording studio from Manor Recording Studios. Photo by author.
Setting up microphone placement. Photo by author.
Page 237. Di Shelley at Winscombe church. Photographer: Mike Martin (I have been unable to trace his whereabouts for permission to use this photo). Image converted to b & w.
Page 239. A general view of the main works in 1977. Photo: Taylor archive.
A large case with the core plate clamped to it. Photo: John Taylor & Co.

Chapter 19
Page 245. The Hemony carillon, Zuiderkerk, Amsterdam. Photographer: Yair Halkai. Creative Commons Attribution-Share Alike 3.0 Unported licence. Image converted to b & w.
Page 249. The large tuning machine installed in 1900. Photo: Taylor Archive.
Page 253. Harold Marcon, bell tuner. Photographer unknown.

Chapter 20
Page 259. A modern view of the tuning shop. Photo: John Taylor & Co.
Page 263. The AC/DC bell awaiting despatch. Photo by author.
Page 265. The Washington carillon assembled in the works. Photo: Taylor archive.
Page 269. John Gouwens, carillonneur at the Culver Academies. Photographer: Gary Mills.
Page 271. Rouen Cathedral carillon. With the kind permission of the copyright holder, Jean-François Claire. Image cropped and converted to b & w.
An 8 inch bell from the Royal Eijsbouts foundry. Photo by author.
A small Taylor carillon bell. Photo by author.

Chapter 21
Page 275. Denison Taylor beside the ten ton "Little John" hour bell. Photo: Taylor archives.
Page 279. Paul Taylor in tuning shop. With the kind permission of photographer Nicholas Sargeant.
Page 285. Paul Taylor & clavier, Washington carillon. Photo: Taylor archive.

Back Cover
Finished bells in the tuning shop, transferring metal from the tilt crucible furnace, lettering a case mould. Taylor's, 2017
Photos: John Taylor & Co.

Conversion tables: Weights & Measures

British Weights

1 lb = 0.463 kilo (kg)
2.2 lbs = 1 kg
28 lbs = 1 quarter (qr) = 12.7 kg
56 lbs = 2 qrs = 25.4 kg
84 lbs = 3 qrs = 38.1 kg
112 lbs = 4 qrs = 1 hundredweight (cwt) = 50.9 kg
5 cwts (¼ British ton) = 254.5 kg
10 cwts (½ British ton) = 509 kg
15 cwts (¾ British ton) = 763.5 kg
20 cwts = 2,240 lbs = 1 British 'long' ton = 1016.047 kg

2,200 lbs = 1,000 kg = 1 metric tonne

British bell weights are always given as tons, hundredweights (cwts), quarters (qrs), lbs.
For example: A bell weighing 10 tons 10 hundredweight (cwts) 3 quarters (qrs) 16 lbs
 = 10 x 2,240 lbs + 10 x 112 lbs + 3 x 28 lbs + 16 lbs = 3,460 lbs = 1,572.7 kg = 1.5727 metric tonnes

U.S. Weights

100 lbs = 1 cwt = 45.4 kg
2,000 lbs = 20 cwts = 1 US 'short' ton = 907 kg

British Linear Measures

1 inch (in) = 25.4 millimetres (mm) = 2.54 centimetres (cm)
12 inches (ins) = 1 foot (ft) = 304.8 mm = 30.48 cm
36 ins = 3 ft = 1 yard (yd) = 914.4 mm = 9.144 cm

About the Author

Mike Milsom was born in Manchester to parents who were Londoners, and the family moved to Loughborough when he was five years old. There was music in the house most evenings when his mother played the piano or listened to records. From the age of seven he had piano lessons and then became a boy treble in the choir at Loughborough Parish Church. His headmistress told his mother that she should apply to Southwell Minster Cathedral for him to become a choirboy. He won a choral scholarship and was in the cathedral choir for three years. On leaving school he went to Cardiff University to study for a Bachelor of Music degree with the aim of applying to become a BBC Trainee Studio Manager. This was not possible as he left the university after the first year. He then became involved in the design, manufacture and sales of high quality audio equipment.

Mike became a bell tuner at Taylor's bellfoundry in Loughborough from 1970-1973 and was asked to re-join the company in 1977. Paul Taylor, the last member of the Taylor family that had been involved in bellfounding for 200 years, was about to semi-retire. Mike was indoctrinated into the mysteries of bellfounding and was made "Bellmaster", a position he held until 1988.

He now lives in Spain with his wife Jane along with her two children and two grandchildren. Together they started a monthly magazine for ex-pats in 2006 and currently he continues to write the articles.

Email: mikejgmilsom@gmail.com

Back cover photos: *Finished bells in the tuning shop, transferring metal from the tilt crucible furnace, lettering a case mould. Taylor's, 2017*
Photos: John Taylor & Co.

Printed in Poland
by Amazon Fulfillment
Poland Sp. z o.o., Wrocław